The Solidarities of Strangers is a study of English policies toward the poor from the seventeenth century to the present that combines individual stories with official actions. Lynn Lees shows how clients as well as officials negotiated welfare settlements. Cultural definitions of entitlement, rather than available resources, determined amounts and beneficiaries. Indeed, industrialization and growing wealth went along with restricted payments to the needy, while universal allowances and insurance systems expan... world wars crippled budgets and drained resou... laws were a "residualist" system, aiding the de... charities covered needs, they went through cyc... that affected men and women unequally. The l... England and Wales has not been a story of continued progress and improvement but one determined by continually changing attitudes toward poverty.

THE SOLIDARITIES
OF STRANGERS

THE SOLIDARITIES
OF STRANGERS

THE ENGLISH POOR LAWS AND
THE PEOPLE, 1700–1948

LYNN HOLLEN LEES
University of Pennsylvania

CAMBRIDGE
UNIVERSITY PRESS

PUBLISHED BY THE PRESS SYNDICATE OF THE UNIVERSITY OF CAMBRIDGE
The Pitt Building, Trumpington Street, Cambridge, CB2 1RP, United Kingdom

CAMBRIDGE UNIVERSITY PRESS
The Edinburgh Building, Cambridge CB2 2RU, United Kingdom
40 West 20th Street, New York, NY 10011-4211, USA
10 Stamford Road, Oakleigh, Melbourne 3166, Australia

© Lynn Hollen Lees 1998

First published 1998

Typeset in Times Roman

Library of Congress Cataloging-in-Publication Data
Lees, Lynn Hollen.
   The solidarities of strangers : the English poor laws and the
people, 1700–1948 / Lynn Hollen Lees.
      p.   cm.
   Includes bibliographical references and index.
   ISBN 0-521-57261-4 (hb)
   1. Poor laws – Great Britain – History.   2. Public Welfare – Great
Britain – History.   I. Title.
   KD3310.L44   1998
   344.42'0325 – dc21   97-613
                                                                       CIP

*A catalog record for this book is available from
the British Library.*

ISBN 0 521 57261 4 hardback

Transferred to digital printing 2003

To: A. L.

I know lives, I could miss
Without a Misery –
Others – whose instant's wanting –
Would be Eternity

–Emily Dickinson

CONTENTS

ACKNOWLEDGMENTS

During the years I have spent studying the poor laws, I have acquired many debts. An American Council of Learned Societies Ford Grant Fellowship permitted me to begin research in Britain in 1985–6, and a fellowship from the National Endowment for the Humanities gave me time in 1993 to do much of the writing. The University of Pennsylvania generously supported my work with a semester of leave in 1992. The staff at record offices all over England answered endless questions and made my search for settlement examinations much easier. I am particularly in debt to the archivists of the Bedfordshire Record Office, the Leicestershire Record Office, the Cambridgeshire Record Office, the Hampshire Record Office, the Lancashire Record Office, the Shropshire Record Office, the West Yorkshire Record Office, the Greater London Council Archive, and the British Library of Political and Economic Science, and librarians of the Guildhall Library, the Manchester City Library, the Borthwick Institute, the Holborn Public Library, the Bradford Library, the Salford Local History Library, and the University of York library. Vincent Walsh kindly loaned his microfilms of Atcham settlement examinations. James Stephen Taylor introduced me to the fascinating correspondence of citizens of Kirkby Lonsdale with Stephen Garnett, and then let me use his microfilms of that township's letters. Both shared their time and materials generously. After asking me to be a consultant on the Charles Booth Archives project, Michael Hughes made available microfilms of Stepney poor law records, which have been an immense help. In England, Paul Thompson allowed me to use materials in the Family Life and Work Experience Archive held by the Department of Sociology at the University of Essex, and Dr. K. M. Thompson of the Leicestershire Record Office gave me permission to see early case records of the Leicester Charity Organization Society. I also wish to thank the Rev. Graham W. Bettridge for permission to quote from the Kirkby Lonsdale Township letters. In my search for prints and cartoons, Joan

Sussler of the Lewis Walpole Library offered enthusiastic, expert help, as did the staff at the Yale Center for British Art, the Library Company of Philadelphia, and the Special Collections Division of Van Pelt Library at the University of Pennsylvania. In particular, I want to acknowledge the regular support of librarians at the Van Pelt Library, who brought in crumbling volumes from storage, cheerfully sent off dozens of interlibrary loan requests, and helped me trace materials in other collections.

Maria I. B. Baganha began the long process of preparing my computerized sample of settlement examinations and other poor law data, which Miriam King and Katherine Hempstead continued. I am grateful to all three for their expertise and good sense. Susan Davis, Catherine Whittaker, and Jeff Duffy helped with research. In the final stages of the project, Kristen Stromberg and Max Grant worked on bibliography and manuscript preparation. Thanks to them all.

Parts of this manuscript have been presented in the form of lectures or seminar talks at the University of Leicester, All Souls College, Princeton University, Harvard University, the University of Pennsylvania, the National Gallery of Art, and Villanova University. Students and colleagues gently pointed out problems in the argument and asked astute questions, which sent me back to my sources. Keith Snell, whose knowledge of settlement examinations is unrivaled, pushed me to clarify muddy sentences and thoughts, and helped me sort out some of the mysteries of poor law procedures. Anne Digby, Joanna Innes, Richard Smith, and Richard Wall commented on work and introduced me to other scholars of British welfare. Several people read drafts of chapters or the entire manuscript and offered excellent advice about revisions in many pleasant conversations. My special thanks go to Mary Fissell, John Gillis, Paul Hohenberg, Seth Koven, Andrew Lees, Mary Poovey, Pat Thane, and James Stephen Taylor. The manuscript was much improved by their suggestions. The academic world at its best operates as a community of concerned scholars and friends; I have regularly found it to be so.

THE SOLIDARITIES
OF STRANGERS

INTRODUCTION

If a society desires to struggle against the evils arising from within that consume it, that society must look into itself, to the relations of exchange, to civic responsibilities, to ethics, to the social contract.

François Ewald

To be alive is to be at risk. Even the most fortunate find themselves ill and too soon old, while fire, flood, disease, and random violence ravage those caught in their paths. Neither virtue nor foresight can effectively shield individuals from the fragility of the human body in a hostile world. Communities, in contrast, can do much to protect their members. They can guard, insure, innoculate, and nurse. They can supply work, food, shelter, and defense. The group can protect – or at least sustain – its members in ways unavailable to most people, because of its greater resources. But should they do so? If the answer is yes, who should receive the benefit of communal protection? And what should they be protected against? These questions have been posed repeatedly as societies have struggled to draw a boundary between communal and individual needs and public and private resources. There has been no single answer given, no universal solution to the conflicting claims of self, family, and community. Indeed, the major political philosophies current since the Enlightenment have suggested quite different answers, although all have acknowledged the responsibility of the state to provide some minimal level of services and protection for citizens.

Those currently hostile to "welfare" and public support for the poor need to recognize that groups, as well as individuals, have an interest in the distribution of goods and services. At a minimum, enough resources have to be allocated to children and to a local labor force in order to permit the survival of the collectivity. Indeed, some economists argue that a cost–benefit analysis leads groups to adopt policies of moderate redistribution.[1] Transference of some income from richer to poorer has been a common survival strategy of communities.

The ways that communities have done so, however, differ greatly. In the early 1970s, Richard Titmuss distinguished among three different strategies. First, the residualist system: States intervene only in extreme cases of need, offering means-tested benefits to those who cannot meet particular emergencies themselves and have no other source of income. Second, the industrial approach: States tie benefits to earnings and contributions, using insurance to shield working individuals and their families from need. Third, universalist benefits: All citizens get payments as a matter of right.[2] Different countries have opted for variants of each of these methods, sometimes covering different groups in different ways. The United States, for example, uses a residualist system to support families with dependent children, but uses a universalist style of payments for the elderly. Britain, on the other hand, gives universal payments to families with young children and to the elderly, but sets the payments so low that those without extra resources have to claim additional, means-tested benefits. German payments to citizens operate largely through insurance plans. Redistribution comes in many different shapes and sizes, depending upon whether states decide to target primarily the needy or to assume that risk is universal and cover everyone as a matter of right. Although struggles between universalists who use a discourse of rights and residualists continue, few political systems are consistent in their types of coverage and definitions of need. Modern states target multiple groups – farmers, homeowners, parents, school children, the elderly, the unemployed, businesses, to name only a few – and give subsidies, some of which are called "welfare" and seen as similar, others of which respond to a different logic. In this book, I will use a narrow definition of welfare: public payments or services given to individuals to help support them. This encompasses both universalist and residualist systems.

In one form or another, Western societies have for centuries supported institutions that have offered aid to the dependent. Churches collected and distributed alms; individuals and families endowed hospitals and orphanages; governments fed or housed people they viewed as dependent. Sometimes kinship groups or villages reallocated land among their members so the larger

---

[1] See for example William J. Baumol, *Welfare Economics and the Theory of the State*, 2nd ed. (Cambridge: Harvard University Press, 1965); David A. Collard, *Altruism and Economy: A Study in Non-Selfish Economics* (Oxford: Martin Robertson, 1978).

[2] Richard M. Titmuss, *Social Policy* (London: Allen & Unwin, 1974).

households would have enough to feed themselves. In early modern times, many cities amassed grain stocks for citizens during seasons of famine, and in rural areas, the maintenance of common lands gave the poor access to pasturage and firewood. Multiple mechanisms, both public and private, have been developed to redistribute some resources to those living on the margins. The widespread adoption of social insurance in the later nineteenth and the twentieth centuries merely continued through different means community support for those in need. The provision of welfare is, therefore, not a modern invention, but a long-term practice of groups to buffer members from the full impact of individual or collective disasters.

Nevertheless, much social science literature, particularly that written from the 1950s through the 1970s, linked welfare and "modernization." Economic growth and the logic of industrialism supposedly produced welfare states.[3] Such unilinear, evolutionary visions of welfare states foundered as scholars looked at more cases over longer periods of time.[4] The work of Peter Flora and Jens Albers, for example, has undermined simplistic correlations between industrial development and comprehensive welfare legislation.[5] Yet evolutionary Whiggish explanations of welfare remain popular; even as sensitive an observer as Abram de Swaan orients his study of North American and European welfare systems toward their twentieth-century shape, linking their evolution to a "collectivizing process" fueled by capitalism, industrialization, urbanization, and state formation.[6] Unfortunately, the blinkered present-mindedness of most theoreticians of welfare does violence to the long and convoluted history of social welfare practices.

---

[3] Harold Wilensky, *The Welfare State and Equality* (Berkeley: University of California Press, 1975); Frederick L. Pryor, *Public Expenditures in Communist and Capitalist Nations* (London: Allen & Unwin, 1968).

[4] The diverse nature of welfare systems has been an emerging theme in recent literature; see, for example, Peter Baldwin, *The Politics of Social Solidarity* (New York: Cambridge University Press, 1990), and Gøsta Esping-Andersen, *The Three Worlds of Welfare Capitalism* (Princeton: Princeton University Press, 1990). By accepting the notion of American exceptionalism, historians of welfare in the United States acknowledged that such institutions could follow several paths of development. See Gaston Rimlinger, *Welfare Policy and Industrialization in Europe, America, and Russia* (New York: Wiley, 1971); Daniel Levine, *Poverty and Society: The Growth of the American Welfare State in International Comparison* (New Brunswick: Rutgers University Press, 1988); Edwina Amenta and Theda Skocpol, "Taking Exception: Explaining the Distinctiveness of American Public Policies in the Last Century," in Francis G. Castles, ed., *The Comparative History of Public Policy* (New York: Oxford University Press, 1989), 292–33.

[5] Peter Flora and Jens Alber, "Modernization, Democratization, and the Development of Welfare States in Western Europe," in Peter Flora and Arnold J. Heidenheimer, eds., *The Development of Welfare States in Europe and America* (New Brunswick: Transaction Books, 1981), 37–80.

[6] Abram de Swaan, *In Care of the State: Health Care, Education and Welfare in Europe and the USA in the Modern Era* (New York: Oxford University Press, 1988).

Historians of welfare working within a Marxist tradition have been able to look backward more successfully and integrate early institutions into a long-run framework of change. Catherina Lis and Hugo Soly, for example, relate poor relief to the evolution of European labor markets from the fourteenth century forward, arguing that "the rise of capitalist relations of production required the construction of public methods of support." Although they astutely point out the many similarities among welfare arrangements throughout early modern Europe, their use of class categories vastly oversimplifies the issue of agency and motivation.[7] Moreover, their insistence upon the use of relief for social control obscures the pragmatic use by the poor of relief for their own purposes.[8] Nevertheless, the point that welfare institutions have been deeply influenced by attitudes to work and linked to the practice of forced labor is an important one.[9] There are good reasons why labor-market-centered approaches to welfare history have had many adherents.

Another body of influential theorists has concentrated less on the question, *why*, than on the problem of *who*. What group or groups were responsible for the growth of welfare institutions? Peter Baldwin distinguishes between "social" approaches to the welfare state, which target workers and/or the middle classes as agents of change, and "Bonapartist" ones, which focus on elites and conservative politicians.[10] Baldwin's own work points to the importance of social coalitions in the passage of welfare legislation in the twentieth century and to the weakness of explanations targeting one social class. Given the long-term history of Western welfare institutions and shifts in their design both before and after transitions to democratic politics, it is difficult to give any one social group credit for their adoption. Aristocratic as well as middle-class politicians took differing stands on welfare depending on time and place. Moreover, recent discussions of both poor relief and social insurance have widened the set of actors that needs to be taken into account. Women's orga-

[7] Catharina Lis and Hugo Soly, *Poverty and Capitalism in Pre-Industrial Europe*, rev. ed. (Brighton: Harvester Press, 1982), 221.

[8] See, for example Olwen H. Hufton, *The Poor of Eighteenth-Century France, 1750–1789* (Oxford: Oxford University Press, 1971); Catharina Lis and Hugo Soly, "Total Institutions and the Survival Strategies of the Labouring Poor in Antwerp, 1770–1860," in Peter Mandler, ed., *The Uses of Charity* (Philadelphia: University of Pennsylvania Press, 1990), 38–67; Lynn Hollen Lees, "The Survival of the Unfit: Welfare Policies and Family Maintenance in Nineteenth-Century London," in Mandler, *Uses*, 68–91.

[9] Other scholars who stress the linkage between welfare payments, labor markets, and work service are Frances Fox Piven and Richard A. Cloward, *Regulating the Poor* (New York: Pantheon, 1971), and George R. Boyer, *An Economic History of the English Poor Law, 1750–1850* (New York: Cambridge University Press, 1990).

[10] Peter Baldwin, *The Politics of Social Solidarity: Class Bases of the European Welfare State, 1875–1975* (New York: Cambridge University Press, 1990), 7, 39.

nizations took active parts in the design of, and agitation for, welfare institutions throughout Europe and North America.[11] Farmers' political groups played a central role in the shaping of the Swedish welfare state.[12] In fact, class-based explanations of welfare institutions deal badly with the large cast of characters actively concerned with the development of such structures.

Recent scholarship on charity, poor relief, and social insurance has diverged sharply from older class-based, linear discussions of welfare, making the welfare story much more complicated but also vastly more interesting. Rather than telling a one-sided tale of either oppression or progress triumphant, Marco van Leeuwen suggests a model of strategic interaction that fits a range of European countries; in it, both elites and the poor act in their own interests, agreeing together upon a particular relief package in exchange for the desired behavior.[13] His approach not only gives the poor some agency, but also draws attention to the ways in which the outcomes of welfare transactions depend both upon the shape of welfare institutions and upon a bargaining process. Other historians embed the notion of bargaining in the processes of state formation and political agitation. Susan Pedersen points to the interactions of "rhetoric and political capacity" to explain different types of family welfare policies.[14] In the British case, the debate was framed by women who had little political power, whereas policies were shaped by male civil servants and trade unions, working together to safeguard male wages. Pedersen's study builds on a burgeoning feminist literature about welfare, which identifies women's contributions to the design and implementation of institutions and points to the gendering of benefits within the supposedly universalist welfare state.[15] Theda Skocpol's revisionist study of U.S. social policy also uses gender effectively to highlight contending visions of welfare institutions. Her "polity-centered analysis" combines attention to political institutions, parties, and social groups whose members have varying goals

---

[11] Sonya Michel and Seth Koven, "Womanly Duties: Maternalist Politics and the Origins of Welfare States in France, Germany, Great Britain, and the United States, 1880–1920," in *American Historical Review* 95:4 (1990): 1,076–1,108; Theda Skocpol, *Protecting Soldiers and Mothers* (Cambridge: Harvard University Press, 1992).

[12] Baldwin, *Politics*, 93.

[13] Marco H. D. van Leeuwen, "The Logic of Charity: Poor Relief in Preindustrial Europe," *Journal of Interdisciplinary History* 24:4 (1994): 589–613.

[14] Susan Pedersen, *Family, Dependence, and the Origins of the Welfare State: Britain and France, 1914–1945* (New York: Cambridge University Press, 1993), 19.

[15] See, for example, Linda Gordon, ed. *Women, the State, and Welfare* (Madison: University of Wisconsin Press, 1990); Jane Lewis, *Women's Welfare, Women's Rights* (London: Routledge, 1983); Carole Pateman, "The Patriarchal Welfare State," in Amy Gutman, ed., *Democracy and the Welfare State* (Princeton: Princeton University Press, 1988), 231–60.

and capabilities. Firmly embedding her analyses in a particular time and place, she shows how social policies are tightly related to state formation and political organizations. But her story is a contingent one; policies change over time as the state changes and as social groups shift their aims and political capacities.[16] Systems can contract as well as expand; they can shift targeted beneficiaries and change methods of support. The current political struggles in the United States over welfare dramatize the accuracy of this point.

Welfare scholarship has moved far away from unilinear, teleological models in which all industrializing societies were seen as moving stage by stage into a homogeneous phase of universal benefit. Although it is true that North American and Western European societies all adopted state-financed, welfare programs for citizens before 1945, they moved toward such institutions at different dates in different ways for somewhat different reasons. Gøsta Esping-Andersen, for example, identifies three sorts of welfare regime: the "liberal" welfare state (Canada, Australia, the United States, and Britain pre-1945), a "corporatist" variety (France, Germany, and Italy), and the "social democratic" type (Scandinavia and Great Britain between 1945 and 1979).[17] Not only benefits, but the mix of public and private control and the impact on labor markets differed greatly among the three types. Moreover, as Daniel Levine has pointed out, the intellectual assumptions about welfare, as well as the justifications for it, have varied from country to country.[18] "Welfare" has multiple meanings, and to understand them requires looking at national stories and national histories. States learned from one another, to be sure, but what we see today resulted from political negotiations among parties, bureaucracies, and citizens as states developed their welfare functions. Furthermore, these welfare bargains are not stable. State after state in the 1990s has trimmed benefits and retreated from mandates, and the trend is far from over. The heyday of universalism was in the 1960s, when economic growth and low unemployment filled state coffers and limited claims. As populations age and regions deindustrialize, the cost of the standard Western "welfare" package has mounted alarmingly, to the point where many voters revolt and call for change. The welfare saga is far from over.

Comparisons enlighten, but they do not explain welfare arrangements as they exist today. The welfare story is as much a local and a national story as an international one, a tale of clients, assumptions, fears, and hopes that is quite different from that of institution building or of a lockstep trajectory to

---

[16] Skocpol, *Protecting,* 41, 58.

[17] Esping-Andersen, *Welfare Capitalism.*

[18] Levine, *Poverty and Society,* 264, 270.

a "better" world. This book tells the story of the English and Welsh poor laws and their supersession by social insurance after three centuries of local bargaining and controversy. In both popular and scholarly lore, the poor laws have taken on the role of the ugly stepmother who oppressed her virtuous, needy children until the good fairy of the welfare state banished her forever. This historical romance of persecution, struggle, and eventual triumph over the forces of injustice underlies much of the early literature on the English poor laws.[19] But this narrative of vice and virtue ignores the widespread acceptance the laws once enjoyed. I shall tell a less dramatic story, in which good and evil play their roles through the eyes of participants whose views determined the legitimacy and functioning of poor law institutions, which Parliament shaped and regularly revised through legislation.

The poor laws were a fundamental structure of the English state for 350 years, and as such they both shaped and were shaped by local communities. Even if welfare policies were formally set at the national level, they were enacted locally, where face-to-face negotiations determined their impact. Therefore, understanding their cultural meaning requires attention to local as well as national arenas of decision making. The poor laws rested upon common understandings of citizenship and social rights, which fluctuated over time and became intensely class divided during the early nineteenth century. As a result, the legitimacy of the laws was often contested and then effectively challenged after 1900. The outcome was the formal abolition of the poor laws and the popular shift to universalist, tax-financed benefit systems. Nevertheless, when destitution did not disappear, neither did means-tested benefits. In the long run, welfare in the United Kingdom retained elements of the earlier poor laws, just as it kept many buildings and personnel from the previous system. Certainly there was change; certainly there were periods and types of improvement, but the long-term continuities of approach – particularly in health care and in the use of means-tested income supplements – are striking.

But other stories can and have been told about the poor laws and the later adoption of social insurance. Most attention has been paid to their administrative frameworks and to professed aims and impacts. Both the political left and the political right have condemned the poor laws periodically since their inception; for example, in the 1780s, Joseph Townsend fired off a blistering attack against the "disgusting . . . parish pay table."[20] The chorus of hostile

---

[19] For a discussion of the romance mode of writing history, see Hayden White, *Metahistory* (Baltimore: Johns Hopkins University Press, 1973).

[20] Joseph Townsend, *A Dissertation on the Poor Laws by a Well-Wisher to Mankind* (Berkeley and Los Angeles: University of California Press, 1971), 69.

voices reached a crescendo in the 1834 Royal Commission report on the poor laws, which blamed outdoor relief for excess population and for the assumed immorality and laziness of rural workers. Some of their conclusions were reechoed in the early twentieth century by Beatrice and Sidney Webb and then by Barbara and John Hammond as part of a Fabian socialist attack on unregulated labor markets and means-tested benefits, and their hostility carried over into their evaluations of outdoor relief.[21] But in the 1960s, debates on the poor laws turned from a political and moral framework to a predominantly economic one.[22] Scholars used local economic data and economic theory to deny that the poor laws had had disastrous effects on local labor markets. In the longer run, the stock of the early poor laws kept rising, as historians pointed to the utility and relative generosity of pre-1834 relief arrangements in contrast to the meanness of the New Poor Law.[23]

The period after 1834 has been evaluated in the light of the welfare state. A Whiggish point of view of an inevitable trajectory away from the unsatisfactory, hated poor laws toward the shining sun of social insurance held sway through the 1960s.[24] But when significant poverty was discovered within the hallowed halls of the welfare utopia, the assumptions of the Whig case crumbled. In consequence, scholars reassessed the early poor laws and argued for generosity of benefit. Continuities of policy post-1945, particularly in the area of public health, were striking.[25] Recently, David Thomson, Keith Snell, and J. Millar have even reversed Whig arguments, arguing that transfer payments to the elderly and to single-parent families were significantly less under the welfare state than they had been in the early nineteenth century

---

[21] J. L. Hammond and Barbara Hammond, *The Village Labourer, 1760–1832* (1912; New York: Longmans, 1978); Sidney Webb and Beatrice Webb, *English Local Government*, vol. 7, *English Poor Law History, Part I: The Old Poor Law* (London: Longmans, Green, 1927).

[22] See, for example, Mark Blaug, "The Myth of the Old Poor Law and the Making of the New," *Journal of Economic History* 23 (1963): 151–84; Daniel A. Baugh, "The Cost of Poor Relief in South-East England, 1790–1834," *Economic History Review*, 2nd ser., 28 (1975): 50–68; Donald McCloskey, "New Perspectives on the Old Poor Law," *Explorations in Economic History* 10 (1973): 419–36. A recent example of this literature is Boyer, *English Poor Law*.

[23] Anne Digby, *Pauper Palaces* (London: Routledge, 1978); K. D. M. Snell, *Annals of the Labouring Poor* (New York: Cambridge University Press, 1985).

[24] See M. B. Bruce, *The Coming of the Welfare State*, rev. ed. (New York: Schocken, 1966); Bentley B. Gilbert, *The Evolution of National Insurance in Great Britain: The Origins of the Welfare State* (London: Michael Joseph, 1966).

[25] Norman McCord, "The Implementation of the 1834 Poor Law Amendment Act on Tyneside," *International Review of Social History* 14(1969): 90–158; M. W. Flinn, "Medical Services Under the New Poor Law," in Derek Fraser, ed., *The New Poor Law in the Nineteenth Century* (New York: St. Martin's, 1976), 45–66.

under the poor laws.[26] Studies of British welfare systems have therefore turned away from what was said to what was done. Local studies of actions have largely replaced examinations of rhetoric and intent, but coverage in both time and space has been spotty. Because most scholars have targeted a particular town, region, or institution for a limited number of decades, getting a broader picture of how welfare systems changed over time has been difficult.[27] Moreover, the lack of attention to gender, the welfare receivers, and welfare bargaining at the local level needs to be remedied.[28] Despite the shelves of books and articles written on the English poor laws and social insurance schemes, we know relatively little about how such institutions operated, how their practices changed over time, and how they were regarded by ordinary people. Moreover, their central importance to the evolution of English and Welsh communities has not been recognized; the poor laws set the limits of membership and pushed some people out. They defined the meaning of social citizenship for a period of over three hundred years.

Why study England and Wales, rather than another example? First, because that particular case shows how compulsory, effective welfare systems could be implemented well before the advent of industrialized societies. The English government in the early modern period had the authority, resources, and fiscal control necessary to design and enforce a workable welfare system for its entire population. As the first such example in Europe, it provides a striking contrast to largely urban, institutional approaches to welfare established in France, the Netherlands, Denmark, and some of the German states. Moreover, the long history of the poor laws provides an opportunity over a period of almost four hundred years to explore the interconnections between welfare policy and changes within the wider society. How did the urbanization of the country and intensified migration affect welfare institutions? What impact did industrialization have upon the functioning of the poor laws? Did widened suffrage, deepened class divisions, and

[26] David Thomson, "The Decline of Social Welfare: Falling State Support for the Elderly since Early Victorian Times," *Ageing and Society* 4:4 (1984): 451–82; K. D. M. Snell and J. Millar, "Lone-parent Families and the Welfare State: Past and Present," *Continuity and Change* 2:3 (1987): 387–422.

[27] Notable exceptions are Snell, *Annals,* and M. A. Crowther, *The Workhouse System, 1834–1929* (London: Methuen, 1983).

[28] Recent works by James Stephen Taylor, *Poverty, Migration, and Settlement in the Industrial Revolution: Sojourners' Narratives* (Palo Alto: Society for the Promotion of Science and Scholarship, 1989), and Lara Marks, "Medical Care for Pauper Mothers and Their Infants: Poor Law Provision and Local Demand in East London, 1870–1929," *Economic History Review* 46:3 (August, 1993), 518–42 are exceptions to this generalization.

intensified awareness of gender change welfare policies? If so, how? Welfare policies spring from wider cultural understandings of rights and duties, which are not static but evolve along with the organization of the state. In the long run, English civil servants, who operated within the intellectual world created by the poor laws, produced the classic defense of a universalist welfare system that gave all citizens certain services and payments. The Beveridge Report of 1942 provided the intellectual underpinnings for postwar welfare legislation, an alternative formulation to the liberal, residualist system established by the poor laws. Just how and why this change took place is a central theme of this study.

English and Welsh welfare systems, therefore, are not merely one case among many that could be isolated for comparative purposes. They helped to define two of the major approaches to welfare adopted in Western countries during the past four hundred years. During the eighteenth and nineteenth centuries, the poor laws offered an influential model for welfare officials in North America, and in the twentieth, the rhetoric of the Beveridge Report was taken up by social democrats in many societies to bolster support for the extension of welfare benefits. English and Welsh welfare practices were widely known, defended, and attacked over a long period in which similar societies in North America and Europe also wrestled with the welfare problem. Although in no sense the only example available, English solutions to the welfare problem loomed large in the fund of ideas available to Western administrators and reformers.

One focus of this study is the definition of community that emerged from the act of almsgiving and the changes that it underwent over time. In contrast to the emphasis placed by Alan MacFarlane and other scholars upon English individualism, I stress the collective ties that bound citizens together, while dividing them along lines of culture and class. Since medieval times, English and Welsh society has supported multiple institutions that reinforced group identities. Manors, open fields, nucleated villages, churches, and parish government drew people together to work, play, worship, and gossip.[29] Law courts, militias, and elections generated occasions for collective celebration and conflict. Whatever the disintegrative forces set free by the nuclear family pattern and by frequent migration, the pressures exerted by collective institutions and rituals remained powerful, although the nature of such pressures and their sources changed over time.

---

[29] Lawrence Stone has argued for the power of collective institutions in England and Wales and for the need to specify in social space and time the pressures for individualism. See Lawrence Stone, "Illusions of a Changeless Family," *Times Literary Supplement* (May 16, 1986), 525.

The poor laws deserve a prominent place in this list of community-building pressures. For several hundred years they provided daily occasions for the reexamination of social duties and social rights by both the haves and the have-nots. Whatever the motivations of the parties involved, the result of welfare transactions was unavoidably a reinforcement of social solidarity on the communal level. Those who gave had to acknowledge obligation to the destitute; those who asked for bread asserted the legitimacy of their need as well as their membership in a self-supporting community. Although the transaction accentuated differences of class and income, the force of law and habit bound both sides in the welfare transaction together into a morris dance of interlocking obligation. Rich and poor faced one another to contest the distribution of local resources and to reallocate them according to some locally recognized standard of need and desert. Each decision brought into question the boundaries of the group and the inequality it was prepared to tolerate. An inherently flexible system, it gave voice to multiple, evolving understandings of social obligation that underpinned the English and Welsh parish. Entitlement is a modern word that points to the terrain within which these struggles over rights and obligations took place.

These regular contests over redistribution rested on evolving notions of social citizenship. I have borrowed that term, of course, from T. H. Marshall, who said that states provided their members with a historically shifting package of rights.[30] Marshall argued from principles of justice and entitlement, rather than those of need. Ignoring differences in rights allocated by gender or by age, his categories are ostensibly universal. He equated British citizenship with civil rights in the eighteenth century, with political rights in the nineteenth, and with social rights in the twentieth, fulfilling liberal wishes for the complete realization of the self. Marshall, however, recognized the poor laws as an early assertion of the principle of universally granted social benefits. I would go farther than Marshall and argue that the poor laws established, as early as the seventeenth century, a condition of social citizenship within local communities for English and Welsh people. Those with clear rights of settlement resided in a locally organized welfare state. Yet the meaning of social citizenship in a hierarchical society with limited political rights was deeply problematic. What poor law grants meant in English and Welsh society was debated publicly and privately over a period of four hundred years.

---

[30] T. H. Marshall, "Citizenship and Social Class," in *Class Citizenship and Social Development,* ed. Seymour Martin Lipset (Garden City: Doubleday, 1964), 65–122; the term citizen according to the *OED* signifies member of a state, a person with the rights and privileges of citizenship, which shifts over time.

The law granted individuals the right to subsistence in a particular place, yet opinion could begrudge that right to people because of character, age, physical condition, ethnicity, or occupation. Were rights to be absolute or conditional? Answers varied, and therefore conflict ensued.

Let me pose explicitly several questions that help to structure this study: How did the communities generated by the poor laws allocate membership and resources? Who set the rules and the limits of obligation? Which needs were legitimate, and which were not, and how did such definitions change over time? Welfare transactions offer a window into the functioning of societies at the local level, one which brings into view the destitute alongside the affluent, the deserving as well as the undeserving.

Welfare bargains highlight the issue of ethnicity within the United Kingdom because the protection extended by Parliament to English and Welsh citizens in their area of settlement did not extend to the other parts of the realm. Ireland lacked any public relief system for the destitute until 1838, and thereafter its citizens received much more limited services than their English counterparts. The country could not afford – and Parliament did not mandate – the cradle-to-grave style of aid provided under the English poor laws. Despite initially similar legislation, the Scottish poor laws developed along a different track from the English, relying on voluntary contributions and excluding relief to able-bodied men or women. Although the Scottish Poor Law of 1844 made administrative changes, it reaffirmed restrictions on aid to the unemployed, and practice changed little from earlier centuries.[31] Scots distinguished their welfare system from that of the English and were proud of the differences. Communities in different parts of the kingdom thus offered their members unequal access to welfare benefits, and this inequality was mandated by the state and accepted by social elites. Welfare constituted a dividing line between English and Welsh on the one hand, and Scottish and Irish on the other. Although it aided migration, it also intensified suspicions of Celtic outsiders. Whatever sense of Britishness might have been fostered by common loyalties to monarchy, army, and nation, welfare systems remained resolutely local, reinforcing ethnic differences until the twentieth century.[32] In the transition from state to nation, welfare arrangements differentiated the citizens of the so-called United Kingdom, rather than drawing

---

[31] Rosalind Mitchison, "The Making of the Old Scottish Poor Law," *Past and Present* 63 (1974): 58–93; R. A. Cage, *The Scottish Poor Law, 1745–1845* (Edinburgh: Scottish Academic Press, 1981).

[32] See Linda Colley, *Britons: Forging the Nation 1707–1837* (New Haven: Yale University Press, 1992), for an analysis of the evolving sense of a British identity.

them together. Some had entitlement, and others did not. The legal status and birthplace of the individual, rather his or her destitution, made the difference.

Despite their title, the poor laws implied less about levels of poverty than they did about local decisions to fund relief claims. Although those who received relief were no doubt poor, it is impossible to compare their economic condition with that of the non-receivers in lower income groups. Did the excluded lack relief because of their resources, their citizenship, or their unwillingness to apply? Without extensive evidence on the numbers and condition of the poor in particular places and at different dates, it is impossible to quantify the proportion of the poor getting aid from the state at a given time, and there is no reason to suppose that overseers throughout the country set uniform standards for either need or payments. To the contrary, standards seem to have shifted markedly over time, and not in a linear direction. Although massive destitution – such as that triggered by rising grain prices during the wars with France, the failure of potato crops in Ireland between 1845–9, or the widespread unemployment among Lancashire cotton workers in 1862–3 – produced large increases in relief expenses and swelled the proportion of paupers in affected areas, it is not clear even in those exceptional cases what percentage of the destitute actually received poor law aid. In any case, it is illegitimate to suppose a direct and tight correlation between changing numbers of people on relief and changing amounts of poverty. One problem is our lack of quantitative information on the sizes and incomes of local populations, an issue that has not disappeared. As late as the 1950s, Richard Titmuss complained bitterly about the British government's unwillingness to ferret out "the hard facts of poverty and dependency," and the same situation persists today.[33]

Quantitative statements about poverty also founder on the indeterminate nature of the concepts involved. What is a need and who ought to define it? What differentiates destitution from less extreme varieties of want? Systematic attempts to measure poverty in terms of caloric intake date from the early twentieth century, and very few such investigations were done. In other cases, judgments about poverty and destitution were subjectively made by individuals whose standards probably varied. The inequality inherent in capitalist societies produces vastly different incomes and access to goods and no agreement about what counts as an intolerable amount of "poverty." Current controversies over definitions of "subsistence" income or entitlement are merely variants of a larger epistemological problem. Poverty itself is a relative con-

---

[33] Richard M. Titmuss, *Essays on "The Welfare State,"* 2nd ed. (Boston: Beacon Press, 1963), 226.

cept, definable only in comparison with a specific, locally relevant standard. When Samuel Johnson traveled in Scotland in 1773, he described a Highland hut where he visited with a local woman.[34] Her home was made of loose stones and roofed with thatch. It had a dirt floor, and it lacked windows and even a hearth. Smoke escaped through a hole in the ceiling. Yet the woman owned goats and some poultry, she raised potatoes and barley, and she could feed her family comfortably with little recourse to the market. Although certainly poor by English standards, she was definitely not poor in comparison with many Highland crofters or Irish cottagers. Our notions of poverty are culturally constructed and need to be related to local norms. The English poor laws rested on the assumption that elected overseers and guardians were the most effective judges of destitution and the needs of local people. Their standards for redress were by definition adequate; the fact that paupers might have disagreed was not considered relevant.

In any case, the English poor laws were never intended to eliminate poverty, which was seen as a normal, God-ordained, and desirable part of the social order. As Joseph Townsend so aptly put it in 1786, "Hunger will . . . teach decency and civility, obedience and subjection, to the most brutish, the most obstinate, and the most perverse."[35] Patrick Colquhoun, writing on indigence in 1806, concurred: "Poverty is therefore a most necessary and indispensable ingredient in society, without which nations and communities could not exist in a state of civilization. It is the lot of man."[36] For both Townsend and Colquhoun, poverty was a goal, encouraging virtue, hard work, and a sense of social hierarchy. The authors of the 1834 Poor Law report also rejected the notion that there was a need to combat poverty, taking only destitution and incipient starvation as their targets; in their view, eliminating poverty was neither necessary nor desirable. Only utopian socialists and idealists in the twentieth century looked ahead to a world without poverty; certainly administrators of the poor laws did not. The surprise and indignation with which politicians and social theorists in Britain have regularly rediscovered that welfare has not eliminated poverty arise directly from a misunderstanding of the function and scope of British welfare institutions.

Welfare regimes are firmly anchored in particular times and in cultural space; they shift in character, expand, and contract. The term, residualist, which I borrow from Richard Titmuss, fits well British practice under the

[34] Samuel Johnson, *A Journey to the Western Islands of Scotland*, ed. Allan Wendt (Boston: Houghton Mifflin, 1965), 23–4.

[35] Townsend, *Dissertation*, 27.

[36] Patrick Colquhoun, *A Treatise on Indigence* (London: J. Hatchard, 1806), 7.

poor laws until 1948, and it describes the aim of recent Conservative governments to whittle down state responsibilities in favor of individual responsibility and private initiative.[37] Change over time in welfare arrangements does not necessarily mean progress. This is especially true in the English case, where the formal continuity of the poor laws concealed major shifts in their operation. First, the formal continuity: Parliament created through the poor laws a residualist welfare system in England and Wales, one that remained largely intact as codified in 1601 until 1948. Next, the changes: During that long period, at least three phases of different policies and targeted populations can be identified. Moreover, the social consensus upon which they were based had to be regularly renegotiated, as attitudes toward work, state, and citizenship evolved. English welfare regimes rested upon assumptions brought into question by the industrialization of the economy, the democratization of the state, and the liberalization and gendering of political discourse. This book tells the story of a residualist poor law.

Phase I. 1601–1834: *Residualism Taken for Granted.* Parishes throughout the kingdom slowly accepted the state-mandated duty to relieve the "impotent poor" and to offer limited amounts of work to the jobless who had a legal settlement. When families and markets failed to provide support, the parish would step in, but only for those with clearly established local claims. Nevertheless, an expansive definition of need that included the problems of large families, inadequate wages, cyclical unemployment for both men and women, and illness conferred legitimacy on the poor laws in workers' eyes and helped to compensate for niggling criteria of eligibility. For the most part, the poor laws were accepted by both givers and receivers. Large-scale opposition by taxpayers appeared only late in the eighteenth century, when wartime shortages triggered massive increases in claims and did not reach Parliament until the years around 1815. The period 1815 to 1834 was one of experimentation, when many parishes restricted grants and worked to redefine the terms of local welfare bargains.

Phase II. 1834–60: *Residualism Refined.* Disgruntled landlords and taxpayers turned away from the more generous welfare regime that had developed in the later eighteenth century. Tightened criteria of eligibility and disciplinary workhouses, which were codified in the Poor Law of 1834, gained support. Relief practices became less generous as they became more gendered. Welfare mechanisms in an era of evolving industrial capitalism became less gentlemanly as renewed emphasis on market mechanisms and

---

[37] Titmuss, *Social Policy.*

self-support led to cutbacks in relief, particularly to adult males. Resistance by workers, first to the adoption of the law and later to its assumptions and tenets, became an active element in popular culture and in local politics, while Liberals and poor law administrators tried to maintain the principles of a residualist system.

Phase III. 1860–1948: *Residualism Reevaluated and Rejected.* The legitimacy of the New Poor Law declined as citizens' rights widened. The adequacy of purely market-driven solutions to the issues of unemployment, industrial accidents, support in old age, health, and infant care came increasingly into question on both the national and the local levels, when the franchise expanded and environmentalist explanations of poverty supplanted moral ones. Meanwhile, newly professionalized staffs and social workers, who built their reputations on expertise and the ability to improve rather than to discipline, transformed poor law institutions from within. Then, too, worker-guardians changed local rules for relief, increasing outdoor aid. Alternative institutions grew in scope, as criticisms of the poor laws mounted. When the Liberal government turned away from poor law reform to social insurance schemes, it broadened alternative welfare structures. By 1948, the poor laws seemed redundant, an affront to the egalitarian assumptions of the Beveridge report, and they were abolished as Parliament adopted universalist criteria for social services and aid.

The story does not end there, however, as the epilogue of this book will recount. Launched with great expectations, the British welfare state foundered on the rocks of inadequate resources and sub-subsistence grants. Despite a wealth of egalitarian intentions, underfunded universal benefits left poverty alive and well, and residualist solutions reemerged in the form of additional benefits. In the long run, British society has given the market major responsibility for providing work and income. After 1909, the state began to set minimum standards for income and services, which were slowly extended to the entire population. Nevertheless, when compared with the Scandinavian countries or those of central Europe, universal benefits in the United Kingdom provide less and means-tested payments provide relatively more to the dependent population. The British variety of welfare capitalism has been resolutely different from that of its Continental neighbors and from that of the United States.

Remember that welfare is a continuing story, not one with a teleologically determined end. Events of the 1990s, in which one industrialized state after another restricts benefits and politicians leap to attack the sacred cows of the recent past, show how historically contingent and vulnerable are consensuses over welfare. They depend upon cultural assumptions and political coalitions that can easily shift. The current conservative swing in Britain, the United States, and much of Western Europe, in combination with aging populations, deindustrialization, soaring medical costs, and unemployment, has unraveled earlier agreements about community support. What was taken for granted in 1960 comes under fire in the 1990s, when the state's ability to pay seems in doubt. Nevertheless, the extent of political willingness to cut back welfare seems to vary among nations. Current enthusiasm in the United States for "ending welfare as we know it" goes far beyond the limited and halting efforts to contain welfare costs that have been enacted by legislatures in Western Europe. Britain's welfare system has two shields unavailable in the United States: almost four hundred years of legally mandated, state support for the destitute, and since 1945, public commitment to universalist entitlements. Where all benefit from the system, all have a stake in defending it. History matters.

PART ONE

RESIDUALISM TAKEN FOR GRANTED, 1700–1834

T HE ORIGINS of the English poor laws lay in the intersection of humanist aspirations with rising economic hardship and state paranoia about the poor. As the numbers of destitute grew, so did attempts to legislate sweeping solutions. In 1531, Parliament ordered vagrants to be detained and punished. Later bills required parishes to put the idle to work, to send poor children into service, and to collect money for the elderly and disabled. The state wanted a well-ordered society where all labored and stayed at home, and it gave parishes the burden of effecting this grand design. Together, alms, work, branding, and beating were supposed to turn the frail and the recalcitrant into model subjects.

This plan, however, quickly ran aground on the rocks of reality. Many parishes ignored the law well into the seventeenth century. Moreover, after adoption, the poor laws operated as a residualist system, usually coming in late and with little. And although the state tried to be a harsh taskmaster, demanding work in return for alms, this provision of the law remained problematic. Overall, parishes supplied work only intermittently and ineffectively. Even if "workfare" seemed a good idea, it had a poor track record. Over the longer run, therefore, some of the harsher elements of the poor laws lost their sting. Parishes enforced vagrancy laws irregularly and unevenly, and concentrated their energies on the elderly and single-parent families, who received alms when destitute, and poor children, who were boarded with families or given apprenticeships. Over time, the activism mandated by Tudor governments declined in most places into a pension system.

"Welfare," as it was practiced in the centuries between the first Tudor laws and the revision of 1834, was neither uniformly harsh nor benign. Some of the poor benefited from relative largesse; others found it punitive and discriminatory. But to concentrate on the issue of benevolence misses a more important point: that of consensus. Once the machinery of the poor law began to operate in a place, it was widely accepted. Both applicants and administrators viewed the laws as legitimate, justices of the peace enforced the poor laws, overseers implemented them, and poor workers used them. English and Welsh communities accepted the responsibility of redistributing their resources to the poorest of the poor, and did so, even if grudgingly.

But for many, this welfare system lost its legitimacy during the political and social crises triggered by the long-running wars with France late in the eighteenth century. With bread prices high, men away in the army, and markets interrupted by blockades, taxpayers decided that the economic cost was more than they were willing to pay. Over the course of several decades, benefits were scaled back and the workhouse reconfigured in many parishes in the hope of deterring all but the most needy. By 1820, major assaults on the poor laws had been mounted both locally and nationally in an effort to delegitimize public support for the poor, despite long-term growth in national wealth. As the country got richer and widened its political system to include the middle classes, it also narrowed public commitments to workers. Encouraged to move in response to shifting labor demand, migrants discovered that settlement in their new parishes was hard to get. Worse, legal entitlement no longer conferred moral entitlement. The poor were pushed to the margins of their communities well before the adoption of the Poor Law Amendment Act in 1834.

1

THE WELFARE PROCESS
UNDER THE OLD POOR LAWS

Duty and Interest are Two as great Obligations as can be laid upon
Mortals, and they both as Powerful advocates call upon the Rich to take
care of the Poor.

John Bellers, 1714

I cannot nor will not be quite lost, while I have a parish to flee two [sic].

Elizabeth Langford, 1809

The poor were a familiar part of the British social landscape in the seventeenth and eighteenth centuries. Mangy beggars and peddlers thronged London streets as drawn by Hogarth or Rowlandson; indeed, the ugly and disorderly poor waylaid the better-off people at every corner. Outside the cities,
they squatted on common land or wandered along the highways, while others wasted away quietly in their tumbledown cottages. After all, as Cobbett
put it, "Extreme poverty is in certain cases inseparable from the life of man."[1]
Poverty was not only tolerated, it was expected, and by some even desired –
for others. But poverty was not ignored. A complicated set of institutions had
developed after the Reformation in Britain, as well as in Europe, for the care
of the poor. Hospitals, almshouses, workhouses, and orphanages multiplied,
and in England mandatory relief was provided for the destitute. Multiple
explanations can be given for these provisions: rising demand from a rising
population in the sixteenth century, the ideological influence of humanism
and of an activist Protestantism, the desires of an interventionist state for
order. All worked together to prod the government to legislate procedures for
action. But the real relief story took place necessarily on the local level,

[1] William Cobbett, *A Legacy to Labourers* (1834; new ed., London: Charles Griffin, 1872), 79.

21

where individual decisions were made. The welfare bargain was a local one, between givers and receivers in a particular political context. Negotiated among unequals, it defined the limits of social obligation and of communal membership in a hierarchical society.

The leap from poverty to dependence upon the state was a large one, just as it is today. At any given time, relatively few of the needy were supported by tax money funneled to them by their parishes. There were many intervening steps between poverty and dependence upon local government for support, steps marked out by the law, by pride and publicity, by common notions of entitlement and community. Welfare was a process, not a thing. It emerged from complex understandings of deprivation and responsibility, some of which were shared and others contested. To be a "pauper" required more than destitution. First, someone had to ask for aid; second, local officials had to acknowledge public responsibility and decide upon a course of action; and, third, the individual in question had to decide whether or not to accept that aid and its social consequences. There were those who dispensed, those who received, and those who were ignored or exiled in times of need.

This chapter explores how some of the poor became paupers. It tells the story of poor law procedures from the early eighteenth century until 1834, a period that I treat as a unit because of the continuity of legal and administrative structures. Although the Parliament passed well over one hundred fifty bills relating to the care of the poor during the eighteenth and early nineteenth centuries, most were local acts or mandated only small changes. None of the measures calling for large-scale reform managed to pass both houses of Parliament until the Whig reform of 1834, which later chapters will explore. Variations over time and space, although not unimportant, will be considered in Chapter 2, but for the moment, let us focus on the welfare process, on the rules of the welfare game as normally played by both the givers and the receivers.

Welfare Laws and Welfare Practice

During the sixteenth century, Parliament passed a series of laws that defined the dependent poor and outlined a procedure to provide for them. As codified in 1601, the poor laws required that in every parish, churchwardens and several of the "substantial householders" jointly serving as "overseers of the poor" were to set to work "all such persons, married or unmarried, having no means to maintain them" or no "daily trade." Children whose parents could not support them were to be apprenticed or given work alongside destitute adults. The proceeds of a special tax on inhabitants and on the occupiers of lands, houses, tithes, coal mines, and woods of the parish should be used to purchase materials for manufacturing, as well as to subsidize "the necessary relief of the lame, impotent, old, blind," and others who could not work.[2] When families could no longer succor their own or when the labor market did not offer jobs, the local community was ordered to step in and become the care giver and employer of last resort.

The Privy Council originally pushed this scheme and worked to extend it to the entire realm, but during the early seventeenth century local officials were slow to levy rates and appoint overseers. In the view of Anthony Fletcher, who has studied local government during the reigns of the Stuart kings, enforcement of the laws increased during the period from 1630 to 1660 and became widespread thereafter.[3] By the early eighteenth century, the laws had become a major concern of Parliament. Backbench activists introduced dozens of local and national regulatory acts that refined poor law practice and provided local exceptions, taking the initiative from a central executive.[4] Members of Parliament, judges, philanthropists, and ordinary people thought about the poor laws. Yet as they tinkered in the interests of improvement, they accepted the structure set in 1601 and put it into practice. Paul Slack credits the legislative process in England for the poor laws. Parliament permitted the negotiation of multiple interests and the implementation of an effective, accepted set of welfare institutions. Whereas humanist theory, Protestant activism, and state desires for social stability prompted action, the precise form of the result required the legitimacy of a representative legislature to implement.[5]

By the seventeenth century, elite opinion recognized three kinds of poor: the worthy, the workers lacking jobs, and the wicked. The rather different needs of all three groups were to be accommodated by the poor law.[6] The most troubling were the unworthy, those deserving punishment rather than relief. Elizabethan law marked out a subset of the population, "rogues and vagabonds," whom local authorities were directed to whip or jail in the interest of moral reform. Deciding whom to lash and to whom to give alms rested

---

[2] 39 Elizabeth, c. 2; see Michael Nolan, *A Treatise of the Laws for the Relief and Settlement of the Poor* (1805; reprint, New York: Garland, 1978), 2:385.

[3] Anthony Fletcher, *Reform in the Provinces* (New Haven: Yale University Press, 1986), 184–8.

[4] Joanna Innes, "Parliament and the Shaping of Eighteenth-Century English Social Policy," *Transactions of the Royal Historical Society,* 5th ser., 40 (1990): 63–93.

[5] Paul Slack, *The English Poor Law, 1531–1782* (New York: Cambridge University Press, 1990), 9.

[6] Paul Slack, *Poverty and Policy in Tudor and Stuart England* (London: Longman, 1988), 22–7, 130.

with local justices and overseers; yet the Elizabethan Privy Council urged an activist approach in the interests of social stability. The inevitable confusion between the two groups emerged clearly in 1662, when an act "for the better Relief of the Poor of this Kingdom" dedicated far less attention to recipients of parish funds than to the "rogues, vagrants, sturdy beggars, or idle and disorderly" who were to be imprisoned or in extreme cases to be transported to the colonies.[7] In much legislation, "workhouse" and "house of correction" were used synonymously. Acts of Parliament to establish local Houses of Industry, in Exeter in 1774, for example, commonly gave their supervisors the authority to take in and to punish the destitute in the neighborhood. Indeed, overseers were allowed to round up begging children and adult vagrants, placing them in the local workhouse to be disciplined through forced labor.[8] Relief, production, and punishment went together under the poor laws. From their beginnings, the poor laws required contradictory responses to poverty: succor and repression, alms and forced labor. These dual directives placed a burden on both administrators and paupers. Which person would be treated in which way, and how should one decide?

Working to impose order through classification and control, the early poor laws tried to divide the poor into the worthy and unworthy, rather than mechanically dividing them by sex or by age. Virtue lay with those who belonged to the local community and who had worked until their bodies could do no more or the local economy could no longer employ them. Disorder and vice came with outsiders, those not known, perhaps with dubious occupations. A law of 1744 specified peddlers, minstrels, jugglers, actors, and fortune tellers, among others, whose unwillingness to work in settled occupations made them suspect.[9] Parliament pushed these distinctions upon local authorities and exhorted them to be vigilant. Although parishes owed relief to their legitimate poor, there remained a penumbra of people, perhaps destitute but considered unworthy, whose entitlement to relief was in doubt. In a variety of cases, authorities had to deal with the ambiguity.

The Making of a Pauper

The Elizabethan Poor Law outlined a simple system of face-to-face encounters between the propertied and the propertyless, set against the backdrop of

---

[7] 13 & 14 Charles II, c. 12.

[8] Sidney Webb and Beatrice Webb, *English Local Government from the Revolution to the Municipal Corporations Act*, vol. 7, *English Poor Law History*, Part 1: *The Old Poor Law* (London: Longmans, 1927), 240.

[9] 17 George II, c. 5.

local divine and secular authority. To serve the local dependent poor, Parliament ordered elected overseers to meet monthly in the church after Sunday service, "there to consider of some good course to be taken." Overseers – positions that normally rotated from ratepayer to ratepayer in a regular sequence – were to decide among giving alms, giving work, or providing a service. Their knowledge was assumed, and their energy and attention coerced by fines for negligence or dishonesty. It was tedious work, avoided by the major landlords and tenants who shifted it onto the smaller property holders.[10] But the poor laws drew a much larger group of people into administrative decisions. Vestry meetings and town councils set local policies; magistrates, who examined applicants and reviewed decisions either individually or in quarter sessions meetings, provided another layer of oversight and action. Paul Slack has called the poor laws a "participatory" system.[11] They forced rich and poor to outline expectations and obligations. The welfare function, a basic element in English political culture, was debated in public.

In "The Pluralist and the Old Soldier," a popular print of the later eighteenth century, a one-legged veteran turned beggar demands charity from a fat vicar, walking along a country road. They meet outside a beautiful, besteepled town, to which the vicar will soon retreat. Instead of alms, the pluralist offers insults and suggests, "Your parish, and some work would you become,/ so haste away, or Constable's your doom." While the ugly, importunate beggar reaches out with hat in hand, the sleek cleric clutches his dark robes and retreats physically from the disabled man and his claims. This strongly anticlerical statement contrasts poor law to Christian charity and citizen to outsider, as it brands the state system of relief inadequate and inhumane. The beggar, who has his valor and state service written on his body, begs for a humanitarian response going beyond that of the law; although he has the last word, his claims are refused.

In 1635, the mayor of Salisbury met monthly with town overseers and churchwardens to tally Sunday donations for the poor and to discuss payments to the destitute. They registered boys to be apprenticed, and to stave off future claims, they called in newcomers to be questioned. Indeed, one alderman reporting a stranger lodged at the Widow Easton's, recommended: "If he may be voided the town, let it be done!"[12] The aldermen ran a tight ship; con-

---

[10] Peter Mandler, "The Making of the New Poor Law *Redivivus*," *Past and Present* 117 (1987): 133.

[11] Paul Slack, *Poor Law*, 48.

[12] Paul Slack, ed., *Poverty in Early Stuart Salisbury*, vol. 31, *Wiltshire Reco Society*, (Warwick: Devizes, 1975), 94, 101.

Figure 1.1. "The Pluralist and the Old Soldier," John Collier, 1770. Wellcome Institute Library, London

trolling local welfare costs meant giving with one hand and exiling with the other.

Local residents could also monitor potential applicants and work to control costs. Thomas Turner, a shopkeeper in East Hoathly, Sussex, was an active vestry member and sometimes overseer of the poor in his village during the 1750s. Discovering in 1756 that a local, unmarried girl was pregnant, he and another man visited her and tried to make her admit her lover's name. When she refused to do so, they took her to a justice of the peace in the nearby town of Lewes so that she could be examined for legal settlement and perhaps be linked to another parish. Unfortunately, from his point of view, she was settled in East Hoathly. Moreover, "[w]ith all the persuasions Mr. Verral, Mr. French, and myself were masters of [we] could not prevail on her to confess the father, though I think we tried all ways to come to the knowledge of him." Unless the father were identified, the parish would have to pay for the child's support.[13]

These public encounters between overseers, vestry members, and the parish poor continued through the eighteenth century. The court case, *King v. Collet*, outlines the weekly relief ritual around 1823 in a southern rural parish where family allowances were granted to the indigent:

The parishioners were accustomed to meet once a week at the parish workhouse, at which meetings all applications for relief were received and where all laborers belonging to the parish, who had not in the preceding week been in constant employment, attended to give an account of their earnings and received such sums as, with the earnings, should amount to a sum deemed competent to their maintenance in proportion to their children.[14]

But by 1823, many country gentlemen had stopped defending a natural right to relief and turned toward laissez-faire economics. *King v. Collet* arose from the court challenge of a landlord who demanded investigation of applicants' incomes and work services from the poor. In this case, consensus had failed, and outsiders were called in to adjudicate.

Over time, many communities discovered that knowledge of the poor was a complex matter; agreement about entitlement proved neither easy nor automatic. Whose standards of destitution or being "out of work" were to be used? And how were overseers to know who "belonged" to the parish and

---

[13] David Vaisey, ed., *The Diary of Thomas Turner, 1754–1765* (New York: Oxford University Press, 1984), 48.

[14] Richard Burn, *The Justice of the Peace and the Parish Officer*, 24th ed., with corrections, additions, and improvements by Sir George Chetwynd, 5 vols. (London: T. Cadell, 1825), 4:174–5.

was therefore eligible for aid in a society where migration was normal? Since overseers changed every year, what should be done to maintain continuity of judgments? Even in 1600, the urban poor were notoriously mobile, and rural laborers circulated from job to job in regions far wider than the single parish. The likelihood that an applicant might be an outsider or unknown to the overseer mounted with the population and geographic size of the parish. Before overseers would admit responsibility for someone, the person's eligibility had to be established.

From at least the later sixteenth century, entitlement derived from what was called "settlement." Originally, in the common law, a person's settlement derived from the location of his or her home, and late sixteenth-century statutes permitted easy acquisition of residence rights. Richard Burn, author of the standard handbook on local administration used in England from the mid-eighteenth to the mid-nineteenth centuries, commented that under Elizabethan law, "the first day a man came into a parish, he was a stranger, the second day he was a guest, and the third, he was an inhabitant."[15] Burn's rather flippant judgment about the ease of settlement in earlier days betrays his own preoccupations with that issue's difficulty in his own times. What constituted legal settlement was explicitly defined by Parliament in the later seventeenth century, and it became progressively more difficult to obtain, although the concept itself remained alive and still influenced poor law entitlements in the twentieth century. A person acquired settlement in a parish and therefore the legal right to poor relief by serving an apprenticeship there, by being hired for a year, by holding a local office, by paying local taxes, or by renting or owning local property. Women acquired their husband's settlements upon marriage, and legitimate children inherited rights from their parents. In other words, the right to full membership in a local community, which included poor law benefits, came through work service of at least a year, through property holdings, and through public service. Access to this right came more easily to adult men than to women, and most easily of all to those with property, who could buy their way in with little difficulty.[16] Nevertheless, it was relatively easy for taxpayers to stop migrants from acquiring local settlement. They could hire workers for periods of less than a year or restrict apprenticeships and the availability of local offices; property owners could

---

[15] Richard Burn, *The Justice of the Peace and Parish Officer*, 2 vols. (London: A. Millar, 1755), 2:191.

[16] For a discussion of settlement laws, see Herbert Davey, *Poor Law Settlement and Removal* (London: Stevens & Sons, 1908); and also Robert Pashley, *Pauperism and the Poor Laws* (London: Longman, Brown, Green and Longmans, 1852).

refuse to lease cottages to those with insecure employment and limited resources.[17]

For the poor, settlement operated as intangible property, an extra resource to be called upon when needed. Application to the parish normally brought added income. Consequently, for tax payers, the comfortable settlement – of people other than themselves – brought a financial risk in hard times. As a result, property owners sometimes tried to limit access to settlement, particularly in the later eighteenth and early nineteenth centuries when destitution skyrocketed. Parliament made the process easier by permitting parishes to remove those "likely to be chargeable." After 1662, people without legal grounds for a settlement who had lived in a parish fewer than forty days could be ejected.[18] By 1692, even this was thought too permissive, and newcomers had to give public notice to the overseers of arrival; their forty-day trial period began only after their presence was announced in church to give everyone the chance to object and to brand them as undesirables.[19] Only those who could get a certificate of future support and good character from their parish of settlement could be absolutely sure that they could move outside their home parish and not face removal. Not until 1795 did people without a settlement gain the legal right to remain in a parish until they actually became chargeable on the poor laws.

The practical impact of such restrictions has been much debated since Adam Smith remarked that the English poor found themselves "cruelly oppressed" by the settlement laws.[20] Norma Landau has recently argued that until 1795, "parish officers used the laws of settlement to regulate the immigration of the poor to their parishes." Using information gleaned from the Kent petty sessions, she concludes that local officials routinely examined newcomers regarding their settlement and would sometimes export those not yet receiving relief. In her view, the surveillance of migrants and their regulation was "an integral component of the economic structures of early modern England," serving to limit newcomers' access to local resources and opportunities.[21] Keith Snell has vigorously challenged this view, stressing the generally high level of migration in England and the lack of a link between

[17] K. D. M. Snell, "Pauper Settlement and the Right to Poor Relief in England and Wales, *Continuity and Change* 6:3 (1991): 398.

[18] 13 & 14 Charles II, c. 12.

[19] 3 & 4 William and Mary, c. 11.

[20] Adam Smith, *The Wealth of Nations* (London: Ward Lock Bowder, 1891), 126.

[21] Norma Landau, "The Laws of Settlement and the Surveillance of Immigration in Eighteenth-Century Kent," *Continuity and Change* 3:3 (1988): 391–420; idem, "The Regulation of Immi-

residence and settlement rights. People had the right to migrate in search of work, and his own reading of settlement examinations suggests that virtually none applied to people who were employed. In Snell's view, the poor could move freely into parishes other than "closed" ones, where rental property was actively restricted, and they could normally remain there unless they became a charge on the poor laws and local officials had an incentive to remove them, which occurred in only a minority of cases.[22] It seems a mistake, therefore, to see the settlement laws and their operation as interfering with labor migration in any effective way. But they had other consequences.

Determining settlement was a burdensome, time-consuming task for parish officials, who could certainly use their right to remove those "likely to be chargeable" as a way of harassing the destitute and encouraging them to move on. Thus, the settlement laws could bring hardship to the poor, and they certainly created mountains of correspondence, endless legal appeals, and much employment for English lawyers. As early as 1786, Sir James Burrow published two volumes of precedent-setting decisions from just the Court of King's Bench on the subject of settlements.[23] As a determinant of local tax rates, the legal liability for relief was a hotly contested topic.

Before destitute persons became paupers, they had to demonstrate need, entitlement, and the willingness to receive parish aid. At least three sets of actions took place: The destitute person had to ask for relief, the responsible parish had to be established, and overseers of the poor had to agree to grant aid under conditions acceptable to the applicant. The would-be pauper was questioned, sometimes investigated, and officially examined before a magistrate, who represented the local landlords and gentlemen; information was exchanged and recorded, and offers were outlined until the pauper accepted or rejected the terms. Before 1834, justices of the peace could also be called upon to review a judgment if a feisty applicant challenged overseers' decisions. A pauper – who was assumed to be a male household head – could go before a justice and swear that he was "very poor and impotent and not able to provide for himself and his family," and that he had been refused relief. The justices could then call the overseers to appear in court and justify their refusal.

gration, Economic Structures, and Definitions of the Poor in Eighteenth-Century England," *Historical Journal* 33:3 (1990): 541–572.

[22] Snell, "Pauper Settlement," 384–5, 399.

[23] Sidney Webb and Beatrice Webb, *Old Poor Law*, 7:328, 334. More extensive treatments of the statutes and the common law cases regulating poor relief and settlement before 1800 can be found in Nolan, *Relief and Settlement*; Sir Gregory Allnutt Lewin, *A Summary of the Law of Settlement*, 1827; James Sculpture, *A Compendium of the Laws Relating to the Settlement and Removal of the Poor*, 1827.

If they did not convince the court of the legitimacy of their decision, the justices could order maintenance for the pauper and his family at a particular rate, although this probably happened rarely.[24] Peter Mandler argues that the landlords worked within an ethic of paternalism, sometimes intervening to support the "natural rights" of the poor. Until they converted to a logic of the marketplace in the years around and after 1817, country gentlemen could interfere in the poor law process in the interest of the applicant. Mandler describes their role, however, as a "weak force exercised at a distance."[25]

The process of decision making could take days or weeks. It might involve the exchange of letters, requests for birth or marriage certificates, and inquiries with landlords, employers, or relatives. Because both overseer and pauper could cite earlier welfare decisions as precedents, the process often required checking past rulings in several parishes. It could also involve lengthy appeals before magistrates as both parish and pauper sought to maintain their "rights" and privileges over a long period of time in which circumstances and personnel had changed. During the later eighteenth century, judges heard cases in which overseers claimed the right to force paupers into workhouses, rather than grant them outrelief as local justices of the peace ordered. In the case of *King v. Carlisle,* which came before the royal courts in 1767, Carlisle overseers eventually won a battle to cut off a relief allowance to Jane Carr, who had received one shilling a week for herself and her two illegitimate children. After granting her outrelief for six months, overseers decided to give her maintenance in the workhouse. She offered to take five pence a week or to support one child and have the other enter the workhouse, but the Carlisle overseers refused to make a deal. Rather than enter the workhouse, Carr appealed to justices at the Cumberland quarter sessions and got an order for support at one shilling a week. But the Carlisle authorities promptly refused the order and appealed it to the Assize court, where their position was upheld: "The defendant was by law empowered to refuse payment of such weekly allowance."[26]

Well before the adoption of the 1834 Poor Law Amendment Act, public charity had moved far away from a simple hand-to-hand transfer of funds from rich to poor. Public "gifts" had lost their spontaneity and their immediacy and had become contested, negotiated, and sometimes litigated pay-

---

[24] Richard Burn, *The Justice of the Peace and the Parish Officer,* 14th ed. (London: T. Cadell, 1780), 4:573–5.

[25] Mandler, *"Redivivus,"* 137.

[26] Richard Burn, *The Justice of the Peace and the Parish Officer,* 19th ed. (London: T. Cadell, 1800), 4:850.

ments. Over time, the granting of relief became an increasingly formal process, depending more and more upon written records and decisions. Yet it still involved intangibles: deference, paternalism, notions about gender, old age and childhood. "Appropriate" relief was a protean, changeable concept, one regularly redefined by applicants and authorities during the granting of welfare, and one whose public definition underwent major changes between 1601 and the repeal of the poor laws in 1948.

Deciding who belonged in the various categories mandated by Parliament required information. Discussing early poor law practice, George Oxley argues that in most parishes decisions were made on the basis of common knowledge, inasmuch as the poor were the neighbors, tenants, and employees of the overseers and justices. Reputation provided whatever details were needed in a society where most people were illiterate and where most business was carried out through face-to-face encounters. He maintains that in the sixteenth and seventeenth centuries, written records served only to prevent fraud and to give decisions "legal validity."[27] Nevertheless, written surveys were sometimes at least ordered, if not enforced. For example, in 1597, the Court of Quarter Sessions in Cornwall directed each parish in the county to prepare a report on its poor, noting those who were incapable of self-support, those who could earn part of their keep, and the kin who could contribute to paupers' maintenance. These surveys were to be used by overseers and justices when deciding about policy and about the levying of poor rates. Towns, too, did censuses of the poor when they were first setting up their poor law administrations; elaborate lists of paupers have survived for Norwich and Ipswich.[28] This impulse to define, to list, and to fix the status and condition of the poor through a written record was atypical in the early days of the poor laws, but it was to become more common during the eighteenth century for a particular category of the poor.

Outsiders had their status defined and remembered through paper and ink, not fickle public memory. A law of 1692 directed overseers of the poor to record in their account books the names and official dates of arrival in a parish of newcomers seeking settlement.[29] Establishing legal settlement, at least from the period after the English Civil War, left a clear paper trail. Enough certificates of settlement, settlement examinations, and orders of removal have survived to show the heavy use of such documents by migrants and by

---

[27] George Oxley, *Poor Relief in England and Wales, 1601–1834* (London: David & Charles, 1974), 52–3.

[28] Webb and Webb, *Old Poor Law,* 7:87; Oxley, *Poor Relief,* 52–3.

[29] 3 & 4 William and Mary, c. 11.

parishes eager to protect themselves from illegitimate claims. Destitute people whose membership in the local community was not common knowledge had to answer questions about birthplace, marriage, apprenticeship, work history, and property rentals, and then to swear to the truth of such details before a justice of the peace. Overseers could then use such documents to justify removal to a parish of legal settlement, and applicants for relief could use them to prove entitlement to aid in a particular place. As the rules for settlement became more complex and many people inherited their settlement rather than earning it themselves, where a person legally "belonged" ceased to be a self-evident matter. Certainly by the eighteenth century in the larger urban parishes, common knowledge and local oral traditions became unsatisfactory guides for decision making, particularly when overseers were caught between taxpayers' demands for cheap relief and the claims of destitute applicants. Written records brought overseers some protection from irate citizens, meddling judges, and importunate paupers. On matters of money and settlement, welfare administrators found themselves drawn into fixed procedures and formal decisions, most of which were designed to separate insiders from outsiders. Other discriminations were less important.

Another step toward formality and fixity arrived with the hiring of paid administrators who investigated claims and oversaw any litigation over the forms and amounts of relief. These parish employees could devote much more time to checking claims than the often reluctant elected overseers they replaced. Ecclesfield in the West Riding hired an overseer as early as 1711, and many other examples can be found in eighteenth-century records. Paid workhouse governors, usually in the towns, took on similar roles. Finally, in 1819, Parliament formally gave parishes the power to hire assistant overseers, which many did during the early 1820s.[30]

Pauper Meets Overseer

The heart of the welfare process lay in the contacts between pauper and administrator, when the official formed an opinion about the entitlements and the character of the destitute person thrust before him. Each gave a performance for the benefit of the other: the pauper to extract aid, the official to strike a wise balance between help and discouragement of additional appeals. These actions had a public face because the process of granting alms was a collective one: Overseers met as a group and had to record their decisions.

[30] Oxley, *Poor Relief,* xx, 45, 128.

Moreover, at least two justices were needed to approve the apprenticing of a child or the punishment of an adult.[31] Individual inclinations were therefore curbed by publicity and the precision of a written record.

When overseers acted alone and without recording their actions, irregularities could and did occur. Consider the case of Harriet Williams, a widowed servant who worked in London much of her adult life in St. George, Hanover Square. In 1829, when unemployed, she went to Exeter, intending to go on to Exmouth to visit her uncle. Unfortunately, she was ill and decided to apply for relief in Exeter. The poor law officer there refused to help her and ordered her carted outside the parish, where she was dumped by a hedge. A farmer found her and walked her through his parish, leaving her on the road, where a gentleman gave her a ride in his gig for a few miles. When Williams fainted, he, too, abandoned her. Some laborers found her and took her to a nearby inn, where she was eventually examined by a poor law clerk and given a few shillings. Williams then disappears from the poor law record, although she probably had a secure entitlement to relief in London and warranted temporary, local aid because of her illness.[32] But as a female without local connections, she was easy to ignore and probably too sick to assert her rights effectively. Whatever she said to the Exeter overseer of the poor had the effect of alarming him about cost and liability, rather than encouraging him to help.

The presentation of a case, therefore, mattered. For the most part, applicants for aid found themselves in the public eye, their claims listed by clerks and examined by justices. They, as well as overseers, tailored performance to expectations. Unfortunately, the written record is virtually silent upon the tone and style of the thousands of such encounters that took place annually. A few sketchy descriptions have survived: All firmly locate power on the side of the overseers, although recognizing the claims of the poor.

In 1784, Thomas Rowlandson drew a picture of a vestry meeting. A group of well-wined and-dined, bewigged officials amuses itself talking and reading while a line of parish supplicants waits on the other side of a heavy table. A young, attractive girl with heavy breasts, possibly pregnant, is being interviewed and ogled, as a distraught, poor man cowers in the background. The space of the vestry room is controlled by the officials who confine the applicants to the standing space near the door. Social difference and dependence are ratified by dress as well as demeanor.[33]

---

[31] 43 Elizabeth, c. 2.

[32] 70A/PO6283, Devon Record Office, quoted by James Stephen Taylor, *Poverty, Migration, and Settlement in the Industrial Revolution: Sojourners' Narratives* (Palo Alto: Society for the Promotion of Science and Scholarship, 1989), 9–10.

[33] John Hayes, *Rowlandson's Watercolors and Drawings* (London: Phaidon, 1972), 90.

Figure 1.2. "The Parish Vestry," Thomas Rowlandson, 1784. Courtesy of the Victoria and Albert Museum

Writing in 1835, Charles Dickens described a similar meeting between a London widow with six children and parish overseers. The board, "who all sit behind great books and with their hats on," query the "miserable looking woman" about her address. Escorted into the boardroom by a fat, parish beadle in a lace-trimmed coat, she answers them obsequiously and claims that her landlady "knows me to be very hard-working and industrious"; the overseer rudely interrupts and orders the beadle to check her story, which if true would gain her the right to enter the workhouse.[34] Dickens's and Rowlandson's paupers defer to local worthies, who barely acknowledge their existence. The price of relief was acknowledged dependence and a submissive air.

Nevertheless, to assume that the destitute were completely powerless in their negotiations with welfare authorities is a mistake. Not only did welfare legislation before 1834 guarantee the very poor certain rights of appeal in the common law courts, but the process of granting welfare was so structured that their participation in it helped to shape outcomes. Gaining poor relief required action, cooperation, and choices, which were then responded to by welfare officials. Although the extent of their power was limited, applicants had a certain latitude within which they could negotiate about outcomes and pressure authorities to give them aid in a congenial form. The parish clerks of St. Martin, Vintry, in London recorded welfare cases in unusual detail, offering us rare glimpses of the welfare process in that parish. In November of 1816, Thomas Morris, who lived and worked in Sawbridgeworth, Hertfordshire, with his wife and seven children, asked poor law authorities to pay his rent so that he could remain in the parish. They contacted overseers in St. Martin, Vintry, the district where he had a settlement, and passed along the request. London overseers could have ignored him, but they then ran the risk of having all nine Morrises sent back to the capital. Instead, two overseers hired a horse and carriage and traveled the twenty-four miles to the Morrises' cottage, where they found the family eating a "poor but homely dinner." Morris had been ill and then was laid off because local employers had chosen to give work to those with settlements in the parish, rather than to migrants. After checking his story, the overseers paid his rent and left the family to their own devices.[35]

Negotiation was even more in evidence in the case of Mary Savage, a widow who managed to extract a great deal of practical help from St. Martin, Vintry, officials over a period of ten years. In 1818, at her request they paid

---

[34] Charles Dickens, *Sketches by Boz* (London, Chapman & Hall, 1850), 2.

[35] St. Martin, Vintry, "Examination of the Poor, 1815–1829," 30 November 1816, Guildhall Library.

to get a copy of her marriage certificate so that she could prove her children were legitimate and get them admitted to the Military Asylum in Chelsea. One daughter was apprenticed by the parish, using local charity funds. Finally, in 1829, Savage came to a vestry meeting and proposed to marry her common law husband, if they would provide a dowry of £5. They gave her £1 at once and the rest after the ceremony, adding another £5 as an apprenticeship fee for her son to his new stepfather![36] She, rather than the overseers, seems to have been orchestrating that set of welfare negotiations. Few probably fared as well as she.

Important elements of the welfare process were completely under the control of the poor. They decided when to ask for aid and when to refuse it. Certainly, hunger and homelessness drove many to request help, but need does not trigger an automatic rush into the arms of welfare authorities. As we see in our own times, many street people keep their distance from shelters and charities; the existence of a service does not guarantee its use or its adequacy to meet the perceived needs of a potential recipient. Remember that a choice between several unpalatable alternatives remains a choice. When in need, the poor could ask relatives or neighbors for aid; they could stop paying rent or pawn household goods. Towns had multiple charities that gave grants of money or food, and local shops often offered credit to former customers. Another response was simply to leave and look for work elsewhere. A few would beg or steal in order to survive. Even if they did not like the alternatives they faced, most poor people had some choices to make.

Also, the poor were the initial source of the information on settlement offered to authorities. Applicants for relief could claim ignorance or conveniently forget pertinent details that might legitimate their removal to an undesirable part of the country. Since relevant records of their history might exist in any one of England and Wales's more than fifteen thousand parishes, it was quite impractical for an overseer or relieving officer to do much to check the story told to him. Unless local people offered additional information, poor law authorities were at the mercy of the pauper's story, which had to be disproved if they wished to reject it.

Applying to poor law authorities was only one of several options whose costs and benefits the poor had to weigh. For some, the cost was too high to pay. Many workers proudly announced in their autobiographies that their families had refused to take aid from their parishes; dependence on public charity was a line they refused to cross. Joseph Arch, born in 1826, the son of a Warwickshire agricultural laborer, remarked that his mother explicitly for-

---

[36] Ibid., 13 May 1818.

bade her children to go to the rectory and get free soup. Although she would accept help from neighbors and friends, she and her husband thought poor law aid or charity reduced them to the level of paupers, a status they and their son vehemently rejected: "The poor man who accepted the sop of parish help, which was cast to him as a bone to a dog, felt that life's heavy burden had been made lighter. . . . And so it was that men, born to be free, and willing to be independent, were turned into parasites."[37] In Arch's representation of himself and his family, self-respect was tied to their right of refusal of aid from social superiors or from the state. Others found ways of reconciling pride and the acceptance of welfare. John Clare, who was born in 1793 in Northamptonshire, the son of a shepherd and farm laborer, remembered that his father, when in extreme poverty, thought more work was the appropriate solution, and he forced his young children to join him at threshing and other farm jobs. At a later point in his life, when his health had broken down, he refused to take a pension but insisted on doing road work for five shillings a week in order not to be "beholden" to the parish.[38] Parish support for him consisted of a public works job, which he would not have gotten if he had not been eligible for poor law aid.

Others lacked a revulsion against poor law aid and turned to it with seemingly little reluctance when in need. During the 1820s, John Castle, his mother, and his siblings drew a weekly parish grant from Great Coggeshall in Buckinghamshire, which enabled them to survive. Once, when unemployed as an adolescent, he and his brother applied to the local guardians for relief and entered the workhouse because they "had nothing to lose." Later in his life, when he could not earn enough as a weaver to support his family, he drew outrelief from Sudbury union. Rather than curse the overseers for what they would not do, he accepted their help gladly. One day when his wife was too ill to permit him to walk several miles to get his grant, an overseer dropped by his house and gave him the money. In his autobiography, Castle pictured the overseer as a divine messenger: "Many such deliverances I had which made my heart praise the goodness of the Lord."[39]

Case records show that many paupers took an active stance vis à vis poor law authorities; they initiated encounters and complained of treatment if it was not satisfactory. John Castle criticized the food in the Witham workhouse

[37] Joseph Arch, *Joseph Arch. The Story of His Life Told by Himself* (London: Hutchinson, 1898), 35–6.

[38] John Clare, *John Clare's Autobiographical Writings*, ed. Eric Robinson (New York: Oxford University Press, 1983), 3, 15–16.

[39] John Castle, "The Diary of John Castle," in John Burnett, ed., *Destiny Obscure* (London: Allen Lane, 1982), 262–3.

and was indignant when evicted because of his complaints.[40] When Joseph Nelson was ill in 1813, his wife went to the overseers in Clayton and demanded more support than the two shillings per week normally granted them. As soon as she was refused, she contacted a local magistrate who summoned the overseers and ordered them to pay her family eight shillings a week until Nelson recovered. A few years later, after Nelson's death, she again negotiated for more money with local overseers in Horton, who were convinced that more had to be done voluntarily or the magistrates would intervene.[41] Not only did she manage to manipulate the overseers, but neighbors successfully pressured doctors and poor law authorities on her behalf. The poor laws operated in local communities where individuals were susceptible to political pressures and legal restraints.

Welfare aid under the poor laws came as the result of application and negotiations in which the destitute took an active part. Although they had little direct power over authorities, they could manipulate the process in limited ways and contract out when it became unacceptable. Citizens with parish settlements had a right to relief, and they knew it. In England and Wales, "social citizenship" with a right to maintenance arrived with the poor laws, not with the Labour government of 1945. But it rested on dual inequalities. Communities in England gave the familiar destitute a secure place at the very bottom of the social ladder, whereas they denied a space and status to those without a settlement. The poor laws ratified this distinction between low status and no status.

The Poor Become "Paupers"

The very commonness of poverty demanded distinctions, differentiation between types and degrees of entitlement. To be sure, poverty had long had multiple representations – witness the long-lived power of words such as "deserving" and "undeserving," "industrious" and "lazy." The Elizabethans thought they had categorized sufficiently by separating the "impotent" from those who could and would work; officials were to weigh bodily strengths, employability, and attitudes, along with settlements, when they responded to needs. But over time, a new representation of the very poor solidified and captured public attention. The dependent poor became "paupers," and moved from a category identified with the human condition to one tinged with the

---

[40] Ibid., 263–5.

[41] Kirkby Lonsdale, "Township Records," 25 January 1813, John Jenkinson to Stephen Garnett, #164; ibid., 21 March 1817, #81, John Haley to Stephen Garnett.

colors of deviance and disreputability. The transition took place in the early nineteenth century.

The noun, "pauper," comes from the Latin adjective, *pauper,* meaning poor, which passed into English through the legal phrase, *in forma pauperis.* A statute of 1495 granted poor people the right to sue without paying for court costs.[42] In this legal sense, a pauper was a person who would swear before a justice to own less than five pounds of property excluding his or her clothes.[43] Such people were then entitled to free legal services and writs so that their access to justice in the courts was not hindered by their poverty. It signaled an economic status, which the state privileged in order to safeguard the legal rights of the poor. Yet the word had other connotations. From the late fifteenth century through the nineteenth, "pauper" also meant simply a very poor person, someone requiring charity. Particularly for novelists and journalists, pauper became a more dramatic word for poverty, which signaled extreme need.

But another, more restricted, much more pejorative sense of the word came into use during the mid-eighteenth century and became dominant by the early nineteenth century. Paupers were first and foremost people in receipt of poor relief, those in care of the state because of their inability to support themselves. The first edition of Richard Burn's manual for justices of the peace calls those receiving parish relief paupers, and Thomas Mendham published in 1775 his comments on the poor laws in the form of "A Dialogue . . . between a gentleman, a pauper, and his friend."[44] Then in 1799, Patrick Colquhoun called for the establishment of "a pauper police" in his discussion of indigence.[45] By the first decades of the nineteenth century, writers discussed pauper laborers, pauper patients, pauper asylums, and pauper graves, all in the context of the potential or actual services of the poor law.

Although in its early usage the word had a clear human referent, over time it became more and more abstract and more pejorative. By the early nineteenth century, "pauperism" slipped into public discourse in sentences reeking of condemnation and moral superiority. William Cobbett complained in 1823 of "the pauperism and the crimes that disgrace this once happy and moral England."[46] Harriet Martineau, while praising discipline and self-help,

---

[42] 11 Henry VII, c. 12.

[43] Sir William Blackstone, *Commentaries on the Laws of England.* 3rd ed., 4 vols. (Oxford: Oxford University Press, 1768), see III: xxiv, 400; quoted in *OED*; Richard Burn, *Justice of the Peace and the Parish Officer,* 29th ed. (London: T. Cadell, 1845).

[44] Burn, *Justice of the Peace and Parish Officer* (London: A. Miller, 1755); Thomas Mendham, 1775; quoted in OED.

[45] Patrick Colquhoun, *A Treatise on Indigence* (London: J. Hatchard, 1806).

[46] *OED*, 1971:II: 570.

warned readers in 1834 of "the indigent who have been pauperized by the undue depression of wages," and witnesses attending the 1834 Royal Commission on the Poor Laws complained of the pauperism in their parishes, which they cleverly attributed to the effects of the laws themselves.[47] Such attacks, to quote Gertrude Himmelfarb, succeeded in "deliberately breaking the continuum of pauper and poor." A rhetoric of exclusion had been codified by 1834.[48] By the 1850s, a host of derivative, rather nasty words had slipped into print. The *Oxford English Dictionary*, for example, notes pauperization, dispauperize, pauperous, and even pauperate! Clouds of "pauperdom" obscured the faces of the destitute.

Not only writers branded the dependent poor as a separate, inferior group, but Parliament ratified the process in law. The ability of the poor to attend open vestry meetings and to vote for overseers of the poor ended in 1818 with the passage of Sturges Bourne's Act, which restricted parish meetings in districts adopting it to ratepayers and gave multiple votes to those owning large amounts of property.[49] Then the Poor Law Amendment Act of 1834 levied similar restrictions on the elections for poor law guardians, and the Reform Bill of 1832 and the Municipal Corporation Act of 1835 formally debarred any person who had received parish relief within the preceding year from voting.[50] Not until the Parliament was prepared to link political participation with national citizenship, rather than property, did the dependent poor gain equal political rights.

Notions of pauperization and pauperism projected deep social fears of corruption and decay onto the bodies of the destitute. Perhaps, many thought, urban pollution and disease came not from economic ill health but from moral failure. In the conception of the pauper, we can see the English wrestling with multiple anxieties. They transferred their hostility to the dirt, disease, and decay of early industrial society onto the figures of the dependent poor. The pauper helped people define their own virtue by representing what they were not. If in 1601 the unworthy poor were vagrants and migrants, by 1834 *all* the dependent poor had become unworthy. How and why this transition took place will be explored in Chapter 3.

---

[47] *Report from the Commissioners for Inquiring into the Administration and Practical Operation of the Poor Laws*, Appendix A, *Reports of the Assistant Commissioners*, Part I. 1834 (44), vol. 28, 635–6.

[48] Gertrude Himmelfarb, *The Idea of Poverty* (New York: Knopf, 1984), 175; see also Mary Poovey, *Making a Social Body* (Chicago: University of Chicago Press, 1995), 11.

[49] Bryan Keith-Lucas, *English Local Government in the Nineteenth and Twentieth Centuries* (London: The Historical Association, 1977).

[50] 3 & 4 William IV, c. 76; 2 William IV, c. 45; 5 & 6 William IV, c. 76.

2

WEEKLY DOLES: COMMUNAL SUPPORT IN THE EIGHTEENTH CENTURY

For town-relief the grieving man applied,
And begg'd with tears what some with scorn denied;
Others look'd down upon the glowing vest,
And, frowning, ask'd him at what price he dress'd?
Happy for him his country's laws are mild,
They must support him, though they still reviled.
George Crabbe, 1810

Responsibility for the poor, as conceived in the eighteenth century, conjures many contradictory images. Philanthropists decorated their tracts with pious pictures of their charitable charges: neatly dressed widows and frail orphans deferring to their bourgeois benefactors. Yet George Crabbe's "grieving man" was reviled while supported, disdained for his "glowing vest." The dependent poor had multiple images in the public eye, representations manipulating the beholder to place vastly differing distances between self and the needy. The poor laws and their subjects shared this ambiguity. Even though a widespread discourse of humanitarianism continued to privilege private and public charity toward the poor, much in public culture suggested profound distrust of the impoverished. They were not respectable even if in some ways deserving. The practice of poor relief during the eighteenth century rested on similarly ambiguous responses – generosity interlaced with suspicion, aid tied to dependence and restriction. In a society where the destitute were always there to be seen and to lay burdens on consciences as well as pocketbooks, it is no wonder that their pictures were drawn in multiple colors.

Dealing with the poor was unavoidable in England and Wales because of the cradle-to-grave benefits mandated by Parliament for the destitute. Whatever the attitudes of the dispensers, the poor laws provided multiple services and a scale of benefits that historians like Keith Snell and David Thomson have called generous.[1] No doubt the public largesse fed public distrust, along with a widespread acceptance of the poor laws themselves. There existed within Britain strong communal pressures for the public support of certain types of poor people. Peter Laslett has pointed to the linkage between kinship organization and collective security. The strongly nuclear structures of British families, combined with high death rates, migration by adolescents, and high proportions of celibates, meant that a large percentage of the population reached old age without kin to help support them. Both Laslett and Richard Smith have suggested a strong connection between British demographic patterns and welfare; the latter permitted the former to function. If the society was not prepared to let destitute elderly starve, which it was not, then the society had to step in when families failed.[2] Both Laslett and Smith point to a wide cultural toleration within Britain for collective support for the elderly.

This chapter explores eighteenth-century welfare practices, as well as popular responses to parish aid. I use the categories of settlement rights, age, and gender to analyze differences in treatment, and I also outline urban and rural variations in welfare strategies. Work as relief, publicly subsidized self-help, is also part of the story. Differences in practice and representation make welfare under the Elizabethan poor laws a contested subject, yet a familiar one in every parish and township of the country.

Numbers of Paupers

Parish officers had no lack of potential claimants for poor law aid. Every village and township had its share of people whose incomes hovered at or below subsistence. Poverty existed in many gradations, all of which are difficult to quantify from a distance of three hundred years. Scholars today, revising Gregory King's estimates from 1688 with local data, judge that cottagers, pau-

---

[1] K. D. M. Snell, *Annals of the Labouring Poor* (New York: Cambridge University Press, 1985), 104; David Thomson, "Welfare and the Historians," in L. Bonfield and K. Wrightson, eds., *The World We Have Lost: Histories of Population and Social Structure* (Oxford: Oxford University Press, 1986), 370.

[2] Peter Laslett, "Family, Kinship and Collectivity as Systems of Support in Pre-Industrial Europe: A Consideration of the 'Nuclear-Hardship' Hypothesis," *Continuity and Change* 3:2 (1988): 153–75; R. M. Smith, "The Structured Dependence of the Elderly as a Recent Development: Some Sceptical Historical Thoughts," *Ageing and Society* 4 (1984): 409–28.

pers, and vagrants accounted for about 24 percent of all English and Welsh households and between 15 percent and 18 percent of the total population at that time.[3] Clearly, a substantial share of workers lived from hand to mouth. Such people "decreased the wealth of the kingdom," and they had to scrounge to feed themselves.[4] But, at any one time, few got aid from the poor laws. Some got help via tax exemptions; others received intermittent charity or gifts from kin. Multiple expedients other than the poor laws kept the poorest sort alive. Despite their obligation to maintain the destitute, parishes were clearly not prepared to support large numbers of people, except during a short-term crisis. Nor were they prepared to transfer major amounts of income to them. In fact, Peter Lindert, using the surveys of King, Patrick Colquhoun, and David Davies calculates that relief payments accounted for only 1.2 percent or 1.5 percent of national income in the period 1685–90, 1.5 percent in 1753–9, and 2 percent in 1802–3; Paul Slack's estimates are similar.[5] Costs clearly rose during the eighteenth century as population increased and the economy entered an unstable period. Yet, at a time when income inequality was extreme and the population's health was precarious, property owners directed only limited social resources into relief of the poor. Parishes therefore had to allocate alms and differentiate among the destitute.

Just how many actually received poor law aid at any point in either the seventeenth or the eighteenth centuries is impossible to determine. Parishes and townships did not keep aggregate statistics, and Parliament first required a national accounting in 1803. Although Parliament paid scrupulous attention to the cost of welfare, it was content to leave its human face undefined and in shadows. In the year between Easter of 1802 and Easter of 1803, the parishes and townships of England and Wales recorded slightly over one million people as relief recipients – a total amounting to 11.4 percent of the population. Yet it is not clear whether overseers counted only the average number of peo-

---

[3] Peter H. Lindert and Jeffrey G. Williamson, "Revising England's Social Tables 1688–1867," *Explorations in Economic History* 19 (1982): 388; see also Tom Arkell, "The Incidence of Poverty in England in the Later Seventeenth Century," *Social History* 12 (1987): 23–47.

[4] King's tables are reprinted in Harold Perkin, *The Origins of Modern English Society, 1780–1880* (London: Routledge, 1969), 20–1.

[5] Nevertheless, these levels were not exceeded by the British state in the modern period until the 1930s. Between 1880 and 1920, social transfer payments in Britain accounted for less than 1.5 percent of Net National Product. See Peter H. Lindert, "Toward a Comparative History of Income and Wealth Inequality," in Y. S. Brenner, Hartmut Kaelble, and Mark Thomas, eds., *Income Distribution in Historical Perspective* (New York: Cambridge University Press, 1991), 221; Peter H. Lindert, "The Rise of Social Spending, 1880–1930," *Working Paper Series* 68, Agricultural History Center (Davis: University of California, 1992): 39. See also Paul Slack, *The English Poor Law, 1531–1782* (New York: Cambridge University Press, 1990), 22.

ple relieved or included everyone who got aid – and there is no reason to expect consistency of practice throughout the country.[6] Nevertheless, 11.4 percent can reasonably be treated as a minimum figure for the average incidence of dependence on the parishes in 1803. Using figures for wheat prices and relief costs as reported to Parliament, Joanna Innes calculates that poor law authorities spent enough annually to supply bread to 8 percent of the English population in 1748–50 and 9 percent in 1776.[7] Using a similar method, Paul Slack argues that the level of relief expenditures in England and Wales would have supported 11 percent of the population in 1783–5 and 15 percent in 1802–3.[8] Of course, many of the dependent poor got help only temporarily, so that the size of the dependent population in any given year would have been significantly larger than these figures.

Local studies, which follow the granting of relief in one area over a longer period of time, indicate a much higher incidence of dependence during difficult years than do the figures for 1803, a wartime year but not one of harvest failure. Tom Arkell found that about 25 percent of the population in two Warwickshire parishes needed some kind of public charity or poor law aid during the 1660s and 1670s. In St. Catherine, Coleman, London, about 23 percent of the population got relief in 1693–4, a period of depression; 25 percent of the adult males in the area of Carhampton in Somerset took parish aid at some point between 1766 and 1776. Over time, most of the laboring poor probably had to apply to the poor law, although we know little about length of dependency and frequency of application. Slack estimates that over a five-year period probably 20 percent of a parish population might well have applied for poor law aid.[9]

These estimates conceal as much as they reveal: Destitution varied significantly between summer and winter, good years and bad, rich parishes and poor. "Average" levels of the incidence of poor law support in a parish or township collapse the variation that made relief so intermittently expensive and choice so painful for contemporaries. The best that scholars can do today is to estimate an order of magnitude for the problem and note large-scale vari-

---

[6] For a discussion of the early poor law statistics, see Karel Williams, *From Pauperism to Poverty* (London: Routledge, 1981), 147, 230.

[7] Joanna Innes, "Social Problems: Poverty and Marginality in Eighteenth-Century England," unpublished paper presented to "The Social World of Britain and America, 1600–1820" (Williamsburg, VA, 1985), 28.

[8] Slack, *Poor Law*, 22.

[9] Arkell, "Poverty," 42; for a survey of sources on the incidence of pauperism in the eighteenth century, see Innes, "Social Problems," 28–31; Slack, *Poor Law*, 25.

ations over time. In the larger towns in reasonably good times, between 5 percent and 10 percent of residents probably got poor law aid, whereas in depression years, the use of welfare and the numbers on poor relief multiplied.
Going to the parish for help was a familiar process for both the urban and the
rural poor during the eighteenth century.

Boundaries

The poor laws created the effective boundaries of their communities. Those
who did not "belong" could be literally excluded through vagrancy laws and
settlement laws, or they could be marginalized more subtly through denial of
relief or implied threats of removal. Still, mechanical divisions between
insider and outsider were routinely blurred by judgments about usefulness in
the local labor market, by pragmatic calculations about time and trouble, and
by compassion. Overseers and claimants daily beat the bounds of the parish
as they negotiated the distribution of relief.

One major fault line marking off insider from outsider derived from occupation and presumed attitudes toward employment. Elizabethan law drew
strong moral distinctions between those who *could* not work or who could
not find work and those whom local authorities judged *would* not work.
Those belonging to this latter category – labeled rogues, vagabonds, and
sturdy beggars – were to receive not alms but the full weight of public punishment. The law branded a broad category of people who moved around the
country – particularly wandering scholars, jugglers, tinkers, peddlers, ship-
wrecked seamen, gypsies, minstrels, players, discharged prisoners, fortune-
tellers, and people who refused to take a job at current wage rates – as
vagrants. Those judged guilty of this crime could be "stripped naked from the
middle upwards and openly whipped until his or her body be bloody and then
passed to his or her birthplace or last residence and in case they know neither
they are to be sent to the House of Correction for a year."[10] In the public eye,
migrating from place to place and refusing to take a settled job signaled danger and disreputability. Lee Beier argues that in Tudor times vagrancy was a
social crime; the state marked out people for punishment and confinement
because of who they were, rather than what they had done. Parish officials
rounded up thousands of vagrants in the late sixteenth and early seventeenth

---

[10] Michael Nolan, *A Treatise of the Laws for the Relief and Settlement of the Poor*, 2 vols. (London: Butterworth, 1805), 2:385, 387; Sidney Webb and Beatrice Webb, *English Local Government from the Revolution to the Municipal Corporations Act*, vol. 7, *English Poor Law History,
Part 1: The Old Poor Law* (London: Longmans, 1927), 351–2.

centuries, goaded by central government diatribes against "masterless men."[11] Parish officers treated them as outsiders to be confined or removed.

The category of "rogue and vagabond" underwent considerable widening in 1744 when Parliament added, to the lists of the disorderly men who threatened to run away and abandon their families, people who "not having wherewith to maintain themselves, live idle without employment, and lunatics or others 'disordered in their senses.'" Wandering women who bore children outside their home parish could be whipped and jailed for up to six months, and beggars' children could be bound as servants or apprentices up to age twenty-one.[12] The law branded as outsiders not only those without settlements and steady jobs, but people whose mental state or family life was judged threatening to the community. "Belonging" to a parish, therefore, was not a simple matter of birthright or property holdings, but it reflected occupation, behavior, and values. It implied cultural conformity, as well as a legal status.

But whatever their occupation and attitude toward work, poor migrants found themselves scrutinized by parish authorities. Peter Clark has drawn attention to the large amount of "subsistence migration" by the poor looking for jobs during the seventeenth century.[13] No wonder town fathers and parish overseers worried about the arrival of seedy newcomers who might swell relief rolls. Although English towns did not control entry and residence in the manner of many German settlements, local authorities would sometimes attempt to block the residence of poor migrants. In 1557, the town council of Colchester in Essex directed citizens not to rent houses, shops, or tenancies to strangers unless it was clear they could be self-supporting.[14] The Durham parish of Pittington, in 1622, went further; its select vestry decreed that "no inhabitant . . . shall receive, harbour and entertain any stranger to be his tenant or tenants into his house or houses before he acquaint the Twelve with his intent, and shall himself and two sufficient men with him, enter into bond . . . to the Overseers that neither his tenant, wife or children shall be chargeable to the parish for five years next following, upon pain and penalty to forfeit ten shillings for every month."[15]

---

[11] A. L. Beier, *Masterless Men: The Vagrancy Problem in England, 1560–1640* (London: University Paperbacks, 1985), xxii, 148; see also Webb and Webb, *Old Poor Law,* 315–16.

[12] Nolan, *Treatise,* 2:49, 65, 66.

[13] Peter Clark, "Migration in England During the Late Seventeenth and Early Eighteenth Centuries," *Past and Present* 83 (1979): 57–90.

[14] Webb and Webb, *Old Poor Law,* 317.

[15] Churchwarden's Accounts of Pittington, Surtees Society, vol. 84 (1888), 84; quoted in Webb and Webb, *Old Poor Law,* 317.

In the later seventeenth century, Parliament gave to parish officials sharp weapons with which to attack the itinerant poor, if they so chose. The legislature branded migration by the poor as threatening and illegitimate: It regretted that "poor persons are not restrained from going from one parish to another, and therefore do endeavor to settle themselves in those parishes where there is the best stock, the largest commons or wastes to build cottages, and the most woods for them to burn and destroy, and when they have consumed it, then to another parish, and at last become rogues and vagabonds."[16] They posited a downward cycle from migration into slash-and-burn agriculture and finally to crime, which they were prepared to break in its initial phases.[17] Parliament empowered overseers, in a provision not repealed until 1795, to remove newcomers who were "likely to become chargeable to the parish." Initially, newcomers had to be removed within forty days or they could stay until they asked for relief, but the problem of their invisibility in larger towns and the difficulty of establishing a time of arrival led to further restrictions. By 1692, in order to qualify for settlement rights, migrants had to give written notice of arrival, which was to be registered by overseers and read aloud in the church. Outsiders were to be publicly identified and recorded, and even if allowed to reside in the short run, they remained in danger of being exported if they asked for relief.

The net effect of settlement laws on migrants has been debated for over two hundred years. Adam Smith's attack on the laws as cruelly oppressive of the poor was countered by John Howlett and Frederick Eden, both of whom doubted that the settlement laws interfered in any significant way with labor mobility.[18] In the 1920s, Dorothy Marshall renewed an attack on settlement regulations. She blamed the laws for indirectly causing vagrancy, splitting up families, and decreasing workers' freedom to move.[19] The Webbs place the laws squarely within the framework of repression, which they see guiding the poor laws. The argument that the settlement laws and their linkage to relief inhibited labor migration has been widely accepted by economic historians,

[16] 13 & 14 Charles II, c. 12.

[17] James S. Taylor makes this point in his article of 1972; see James S. Taylor, "The Unreformed Workhouse, 1776–1834," in E. W. Martin, ed., *Comparative Developments in Social Welfare* (London: Allen & Unwin, 1972), 57–83.

[18] Adam Smith, *The Wealth of Nations* (London: Routledge, 1891), 126; John Howlett, *An Examination of Mr. Pitt's Speech* (London, 1796), 14; Frederick Eden, *The State of the Poor* (London, 1797), 1:297.

[19] Dorothy Marshall, *The English Poor in the Eighteenth Century* (London: Routledge, 1926), 248–9.

but has recently been effectively challenged by George Boyer, who shows that poor relief payments had little or no effect upon economic growth and therefore could not have slowed the movement from agricultural counties into urban areas.[20]

But whatever their net impact on economic growth, the settlement laws clearly shaped the members of local communities and their sense of themselves. If overseers ignored settlement laws and offered relief to all, then migrants cannot be considered to have been marginal to local society; but if the laws guided welfare policy, then newcomers with various social characteristics were excluded. Three issues need to be confronted: the purpose for which the laws were used; the types of people who were examined and removed from their parish of residence; and the incidence of the laws' enforcement. These problems are difficult ones, for the central government in the seventeenth and eighteenth centuries collected no systematic data on removals, examinations, or migration. Moreover, the local documents that remain cannot be shown to be representative either of the poor who received or applied for relief or of migrants as a whole. At most, they describe a group of destitute people that attracted the attention of local officials for which a paper trail survives.

The settlement laws generated three sorts of materials: examinations of a poor person's parish of legal residence, certificates acknowledging settlement and a responsibility for relief, and orders of removal for a person back to his or her parish of settlement. Records are probably particularly incomplete for locally settled paupers well known by the overseers. Why go through an elaborate procedure to determine settlement, when an individual's local rights were acknowledged by all parties? Poor law settlement documents are therefore biased toward outsiders, whereas the locally settled are underrepresented. They give a good picture, however, of the workings of the law and its targets for removal.[21]

Consider the case of Thomas Hampson, a wheelwright born in Staffordshire, who had acquired a settlement via apprenticeship in the parish of Lee. He moved, after completing his indentures, to Rutland, where he worked for a time and married. Overseers threatened him with removal, so the couple

---

[20] George R. Boyer, *An Economic History of the English Poor Law, 1750–1850* (New York: Cambridge University Press, 1990), 192.

[21] For an evaluation of the various sources pertaining to settlement and of the problems and possibilities inherent in their use, see K. D. M. Snell, "Settlement, Poor Law and the Rural Historian: New Approaches and Opportunities," *Rural History* 3:2 (1992): 145–72.

moved to Royston in 1735, where he worked for a weekly wage that would not gain him a new settlement. Within a few weeks of his arrival, local overseers hauled him before a justice, discovered his settlement, and shipped him and his wife back to Lee. Despite his employability, they wanted to take no chances. E. M. Hampson decided that in Cambridgeshire, "married men with families were the prey on which the vultures swooped mercilessly."[22] Norma Landau estimates that at most 9 percent of the three thousand men whose settlement cases were considered by the Kent petty sessions during the eighteenth century were single.[23] Married men, even younger ones without children, constituted a threat to parish budgets, and overseers targeted them for attention.

Norma Landau's analyses of settlement cases reviewed in Kent between 1723 and 1795 give some additional details on the male populations that the overseers investigated. The vast majority of the men who were examined and removed had migrated into a Kent parish from less than thirty-five miles away. In the countryside, most were laborers, although in the small towns overseers targeted equal numbers of craftsmen or tradesmen and unskilled workers for investigation. A sizable share of the men examined were married; indeed, a majority of them had children. In Kent, overseers marked out the more expensive migrants to maintain and sent away the ones who were relatively cheap to remove. Landau argues, however, that young, just-married workers were also examined in Kent because, in her opinion, overseers used the settlement laws to monitor migration and to lay the groundwork for future removal. Kent towns seem to have become much more lax in their surveillance of skilled workers and useful migrants by the later eighteenth century.[24] Her work demonstrates the possibility that settlement laws could be used to regulate migration; however, without data on base populations and their employment status, it cannot be shown that her cases represented a significant proportion of local migrants or that these migrants were examined before they became destitute or unemployed.[25]

Overseers also worked to export women and children. The widow and chil-

[22] E. M. Hampson, *The Treatment of Poverty in Cambridgeshire, 1597–1834* (New York: Cambridge University Press, 1934), 138.

[23] Norma Landau, "The Laws of Settlement and the Surveillance of Immigration in Eighteenth-Century Kent," *Continuity and Change* 3:3 (1988): 412.

[24] Norma Landau, "The Regulation of Immigration, Economic Structures and Definitions of the Poor in Eighteenth-Century England," *Historical Journal* 33:3 (1990): 541–72.

[25] K. D. M. Snell, "Pauper Settlement and the Right to Poor Relief in England and Wales," *Continuity and Change* 6:3 (1991): 375–415.

dren of William Godfrey, who died in Kingswalden, Hertfordshire, in 1687, were one such household. He had lived in that parish for about two years, renting a cottage and paying poor rates. His wife did labor service to pay their highway rate; as a result, they were included on local tax lists. Nevertheless, as soon as Godfrey died, overseers complained to the justices of the peace about the potential chargeability of the family and challenged its right of settlement.[26] In general, women were at a higher risk of removal by poor law authorities than were men. Because of their low wages and relatively high rates of unemployment, they cost more to relieve when destitute than did men, and their utility to local economies was usually lower. Hampson estimates that a third of the removal orders issued in Cambridgeshire between 1660 and 1834 were for pregnant women.[27] In Kent, women whose settlement cases were reviewed by the petty sessions courts were much more likely to be removed than their male counterparts: Seventy percent of the female examinees considered at the Sittingbourne and Sevenoaks petty sessions during a set of sampled years were removed, while only 23 percent of the male examinees got the same treatment.[28]

Such a sustained attack on outsiders seems to have been unusual. Despite overseers' harassment of married men and female-headed households, they did not actually eject very many people from their parishes. During the eighteenth and early nineteenth centuries, only between 2.3 percent and 5.3 percent of all the funds assessed and levied for poor relief went into the removal of the destitute. In fact, Snell estimates that in southern and eastern England under the old poor laws, an annual average of fewer than two people per year were removed from each rural parish.[29] The threat of removal for any individual pauper was a real one, however, and overseers were more than capable of using it to deter migrants from applying for relief or to prod them to move elsewhere. The settlement laws gave administrators a weapon to help rid their parish of unwanted outsiders. They could be invoked in times of high unemployment and ignored during periods of labor shortage. Forced into directing broadly conceived welfare schemes for their own too ample poor, overseers drew the line at fully incorporating outsiders. Migrants could stay if they were needed for work and were not on relief, but they did not have to

---

[26] Marshall, *The English Poor,* 166, 272–3.

[27] Hampson, *Treatment,* 140.

[28] The data from Sittingbourne covers the years 1723–6, 1760–4, and 1789–92, whereas the Sevenoaks records pertain to 1708–10 and 1717–25; see Landau, "The Laws of Settlement," 401, 405.

[29] Snell, "Settlement, Poor Law and the Rural Historian," 155, 157.

be treated equally. They were marginal to local society, and the settlement laws were administered in order to keep them that way.

Relief to the Deserving

Not all destitution was equal, even among the settled poor. The elderly had the best chance of seeing the benign side of parish relief. As part of the "impotent poor," they could be maintained without menacing public virtue or public order, and they were the group most threatened by the strongly nuclear organization of the English family. In a society where the social rules mandated a separate residence for each married couple, the normal calamities of the life cycle left many people alone and unable to care for themselves. Rather than change the cultural rules of the kinship system, the English opted early for communal support of the demographically isolated. Tim Wales argues that the pensioning of the elderly in England rose in the later seventeenth century and early eighteenth century at a time when the proportion of elderly in the society was also on the rise. In the parish of Hedenham, Norfolk, Lydia Puncher was on relief for over thirty years, beginning when she was widowed, probably in her fifties. Although the incidence of such cases is impossible to calculate for the country as a whole, Wales judges that in Hedenham, "the parish was more important than children in supporting the aged poor."[30]

Elderly applicants were commonly given a pension. Not only were rents paid, but nursing services offered and shelter given in parish cottages or the workhouse. Parish account books for the poor list charges for fuel, tobacco, shoes, shrouds, and spectacles, much of which was funnelled to elderly pensioners.[31] Overseers gave straw for cottage thatching and seed potatoes for gardens to those with clear entitlements and good local reputations. From the second half of the seventeenth century, allowances in Norfolk rose, on average, to approximately one shilling per head per week, a sum Wales says the poor could survive upon. In his judgment, paupers' standards of living were comparable to those of day laborers who had to support a family.[32] Because

---

[30] Tim Wales, "Poverty, Poor Relief and the Life-Cycle: Some Evidence from Seventeenth-Century Norfolk," in Richard M. Smith, ed., *Land, Kinship and the Life Cycle* (New York: Cambridge University Press, 1984), 385.

[31] Snell, *Annals*, 106–7.

[32] David Thomson reaches a similar conclusion using data for the early nineteenth century. He finds that, around 1834 grants to the elderly in the parishes he studied amounted to full maintenance. In his opinion, the elderly were treated generously under the Old Poor Law, which provided them with the equivalent of a laborer's wage. David Thomson, "The Decline of Social

many of the elderly lived with kin, small subsidies could go far in maintaining them.[33]

The issue of the incidence of relief to the elderly is difficult to resolve given the limited amount of research that has been done, but available figures indicate that the extent of dependency was probably high. A census of the poor taken in 1601 in Cawston, a small market town in Norfolk, included twenty-one households headed by people over age sixty. All were either paupers at the time of the census or in great danger of becoming dependent because they lacked both cows and their own cottages with a garden. They represented 12 percent of the households in the parish.[34] Mary Fissell, who has studied the parish of Abson and Wick near Bristol, reports that for the period between 1760 and 1803, about 50 percent of the elderly were on relief when they died. Moreover, about 17 percent of all people on relief were elderly, and 30 percent of all funds went to them during those years.[35] Not only did the elderly constitute one of the largest groups receiving welfare aid, but they also received proportionately more than their share of relief funds. At the age of seventy-four, Margaret Phillips, a lame, widowed fruit seller, got a pension from St. Martin, Vintry, which she kept until she entered a parish workhouse permanently at age eighty-eight.[36] The English welfare system privileged those at the end of their life cycle who remained in their parish of settlement.

It also privileged children. Not only was each parish responsible for the children of people legally settled in it, but the parish had to support illegitimate children born within its boundaries. Unfortunately, orphans, deserted children, and the illegitimate found that the mercies of the parish were not very tender. Infants had to survive the process of being put out to nurse, and, after 1722, those of primary school age in the larger towns found themselves locked away in workhouses or houses of industry. Unfortunately, both meth-

Welfare: Falling State Support for the Elderly Since Early Victorian Times," *Ageing and Society* 4:4 (1984): 451–82.

[33] Thomas Sokoll, "Household and Family Among the Poor: The Case of Two Essex Communities in the Late Eighteenth and Early Nineteenth Centuries," Ph.D. thesis, Cambridge University, 1990, 7.

[34] Wales, "Poverty," 370, 392–3.

[35] Mary E. Fissell, "Widows and Welfare Mothers in Eighteenth-Century England: Some Life-Cycle Considerations of Poor Relief," unpublished paper presented to the Tenth International Economic History Congress (Leuven, Belgium, 1990), 37–40; idem, "The 'Sick and Drooping Poor,' in Eighteenth-Century Bristol and Its Region," *Social History of Medicine* 2 (1989): 5.

[36] James Stephen Taylor, *Poverty, Migration, and Settlement in the Industrial Revolution: Sojourners' Narratives* (Palo Alto: The Society for the Promotion of Science and Scholarship, 1989), 128–9.

ods served more effectively to thin the ranks of the poor than to rear the young to habits of industry and virtue. Jonas Hanway, a London philanthropist and reformer, stated flatly that "parish officers never intend that parish children should live." Indeed, London statistics bore out his claim: Of more than 2,300 children taken into London workhouses between 1750 and 1755, only 7 percent survived until the end of that period. Hanway was so furious at their treatment that he goaded Parliament in the 1760s into passing acts requiring London parishes to send all children under six into the countryside at least three miles outside the metropolis.[37] The luckier parish children had relatives who could be paid by the parish to be responsible for them. In 1815, the London parish of St. Martin, Vintry, sent five-year-old William Smith, an illegitimate child whose mother had abandoned him, into Farnham, Surrey, to be nursed. Relatives kept an eye out for him, however, and he was later apprenticed to his uncle at age fourteen. When their widowed mother abandoned them in London in 1826, Henry and Mary Aprins were sent by their parish to an aunt, who took care of them for six shillings a week until they both reached age twelve. At that point, the parish helped Henry get a job as a yearly servant in London's West End.[38] Since all three of these children had spent their infancy with their mothers, they escaped the ministrations of ill-paid, unmonitored wet nurses under whose care children died like flies.

Parish children who neither perished nor ran away received a rudimentary education and an apprenticeship. Charity schools and workhouses worked together to keep children from vagrancy by offering shelter, along with Christianity, reading, and industrial training. In London, they wore uniforms, marched to church together, and heard multiple sermons on the need to abjure nasty habits and remain clean and tidy, while their teachers took every opportunity to remind them of their inferior heritage and negligible prospects.[39] The less lucky found themselves in ramshackle poorhouses watched over by elderly paupers who could barely take care of themselves.

Jobs as servants or apprenticeship to local tradesmen awaited those who managed to survive the dirt and inattention. Most commonly, during the seventeenth and eighteenth centuries, children were bound to local craftsmen in

---

[37] Quoted by Roy Porter in *English Society in the Eighteenth Century* (London: Penguin, 1982), 147; Webb and Webb, *Old Poor Law*, 271.

[38] St. Martin, Vintry, "Examinations of the Poor, 1815–1830," ms. 2847, cases 14, 28, Guildhall Library, London.

[39] For an account of the charity school movement in London, see Dorothy George, *London Life in the Eighteenth Century* (London: Routledge, 1930), 220–3.

return for money. The master received a small premium and in return was to feed, clothe, and instruct the child, making him or her a member of the household during the period of training. In 1745, the vestry of St. Giles in the Fields bound Margaret Neale, age eleven, "a poor child of the parish," to a hat maker in the City of London, to learn "the art of binding hats and housewifery," until age twenty-one. Humphrey MacDonnell, age twelve, was apprenticed to a Southwark fisherman to serve until age twenty-four.[40] Both sexes received similar treatment, although apprenticeship registers for southern counties listed almost twice as many boys as girls, and their distribution among trades was not identical.[41]

Despite the formal obligations of care, education, and concern, many of the masters looked for cheap labor, while the overseers turned a blind eye. In 1768, Sir John Fielding charged: "The chief view of the Overseer is to get rid of the object and fix his settlement in another parish."[42] Richard Burn, a Westmorland justice and overseer who observed the process firsthand in the north, agreed.[43] Contemporaries freely admitted that they bound pauper children to virtually anyone as long as a master lived outside the parish; they also promptly forgot any need to oversee the arrangement. In any case, parish children were unlikely to be sent into any but low-skilled, badly paid occupations. Not only were the premiums for pauper children lower than those paid by parents for entry into the more prestigious trades, but pauper children were generally younger and less well educated than their better-off peers.

Although over the long run apprenticeship declined as a general practice, parishes continued to bind both male and female children as apprentices.[44] During the seventeenth century, the town of Southampton indentured 367 adolescents; most went into the clothing industry, although both boys and girls were also sent into skilled trades and shops producing food or drink. Keith Snell, who compiled apprenticeship records from a wide sample of parishes in southern agricultural counties, reports that in those areas during the eighteenth century, the most common occupations for apprentices were in husbandry or clothing production. Young girls most often became servants, although a lucky few found themselves training as papermakers, clerks,

---

[40] St. Giles in the Fields, "Apprenticeship Indentures, 1745–1823," P82/GIS; 1/1–8, Greater London Record Office.

[41] Snell, *Annals,* 279–82.

[42] Quoted in Webb and Webb, *Old Poor Law,* 198.

[43] Richard Burn, *The History of the Poor Laws* (London: A. Miller, 1764), 121; see also Webb and Webb, *Old Poor Law,* 198–9.

[44] Snell, *Annals,* 228–30, 233.

dyers, or watchmakers. It was a lottery in which chance and overseers' inclinations played a major part.[45]

Worse fates than an apprenticeship into drudgery or a declining trade awaited parish children, however. Fictive "indenture" into a textile factory or other manufacturing shop became common in the later eighteenth century until Parliament regulated the practice in the early nineteenth century, and eased conditions of labor supply largely eliminated it. Parishes also assigned children to local tradesmen as apprentices or merely workers; ratepayers had to take them in or pay for an exemption. In both of these cases, overseers hustled children out of the workhouse into the labor market under essentially unsupervised conditions, perhaps hoping for the best but certainly ignoring the potential for exploitation.[46] Those without parents or kin to look after their interests did not find parish overseers effective substitutes.

The Elizabethan poor laws were formally less concerned with distinctions of gender than with those of age. Indeed, the law of 1601 did not mandate different treatments for men and women. Females, if healthy and adult, belonged in the category of those who ought to work to maintain themselves, although women with young children were classed as part of the impotent poor deserving of support. Elderly women and very young ones had the same rights as males did to poor law aid. In addition, most of the legal provisions of settlement law applied to women as well as men. Women could earn their own settlement through service, rental, or apprenticeship, although cases of the latter two types are not common. Yet the law made one major distinction between adult women and men: The law gave married women the settlement of their husbands. Just as wives lacked independent legal personalities, they had no independent rights to welfare. Although this practice avoided the breakup of destitute families applying for aid, it privileged male employment histories, kin, and migratory patterns over those of the female. At marriage, a wife's settlement history became irrelevant, and she, as well as the children, became subject to whatever claims her husband, or his father, had managed to establish.

Despite the Elizabethan law's apparent lack of concern for differences of gender, it is clear that females constituted a problematic group for poor law authorities. In practice, sexual difference mattered because gender mattered to the wider society. In particular, the notion of female dependency, com-

---

[45] Ibid., 279–82, 286.

[46] For a discussion of child apprenticeship under the Old Poor Law, see Webb and Webb, *Old Poor Law,* 196–211.

monly applied to mothers of young children and widows, legitimated aid to women at points of the life cycle when men were not as readily considered for automatic eligibility. The law privileged women over men because of their child-bearing and child-rearing functions. But at the same time, overseers knew that dependent females with children menaced parish budgets. Even single females, who might produce illegitimate children and thereby burden the community with another mouth to feed for life, constituted potential threats. Women in the child-bearing and child-rearing years, therefore, became special cases for poor law attention. Overseers combined relative generosity to married or widowed females who had children and settlement with high-handed repressiveness against those without clear rights or a powerful protector.

Examples of relatively well-treated females are easy to find. In 1815, St. Martin, Vintry, gave Susan Boston, a forty-nine-year-old widow who supported two children, a pension of three shillings a week, even though she did not live in the parish. Her husband had kept a well-known pub on Brickhill Lane, and her entitlement was not questioned.[47] The overseers of St. Martin also took relatively good care of Hannah Tapsel, a forty-three-year-old widow with two young children. A laundress and seamstress, she was listed in parish records as "an industrious woman," who had earned her settlement herself by renting a room in the parish and paying rates on it. As a result, they gave her four shillings a week from 1815 until her death in 1818 and then paid relatives generously to raise her two boys.[48] When entitlement was clear, female-headed households and elderly women fared rather well under the old poor laws. Keith Snell estimates that poor law subsidies for single-parent households (most of which were female-headed) in rural Yorkshire around 1800 amounted to about 78 percent of the average income of their employed neighbors; in 1809, in southern parishes such as Terling, the rate reached 95 percent.[49]

When they could get away with it, however, overseers used their authority to browbeat women (and men) to get them off welfare rolls. Coercing marriage and deporting them to their parishes of official settlement were two common tactics. Consider the case of Esther Herbert, a parishioner of the west London parish of Fulham, who in 1793 was pregnant with Samuel

---

[47] St. Martin, Vintry, "Examinations," case 4.

[48] Ibid., case 30.

[49] K. D. M. Snell and J. Millar, "Lone-Parent Families and the Welfare State: Past and Present," *Continuity and Change* 2:3 (1987): 407–8.

Gillingham's child. Parish officers, she later claimed, threatened to send her to prison for a year if she would not marry her child's father, and they threw him in jail to gain his consent. After both agreed to the proposal, the overseers provided a license, marriage at the parish church, and a wedding dinner. Unfortunately for the parish's plans to end their liability, Gillingham ran away after the dinner, leaving his new wife in parish hands.[50] Overseers would export pregnant women to their home parishes when they could, pay them to marry their lovers or seducers, or if all else failed, sue the fathers of their children for support payments.

Nevertheless, parish money in large amounts flowed to women, particularly in the later eighteenth century, when the rate of illegitimacy rose sharply. Bastards had to be maintained by the parish of their birth, and overseers, mothers, and fathers were aware of this fact. Mary Fissell has calculated that about 50 percent of poor law payments between 1760 and 1803 in the rural parish of Abson and Wick went to unwed mothers and elderly women, who made up only about 20 percent of the people on welfare in that parish during those years. The amount of aid to women there, in fact, skyrocketed during the last quarter of the eighteenth century: It rose by 524 percent, whereas the amount given to men decreased by 40 percent.[51] Earlier, the parish had been able to keep costs down by forcing marriages and granting only temporary payments, but by the 1770s and 1780s, levels of female pauperism in the parish increased sharply.[52] Over time, Abson and Wick multiplied regular weekly pensions to local women, to the elderly, as well as to the mothers of bastard children. Whether this reflects changes in need or in policy is problematic, of course.

Women who lacked local entitlement were particularly vulnerable. Nicholas Rogers's study of people charged with vagrancy in London in selected years between 1757 and 1799 reveals that before the 1790s, the vast majority of those charged were female. In fact, they outnumbered men among prosecuted vagrants by a ratio of 3:1 in 1757, 1758, and 1777 and by 2:1 in 1764, 1765, 1772, and 1783. Some were wayfarers like Elizabeth Croucher, found near Chiswick "laying all night in ye open air in ye great road." She was arrested and ordered whipped. More commonly, the women arrested resembled Letitia Coleman, a mother with three small children, who

---

[50] Taylor, *Poverty*, 28.

[51] Fissell, "Widows and Welfare Mothers," 10.

[52] Mary E. Fissell, "Gender, Life Cycle, and the Old Poor Law," unpublished paper (Manchester, 1991): 14–17.

turned to begging after her husband was impressed into the navy. Sarah Hancock, a young servant from Warminster, held several jobs in the London region around 1757, but authorities found that she had "been some time out of place and had been reduced to great Distress and not having [the] wherewithal to procure Lodging has been obliged to Lodge in outhouses [and] Barns." Women without local kin and a job were at risk; legally, they could be jailed, transported, or more commonly passed out of London back to their place of settlement. As outsiders, they had no local rights, despite their obvious need and similarity to settled paupers.[53]

Gender was quite relevant to overseers' decision making under the old poor laws, even if clear differences in treatment for men and women were not formally mandated. Their reproductive functions set female paupers apart from male ones in poor law practice, and their lack of local political rights and, usually, property made women particularly vulnerable to official pressures. Although they gained from common ideas of dependency, they lost in the area of common civil rights: free choice of residence, spouse, and settlement through work.

Ideas about gender also shaped the treatment of males by parish authorities. The notion that men as husbands and fathers needed to earn enough to maintain their families was widely accepted in England by the later eighteenth century. Margaret Escott has surveyed the records of Binfield, Berkshire, looking at charities as well as poor relief. Local households had the right to payments from a variety of local funds, if they were judged to demonstrate "desert." In the books of charities, men with children were judged the equivalent of elderly widows. A grant of £3 3s. went to the Widow Burgess, "sober and industrious," and to Richard Morris, a farmer "industrious & sober & burthen's with a large Fam'ly." Grants of £1 went to Abraham Bolton, a "very industrious Labourer & sober man with a family of five children," and to John Payne Bricklayer, "sober and industrious with five children," and to the wife of John Morton, labourer, "whose decent appearance amidst the burthen of a large family is very exemplary."[54] Similar criteria of worthiness applied to both males and females, and they got similar grants. Although local notions of sex roles differed, entitlement was extended to the worthy of both sexes. Industry and attention to one's children mattered for

---

[53] See Nicholas Rogers, "Vagrancy in Eighteenth-Century London," unpublished paper (1983) 5, 7, 9–12.

[54] Margaret Escott, "Charity and Poverty in Binfield Berkshire, 1775–1875," unpublished paper presented at the Tenth International Economic History Conference (Leuven, Belgium, 1990), 6.

both men and women, and many parishes used the poor laws to keep the households of the working poor from destitution. Over 90 percent of the parishes in England and Wales claimed in 1824 to give child allowances to large families, and 41 percent offered aid to supplement low wages.[55] Males with many children were felt to be among the deserving poor in the later eighteenth century, as long as they met certain criteria of industry, sobriety, and relative independence. If women had the responsibility for child rearing, men had that of child support, and under the old poor laws, parishes were committed to maintaining those functions. If poverty undermined a man's ability to provide for his children, overseers in the later eighteenth century were prepared to grant him welfare aid. They worried less about assigning blame for his low income than about the subsistence needs of his household.

These conceptions of gender roles also shaped another element of parish welfare policies: that of the provision of work. The acceptance of a roughly equal work obligation for men and for women that had existed during the seventeenth century changed during the eighteenth to encourage different sorts of treatment. In southern agricultural counties, farm-laboring jobs were provided for unemployed men, but not for women. Over time, overseers shifted their interpretations of the work requirement to conform with their attitudes toward gender.

Work and Welfare

Because the poor had to work to survive, why shouldn't paupers do likewise? In this case, moral, spiritual, and economic considerations all pointed in the same direction. For Thomas Sherlock, Bishop of London, "labour is the Business and Employment of the Poor: it is the Work which God has given him to do."[56] Around 1800, Patrick Colquhoun echoed this connection between poverty and work. Poverty is the state of those who must labor. Only when people could not work or would not work was there a problem calling for state intervention.[57] Faith in labor as necessary for a healthy state marked the attitudes of a broad group of philanthropists and reformers stretching from the arithmetricians in the later seventeenth century to the political economists of the late eighteenth and early nineteenth centuries. In 1795, Sir Frederick

[55] See Williams, *Pauperism*, 151.

[56] Quoted in Donna J. Andrew, *Philanthropy and Police* (Princeton: Princeton University Press, 1989), 25.

[57] Patrick Colquhoun, *A Treatise on Indigence* (London, 1806), 7; see also Gertrude Himmelfarb, *The Idea of Poverty* (New York: Knopf, 1984), 68–9, 77–8.

Eden quoted with approval Charles Davenant's judgment from the 1690s: "It is a justice we owe to the commonwealth not to suffer such as have health, and who might maintain themselves, to be drones, and live upon the labour of others." For Davenant, providing work in manufacturing was "the highest of all charities."[58]

For both men and women whose poverty stemmed from unemployment, the Elizabethan poor laws prescribed publicly provided manufacturing jobs. Putting the poor to work so that they could earn their bread seemed a logical solution to reformers and local poor law officials for much of the eighteenth century. Donna Andrew has shown how a large group of London philanthropists and merchants active around 1700, among them John Cary, John Bellers, and Sir Joshua Child, built employment into their charitable schemes. Utopian schemes for colonies where workers produced food and goods in abundance poured easily from philanthropists' pens.[59] "Workfare" has had a seductive appeal for centuries.

The heyday of English workhouses as miniature factories came in the late seventeenth century and the eighteenth century, when parishes all over the country set up institutions to house and employ the poor. Between 1696 and 1712, fifteen towns, including Bristol, Norwich, and the City of London, built residential workhouses in which, city fathers hoped, the poor could be disciplined to earn their own living.[60] Textile production and pin manufacturing were among the earliest trades practiced. In the following decade, the Society for the Promotion of Christian Knowledge encouraged dozens more rural parishes to set up workhouses, and by the 1770s, a national enumeration of workhouses listed about two thousand such institutions in England and Wales with a combined capacity of about ninety thousand places.[61] In Essex by the 1770s, one of every three parishes had a workhouse; in that county, inmates commonly spun wool, hemp, and silk; others made sacks or picked apart ropes to produce ship's caulking.[62] In the 1760s and 1770s in Norfolk and Suffolk, several groups of parishes pooled their resources to set up massive Houses of Industry for the local poor, where inmates raised food or made nets

---

[58] Quoted in Andrew, *Philanthropy*, 26.

[59] Quoted in ibid., 28.

[60] Timothy Virgil Hitchcock, "The English Workhouse: A Study in Institutional Poor Relief in Selected Counties 1696–1750," D. Phil. thesis (Oxford University, 1985).

[61] Taylor, "Unreformed Workhouse," 61.

[62] E. G. Thomas, "The Treatment of Poverty in Berkshire, Essex and Oxfordshire, 1723–1834," Ph.D. thesis (University of London, 1971).

and sacks. Others spun hemp and wool for Norwich manufacturers. Surviving plans of the buildings show rooms allocated to spinning, sack making, hemp dressing, tailoring, and shoemaking.[63]

The rules of the St. Marylebone workhouse make clear the connection between work and production of goods for sale. The parish employed a Taskmaster to supervise paupers, who worked for ten and a half hours daily in the summer and "as long as they could see" in the winter. The Taskmaster got free room and board for himself and his family, plus 10 percent of the sale price of the goods produced. In 1798, he claimed to have earned £152 from the proceeds from the spinning and winding of yarn, oakum picking, shoemaking, and tailoring that went on under his supervision.[64] Approximately half of the almost nine hundred inmates of the institution had been set to work under his care. The regulations of the Aylsham, Norfolk, workhouse from 1788 indicate a similar regime for the poor: work from 7:00 a.m. until noon and from 2:00 p.m. till 7:00 p.m. Those who earned more than their upkeep were to be given the profit.[65]

Relatively few records of these early businesses remain, and they cover scattered places and years. Yet they all tell a similar story. It is clear that overseers regularly tried to produce simple products to be sold in the marketplace. The merchant who planned the Bristol workhouse for young women claimed that in the later 1690s the venture earned about six pounds per week from the sale of the yarn spun by the one hundred female inmates.[66] Chelmsford poor law account books recorded a profitable sack-making business that sold goods to local farmers from 1755 to 1768. E. M. Thomas locates the bulk of the manufacturing experiments in eighteenth-century Essex, Berkshire, and Oxfordshire in textile-producing areas. He says that they continued in times when trade was flourishing and then collapsed with the ending of rural spinning.[67] As long as the manufacturing sector was dominated by handicraft production and included many products made with low-skilled labor, paupers could compete with workers in the larger labor market. This point is reinforced by the frequent references in the records to the "farming" of paupers.

---

[63] Anne Digby, *Pauper Palaces* (London: Routledge, 1978), 38, 42–3.

[64] A. R. Neate, *The St. Marylebone Workhouse and Institution, 1730–1965* (London: St. Marylebone Society, 1967), 9.

[65] Jerry Crowley and Andy Reid, *The Poor Law in Norfolk, 1700–1850: A Collection of Source Material* (Ely: EARO Resource and Technology Center, 1983), 50.

[66] Ivy Pinchbeck and Margaret Hewitt, *Children in English Society*, 2 vols. (London: Routledge, 1969), 1:163–4.

[67] Thomas, "Poverty in Berkshire," 102–3.

Overseers contracted with local entrepreneurs to employ the parish poor at a given rate per head. The contractor could then use the paupers at will in whatever form of production he wished.

Discipline for production went hand in hand with discipline for reformation. Rules of the Aylsham workhouse in Norfolk in 1788 illustrate conditions in one of the larger, better-run institutions. Inmates' time was rigidly allocated, and they were to be clean and deferential. Drunkenness, swearing, and other forms of misbehavior were punished with the loss of the next meal or, for repeated offenses, a restricted diet. On the other hand, paupers could wander the grounds belonging to the workhouse and they were sometimes allowed to leave on Sundays. Moreover, they were reasonably well fed according to contemporary dietary standards, and the rules indicated that beer or other liquor would be allocated by the committee "from time to time."[68]

Public plans to make paupers self-supporting usually failed. Virtually all the studies of workhouse businesses argue that these fledgling enterprises lost money in the medium or longer run. Most workhouse inmates were children or the elderly; others were disabled or ill. Because healthy adults rarely entered the workhouse except in times of depression, their labor appeared at times when it was most difficult to sell whatever was produced. By 1723, when Parliament authorized the general building of workhouses so that relief all over England and Wales could be made contingent on entry, pamphleteers regularly noted the lack of profitability in workhouse enterprises. They were assumed not to be self-supporting.[69] Overseers in Tiverton, Devon, recounted how in 1740 parishioners had subscribed funds for a large woolen manufactory to employ the poor. Within a year, problems of wasted materials and overly large inventories discouraged parish authorities; so they sold all the materials and closed the factory.[70] Cambridgeshire workhouse account books indicate that maintenance costs for paupers far outstripped the small profits of workhouse enterprises.[71] Beatrice and Sidney Webb found that the repeated attempts to make the poor self-supporting were a "uniform failure." They calculated that profits were negligible – only about one pence per day per worker, or scarcely more than the cost of materials and supervision.[72] In

---

[68] Crowley and Reid, *Poor Law*, 50.

[69] Hitchcock, "The English Workhouse," 121.

[70] Eden, *State of the Poor*, 2:143.

[71] Hampson, *Treatment*, 97, 110.

[72] Webb and Webb, *Old Poor Law*, 1:222–6, 233.

Dorothy Marshall's opinion, too, it was clear by the mid-eighteenth century that the workhouse poor could not earn enough to support themselves.[73]

It is important to keep in mind that these islands of unfree, pauper labor represented only a small proportion of the English workforce. Most workhouses outside of London and East Anglia were small buildings and held on average between twenty and thirty inmates. The larger houses, which relatively few places built, housed perhaps one or two hundred people in the 1770s. James Taylor has calculated from a parliamentary return of the 1770s that the total of about two thousand workhouses at that time could accommodate only about ninety thousand people.[74] If half of these spaces, a generous allowance, were filled with people who took part in workhouse production, they represented less than 1 percent of the total English population at the time. Little had changed by 1803; less than 10 percent of all paupers, or eighty-three thousand people, lived in workhouses. Only a fraction of that group would have been manufacturing goods for sale.[75] Production for profit in the workhouse was a quantitatively insignificant labor arrangement, although one whose appeal remained virtually untarnished throughout the eighteenth century.

The repeated use of pauper labor points to a significance far wider than the money generated. Not only did it carry out the precepts of the 1601 poor law, but it guaranteed good order among the destitute by keeping them occupied. Moreover, paupers who worked contributed to their communities and affirmed their solidarity with other citizens through production. All jointly helped to increase the wealth of the group. In a society with a hypersensitive fear of idleness, work kept paupers within a moral community of citizens, which incorporated men and women, young and old. The poor laws, as interpreted in the eighteenth century through houses of industry and manufacturing for profit, imposed a rough equality on the destitute, overriding differences of gender and age.

Welfare in Countryside and Town

Even though poverty was ubiquitous in Britain, it had different faces in the cities and on the land. In the high culture, the rural poor were peasants, part

---

[73] Marshall, *English Poor,* 145, 161.

[74] Taylor, "Unreformed Workhouse," 62–3; Neate, *Marylebone Workhouse,* 8.

[75] Williams, *Pauperism,* 149–50.

of an agricultural society where ladies bountiful brought baskets to the destitute. Mythic visions of contented laborers toiling at harvest both described
and prescribed a way of life where deference and hard work were to be
rewarded by the generosity of the rich.[76] Inequalities could be erased by alms,
whereas ownership of property remained untouched.

In rural areas, the relief regime was organized around face-to-face encounters of overseers with their neighbors. They tailored help to need, being well
aware of health, family status, and employment among applicants. R. P. Hastings describes the poor law in the North Riding of Yorkshire in the later eighteenth century as offering "effective social service."[77] What did overseers
offer to the North Riding poor? For the most part, money. Not only those who
could not work, but cyclically or seasonally unemployed men also, received
weekly grants, which were sometimes adjusted to reflect food prices. A few
parishes arranged jobs with local farmers for the unemployed, offering wage
subsidies to those whose earnings were judged below subsistence; giving
allowances to large families appears to have been common. Overseers paid
rents and built or leased cottages for the poor. Moreover, they bought fuel,
paid for new windows and thatching, and sometimes purchased furniture.
Although relief in kind was less common than grants of money, during years
of bad harvests, for example, 1795–6 and 1799–1801, some parishes distributed grain, bread, or potatoes. Most relief in the county was clearly outdoor
relief.[78] North Riding parishes also provided medical relief to the poor. Many
account books include occasional payments to doctors, whereas the largest
townships hired an apothecary or an apothecary surgeon to tend the poor for
an annual fee.[79]

Overseers in rural areas of the south and east acted similarly to those in the
North Riding. Pensions for the elderly, the disabled, widows, and children
were common, as were payments to poor families for clothes, rents, fuel, and
furniture. The overseers paid for smallpox inoculations, shoes, shrouds, beds
and spectacles. Except in Norfolk and Suffolk, where groups of rural parishes

---

[76] John Barrell, *The Dark Side of the Landscape* (New York: Cambridge University Press, 1980);
Christiana Payne, *Toil and Plenty* (New Haven: Yale University Press, 1994).

[77] Hastings calculates that around 1801 the poor laws supported about 8.8 percent of the county's
population, significantly less than the national rate of 11 percent; R. P. Hastings, "Poverty and
the Poor Law in the North Riding of Yorkshire, c. 1780–1837," *Borthwick Papers* 61 (York:
Borthwick Institute of Historical Research, 1982), 1–7, 32.

[78] In 1802–3, for example, under 4 percent of the area's poor received indoor relief.

[79] Hastings, "Poverty," 13–15, 21–2.

had built large houses of industry, very few of the poor had to enter a work-house.[80] For the most part, they received outdoor relief, which took into account their family size, physical condition, housing, and age. When Parliament asked overseers in 1824 for information about their aid to low-paid and unemployed workers, 155 agricultural parishes replied. Just over 50 percent claimed that they supplemented wages out of the poor rates and 95 percent said they gave child allowances; only 5 percent asserted that they provided neither form of relief.[81] Keith Snell characterizes the welfare system of the old poor law in the south and east as being "generous and widely encompassing."[82]

Jobs were also part of the welfare strategy in the rural north and south. The unemployed in North Riding townships could apply to the overseers for jobs or for materials to manufacture at home, and many districts hired men during the winters for road repair or stone quarrying. Indeed, some vestries functioned as employment exchanges, helping to arrange employment in the area or in the West Riding and in Lancashire. Efforts to encourage the employment of agricultural laborers on parish farms began in Allerton in 1795–6 and spread in the region after 1815, persisting into the mid 1830s. In addition, overseers bound pauper children as apprentices to craft occupations or sent them into Lancashire textile mills.[83]

Overseers in the south and east chose several forms of work relief: They supplied raw materials to the poor in their homes, provided parish jobs, started industrial workshops in "houses of industry," and arranged for local employers either to hire the unemployed themselves or to pay extra taxes to subsidize their wages.

The distinctive feature of poor relief during the later eighteenth and early nineteenth centuries in the south and east was the widespread provision of agricultural work on local farms primarily to married men, sometimes in combination with income subsidies. The so-called Speenhamland system, a sliding scale of wage subsidies pegged to grain prices and to family size, has attracted the most attention. This particular method of increasing the incomes of the poor, recommended to poor law authorities by Berkshire justices of the peace in 1795, was only used intermittently in crisis years by a few parishes

---

[80] For a description of these institutions, see Digby, *Pauper Palaces.*

[81] Williams, *Pauperism,* 151.

[82] Snell, *Annals,* 104–5.

[83] Hastings, 20–2.

even in Berkshire, but other tactics to raise the incomes of the poor, such as the roundsman system, child allowances, or other forms of wage subsidy, seem to have been widespread.[84] The male breadwinner was the central figure in these schemes, however. By the later eighteenth century, poor law work regimes were gendered.

When women's access to agricultural jobs diminished, so too did parish hiring of them. Keith Snell has shown how agricultural work became more sexually specialized during the second half of the eighteenth century in the southeast of England, as grain production rose and scythes and cutting hooks were introduced. Employers hired fewer women for laboring tasks, relegating them to lower-paid, off-season employment, whereas men took over the major harvesting work.[85] When southern rural parishes had to cope with rising seasonal unemployment and destitution at the end of the century, overseers concentrated their work relief on men. If using the roundsman system, parishes sent their unemployed male laborers around the parish to local farmers to find work. The successful were paid by the farmers; the unsuccessful got parish money at a slightly lower rate. Many parishes used this method of subsidizing the unemployed at least as early as the 1760s and 1770s. The roundsman system appeared in Tysoe, Warwickshire, in 1763 and may well have been used earlier. Farmers paid about six-sevenths of a weekly wage to the men sent to them, while the parish added about two pence a day in supplement.[86] In 1797, Sir Frederick Eden described the practice in a Leicestershire parish as follows: "In the winter and at other times when a man is out of work, he applies to the Overseer, who sends him from house to house to get employ; the housekeeper who employs him is obliged to give him victuals and 6 d. a day; the parish adds 4 d. . . . for the support of his family."[87] An alternative scheme, the labor rate, came into use during the 1820s; it sim-

[84] Mark Neuman, "Speenhamland in Berkshire," in Martin, ed., *Comparative Development in Social Welfare,* 100, 102. George R. Boyer, *An Economic History of the English Poor Law, 1750–1850* (New York: Cambridge University Press, 1990), gives an economic interpretation of these practices; see p. 43. Under the Speenhamland system, parishes set a scale of subsistence costs according to family sizes and bread prices and then gave male family heads additional money to bring their incomes up to the necessary standard. Recent research, however, indicates that this relatively expensive scheme was used only intermittently, during years of harvest failure when bread prices were exceptionally high, for example, in 1795 and in 1800–1.

[85] Snell, *Annals,* 58–64.

[86] See Webb and Webb, *Old Poor Law,* 190–1; Hampson, *Treatment,* 100; A. W. Ashby, "One Hundred Years of Poor Law Administration in a Warwickshire Village," *Oxford Studies in Social and Legal History* (Oxford: Oxford University Press, 1912), 155–8.

[87] Eden, *State of the Poor,* 2:384.

ply assigned the unemployed to local taxpayers, who hired them at a rate determined by their age and marital status and subsistence costs. Property owners had to take on additional employees in proportion to their tax assessment. Here, too, the jobs seem to have been reserved for men.[88] Although laboring families survived through the work and contributions of all their members, overseers began to privilege men's access to work in rural areas of the south and east during the later eighteenth century. In so doing, they followed the outlines of economic change in their region, but they also ratified it with public policy. Behind the notorious Speenhamland system of parish grants in aid of wages lies the notion of a male family head supporting his dependents. He applied for aid, and he received it in proportion to the size of "his" household.

The economic pressures of hard times and the labor needs of local farmers clearly shaped poor law policies in rural areas. But much more than income was at stake. The poor law maintained a social order of deference and dependence, of female next to male, of laborer and farmer, of the propertyless and the propertied. The poor law helped to maintain arcadia in its condition of "traditional" harmony and social peace.

But if "God made the country and man made the town," to quote William Cowper, urban poverty had different origins and required different treatments. Overseers in London, Liverpool, and Manchester had to deal with hundreds of the destitute in a period when their rural counterparts confronted only a few, relatively well-known faces. Moreover, overseers found it much more difficult to notice newcomers. Too busy to chase destitute strangers in good times, they had to cope with them in the bad. Sending them all back was too expensive, but ignoring them did not work either. Their fevers menaced the respectable, and their begging annoyed. Urban destitution seemed to demand stronger measures than its rural variant. Nestled in back alleys and on trash-filled streets, it reminded citizens all too well of the darker side of urban life. Containment emerged early as an urban strategy.

Urban parishes had the same sets of legal responsibilities and remedies available as did rural ones, but they in fact had greater assets to throw into the struggle against destitution. If they had more of the poor, they also had more of the rich and an infrastructure of charities and institutions designed to care for their dependent populations. More than in the countryside, urban overseers sought collective, institutional solutions for the burden of the poor.

---

[88] Boyer, *Economic History*, 17–18.

A few of the more energetic cities, Bristol being the foremost, moved early to rationalize poor relief by centralizing it. To stop each city parish from pushing its destitute across the street to another jurisdiction, the town government organized the Corporation of the Poor to dispense welfare throughout the city using the combined tax revenues of all parishes.[89] With the addition of a workhouse, sick wards, and an infirmary, the town moved quite early to institutionalize many of its poor. Wards at the infirmary were packed with the maimed and the broken down. Since few of the corporation's records have survived, it is impossible to estimate the incidence of institutional care in the city, but it was certainly much higher than that of the average rural parish. In the early 1780s, about 5 percent of Bristol's population used the infirmary each year, and many more got medical help or other support from the poor law. Mary Fissell estimates that over the course of their lifetimes, a high proportion of the Bristol poor got free medical care, from either the infirmary or poor law services. In Bristol, a major function of the poor law was to support workers with chronic or serious illnesses and to provide care as needed.[90] Long before the adoption of National Health Insurance, public provision of free medical care was part of the welfare services offered by the state. The urban poor had access to what contemporaries deemed sophisticated medical care; the rural poor, for the most part, did not.

By the mid-eighteenth century, London, of course, had an even more elaborate set of institutions for the depender poor. In addition to several hospitals and infirmaries, there were asylums for female orphans, a foundling home for illegitimate children, childbirth facilities for poor women, soup kitchens, and various reformatory homes for "penitent prostitutes." The Marine Society took in street boys, educated them, and packed them off to the navy.[91] Although the funding of these charities was private, their clients were essentially the same as those of the poor law, and the problems they addressed were identical to those of the parish welfare machinery. Their founders differed from parish overseers primarily in the strength of their activist impulses,

---

[89] Webb and Webb, *Old Poor Law,* 118–19.

[90] Burial registers for the parish of SS. Philip and Jacob between 1784 and 1814 indicate that in sampled years 40 percent of all those dying from consumption and 25 percent of those succumbing to smallpox were receiving poor law aid in the last weeks of their life; Fissell, "The 'Sick and Drooping Poor,'" 37, 50–1.

[91] For a discussion of London's charities in the eighteenth century, see Donna T. Andrew, *Philanthropy and Police: London Charity in the Eighteenth Century* (Princeton: Princeton University Press, 1989), and also David Owen, *English Philanthropy, 1660–1960* (Cambridge: Harvard University Press, 1964), 36–60.

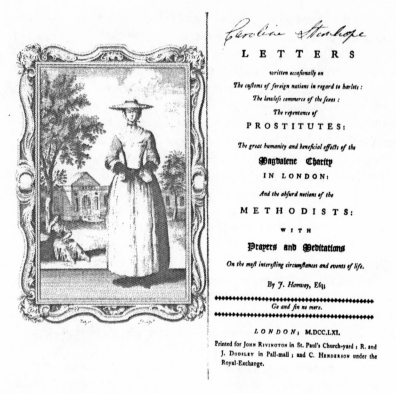

Figure 2.1. "The Repentance of Prostitutes," 1761. Courtesy of the Print Collection, Lewis Walpole Library, Yale University

aggressively prodding their charges toward the goal of independence and virtue.[92] Reformation of character had emerged as a central purpose within the growing realm of private philanthropy. Even if individually destitute, the London poor collectively were well endowed.

The publicly funded counterparts of charitable institutions to reform the poor were the workhouses. The London workhouse, founded in 1698, took in children and taught them religion, reading, and simple manufacturing skills, until early adolescence, when its charges were apprenticed to whatever masters the overseers could find. Quite well financed by the City's Corporation of the Poor, it had workrooms, a school, sick wards, and special areas for

---

[92] Owen, *Philanthropy*, 77.

infants and their nurses. In the early eighteenth century, about one hundred children entered per year.[93]

By the mid-eighteenth century, the metropolis had multiple workhouses, although many soon became, in George Rudé's opinion, "dumps and doss-houses for the destitute and unemployable."[94] Overcrowded and tumble-down, they offered inmates little more than food and shelter of an unpalatable sort. After 1767, Parliament forbade parishes to keep children under six in them for more than six weeks, ordering that young paupers be put out to board with families in the countryside.[95] During the second half of the century, many workhouses were rebuilt, enlarged, and reformed to fit a burgeoning clientele of the destitute. In 1775, the parish of St. Marylebone began to construct a two-story, Georgian-style quadrangle of buildings, designed to hold a thousand paupers. From its board room and offices, the Directors and Guardians of the Poor masterminded the dispensing of relief to the parish poor, whisking as many as possible into the house to be under the watchful eye of the workhouse Master and Matron.[96]

What Michel Foucault has called "the great confinement" menaced the English urban poor far more than their rural counterparts. Particularly in the metropolis, much charity tended to flow within the walls of institutions, where the givers could exact a disciplinary quid pro quo for their largesse. It is best, however, not to exaggerate the impact of such institutions; even if their aims were vast, their successes were small. Their human material often proved intractable – preferring the boozy companionship of friends to the soup-and-gruel regime of the workhouses. Welfare confinement lacked the compulsion of the gulag; people could and did walk away, and the state did not pursue them. Those who remained in overseers' clutches over the long run were the decrepit and the dysfunctional about whose reformation no one much cared.

In any case, the vast majority of the urban poor remained outside institutions. In Manchester in 1785, at a time when the workhouse held at most between one hundred and two hundred inmates, five hundred families received outdoor relief, and many others would have gotten occasional or spe-

---

[93] Stephen M. Macfarlane, "Studies in Poverty and Poor Relief in London at the End of the Seventeenth Century," D. Phil. thesis (Oxford University, 1982), 290–301.

[94] George Rudé, *Hanoverian London* (Berkeley and Los Angeles: University of California Press, 1971), 139.

[95] For a discussion of London poor law institutions, see ibid., 138–41: Dorothy George, *London Life in the Eighteenth Century* (London: Kegan Paul, Trench & Truebner, 1930), 218–20.

[96] Neate, *Marylebone Workhouse*, 6–9.

cial grants from overseers.[97] James Taylor estimates that only about 20 percent of those on permanent relief lived in workhouses around 1800.[98] Even
in London, overseers gave money and gifts in kind to most of the destitute
who were reasonably healthy and had clear settlements. In the Thameside
parish of St. Martin, Vintry, settlement records from the period 1815–26 give
the outcomes of welfare decisions. Showel's workhouse on Bear Lane
housed the sick, the elderly without kin who could care for them, women
needing shelter during childbirth, and a few refractory people that overseers
wanted to punish. The seriously ill went to St. Thomas Hospital. Those who
were institutionalized formed a small subset of the parish's dependent population, but an important set, for they illustrated the fate of the weak and the
disorderly.

Mary Ann Griffin was one such person; for her, vagrancy and illness paved
the way into the workhouse. A middle-aged spinster who sold ribbons and
other small goods on the street, she lived outside the City in a Highgate lodging house. St. Martin, Vintry, acknowledged responsibility for her because
her father had earned a settlement in the parish sometime around 1785. In
1815, Griffin was picked up in St. Pancras for begging and vagrancy. Magistrates sent her to a central London house of correction for a week and then
passed her back to St. Martin, Vintry, where she got casual relief from the
parish and then dropped out of sight for a few months. During the winter of
1816, she came to the overseers for medical help. Diagnosed as having
"gravel and stones," she accepted an order for the workhouse, in which she
stayed for five years. Parish authorities seem to have accepted the notion that
she could not support herself, and they were willing to take care of her indef-
initely. When she was about fifty, Griffin decided to try her luck outside the
workhouse; so she discharged herself and negotiated a pension of 2s. 6d. per
week from the parish and managed to survive for four years, living outside
the parish in Whitechapel. But in 1824, she had an "apopleche fit" that left
her speechless. Somehow her illness was brought to the attention of St. Martin overseers, who admitted her again to the workhouse and then sent her on
to St. Thomas Hospital for medical care. At some later date, she returned to
the workhouse, where she died two years later.[99] In Griffin's story, we see a
typical encounter of urban pauper and parish under the old poor laws. The

---

[97] George B. Hindle, *Provision for the Relief of the Poor in Manchester, 1754–1826* (Manchester: Cheatham Society, 1975), 19–26.

[98] Taylor, "Unreformed Workhouse," 63–4.

[99] St. Martin, Vintry, "Examinations," case 56.

destitute with clear settlements got support deemed appropriate to their sex, age, and physical condition. For those who could take care of themselves, welfare generally meant outrelief. Those who ended up in institutions were the children, the old, and the sick who could not take care of themselves. Institutionalization under the old poor laws was less a cultural drive to normalize a deviant population than a pragmatic solution to the welfare needs of many destitute people who lacked family support systems and who required more than an income subsidy. If the choice was between leaving such people on the streets and assuming a quite impersonal responsibility for their care, overseers turned to the latter solution. Communities stepped in when kin could or did not, and town overseers had few reservations about distancing themselves from the poor, few of whom they knew or had to conciliate.

By Right

During the eighteenth century, the poor laws continued to enjoy legitimacy, if not popularity, among taxpayers. Relief was a duty, an appropriate public function, even if it cost too much and often rewarded the unworthy. But what compromised the poor laws among the propertied brought them favor among the poor, who longed for a moral universe of greater justice and equality. For them, the poor laws represented a redemptive time and social world. John Clare, the laborer poet, contrasted the meanness of a contemporary "Farmer Thrifty" with predecessors who "made as equals not as slaves the poor." In a past golden age, "[e]ach guest was welcomd and the poor was fed / Were master son and serving man and clown / without distinction daily sat them down." Writing in the early 1820s, Clare knew he did not live in such a world, but he defended it with a powerful appeal, arguing that those who "stinted the pauper of his parish fare" made a mockery of English liberty and freedom.[100] The currently debased poor law required refining to an earlier purity.

Clare's rhetoric rested on an expansive vision of popular rights, which was conservative in its acceptance of social hierarchy but radical in its critique of what he saw as contemporary practice. Like William Cobbett, he defended laborers' rights against the meanness of a market economy and its devotion to profit at the expense of generosity and charity. Clare's poem represented the claims of the poor in terms of abstract qualities – right, justice, equality – worthy of a French republican. He had, in fact, lived through the period of the French Revolution and the growth within England of popular radicalism. Its

---

[100] John Clare, *The Parish* (New York: Viking, 1985), 33, 57.

language of the rights of Englishman was ready-made for those who would challenge the established order in the name of the poor.

John Clare used a similar language of rights in his blistering attack on parish officials who met to "fleece the poor" and rob the feeble. He exhorts:

> Hurt not the poor whom fate forbad to shine
> Whose lots were cast in meaner ways then thine . . .
> Take that away which as their right they call
> and thourt a rogue that beggars them of all.[101]

Clare seems to have had a standard of just maintenance for the poor that, when stinted, enraged him. In the community he describes, the poor are taxed rather than relieved appropriately by Farmer Cheetum and Old Saveall; more generous ways had died out years before with the last vicar and the hunting squire. But even if he thought a moral economy dead, he did not stop defending it.

Ordinary people had multiple sources for a similar language of rights. E. P. Thompson, in his *Customs in Common,* describes a "rebellious traditional culture" that was deeply conservative. He reminds us that the concept of prescriptive right, which created property from ancient usage, worked for the poor as well as the rich. In a society where "time immemorial" could be derived from twenty years of practice, the way stood clear for residents to defend in local courts their access to resources. Commons rights, the right to a footpath, and the right to glean were repeatedly invoked in eighteenth-century discourse. Because common law rested on the basis of customary law, headway in the former venue could be made by defense of the latter, which could be derived from collective memory. In the battles over access to common land, to gleaning, and to the cutting of turf and timber, laborers asserted their vision of local custom, which Thompson sees as deeply imbued with a concept of right.[102] For him, the land of England was a contested space where forests, commons, footways, and roads provided occasion for struggle between a community and defenders of private property.

Customary rights remained alive in English popular imagination throughout the eighteenth and well into the nineteenth century. Supported by a calendar of festivals, a language of entitlement, and a vocabulary of group action, as well as collective memory, local people regularly reasserted what they saw as collective privileges. To be sure, a widening gap between the cul-

---

[101] Ibid., 81.

[102] E. P. Thompson, *Customs in Common: Studies in Traditional Popular Culture* (New York, New Press, 1991), 9, 126.

tural assumptions of the propertied and those of the poor meant that these claims were often contested, but workers could easily adapt custom to defend their ideas of right. The result was an actively defended moral economy where custom was brought in on the side of the poor.[103]

The right to subsistence remained one of the most pressing of these popular claims. Bob Bushaway has described the vitality in southern England through the nineteenth century of ritual applications for food and drink by the poor. On Shrove Tuesday, bands of young boys went from house to house demanding pancakes or other donations. In the fall and early winter, on the feasts of All Souls, St. Clement, St. Catherine, St. Andrew, and St. Thomas, groups of poor laborers walked around their parishes asking for doles of food and money. One of the standard rhymes, recorded in the late nineteenth century, began: "Soul day, Soul day / We be come a-souling. / Pray good people remember the poor / and give us a soul cake." Bushaway notes recorded examples of such claims for the counties of Cheshire, Shropshire, Staffordshire, Worcestershire, Sussex, Kent, and Buckinghamshire.[104] Particularly in the winter and times of low employment, other holidays produced similar claims for charity and support. In December of 1799, William Holland, a Somersetshire parson, noted in his diary visits by those claiming food:

December 23: The poor came for meat and corn this cold weather and against Christmas season. Some very thankful and some almost saucy. . . . December 24: Much harried by the Poor of the Parish who come for Christmas Gifts. Many persons rather in affluence came but this is not right because it takes from those who are real objects.[105]

Clearly his notion of local right and those of the applicants varied, but he handed out food nonetheless, reinforcing the custom for the following years.

Communal membership brought customary access to free food in other ways. Gleaning after the harvest was a right granted in many areas to local parishioners. When the last sheaves had been cut, local laborers' families could scour the fields, picking up loose stalks of grain. Although increasingly challenged by landlords, the custom was defended actively in many areas well into the nineteenth century. It represented a considerable income sup-

---

[103] The phrase was originally used by E. P. Thompson, but has since become a standard concept of analysis among many social historians of the eighteenth century. See Edward P. Thompson. "The Moral Economy of the English Crowd," reprinted in *Customs in Common,* 185–258.

[104] Bob Bushaway, *By Rite: Custom, Ceremony and Community in England 1700–1880* (London: Junction Books, 1982), 170, 182–5.

[105] Jack Ayres, ed., *Paupers and Pig Killers: The Diary of William Holland, A Somerset Parson, 1799–1818* (Gloucester: Sutton, 1984), 23.

plement for the poor. Even when the practice lost sanction under the common law after a celebrated court case of 1788, it could still be defended via manorial custom or village bylaw. There is some evidence to indicate that gleaning was to be limited to the local poor. In Raunds, Northamptonshire, in 1740, a family was prosecuted for gleaning without a settlement; later a local bylaw prohibited the practice among those with nonresident relief certificates.[106]

Workers had a language of rights available to them through the common law, through custom, and through radical politics. Not only did they absorb it, but they used it effectively to justify claims of support. During his investigations of the poor laws for the Royal Commission in the early 1830s, Edwin Chadwick interviewed a Sussex farm worker with six children who received a weekly grant from his parish to supplement his wages. Chadwick guided the man through some elementary lessons in political economy.[107] Chadwick, who received sufficient agreement with his own views to regard the man as a good witness, presented the interview in the form of a transcript, giving the laborer a semi-independent voice. Yet rather than parroting stock criticisms of lazy paupers and lax overseers, Chadwick's informant gave an articulate defense of a moral economy in which a right to work and a right to adequate, dignified relief ought to be guaranteed by the central government. Although Chadwick controlled the interview and its reporting, he had little to gain from the invention of ideas that fundamentally contradicted central tenets of poor law reformers. Perhaps Chadwick listened, but he did not hear.

The laborer, who asked for anonymity in order not to be penalized by his parish, told Chadwick that local workers had been discussing the poor laws and were quite impatient for changes to be made. In their view, "the Government won't do a thing for the poor man or they would have done it before." Their wish, he said, was for "regular husbandry work at fair wages. . . . There would be an act passed to force the farmers to employ them on the lands at the usual prices the [regularly employed] workmen are receiving now, which I am confident would give good satisfaction to all those that are not surplus." He and his friends wanted a farmer to be compelled "to employ the right number of hands to cultivate his farm." He talked about the need to create jobs for ditching, mending, and other types of intensive cultivation. In contrast, parish jobs signified for him a loss of status, and he told a story of a nearby village where four men assigned to drag parish carts from place to

---

[106] Thompson, *Customs in Common*, 139.

[107] *Report from His Majesty's Commissioners for Inquiring into the Administration and Practical Operation of the Poor Laws, 1834*, Appendix A, part III. Evidence collected by E. Chadwick, Parliamentary Papers, 1834:xxviii, 14.

place had horses' hoops and bells placed on their heads. In his eyes, the poor became dumb animals when they fell into the clutches of the parish. His strongest attacks targeted the poor law overseers, who, he claimed, did "all parish business now by favour." In place of fair wages for steady work, the "Parish money is now chucked to us like a dog." When asked what changes in the poor laws the laborers had discussed, he replied: "They have hopes that Government will take it in hand, as they would then be contented with what was allotted to them; they would be sure that they would have what was right, and would not be driven about by the overseers."[108] The laborers were offering no specific designs for reform. Their limitless confidence in a central bureaucracy, however, certainly should have appealed to Chadwick's taste, but the wider message cut directly against Chadwick's support for a free labor market.

The language of right in relation to work, wages, and relief surfaced occasionally among middle-class witnesses as well, who bristled at the notion. Thomas Whately, the rector of Cookham, Berkshire, told Edwin Chadwick in 1834 that under the old poor laws, because of the income subsidies paid to laborers, "Wages were no longer a matter of contract between the master and the workman, but a right in the one and a tax in the other."[109] In Swallowfield, Berkshire, an attempt in 1829 to force paupers into a reformed workhouse allegedly led to a protest by local laborers and an appeal for help to the magistrates. They were reported to have demanded as "a right" that parish jobs extend only from eight in the morning until four in the afternoon. They allegedly expected the magistrates "to protect the poor man" and to order that they would have their salaries made up from the parish as in the past.[110] Even before the days of Josiah Bounderby, employers feared that lazy workers wanted turtle soup with a golden spoon!

Many workers looked upon the poor laws as offering social insurance, which indeed they did. Despite all the problems and the niggling meanness of overseers, the laws offered a shelter in bad times. They were a valuable resource to people well aware of the dangers of unemployment, illness, and early death. Jane Boothman, who was settled in Kirkby Lonsdale, but living outside the parish in 1812, wrote to the overseer when her allowance to pay her rent was late. Because "work is bad and meat is dear and the one and 6d you alow me is Litel enugh for hous rent in this place," she had decided to

---

[108] Ibid., 14–15.
[109] Ibid., 23.
[110] Ibid., 35.

return to her home parish. "You had a workhous. Should like to come to it with my litel girl til times doth mend." She knew she was eligible for relief in Kirkby Lonsdale and could count on receiving food and shelter there upon application to the overseers.[111] Elizabeth Langford, also from Kirkby Lonsdale, regularly requested and received relief for herself and her children from that parish between at least 1819 and 1825. Her frustrations with the overseers and their grants were many, and no doubt she disliked many of the people and procedures with which she had to contend. Yet, in 1819, when announcing her willingness to be removed from Preston back to her home parish, she added, "I cannot nor will not be quite Lost while I have a parish to flee two."[112] She and the hundreds of other people settled in Kirkby Lonsdale knew they had a claim for relief from their parish. They wrote to the overseer asking for money for rent, clothes, food, and medicines. They claimed allowances for child support or temporary payment when out of work. The combination of their need and their communal ties brought them entitlement, and they knew it.

Workers went to great lengths to confirm and to establish a settlement. They kept apprenticeship indentures and old rent receipts; they could recite the dates and farms of yearly hirings, as well as the settlement histories of parents. In 1775, Joseph Polyblank, an elderly carpenter, claimed a settlement in West Alvington, Devon, on the basis of having rented property there in 1755, and he had convincing proof of the amounts he had paid. More importantly, he also offered evidence that during the years he had lived in Plymouth and served as Town Cryer, he had never gained a settlement. He seems to have been well enough versed in settlement law to know what to avoid doing as well as what was necessary to establish entitlement.[113]

Of particular importance in establishing entitlement was the memory of earlier encounters with the poor law. Because earlier relief grants acknowledged a parish's assumption of responsibility, workers remembered the times and places of welfare grants. Wives learned from husbands the particulars of their settlement history so that they could give overseers confirmable stories. Ann Smith, who was examined in Mitcham, Surrey, in January of 1801, told the magistrate that she "heard her father Jos. Smith say that his settlement is in Kingston upon Thames, and he is now in the workhouse and acknowledged

---

[111] Kirby Lonsdale Township Letters, WPR/19, 24 May 1812, piece 184.

[112] Ibid., 10 May 1819, piece 24.

[113] "In-House Poor Account Books, 1775, West Alvington, Devon," 818a/PO1–3; quoted in Taylor, *Poverty*, 52–3.

a pauper there." By telling authorities that she had also had relief from Kingston upon Thames, she strengthened her case for acknowledgment from that parish. Also in 1801, Sarah Gaston, a widow, told the Mitcham magistrate that her husband claimed settlement in Wandsworth because he had served an apprenticeship as a carpenter in that parish. Mary Williams, a widow also living in Mitcham, Surrey, linked her settlement in Cranbrook, Kent, to her husband's having worked there as a servant for a year. Although this history took place before they were married and possibly before they had met, she could supply authorities with the name of the hiring farmer.[114]

Entitlement to support from the poor laws was carefully guarded and valued by the poor. Keith Snell has argued that parish settlement and the right to relief formed part of the "moral economy" of the poor, and I would agree.[115] For people with few resources, having a settlement could make the difference between starvation and survival. Charles Varley, clearly a farm laborer who planned ahead, described in his autobiography of 1768 his efforts to secure clear entitlement to relief at the time when he had recently married and could no longer be hired as a live-in servant on a yearly contract.

My greatest trouble was that we had no settlement. . . . Neither could we gain a settlement, as we were married; . . . we might perish for want. Whereupon I was determined to go to be a farmer's servant for one year: in order to gain a settlement, my wife and I were to part for that year, and then to meet as strangers, and to be married in the parish church where I had served my year.

He followed the plan, leaving London for the country, where a farmer hired him for twelve months, thus providing the necessary entitlement for relief. His "remarriage" in the parish church, which would have been registered there along with the names of witnesses, offered clear proof of his local ties and gave him and his family a permanent insurance policy.[116]

Much of the evidence for the notion that the poor claimed a right of subsistence from their parish needs to be inferred from their behavior. The issue of support through the poor laws seems sometimes to have been a trigger for the riots that periodically convulsed the English countryside. E. P. Thompson has argued persuasively that in the eighteenth century, customs

---

[114] For these and other similar examples, see Blanche Berryman, ed., *Mitcham Settlement Examinations, 1784–1814,* Surrey Record Society, vol. 27, (Castle Arch: Surrey Record Society, 1973), 92–3, 96.

[115] Snell, *Annals,* 112.

[116] Charles Varley, *The Modern Farmer's Guide, by a Real Farmer* (Edinburgh: J Reid, 1768), xxv–xxvi; quoted in Snell, *Annals,* 98–9.

were "endorsed and sometimes enforced by popular pressure and protest."[117]
Defense of a moral economy led directly to action in the streets and market-
places. In 1765, people rioted in East Anglia against the introduction there of
large workhouses, which would house the poor of several incorporated
parishes. The rioters said they would "fight for their liberties," one of which
was to be relieved in their own parishes. They wanted to destroy the workhouses, and they claimed divine sanction for their attacks.[118] In 1765, the
House of Industry at Saxmundham in Suffolk was pulled down, as was the
partially built workhouse in Bulcamp a few miles away. A crowd of at least
150 attacked the walls with pitchforks, poles, and sticks, one of their leaders
shouting, "My lads work away, work away. Let's pull Hell down to the
Ground, pull Bulcamp Hell down to the ground."[119]

In the eighteenth century, such direct and bloody defenses of customary
forms of relief were rare, but active defense of a right to subsistence was not.
In the food riots between 1795 and 1801, parish overseers and their policies
toward the poor were frequent targets. Just as mobs pressured farmers and
merchants, forcing them to sell food at "just prices" locally, they attacked
overseers to influence the form and timing of subsidized sales and food handouts. In 1801, in Winkleigh, a group of men denied aid by the overseer forced
the public sale of subsidized barley. In Odiham, a rough sense of equalitarian
justice seems to have produced this anonymous letter to local farmers: The
poor were "[d]etermined if thare be Starvation it shall be a General thing and
not a parcial one for Both Gentle and Simple shall Starve if any Do." Another
note, that a Brent farmer received in the name of the "poor of this Parish"
threatened the burning of barns, wheat mows, and potatoes if "some provision . . . is not made."[120] In years of famine, people claimed a share of local
provisions via subsidized sales.

Workers suffering in the famine years of 1795–6 and 1801 appealed to
magistrates or local overseers to raise wages. After confronting a mob armed
with sticks who threatened to stop work unless they "lived better", a Lewes
magistrate in 1795 ordered overseers to increase relief; a similar demonstra-
tion took place in East and West Rudham in Norfolk. At the same time in

---

[117] Thompson, *Customs in Common*, 3.

[118] A. J. Peacock, *Bread or Blood: A Study of the Agrarian Riots in East Anglia in 1816* (London: Gollancz, 1965), 32; see also M. D. George, *England in Transition* (London: Penguin, 1965), 89–99.

[119] SP 37/4, Public Record Office; quoted in Charles Tilly, *Popular Contention in Great Britain, 1758–1834* (Cambridge: Harvard University Press, 1995), 178, 180.

[120] Roger Wells, *Wretched Faces* (New York: St. Martins, 1988), 165.

Eatonbridge, Kent, laborers surrounded the house of the overseer of the poor, pressuring him to call a vestry meeting that could order higher wages. Awareness of the link between riot and relief levels led Devon magistrates in 1801 to order subsidized food sales in the disturbed areas.[121] John Bohstedt argues that in areas like Devon, where tight social networks of both horizontal and vertical ties existed, popular action successfully enforced workers' notions of just wages and prices. He describes "community bargaining by riot." This vision of a moral economy necessarily encompassed the poor law in a society which guaranteed local people relief from destitution. The laborers of Crediton, Devon made this linkage for themselves in 1795. In a handbill appealing for higher wages, they announced:

> God Bless our Gracious King and send
> Health and Prosperity many his Days attend
> May his Ruleing Subjects Humanity then show
> Any Pay unto the Poor what they to them do owe.[122]

During the eighteenth century, the weekly dole became fixed in the popular imagination as part of the rights of the English. Just wages and prices could guarantee subsistence, but so could the parish in hard times. The defenders of a "moral economy" chose to battle adherents of a market economy over countless issues of customary right, and the operations of the poor law provided a fertile territory for such contests. In the arena of the poor laws, they won many of their battles, despite hostile overseers and low allowances. Hungry English workers often showed themselves to be pragmatists: Half a loaf was better than none.

[121] John Bohstedt, *Riots and Community Politics in England and Wales, 1790–1810* (New York: Cambridge University Press, 1983), 193.

[122] H.O. 42/34; quoted in ibid., 189.

3

EXCLUDING PAUPERS, 1780–1834

The chief objects of the statute of Elizabeth were to make the able-bodied, who were indolent and turbulent, conform to habits of industry. The effects of the law – as it was recently administered . . . were to render the industrious indolent, vicious, and turbulent [and] to endanger the safety of all property.

Edwin Chadwick, 1833

Entitlement is a fragile, often contested conception in times of change, resting as it does on notions of legitimacy and custom. In a society where the law proclaimed that property was king, the propertyless inevitably found themselves in a precarious position. The traditional legitimacy of subsistence rights often proved a weak tool with which to attack the high fence of private property and the well-oiled machine of the market economy. Alternative conceptions of community and different visions of rights and duties confronted one another in Britain during the later eighteenth and early nineteenth centuries. Law, custom, rhetoric, and the graphic arts, as well as the brute facts of relative power, were brought into play in the struggles for legitimacy. Alongside the battles that flared in local markets and in the workplace, in vestry meetings and courts, confrontations emerged on the printed page, as writers and artists defended different visions of a moral order and its social embodiment. The responsibility for poverty was a contested topic, and bitterly so as the numbers of poor grew.

By the early nineteenth century, the destitute had lost much of the legitimacy that they had earlier enjoyed in communal eyes. Acknowledgments of need became secondary to judgments of inadequacy and immorality, as work and production became glorified in the public eye. Why should the state subsidize loafers? many asked. Since the invisible hand of the market would guarantee work and adjust wages to the labor supply, why not let it, rather than the taxpayer, feed the poor? From that vantage point, welfare seemed a responsibility guaranteed by individual initiative and the marketplace, not the public purse. As theories of poverty and pauperism shifted, so did policy toward the destitute. Work, confinement, and discipline became central to the evolving political economy of welfare long before the passage of the New Poor Law.

Poverty and Economic Change

Although by 1800, output in both British agriculture and industry was expanding faster than population, economic growth was slow, and benefits were unequally distributed.[1] Consumption levels of goods and services changed little on average between 1760 and 1820, and the wartime shortages and inflation meant intermittent hardship for many.[2] Evidence of those who were being left behind in the race for higher incomes gave pessimists much about which to brood. Even if metal production was spreading in Shropshire, much of Wales remained dependent upon backward, subsistence agriculture. Although textile manufacturing boomed in the north, it shrank in the West Country and East Anglia. As wheat prices rose, so did the enclosure of commons and waste land, which cut into the incomes of cottagers and laborers. Significant groups in the population lost income and security when their areas deindustrialized or their access to land diminished. Some could and did migrate to more prosperous places, multiplying the numbers of strangers who might apply for relief in hard times. Moreover, the dislocations of wartime, trade blockades, and bad harvests intensified the economic problems of the poor during the second half of the century. The gains from industrialization took a long time to arrive, if you happened to be born a low-skilled worker in the later eighteenth century. Jeffrey Williamson's generally optimistic reading of income fluctuation shows essentially no change in real full-time earnings between 1797 and 1827 for English farm laborers and relative stability of real wages until 1819 for men in a mixed group of urban and factory jobs.[3]

---

[1] The best statement of the slow growth hypothesis is in N. F. R. Crafts and C. K. Harley, "Output Growth and the Industrial Revolution: A Restatement of the Crafts-Harley View," *Economic History Review* 45 (1992): 703–30.

[2] Roderick Floud and Donald McCloskey, *The Economic History of Britain Since 1700*, 2 vols., (New York: Cambridge University Press, 1981), 1:136.

[3] Jeffrey G. Williamson, *Did British Capitalism Breed Inequality?* (Boston: Allen & Unwin, 1985), 17. Family incomes also have to be considered, and on this point the evidence is mixed because women's and children's earnings varied over time and among occupations. In the agricultural sector, Jane Humphries and Sara Horrell estimate that when the earnings of all members are taken into account, family incomes rose on average between the 1790s and 1830. See Sara Horrell and Jane Humphries, "Old Questions, New Data, and Alternative Perspectives:

The major signal contemporaries had about the extent of poverty came from the cost of the poor laws. Yearly expenditures on poor relief, as reported to Parliament, were more than five times as great in 1803 as they had been in 1750. George Boyer has calculated real poor relief expenditures for five parishes in Essex between 1760 and 1830; in all, the trend line rises steadily between the mid-1760s and the late 1790s, with "substantial increases" in the later 1770s and 1780s.[4] Joanna Innes did similar calculations for seven parishes with different economic bases. In all of them, the cost of supporting the local poor, which had been relatively constant before 1750, moved sharply upward thereafter. Relief costs peaked for most in the decade 1785–95.[5]

In the county of Norfolk, whose economy was based upon the combination of agriculture and textile production, average annual relief costs approximately tripled between 1775 and 1802 and then continued to rise. The cost to parishes of poor law relief continued to increase sharply until 1820, far outstripping population increase, and remained above the 1802 level until poor law reforms of 1834 mandated cutbacks in aid.[6] Boyer calculates in fact that real per capita relief expenditures rose at rates between 1.1 percent and 2.2 percent annually from 1748–50 to 1818–20.[7] For decade after decade, more and more people moved onto local relief roles, and the cost of supporting them exploded. Even if Liverpool merchants, Shropshire ironmasters, and wheat-producing farmers were thriving, growing numbers of both rural and urban workers could not support themselves on their wages.

In any economy, the balance between population and resources determines the average real incomes of inhabitants. This balance was shifting in the later eighteenth century because of both demographic growth and increases in agricultural and manufacturing production and trade. Focus for a moment simply upon population. A territory that had housed 5.8 million people in 1751 sheltered 8.7 million in 1801 and 16.7 million in 1851. In fact, from the 1660s, gross reproduction rates climbed in England, reaching a peak in 1816. People married at younger ages, and women bore more children during their

Families' Living Standards in the Industrial Revolution." *Journal of Economic History* 52:4 (1992): 849–80.

[4] George R. Boyer, *An Economic History of the English Poor Law 1750–1850* (New York: Cambridge University Press, 1990), 26–7.

[5] Joanna Innes, "Social Problems: Poverty and Marginality in Eighteenth-Century England," unpublished paper presented to "The Social World of Britain and America, 1600–1820" (Williamsburg, VA, 1985), 72, 74.

[6] Anne Digby, *Pauper Palaces* (London: Routledge, 1978), 84.

[7] Boyer, *Economic History*, 29.

fertile years.[8] As a result, on average, each adult had to support a rising number of dependents, a demographic burden on the working population that did not begin to decline until 1826.[9]

Unfortunately, this sharp rise in the population may well have exceeded productivity gains during the later eighteenth century, at least insofar as those gains affected workers' incomes. Although economists estimate that per capita incomes for the English population as a whole rose markedly during the later eighteenth century, the questions of distribution and purchasing power have to be considered.[10] The evidence on this point is scattered, but several scholars argue the pessimistic case cogently. After investigating wage and price figures, both R. D. Lee and George Boyer insist that during the second half of the eighteenth century, the average real wages of laborers declined; Lee thinks that a redistribution of income took place, away from laborers toward capitalists and landlords.[11] That landlords and manufacturers took rising shares of national income from the mid-eighteenth century to the mid-nineteenth century seems clear from Lindert and Williamson's work on income distribution.[12]

Economic changes transformed rural society fundamentally in the south and east between 1750 and 1850. Teenagers had formerly taken jobs as farm servants between puberty and marriage, working on a year-long contract, which brought room and board as well as settlement rights. They joined not only a patriarchally run household but a local community, and gained rights within it. After 1815, this practice quickly atrophied in the south and west, where the increased sizes of farms and increased food costs made canny farmers unwilling to take in large numbers of hungry teenagers, when day workers were easily available.[13] Although social conservatives lamented the transmutation of servants-in-husbandry into mere farm laborers in the 1820s, they could do little to stem the decline in yearly hirings. When given the

[8] E. A. Wrigley and R. S. Schofield, *The Population History of England, 1541–1871* (New York: Cambridge University Press, 1989), 208, 431. See also R. D. Lee and R. S. Schofield, "British Population in the Eighteenth Century," in Roderick Floud and Donald McCloskey, eds. *The Economic History of Britain Since 1700*, 1:21–4.

[9] Wrigley and Schofield, *Population*, 443.

[10] Phyllis Deane and W. A. Coale, *British Economic Growth, 1688–1959*, 2nd ed. (New York: Cambridge University Press, 1967), 78.

[11] Lee and Schofield, "British Population," 29; Boyer, *Economic History*, 44–5.

[12] P. H. Lindert and J. G. Williamson, "Reinterpreting England's Social Tables 1688–1867," *Explorations in Economic History* 20:1 (January 1983): table 2.

[13] Ann Kussmaul, *Servants in Husbandry in Early Modern England* (New York: Cambridge University Press, 1981), 120–1.

choice between a society of hierarchically ordered ranks in which they provided protection and paternal care and a market-driven society of employer
and employee, farmers opted increasingly for the latter, but many workers
preferred the former. Eric Hobsbawm and George Rudé link the bloody confrontations of the Captain Swing riots to laborers' anger against farmers who
refused to provide steady employment and living wages.[14] Rights, duties, and
deference atrophied together as the market economy gained ground.

George Boyer points out that farm laborers' families in the south and west
during the later eighteenth and early nineteenth centuries typically had three
sources of income: a small bit of land for growing food, employment as a day
laborer on large farms, and wages from proto-industrial production. Then two
of these three sources collapsed. The long-term rise in grain prices made
farmers less willing to lease land to laborers at a favorable rate, and many lost
land with the enclosure of the commons. Moreover, the contraction of many
forms of proto-industry, which started in the later eighteenth century,
decreased the earnings of wives and children.[15] Hand spinning ceased to be
profitable in the later eighteenth century, and other trades contracted after
1815. By the early 1830s, not only had the wages of framework knitters and
handloom weavers plummeted, but job opportunities in pillow lace making
and in straw plaiting shrank.[16] Families increasingly relied on the earnings of
male laborers, who found that they were unemployed during winters and
slack seasons.

Robert Allen has traced changes in male employment patterns in the south
Midlands between 1676 and 1831. At the earlier date, he estimates that about
73 percent of all adult males worked full-time in agriculture, and 25 percent
were craft, service, or industrial workers. By 1831, the share employed in
agriculture had shrunk to around 50 percent, of which about half was
employed only part-time. In addition, he thinks that the labor market in agriculture for women contracted just as sharply; a sector that around 1700
employed 40 percent of adult females full-time offered such jobs to only 16
percent in 1831. Moreover, Jane Humphries asserts that agricultural modernization cost women and children jobs and income when, with the enclosure

---

[14] Eric Hobsbawm and George Rudé, *Captain Swing* (London: Lawrence & Wishart, 1969).

[15] Boyer, *Economic History*, 31.

[16] Robert C. Allen, *Enclosure and the Yeoman* (Oxford: Oxford University Press, 1992), 243–7;
See also K. D. M. Snell, *Annals of the Labouring Poor* (New York: Cambridge University Press,
1985), and Ivy Pinchbeck, *Women Workers in the Industrial Revolution, 1750–1850* (London:
Cass, 1969).

of the commons, they lost grazing and wood-gathering rights. Their contributions to family income plummeted when their families no longer had free access to village land.[17] In as much as cottage industrial production, or proto-industry, increased less than the decline in agricultural work and emigration out of the district seems to have decreased between 1751 and 1831, Allen argues for the existence of a large pool of surplus labor in the region. In his view, the south Midlands resembled an underdeveloped country, where a premature modernization of agriculture "caused nothing but poverty."[18] The effects of agricultural modernization on the English labor force are hotly debated, but the negative impact of seasonal employment and shrinking job opportunities for women and children seems clear.

Of course, not all rural areas of England and Wales housed an agricultural proletariat. In Wales and northern upland areas, small farms continued to be economically viable. Farmers in pastoral regions such as Cumberland, Westmorland and North Yorkshire, who had to compete with factory towns for labor, continued to hire by the year. In any case, urban growth in Lancashire, Yorkshire, Derbyshire, and the west Midlands, not to mention London, meant jobs and higher wages for thousands of artisans, servants, and factory workers. But as Elizabeth Gaskell reminded contemporaries in 1855, North and South were two separate countries. While poverty could be found in each, it had a different face.

From the standpoint of the landlord or the industrial entrepreneur, the English economy was indeed thriving between 1780 and 1840: after all, grain prices and rents were high, on average trade was expanding, and textile and iron production had increased explosively. Early industrialization brought many gains, especially to capitalists, professionals, and property owners. A thick stream of golden profits flowed into the pockets of the merchants and bankers. Yet low-skilled workers, particularly in rural areas, stood apart from the processes of investment and market sales that brought prosperity to owners. Squeezed by declining family incomes and increasing family sizes, laborers were untouched by the rich culture of commodities being generated in the cities and factory towns. Among the poorest, parish pay substituted for mar-

---

[17] Using family budget data and recent indices of living costs, Horrell and Humphries estimate that real family income in Britain was roughly stable from 1791–5 to 1816–20; thereafter its growth rates lagged well behind those of male wages because of declining opportunities for women and children to earn and falling poor law subsidies. Horrell and Humphries, "Old Questions," 865, 871.

[18] Allen, *Enclosure*, 249–51, 262.

ket wages during seasonal layoffs and cyclical downturns. Unfortunately for the dependent poor, the moral bases of their entitlement to welfare weakened as the middling classes reanalyzed their commitment to support the destitute.

A Rhetoric of Vice and Virtue

During the later eighteenth century, poverty occupied the public mind. Philanthropists and reformers rushed their answers to the destitution problem into print. Why were so many poor? Was it their fault or that of the economy? Whether the dictates of the market or of Christian charity should bind citizens together was a vexing issue. Contending ideas battled in a public arena, then, as in our own times.

Poverty was accepted as inevitable by most social analysts well beyond the time of Adam Smith's *Wealth of Nations*.[19] Joseph Townsend, a Wiltshire rector, geologist, and travel writer, argued in 1786 that hunger tamed the character and led individuals into "decency and civility, obedience and subjection." He then coupled his defense of poverty with diatribes against existing public policies toward the poor: "Nothing in nature can be more disgusting than a parish pay-table, attendant upon which in the same objects of misery are too often found combined snuff, gin, rags, vermin, insolence, and abusive language."[20] Whereas self-help and charity engendered virtue, the public purse produced vice. Although Townsend's position was an extreme one, it found sympathetic readers. The work was translated into French, and it was reissued in 1816 in England. Moreover, Thomas Malthus read it and cited it approvingly in the 1803 edition of his *Essay on the Principle of Population*. Townsend spoke in terms of moral abstractions and natural laws into which he infused biological arguments about a struggle for survival. Foreshadowing Malthus and Darwin, he argued that population would expand to a level where wants would equal the means available for subsistence; only hunger could prove a check to curb its growth. Anything that alleviated hunger tended to produce more poverty in the longer run. As a result, "these laws, so beautiful in theory, promote the evils they mean to remedy, and aggravate the distress they were intended to relieve."[21] Townsend recommended charity to encourage deference and gratitude among the poor; in short, alms in return

---

[19] For a general discussion of attitudes toward poverty in the later eighteenth century, see Gertrude Himmelfarb, *The Idea of Poverty* (New York: Knopf, 1984), chs. 2 and 3.

[20] Joseph Townsend, *A Dissertation on the Poor Laws by a Well-Wisher to Mankind* (Berkeley and Los Angeles: University of California Press, 1971), 27, 68.

[21] Ibid., 17.

for moral reform. His linkage of poor law payments to character and of poverty to behavior found an enthusiastic audience.

Townsend's abolitionist sentiments were unusual in the 1780s and 1790s; at that time, much of the discussion of the poor laws came from agricultural and administrative reformers, who took an empirical, rather than a moral approach to their subject. Joanna Innes, who calls the Board of Agriculture, founded in 1794, a "think tank" for rural problems, argues that discussions of the role of agriculture in the national economy at that time produced a rising interest in rural poverty. In addition, would-be reformers like Thomas Gilbert circulated drafts of new legislation and carried on a wide correspondence with people involved in poor law administration around the country in an effort to collect information.[22] In 1795, Arthur Young collected statistics on rural relief levels and local relief practices, via questionnaires in the *Annals of Agriculture*. When he formulated his own remedies for scarcity and want, he settled on the provision of potato gardens and grazing rights. He argued that laborers with land did not become paupers; self-help in a framework of publicly provided resources could cure a large share of the poverty problem.[23] Nevertheless, he considered poverty a necessary discipline to keep the noses of the poor to the inevitable grindstone of labor.

A strong moral framework condemning human weaknesses underlay many of the empirical analyses of poverty published in the later eighteenth century. In 1797, Sir Frederick Eden produced his multivolume work, *The State of the Poor*. An enthusiast for free trade and large farms, he collected family budgets and information on housing, diets, and dress in an effort to show that workers had sufficient resources to live decently. His investigations of local relief practices showed the inadequacy and unprofitability of public employment schemes, which supported his faith in free markets and his call for poor law reform. In his view, permanent national relief schemes fostered dependence and increased the demand for aid. The poor laws had unfortunate moral consequences: They undermined the desire to acquire property, weakened ambition, and encouraged dishonest administration. He too saw a linkage between moral decay and the poor laws.[24] The Enlightenment-style empiricism of both Young and Eden was compatible with serious criticisms of the

[22] Joanna Innes, "The Invention of Rural Poverty in Eighteenth-Century England," talk given to the Oxford Seminar on Poverty, All Soul's College, 6 June 1991.

[23] J. R. Poynter, *Society and Pauperism: English Ideas on Poor Relief, 1795–1834* (London: Routledge, 1969), 47, 98–102.

[24] Sir Frederick Morton Eden, *The State of the Poor: Or, a History of the Labouring Classes in England*, 3 vols. (London, B. & J. White, 1797), 1:444–50, 467.

poor law and a strong belief in encouraging the independence of laborers via self-help. One important strand of this argument derived from the conviction, held strongly by Eden, that the poor became indigent because of their own spending patterns and refusal to save. If this assumption was granted, then the way lay open to announce that the poor had in their own hands the means of their salvation through moral reform.

This route was promptly taken by the charitable, who were determined to make the poor more self-reliant. Donna Andrew points out that public support for London's major charities, such as the Foundling Hospital and the Lambeth Asylum, plummeted during the 1770s and 1780s. Givers turned to new "charities of self-help" like the Sunday school movement, the Philanthropic Society, and the Society for Bettering the Condition and Improving the Comforts of the Poor. Such groups relied aggressively on education, vocational training, and personal contacts to encourage thrift, piety, and virtue. "For the fervent and involved philanthropists, . . . true charity involved the improvement of the nation's morals and manners, as . . . the only sphere in which charity had not been replaced by the operations of the market."[25] In the charitable sphere, as in other public forums during the later eighteenth century, virtue rather than need became a major preoccupation.

At this time, thousands of Sunday schools dedicated to the teaching of virtue, sobriety, and industry sprang up all over the country.[26] To speed the process, the Society for the Support and Encouragement of Sunday Schools was founded in London in 1785, its work touted as necessary for the reformation of popular morals. Evangelical churchmen and philanthropists also founded the Society for Bettering the Condition and Increasing the Comforts of the Poor in 1796, which taught that economic improvement would follow from a shift in habits. Its early reports recommended punctuality, piety, frugality, and abstinence, for it noted "sinning is a very expensive occupation." Its publications praised the supervirtuous who managed to survive without poor law aid despite overwhelming odds and called for punishment of those drones and frauds who abused the charitable. Its adherents had a vision of independent workers aided in their struggle for survival by middle- and upper-class philanthropists, who would teach them among other things about such marvels as white-wash, rice puddings, and oxtail stews, thereby converting them to civility.[27]

---

[25] Donna T. Andrew, *Philanthropy and Police: London Charity in the Eighteenth Century* (Princeton: Princeton University Press, 1989), 156, 196.

[26] Thomas Laqueur, *Religion and Respectability: Sunday Schools and Working-Class Culture, 1780–1850* (New Haven: Yale University Press, 1976).

[27] Poynter, *Society,* 91–7.

This shift in public notions about charity was accelerated by growing awareness of classical economic theory and the linkage made between poverty and poor laws in the writings of Thomas Malthus. If, as Malthus argued, population tended to increase faster than the means of subsistence, workers were inevitably condemned to lives of privation. Wars, diseases, and famines operated to check population growth and therefore could lessen pressure on resources and arrest declines in wages. In contrast public benevolence to the poor, such as relief offered through the poor laws, eventually made conditions worse because it encouraged the poor to have more children and helped them to stay alive. In other words, the poor laws "may be said therefore in some measure to create the poor which they maintain."[28] In the 1798 version of his *Essay on Population,* Malthus assumed that every increase in productivity would soon be followed by a corresponding rise in population so that incomes would be pushed back to the subsistence level. Improvement in living standards for the masses lay largely outside human control. In later revised versions of the theory, in 1803 and after, Malthus admitted the possibility that the deferring of sexual gratification could lower the rate of demographic growth, but he continued to link sexual intercourse to vice and poverty to moral degradation. Over time, his attitude toward the poor laws hardened. He called for their abolition, claiming that once the poor learned that they had to depend upon their own resources, they would mend their ways and practice virtue.[29]

Gertrude Himmelfarb argues that the *Essay on Population* "decisively shaped" social attitudes and policies in Britain for half a century. The book went through multiple editions, inspired dozens of critiques and commentaries, and became one of the defining texts of its generation as its view of political economy supplanted that of Adam Smith.[30] Malthusianism and the hostility to the poor laws it fostered set the intellectual tone for debate on the poor laws well into the 1840s. Although not everyone accepted the policies Malthus recommended, his view of the futility of poor relief had to be confronted, as did his notion that the poor laws undermined the independence and self-respect of the destitute. Such ideas became staple arguments among would-be reformers in the period between 1800 and 1830.

Patrick Colquhoun, the London police magistrate who was actively involved both in the Mendicity Society and in the Society for Bettering the Condition and Improving the Comforts of the Poor, wrote on poverty and its

---

[28] Thomas Malthus, *Essay on Population* (1798), 83–4; Poynter, *Society,* 152–3.

[29] For a discussion of Malthus's evolving views on the poor laws, see Poynter, *Society,* 157.

[30] Himmelfarb, *Poverty,* 101, 133.

remedies, arguing his case on the basis of a pessimistic view of both economic change and the human character. He accepted poverty as the normal condition of those who have to work for a living and disavowed any state responsibility for what he regarded as a basic fact of life, necessary for society because without it none would work. Only indigence, the extreme position of those who could not work to provide subsistence for themselves, required state action. Although he admitted that there were many innocent causes of indigence, he also recognized a series of moral failings that led directly to economic ruin. For him, idleness, vice, and indigence had a close connection.[31] Patrick Colquhoun set his discussions of indigence within a framework where personal responsibility loomed large. When he listed causes of indigence, he found eight innocent and unavoidable ones, twenty-one that arose from chance and the operation of the economy, and then twenty-six "culpable causes," such as sloth, drink, and immorality, which led to crime.[32]

When Samuel Whitbread, a Whig reformer, introduced a bill into Parliament for poor law reform in 1807, he paid tribute to Malthus for having educated the public to the defects of existing law. Although he had earlier been an enthusiastic supporter of minimum wage legislation and active government attempts to combat wartime poverty, he now admitted:

It is an assertion now pretty generally made, that the system of our Poor Laws is certain to degrade those whom it was intended to exalt, to destroy the spirit of independence throughout our land; to hold out hopes which cannot be realized, to encourage idleness and vice; and to produce a superfluous population, the offspring of improvidence and the early victim of misery and want.[33]

The Malthusian argument had penetrated the chambers of Parliament and shaped the responses of men who earlier had rejected the arguments of the political economists. By 1820, many prominent theologians and moralists had accepted the Malthusian model. Thomas Chalmers, the Glasgow clergyman who targeted paupers for venomous attack, argued the case for abolitionism in sermons and tracts.[34] In the pages of the *Quarterly Review, Blackwood's Magazine,* and the *Edinburgh Review,* intellectuals thundered about public policy toward the poor, conducting their debates under Malthus's giant

---

[31] Patrick Colquhoun, *A Treatise on Indigence* (London: J. Hatchard, 1806), 8, 10, 232.

[32] Patrick Colquhoun, *The State of Indigence and the Situation of the Casual Poor in the Metropolis Explained* (London: H. Baldwin, 1799), 7–8; idem, *A Treatise on Indigence,* 11.

[33] Quoted in Poynter, *Society,* 208.

[34] Thomas Chalmers, *Tracts on Pauperism* (Glasgow: William Collins, 1833); Thomas Chalmers, *The Christian and Civic Economy of Large Towns* (Glasgow: J Starke, 1821–6).

shadow.[35] Justices of the peace, local vicars and overseers, agricultural reformers, and budding philanthropists, as well as the major social philosophers of the period, felt compelled to comment upon poverty. To quote Sidney Smith, "[E]very man rushes to the press with his small morsel of imbecility; and is not easy until he sees his impertinence stitched in blue covers."[36] The growing conviction that the poor laws themselves produced the pauperism they were intended to relieve undermined support for compulsory, public relief and linked dependence on the parish to depravity. The lines between the deserving and the undeserving poor were being redrawn, with paupers clearly placed on the wrong side of the tracks.

Representing the Poor

The representation of poverty in the cultural productions of the middle classes shifted dramatically between 1750 and 1820, pushing the poor from the center to the periphery of the communities they inhabited. This is easiest to see in satirical prints, which were immensely popular among both fashionable and not so fashionable people. Bound, they appeared in gentlemen's libraries; in single copies, they were pasted on screens or hung in middle-class homes. Others found their way onto the walls of gin shops and ale houses. Dorothy George sees in them "virtually the only pictorial rendering of the flow of events, moods, and fashions," and she claims that "they reflect the social attitudes of the day."[37]

Early in the eighteenth century, Hogarth had placed both poverty and vice in the middle of the society he drew. Gin Lane lay in London, as did the haunts of Moll Hackabout, Tom Rakewell, and the idle apprentice. Even those who chose a straight and narrow path to virtue remained only a few steps away from the poor. Hogarth's industrious apprentice was confronted by beggars on his wedding day, and the poor entered the Guildhall to plead for alms when he became Lord Mayor. Neither artists nor writers in early and mid-eighteenth-century Britain exiled the poor from the society they described or reduced them to shadows on the sidelines; much of the edge of their humor lay in interaction and in an awareness of ambiguities. In 1751,

---

[35] A. W. Coats, *Poverty in the Victorian Age, I: English Poor Laws, 1807–1833* (London: Gregg International Publishers, Ltd., 1973).

[36] Sydney Smith, "Poor Laws," *Edinburgh Review* 65 (January 1820): 91–2.

[37] M. Dorothy George, *Hogarth to Cruikshank: Social Change in Graphic Satire* (London: Penguin, 1967), 13, 17.

Samuel Johnson wrote in the *Rambler* of a garret where he lived, posing as an urban antiquarian anxious to trace the social origins of the "smoky memorials" on the ceiling. His landlady had rented his room to bankrupt tailors, sickly women, pyromaniacal authors, counterfeiters, and ladies of dubious reputation before he entered into possession of it. As he said, "A single house will show whatever is done or suffered in the world." None of the inhabitants had a monopoly on either virtue or vice.[38]

But, by the 1790s, much of the easy interaction and moral ambiguity of the earlier period had vanished. Even artists more sympathetic to the poor than Hogarth had reduced the destitute to skeletal figures shunted to the sidelines of their society. Not only had the poor lost much of their impish vitality, but their individuality faded into pale images of want and deprivation pushed outside the world of the respectable. Unable to challenge the propertied directly, they appear in windows and at doors, importuning from a distance.

James Gilray, in "John Bull's Progress," comments on how the state produced destitution. In a four-panelled cartoon, he shows a fat, happy John Bull, surrounded by his thriving family in a snug, property-filled cottage. But John Bull goes off to war, forcing his family to pawn all their tools and other property in order to feed themselves and to pay their taxes. Finally, a skinny, crippled Bull returns to find a skeletal family huddled in an empty room. They have become animal-like, gnawing on turnips. The objects around them, and their family by implication, are broken beyond repair. They cringe away from Bull, affection transformed into fear. The war turned a prosperous household into a group of outcasts, unfit for work and unable to return to the normal patriarchal order of the past.[39] Although Gilray's main target is surely the state, his vision of the victimized pushes them firmly outside the boundaries of respectability and shows them isolated from a wider community. In the wartime cartoons, rich and poor occupied separate spaces. Moreover, the impoverished are immediately distinguishable from the middle and upper classes by their dress and their shapes: Their gaunt angularity contrasts sharply with the bulbous, bewigged outlines of the comfortable. A vision of a society separated into distinct and hostile groups has replaced the more fluid, ambiguous worlds of Defoe and Hogarth.

James Gilray's cartoon of 1795, "Substitutes for Bread," focuses on a dinner where fat officials gorge themselves on piles of money in the shape of Turtle Soup, venison, and fish, while ghostly, almost faceless poor peer in the

---

[38] Samuel Johnson, "The History of a Garret," *The Rambler* 161 (October 1, 1751).

[39] LW 793/6.3/1; see also LW 794/2.14/1, Lewis Walpole Collection, Farmington, Connecticut.

Figure 3.1. "John Bull's Progress," James Gilray, 1793. Courtesy of the Print Collection, Lewis Walpole Library, Yale University

window, asking: "Grant us the Crumbs which drop from your table!" They wear caps reminiscent of the revolutionary *bonnet rouge,* and wave sticks in a mildly menacing manner. Contemporaries would not have missed the analogies to Parisian mobs and their direct modes of action. Their petition for help, Gilray announces, comes from the "Starving Swine," who benefit not at all from the announced attempt at public charity.[40] Gilray, for all his sympathy for the poor, shows them as a marginalized group whose politics are suspect and whose humanity is doubted.

In the decade following the end of the French wars, cartoonists depicted a society where public spaces belonged to particular social groups. Park scenes by Thomas Rowlandson show a socially homogeneous crowd. In his depiction of Kensington Gardens in 1815, guards at the gates kept out the "rab-

[40] LW 795/12.24/1

[41] George, *Hogarth to Cruikshank,* 167, 169.

Figure 3.2. "Substitutes for Bread," James Gilray, 1795. Courtesy of the Print Collection, Lewis Walpole Library, Yale University

ble."[41] In the wildly popular *Life in London,* published in 1821, Robert and George Cruikshank followed Tom, Jerry, and Bob on a trip through the metropolis.[42] They went to Covent Garden, Almanack's, and Vauxhall, but to find the poor, they traveled to different places – East Smithfield alehouses and a cellar in the St. Giles slums. There they found groups of leering grotesques, brawling Irish, and drunken women. In the world of Tom and Jerry, the poor lived apart and had to be sought in their native habitats. Exiled to slum streets and cellars, they matched their surroundings. These comic depictions of the poor permitted a glimpse of a population increasingly condemned by the middle classes but one used for entertainment and moral counterexample.

The tendency to marginalize the poor appears also in those novels of the early nineteenth century whose authors broke away from the conventions of romanticism and genteel stories of polite society. Some of the earliest of these treatments focus on the Celtic fringes, whose populations were both figura-

---

[42] Pierce Egan, *Life in London, or, the Day and Night Scenes of Jerry Hawthorne Esq. and His Elegant Friend, Corinthian Tom, Accompanied by Bob Logic the Oxonian in Their Rambles and Sprees Through the Metropolis* (London, 1821); the series is discussed in George, *Hogarth to Cruikshank,* 169.

tively and literally on the edges of the United Kingdom. In these early novels, the Celtic poor were given the vices against which the authors wished to
warn readers. They are literally un-English and are kept far away. In Maria
Edgeworth's *Absentee,* published in 1812, Lord Colombre learns about the
consequences of his family's long and expensive residence in London. Left
to themselves and to the care of rapacious agents, their Irish tenants live in
squalor and turn to drink. Watching a meeting of tenants and agent, Lord
Colombre "endured the smell of tobacco and whiskey, and the sound of various brogues, the din of men wrangling, brawling, threatening, whining,
drawling, cajoling, cursing, and every variety of wretchedness." He decides
to save them by returning to his estates and by teaching them habits of civility.[43]

Elizabeth Hamilton displays a similar attitude in the *Cottagers of Glenburnie,* published in 1808. In it, a distressed gentlewoman goes to live in a
Scottish village, where she finds thatched huts, dunghills, and animals within.
Appalled by the dirt and the lack of attention to it, she immediately begins to
agitate for change. Example and gentle suggestion are her preferred mode of
attack, but she finds the people lazy and unconcerned. Moreover, she brands
their morals deficient: "Lying is too generally considered by the poor as a
very slight offense, or rather indeed as an excusable artifice, often necessary,
sometimes even laudable. It is truly shocking to find the prevalence of this
vice in a country that boasts of the degree of instruction given to the poor."[44]
In the end, a new school brings improvement in behavior, after the gentlewoman instructs the master in the best English standards. She travels to the
margins of her society and brings civility to the poor, who without her example live disorderly, immoral lives. For Hamilton, dirt signaled both a physical
and a moral pollution, which had to be defeated. She and Edgeworth took
descriptions usually reserved for the urban lower classes and applied them to
the poor at the margins of British society. Their work typifies a widening
attack upon the manners of the poor, whose wretchedness is blamed, at least
in part, on their immorality.

By the early nineteenth century, painters and writers commonly placed the
poor within highly conventional morality tales, in which anything but superhuman virtue was branded deficient. John Barrell argues that, by 1800, English painters developed a new set of representations for the rural poor in
which work signaled virtue. Artists neutralized and denied the threat posed

[43] Maria Edgeworth, *The Absentee* (London: J. Dent, 1972), 242.

[44] Elizabeth Hamilton, *The Cottagers of Glenburnie* (New York: E. S. Sargeant, 1808), 337.

by starving laborers by picturing them as docile, happy peasants, fully employed on the land of their masters.[45]

Work and virtue flowed together in the work of essayists and novelists, too. Hannah More made her lower-class characters into caricatures of good and evil so that her readers would find it easy to choose their role models. Tawney Rachel, a gypsy fortune-teller who cheated and defrauded people, could be judged next to the happy Shepherd of Salisbury Plain, who lived on one meal a day and refused all beer on principle. Another paragon of virtue, "Diligent Dick," announced, "I have a wife and seven children. I rise with the lark, and lie down with the lamb. I never spend an idle penny or an idle moment; though my family is numerous, my children were never a burden to me. . . . Sir, the richest man in England is not happier than I."[46]

Jane Taylor, an engraver and writer who published several volumes of verse for children between 1804 and 1808, set a similar tone. She tells of "Dirty Jim," who couldn't keep clean, concluding, "The idle and bad, / Like this little lad, / May be dirty and black to be sure; / But good boys are seen, / To be decent and clean, / Altho' they are ever so poor."[47] The good poor never complained and, of course, never stopped working; they remained contented, whatever their lot, and smiled at adversity. But they were said to be in the minority: Witness her tale of "The Gleaner," in which little Mary gleans grain in a field, never flagging despite the heat.

> Poor girl, hard at work in the heat of the sun,
> How tired and hot you must be;
> Why don't you leave off, as the others have done,
> And sit with them under the tree?
>
> Oh no! for my mother lies ill in her bed,
> Too feeble to spin or to knit;
> And my poor little brothers are crying for bread,
> And yet we can't give them a bit!
>
> Then could I be merry, and idle, and play,
> While they are so hungry and ill?
> O no, I had rather work hard all the day,
> My little blue apron to fill.[48]

[45] John Barrell, *The Dark Side of the Landscape: The Rural Poor in English Painting, 1730–1840* (New York: Cambridge University Press, 1980), 16, 86–7.

[46] Hannah More, *Cheap Repository Tracts* (Boston: E. Lincoln, 1802), 4, 208–9.

[47] Jane Taylor, *Prose and Poetry* (London: Humphrey Milford, 1925), 42.

[48] Ibid., 35.

Such tales had their visual equivalents in the paintings of George Morland, who in his paintings "The Comforts of Industry" and "The Miseries of Idleness" from 1790 contrasted the good and the bad poor. Whereas the former lived in tidy, rural cottages where they remained cheerful and loving, the latter found themselves in tatters in city garrets. The disorder of their clothes mirrored the disorderliness of their children. For Morland, character could be read in the state of one's clothes and the standard of housekeeping. But taken together, his paintings show a divided society – urban and rural, rich and poor, deferential and discontented. His romanticized paintings of charitable acts tell only part of a much more complex social story.[49] But the predominant message of pastoral painting confirmed the tight connection of work and virtue.

Harriet Martineau made this message explicit in her story, *Cousin Marshall,* published in 1832 as part of the *Illustrations of Political Economy.* She tells the story of the four Bridgeman orphans, two of whom were placed in a workhouse by relatives who could not offer support. Ned, the oldest, felt himself disgraced by the move, and he ran away as soon as he was able. Working as a farm laborer, he soon won the respect of his employer, and he became and remained independent through his fierce determination and energy. He managed to save money and gave it to cousin Marshall for the support of his sisters. Alas, his younger sister, Jane, lacked his ambitions. While in the workhouse, she had her head turned by the jokes and habits of the female paupers, who convinced her that work was silly because the parish had to provide support. Jane, of course, came to a bad end, bearing an illegitimate child and wasting her life. The heroine of the story, cousin Marshall, supported her own large family, provided for the Bridgeman children as best as she could, and remained independent until her death at eighty-one. Martineau carefully contrasted her stoic virtue against the wiles of the paupers who faked illnesses and lied about the numbers of their children to gain more relief. Martineau saw dependence upon the poor laws as scandalous, and she did not hesitate to brand those who took public alms as degraded. In her words, the tendency of the poor laws was "to encourage improvidence with all its attendant evils, – to injure the good while relieving the bad, – to extinguish the spirit of independence on one side, – and of charity on the other, – to encourage peculation, tyranny and fraud, – and to increase perpetually the evil they

[49] Josephine Gear, *Putting the Poor in Their Place: A Brief Guide, Exhibition at the University Art Gallery, SUNY Binghamton,* 7–20 April 1986 (Binghamton: The Gallery, 1986). See also Barrell, *Landscape.*

are meant to remedy."[50] In other words, the poor laws produced indigence and led the poor into immorality.

. In this rhetoric of virtue and vice, the poor stood condemned for accepting that which the Tudor state had decreed parishes had the obligation to provide. Those who applied for aid within normal channels found themselves suspected to be "welfare cheats." Neither residence nor need brought entitlement. This shift in attitudes toward poverty, which emanated from the reforming middle classes, pushed the poor outside the bounds of respectable society if they dared to apply for parish aid. By the early nineteenth century, the poor had lost their entitlement to public support in the eyes of the propagandists for a new public morality.

"Work, Boys, Work and Be Contented!"

The rural poor law regime of pensions for the elderly and apprenticeships for children began to crumble in the later eighteenth century when large numbers of unemployed adults swelled the relief rolls. As wartime inflation, industrialization, and agricultural restructuring disrupted the English economy, overseers had periodically to deal with many more healthy adult claimants. But they had few effective methods to combat mass poverty or mass unemployment. Their standard response to destitution – money allowances – raised taxes sharply, infuriating ratepayers. Moreover, their major alternative, employment in a workhouse factory or "house of industry," did not fare well during cyclical downturns in the economy. Demands for aid increased just as markets for products declined. In any case, by 1780, workhouse labor could no longer compete with mechanized production. Factory spinning quickly lowered the price of thread and doomed hand production. Then the introduction of power looms into cotton factories in the 1820s brought down cloth prices. Typical products of workhouse labor commanded less and less in the marketplace. Moreover, the collapse of the cottage manufacture of other simple goods meant that overseers had few alternative industries into which they could shift pauper labor. In any case, they lacked the capital, the facilities, and the will to maintain a regime of production for profit. M. A. Crowther argues that, by 1815, most workhouses only rarely offered work to the able-bodied. Even the East Anglian parishes that had built elaborate "houses of industry" had retreated from manufacturing.[51]

---

[50] Harriet Martineau, *Cousin Marshall,* (London: Charles Fox, 1832), 191.

[51] M. A. Crowther, *The Workhouse System, 1834–1929* (London: Methuen, 1983), 28.

Yet state-provided work was the cornerstone of the Elizabethan poor law, and state interference in the work process was considered normal.[52] Sound political practice and Protestant ethics pushed local officials in the same direction. Indeed, work as the solution to the welfare problem became even more popular during the later eighteenth century as faith in the all-embracing power of labor markets and in individual responsibility grew. Why give money to those who were capable of helping themselves? The difficulty, then as now, was to square theory and practice, and private entrepreneurs could help solve the problem.

A work requirement was easiest to enforce among dependent children, but apprenticeship became more difficult as the scale of destitution increased and the institution itself declined. What to do if you had dozens of children, rather than one or two, to place? Not only were the supervisory costs high, but artisan households with several children of their own had a limited capacity for expansion. Then, as guilds lost their control over access to trades and training, the social meaning of the practice changed drastically and its scale declined. Moreover, overseers could no longer delude themselves that apprenticing a child to a tailor or a shoemaker would give that child access to a skilled occupation. Why spend money to send children to be unpaid laborers in trades where conditions of access were essentially open? Although the practice of settling adolescents with local craftsmen lived on into the twentieth century, it waned in popularity and in effectiveness.

Proto-industrialization had provided new outlets for child labor in several parts of the country. Small masters in the iron trades in the Birmingham and south Staffordshire regions took multiple apprentices into their workshops during the later eighteenth century, using them to make nails, bolts, screws, and other small objects. At least one stocking manufacturer in Nottingham around 1730 ran his workshop on the labor of two dozen pauper apprentices.[53]

The early factories provided a popular alternative for overseers. Owners of the many rural textile mills needed workers, and too few could be found in their local labor markets. As a result, large numbers of poor children were sent into the factories as "apprentices." Just how many went is impossible to

---

[52] For a discussion of the regulated quality of ordinary labor in Britain before 1800, see Robert J. Steinfeld, *The Invention of Free Labor* (Chapel Hill: University of North Carolina Press, 1991).

[53] Ivy Pinchbeck, *Women Workers and the Industrial Revolution, 1750–1850* (London: Cass, 1969), 17, 272–3; Sidney Webb and Beatrice Webb, *English Local Government from the Revolution to the Municipal Corporations Act,* vol. 7, *English Poor Law History, Part 1: The Old Poor Law,* (London: Longmans, 1927), 200.

discover because arrangements were made in the parishes of origin, and many of the indenture documents were destroyed. Yet the practice seems to have been widespread by 1780, when silk manufacturers contracted for children and when demands from the early cotton manufacturers mounted. By that time, the Webbs claim, children were carried off "literally by cartloads" from London workhouses.[54] Critics of the system in the 1790s charged that mills in the Manchester area got most of their young workers as parish apprentices. Eden's survey of 1797 listed parishes from Cumberland, Chester, Derbyshire, Nottingham, and Lancaster as sending children into cotton and silk mills, and it did not include data on all the counties with a substantial manufacturing sector.[55] The first centrally collected data come from an 1815 Parliamentary investigation, which reported that, over a ten-year period, about fourteen hundred children had been sent to the cotton factories from a group of fifty London parishes.[56]

After that point, the practice declined rapidly according to most historians. Parliament, which had begun to regulate parish apprenticeship in 1802, barred London overseers from sending children more than forty miles away and levied other restrictions on the practice. In any case, the rising substitution of steam engines for water wheels meant that mills could be built in urban areas where free labor was abundant and cheaper.[57] The solution of binding pauper children to factory masters decreased markedly by the 1820s, although a few London parishes and Midland parishes continued to do so on a limited basis.[58]

For a period of around thirty years, however, parish overseers and factory masters struck a mutually beneficial bargain at the expense of their young charges. Hundreds of children found themselves taken away from relatives and sent long distances for periods ranging from ten to fifteen years. Living in dormitories near the factories, they found that not only were their daily schedules strictly controlled, but they had no freedom to leave and received no wages. Unsupervised by either the government or parish authorities, their levels of training, education, and treatment were the choice of the entrepreneur. Twelve- to fourteen-hour days were considered normal, and the chil-

---

[54] Webb and Webb, *Old Poor Law,* 201.

[55] Eden, *State of the Poor,* 2:33–42, 45–135, 294–373, 565–583.

[56] Ivy Pinchbeck and Margaret Hewitt, *Children in English Society* (London: Routledge, 1969), 1:255.

[57] Ibid.

[58] St. Giles in the Fields, "Director's Minutes," vol. 1: 7 June 1831; 7 June 1836; see also *The Leicestershire Mercury,* 21 February 1857.

dren's education was generally confined to Sunday school and Bible reading. Little better than slaves for the duration of their apprenticeship, they represented the extreme case of unfree labor among English citizens during the modern period. During their apprenticeships, they were literally exiled from their home communities and put out of the sight and mind of the parish that had legal responsibility for them.

Orphaned or abandoned children, however, did not make up the bulk of the pauper population. Unemployed adults and their families presented the major problem for overseers. What to do with the scores of laborers thrown out of work in the winter or in a trade depression? Work services for adult males became a central part of the welfare regimes in rural areas in the later eighteenth century.[59]

Mark Blaug reminds us that the subsidies offered by the poor laws went along with a substantial increase in labor control. Blaug argues that "allowances-in-aid-of-wages were almost always associated with the roundsman system, modified by the use of the Labor Rate."[60] Under the "roundsman" scheme, overseers assigned unemployed workers in rotation to local taxpayers who had to feed them and offer a small wage; the employers, farmers for the most part, could use the workers at will on their property. Poor law funds were used to bring laborers' wages up to a locally determined standard of subsistence. Parish officials used this plan to split the labor costs of the unemployed between local employers and the ratepayers in Tysoe, Warwickshire, in 1763, in Bedfordshire in 1758 and 1781, and in Cambridgeshire in 1792; these few examples from parishes whose local records have been studied probably represent only the tip of an iceberg of similar arrangements that became widespread in agricultural areas during the later eighteenth century.[61] Work tests forced farmers to employ local labor or to pay via the rates; meanwhile, the lazy would refuse such work and disappear from the relief rolls.

The labor rate plan for subsidizing the rural poor became popular during the 1820s. Under it, ratepayers were assessed proportionate shares of the winter wage bill for laborers, assuming each earned a subsistence income. Employers then had the choice of paying the parish directly or hiring enough

[59] Daniel A. Baugh, "The Cost of Poor Relief in South-East England, 1790–1834," *Economic History Review,* 2nd ser., 28 (1975): 50–68.

[60] Mark Blaug, "The Myth of the Old Poor Law and the Making of the New," *Journal of Economic History* 23:2 (June 1963): 156.

[61] Ashby, "One Hundred Years," 153–7; F. G. Emmison, "The Relief of the Poor at Eaton Socon, 1706–1834," *Bedfordshire Historical Record Society Publications* 15 (1933): 50; Hampson, *Treatment,* 191.

local workers at a publicly determined rate to account for their share of the total expense. Officials in about 17 percent of the parishes in the Speen-hamland counties of the Midlands and south and 10 percent in the non-Speenhamland counties, mostly in the north and west, claimed to be using that method of poor relief when they were surveyed in 1832. About 8 percent of the surveyed parishes continued to use the roundsman system.[62] This direct evidence of the incidence of these labor systems comes well after the peak periods of their use during the Napoleonic Wars and the early 1820s. It seems likely that outdoor relief in agricultural areas after 1780 regularly included demands for work service on the part of the poor. The parish might employ them on the roads, paying out of the rates, or they were apportioned among local farmers. When Rev. Lowe of Bingham in Nottinghamshire began to reform the local poor, whom he described as "completely pau-perised," he found 103 roundsmen on the parish books and 78 people receiv-ing other forms of outdoor relief. Work service and subsidies went together; they were not alternatives.[63]

When Sidney and Beatrice Webb categorized the "stages" of the old poor laws, they isolated a period in the later eighteenth century when the direct exploitation of pauper labor of all ages increased: "In one way or another the Parish sought to transfer to some employer – if need be, by compulsory allo-cation – the duty of enforcing labor and discipline on the poor; and the steadily increasing capitalist developments in industry and agriculture seemed to enable this to be done with all but those who were completely impotent."[64] They saw this period coming to an end around 1796, with the widespread adoption of grants-in-aid-of-wages. Yet as we have seen, subsi-dies were compatible with efforts at labor control, which continued in the early nineteenth century. In any case, the widespread apprenticing of children to factory owners continued until 1815.

In welfare practice, relief became increasingly tied to work service because of its disciplinary and reformatory functions. In 1819, Parliament gave overseers and churchwardens the power to buy or rent up to twenty acres of land so that they could put to work unemployed men needing aid.[65] Local records for the years after 1815, as well as testimony before the Poor Law

---

[62] Boyer, *Economic History,* 17; Mark Blaug, "The Poor Law Report Reexamined," *Journal of Economic History* 23 (1964): 236–7.

[63] Webb and Webb, *Old Poor Law,* 257.

[64] Ibid., 400.

[65] 59 George III, c. 12, sec. 12–14.

Commission of 1834, show that extensive claims were made for work service by the unemployed. Around 1824, Plymouth and Brighton used paupers to remove dung and night soil from their towns. Norwich used pauper labor to pave streets in 1826. Ten London parishes gave paupers work cleaning the streets in 1832.[66] Thomas Pearce, a Sussex farm laborer, told Edwin Chadwick around 1832 that if he were to lose his job and then go to his parish for relief, "they would put me on the roads."[67] Male paupers and adolescent children had to work for their welfare payments. In this period, gender and age became increasingly important in the shaping of welfare aid.

Reformist parishes, which tried to lower poor rates after the end of the wars with France, made work the mainstay of their more intensively deterrent systems. Peter Mandler argues for a change in the labor test at this time when many country gentlemen abandoned earlier paternalist schemes for reliance on the labor market to solve the poverty problem. By offering only hard, unappealing jobs, they hoped to pressure workers to reenter the normal labor market.[68] During the 1820s in the parish of Swallowfield, Berkshire, overseers offered the unemployed low-paid task work at a gravel pit. In Bishop's Hatfield, Hertfordshire, unemployed males under age fifty did road work for below-market wages.[69] Thomas Whately of Cookham, Berkshire, announced with pride to the Poor Law Commission that when able-bodied workers applied for relief, they got lower wages for more effort than would be demanded in the free labor market. The aim was "to let the labourer find that the parish is the hardest taskmaster and the worst paymaster he can find and thus induce him to make his application to the parish his last and not his first resource."[70] In Whately's opinion, parishes and the labor market could jointly solve the welfare problem, and induce virtue in the process.

Both power and behavior were clearly at issue. Even if parishes kept paupers from starving in bad years, they determined that there would be no cakes and ale for the unemployed. The symbolic value of work as a sign of good faith, of good behavior, of participation in productive activity continued to loom large. For adult males, welfare aid had changed from an entitlement to

---

[66] Webb and Webb, *Old Poor Law,* 231–2.

[67] *Report from His Majesty's Commissioners for Inquiring into the Administration and Practical Operation of the Poor Laws, 1834,* Appendix A, part III, Parliamentary Papers, 1834: XXVIII, 17.

[68] Peter Mandler, "The Making of the New Poor Law, *Redivivus,*" *Past and Present,* #117 (Nov. 1987), 131–157.

[69] *Report . . . on the Poor Laws, 1834,* Appendix A, III, 35, 63.

[70] Ibid., 25.

a form of labor discipline. Identifying work and family support as a male activity, overseers were determined to extract from men a hefty quid pro quo for aid and to encourage reformation of behavior. Welfare decisions became increasingly shaped by common notions of gender along with those of moral reformation.

Discipline, Deterrence, and the Workhouse

Vagrants were an early group to be force-fed with increasingly heavy doses of discipline. Constables picked up the destitute on the streets, took them before magistrates, and then either jailed or sent away those without local claims. Although authorities had done similar things in the seventeenth century, the Vagrant Removal Costs Act of 1700, as it was implemented in succeeding decades, gave local officials a new set of tools to spread the cost and to implement it effectively.[71] As a result, in London, poor Scots and Irish, unemployed servants from the provinces, and runaway apprentices, as well as widows and orphans without local rights, were sent home in increasing numbers during the mid- and later eighteenth century. Middlesex parishes that passed home only about 700 vagrants per year during the 1760s, removed an average of 2,500 annually between 1786 and 1790, and sharply increasing numbers after 1815. In 1819–20, contractors reported 6,689 vagrants passed home for whom they requested payment.[72] Nicholas Rogers calls the vagrancy laws "the last disciplinary arm of a disciplinary code," and he notes how the London workhouse was used as a house of correction for about 500 vagrants each year around 1750.[73] After 1780, demands for more aggressive attacks on vagrants multiplied along with the cost of relief. The Evangelical Proclamation Society organized a national conference on vagrancy and lobbied for new legislation, which, after passage in 1792, mandated a minimum jail sentence for vagrants. Thereafter, "rogues and vagabonds" had to be jailed for seven days in a house of correction or whipped.[74] Rogers's investigation of this group shows them to be little different from the destitute and the homeless regularly relieved under the poor laws. The majority were women, people arrested because "old age, family breakdown, the sexual divi-

---

[71] Innes, "Parliament," 73.

[72] Nicholas Rogers, "Policing the Poor in Eighteenth-Century London: The Vagrancy Laws and Their Administration," *Histoire sociale, social history* 24 (May, 1991): 141–2.

[73] Nicholas Rogers, "Vagrancy in Eighteenth-Century London," unpublished paper (1983), 25; idem, "Policing," 134–5.

[74] Rogers, "Policing," 136.

sion of labor and the fortunes of war intensified the normal hazards of working life in service and in the petty trades and pushed them into a desperate poverty."[75] These were the normal clients of welfare offices; they differed only because their settlement rights were elsewhere. But parishes had a decreasing tolerance for those they considered dangerous riffraff, and they moved to exclude, to confine, and to discipline them.

The Enlightenment idea that people could be transformed by institutions had given birth, in Britain in the 1760s, to a host of asylums dedicated to reforming prostitutes, street urchins, and illegitimate children. In 1780, Jonas Hanway, noted for his charities to redeem prostitutes, called for imprisoning the insubordinate poor to force them into industry and humility. More police, penitentiaries, houses of industry and Sunday schools were wanted, he argued, because "[l]iberty cannot stand without virtue."[76] Once in sanitized settings, the socially deviant would supposedly absorb discipline, order, and Christian morals via osmosis. Behavioral reform seemed to require institutionalization for the deviant. Andrew Scull has described the growth in Britain during the early nineteenth century of large-scale asylums that came to house "the mad".[77] Workhouses and prisons can also be added to this list of places that formed a "carcereal archipelago" to discipline and punish, partly through work.[78] That such purposes lay in the forefront of the public mind can be seen in the example of Jeremy Bentham, the much-admired utilitarian philosopher. He looked forward to a society where reformed prisons and workhouses would serve as "a mill to grind rogues honest and idle men industrious."[79] Work was one of the grinding stones through which such transformations were to be effected.

The functions of deterrent workhouses and their disciplinary message were sharpened around the turn of the century. Jeremy Bentham, who had unbounded enthusiasm for large-scale schemes bringing compulsory moral improvement, wrote in 1798 *Pauper Management Improved*. He called for a National Charity Company financed through both stock sales and government funds, which would build houses of industry to oversee the return to discipline and productivity of the poor. Each house would provide living and

---

[75] Rogers, "Vagrancy," 21.

[76] Quoted in Rogers, "Policing," 136.

[77] Andrew T. Scull, *Museums of Madness: The Social Organization of Insanity in Nineteenth-Century England* (London: Allen Lane, 1979).

[78] The phrase is, of course, Michel Foucault's. See Michel Foucault, *Discipline and Punish* (New York: Vintage, 1979), 297.

[79] Jeremy Bentham, *Collected Works of Jeremy Bentham*, 11 vols. (Edinburgh: William Tait, 1843), 10:226; quoted in Scull, *Museums*, 36.

working space for two thousand people under the complete control of the governor, who could observe them constantly in their cells through his innovative circular, panopticon design. Bentham exuded optimism: "Morals reformed, health preserved, industry invigorated, instruction diffused, public burthens lightened, Economy seated, as it were upon a rock, the Gordian knot of the Poor-Laws not cut but untied, all by a simple idea of Architecture!"[80] Bentham's scheme would reform wayward individuals through work; long hours of labor combined with restricted diets and spartan accommodations would convert social dross to sterling. Bentham proposed the imprisonment not only of the current set of paupers, but also of unmarried mothers, beggars, criminals' families, disorderly apprentices, debtors, and children not in school – not only masterless men, but those who had strayed in any way from paths of deference and respectability. Confinement and commercial exploitation would follow. The combination of profits and social benefit, he hoped, would make his scheme irresistible. Bentham's plan took the common practice of paupers producing for profit, grafted it onto the clientele of the familiar mixed workhouse, and then called for intensified discipline and supervision in order to force moral reform and high levels of output. Paupers would not only be educated and trained to contribute to the economy, but also be used to mass-produce new inventions. Within their walls, capitalism and social engineering thrived in tandem. Bentham envisaged the redesigned workhouses as centers for social and economic experimentation.

A synoptic version of Bentham's plan appeared in the *Annals of Agriculture* in 1797–8, and he habitually circulated drafts of his writings among various influential politicians and writers.[81] Although the full version of his schemes remained unpublished, his *Pauper Management Improved* was reissued in 1803 and 1812; it found no immediate enthusiasts or investors, but the work testifies to the widespread faith in social engineering to be found among the disciplinarians of the poor, which did not die out but carried over into the 1820s and 1830s. Note the plan advocated by Rowland Hill in a pamphlet of 1832, *Home Colonies: Sketch of a Plan for the Gradual Extinction of Pauperism and for the Diminution of Crime.* He recommended the creation of work colonies for paupers where they would farm and produce objects for themselves and for sale. Each would house about ten thousand people who would be detained there in temporary slavery and taught skills along with punctuality and classical economics. Women were to learn domestic econ-

---

[80] Quoted in Himmelfarb, *Idea of Poverty,* 79.

[81] Poynter, *Society,* 107–8.

omy, and children were to be educated. People would be free to leave only after learning industry, self-support, and good habits. His scheme, he thought, would recommend itself to the government because of its ability to organize the "present degraded classes" and because of the "enlightened direction" in which their energies would be employed.[82]

Echoes of Bentham's efforts to classify and confine the poor appear in schemes for reforming workhouses in the 1820s. After George Nicholls, a retired officer of the East India Company's merchant marine service, became overseer for Southwell in Nottinghamshire in 1821, he and a group of other like-minded officials ordered that the workhouse be "enclosed by walls sufficiently high to prevent persons entering or leaving the premises without permission." They ordered that the sexes be kept separate, that inmates be divided into various categories, and that diet and time be regulated. Those inside the walls worked at crushing bones, digging holes, or breaking stones – all punitive tasks calculated to deter applicants. Relief outside the workhouse was restricted and, for men, linked to forced labor on the roads. The parish also tightened restrictions on unmarried mothers in order to induce "greater restraint" in their sexual practices.[83]

The parish of Cookham in Berkshire introduced similar changes in its poor law practices in the early 1820s. The local vicar, Thomas Whately, proudly described the new system to Edwin Chadwick in 1834. Its centerpiece was increased use of the workhouse, where all paupers who were not sick or elderly were classed as "the idle, the improvident, vicious." Whately then added, "This class actually comprehended the whole of the able-bodied paupers." They found themselves heavily restricted: Their food was limited to bread and cheese, they could not leave the workhouse, and they could not receive visitors without a written order from an overseer. Forced labor, trenching an acre of "hard gravelly ground," was required of them. Whately noted that normally they would have had "an influx of paupers applying for work whenever the ground was closed by frost or snow," but that they were "got rid of" and "silenced" by the offers of the workhouse and specific labor tasks.[84] Within a few years, a select vestry in Swallowfield, Berkshire, made similar changes. No able-bodied paupers going into the workhouse could leave it without permission; their diet was to be limited to one pound of

[82] Rowland Hill, *Home Colonies: Sketch of a Plan for the Gradual Extinction of Pauperism and for the Diminution of Crime* (London: Simpkin & Marshall, 1832), 9–10, 25–6, 49.

[83] George Nicholls, *A History of the English Poor Law*, vol. 2, new ed. (New York: Putnam & Sons, 1898), 231–3; Webb and Webb, *Old Poor Law*, 257.

[84] *Report on the Poor Laws, 1834*, Appendix A, part III, 25–6.

cheese and a gallon loaf of second-quality bread per week, although this regulation seems not to have been enforced. The parish also increased pressure on laborers to enter the workhouse by refusing to pay rents, to give cash allowances, or to provide clothing for poor families. Hard labor at low wages outside it or hard labor for free within it were the alternatives; not surprisingly, Chadwick was told that in 1834 no able-bodied laborers had chosen the workhouse.[85]

Around 1820, the Marquis of Salisbury superintended the adoption of deterrent workhouses in areas of Hertfordshire near his estate. Over the next decade, the parishes of Bayford, Bishop's Hatfield, Essendon, Hertingfordbury, Little Berkhampstead, Sandridge, Swallowfield, Watton, and Welwyn hired paid officials to run reformed workhouses and tighten the screws on local paupers. The most extensive changes took place in Bishop's Hatfield, where John Bridgens, who had been a drill sergeant and paymaster in the Coldstream Guards, took over as permanent overseer. The local workhouse was enlarged and reorganized to deal with the poor, who were denied outdoor relief unless they were ill. Paupers found themselves segregated by age and sex, confined within the house, and put to bed by 9:00 p.m. Their diet was mostly bread, cheese, and milk porridge, with suppers of pea or rice soup. Meat and potatoes appeared on the menu three times a week, unless a pauper had been guilty of disobedience or other offenses, which reduced him or her to bread and cheese only. In addition, they were put to work during a twelve-hour day in summer and ten hours in winter.

Bridgens's aim was less to relieve poverty than to limit the extent of welfare provided in the parish. In his opinion, rigid enforcement had proved the key to success. "The orders must be most strictly attended to, or the slightest relaxation is sure to let in a flood of pauperism." He admitted that local people would not carry out his orders to the letter, but outsiders and others of "military habits" could manage the task.[86] In Bishop's Hatfield, the Elizabethan poor laws had been reorganized and redefined. Instead of property owners relieving people whom they knew by providing money and services, outsiders were paid to minimize the cost to the ratepayer, to move paupers out of sight, and to return them to productive labor. The settled poor of the parish, whose entitlement went unchallenged, faced the prospect of a regimented workhouse and hard labor if they dared to ask for alms. Although the right to

---

[85] Ibid., 34.

[86] Ibid., 65–6, 68.

subsistence survived, its link to concepts of liberty, a moral economy, and a functioning community had been deliberately repudiated.

During the later eighteenth and early nineteenth centuries, both the theory and practice of public relief changed markedly. Outdoor relief was supplemented by a variety of labor-exploiting schemes that relied on private entrepreneurs in the factories or on their own farms to oversee paupers. Gradually, disciplinary workhouses began to replace production for profit within a "house of industry." As the work-less became in the public mind the work-shy, the goals of parish-provided labor changed from profit and production to the reformation of character. Over time, mass poverty triggered a general revulsion against outdoor relief and against the needy, who were slowly pushed to the margins of their communities and were told that to eat they had to labor.

These changes took place well in advance of the 1834 revision of the poor laws. Their extensive appearance in agricultural parishes of the rural south substantiates a link between welfare practice and the multiple and especially heavy pressures on the poor law in those areas, triggered by the reconfiguration of local economies and by the pressures of foreign wars. Those districts in particular, but also the towns, offered fertile ground for a new welfare regime. The shift to new patterns of labor discipline was adopted easily because of the transformation in attitudes toward poverty circulating in British public culture in the later eighteenth century. In the public eye, the poor had lost their moral entitlement to what was seen as a free lunch.

PART TWO

RESIDUALISM REFINED AND RESTRICTED, 1834–60

INTERMITTENT attempts by Parliament between 1790 and 1830 to reform the poor laws had foundered on the rocks of indecision and division. Despite widespread enthusiasm for self-help, no majority could be mustered for abolition, and other piecemeal changes lacked sufficient supporters. During the high point of abolitionist sentiments in 1817, after a committee of the House of Commons had issued a report condemning the poor laws, the prime minister ignored their analysis and promptly appointed a study group in the House of Lords, which called for the maintenance of current practice. When pressed to a vote, the propertied chose to reaffirm that they were their sisters' – and to some extent also their brothers' – keepers.

Yet, by 1830, the world in which the poor laws operated bore little resemblance to Elizabethan times, when Parliament had mandated public support for the destitute. The British had recently defeated the French in a worldwide war. A strong, imperialist state had been forged in the fight against Napoleon in Europe and Tipu Sultan in India, and it had developed both the tools and the styles for interference, which could be used at home as well as abroad. At home, the age of great cities had arrived, bringing with it cholera, an expansion of radical politics, and heightened fear of crime. All of these threats called for a public response. Increasingly, the poor became not objects of compassion, but targets of distrust and fear. Thomas Chalmers's judgment of urban Britain as a "territory of wickedness" drew a direct connection between poverty and depravity. The poor had changed from neighbors in a face-to-face society to strangers who menaced the respectable through their disorderly lives. Something needed to be done, but what?

How could communal obligations be maintained for people whom many regarded as having broken the bonds of community? Luddite attacks, riots, suffrage demonstrations, and the growth of trade unions testified to the decline of deference. Earlier social hierarchies had been challenged to the point where they could not survive unaltered. Some sort of reconstruction was necessary, and it had to incorporate the tenets of political economy and changing attitudes to the poor, as well as popular rejections of elite authority. Mental revolutions went along with industrial and political ones.

When Parliament rewrote the poor laws in 1834, it signaled a massive shift away from the social consensus of the old regime in England and Wales. For a welfare system that bound communities together, admittedly in an asymmetrical form, it substituted an arrangement that shifted paupers outside the limits of the polity. It replaced a system that had given relatively equal weight to male and female destitution with one that discriminated against men and assigned benefits according to attitudes to gender. Work became a punishment, rather than a means of self-support. Under the new law, the poor were marginalized, rather than incorporated, and, slowly, their general approval of poor law aid changed to hostility. In 1834, residualism was renegotiated in terms that many of the poor found unacceptable.

Between 1834 and roughly 1860, a much more strongly disciplinary style of welfare was widely adopted in England and Wales. Pressure for this drive for discipline came not only from Parliament and administrators, but also from a public culture that represented the poor as racially and morally different. Social statisticians, who reduced the destitute to numbers, which could be manipulated, averaged, and disregarded, also had a hand in this transformation. The next three chapters trace the reconstruction of welfare in England and Wales from the parliamentary investigations of 1832–4 through the 1850s, noting shifts of theory and practice among elites as well as workers.

4

CLASSIFYING AND CONFINING PAUPERS, 1834–60

But what is knowable is not only a function of objects – of what there is to
be known. It is also a function of subjects, of observers – of what is
desired and what needs to be known. A knowable community . . . is a
matter of consciousness as well as of evident fact.

Raymond Williams, 1970

The decision by the Whig government in 1832 to reform the poor laws after
carrying out a nationwide investigation of their theory and practice led to
quick action. After dozens of witnesses had their say in front of a Royal Commission, Edwin Chadwick and Nassau Senior promptly wrote a report, and
the Parliament swiftly legislated the Poor Law Amendment Act of 1834,
which grouped parishes into unions managed by elected guardians, mandated
the building of workhouses and improved pauper education, and forbade
"outdoor relief" to able-bodied workers. In the following years, a central
Poor Law Commission and, after 1847, the Poor Law Board worked to enforce the redesigned system. The "New Poor Law" and its moral imperatives
replaced the old.

Just what this change meant was hotly debated at the time, and disputes continue today. Was the New Poor Law cruel?[1] Did it sharply contract the rights
of the poor or merely clarify existing paternalist practice? Did it represent the
triumph of middle-class devotion to classical liberalism and self-help?[2] Con-

---

[1] The controversies about the intentions of the framers and their success in forcing the poor into
"bastilles" continue in the articles of David Roberts, "How Cruel was the Victorian Poor Law?"
Historical Journal 6:1 (1963): 97–107, and Ursula Henriques, "How Cruel Was the Victorian
Poor Law?" *Historical Journal* 11:2 (1968): 365–71.

[2] The case for a utilitarian, liberal poor law was advanced by Sidney Webb and Beatrice Webb in
their *English Local Government*, vol. 7, *English Poor Law History, Part II: The Last Hundred
Years* (London: Longmans, 1929), and by H. L. Beasles, "The New Poor Law," *History*, N.S.
15 (1930–1), whereas Anthony Brundage argues for continuity of practice and landlord control
in *The Making of the New Poor Law* (New Brunswick: Rutgers University Press, 1978).

sensus has yet to emerge on what actually happened, as well as what theory lay behind day-to-day administration. The questions of motive, as well as of social agency, have been revitalized by Peter Mandler, who points to the land-lords and to their defense of property rights within the context of classical lib-eral economic theory.[3] A wide swath of rural society – Tory landlords, local officials, and clergy – played active parts in changing the poor laws, and their enthusiasms were echoed by many in the cities. Property owners wanted to change the social welfare system away from its basis in an ideology of natural rights and bring it into conformity with notions of self-help and a free labor market. To the question, What ought the state do for the poor? they answered, "less."

Their defense of property rights was underpinned by what they thought they knew about poverty. Indeed, the poor law of 1834 rested upon changed representations of the poor and of the social disease, "pauperism," that circu-lated widely in England during the 1830s. This chapter examines knowledge of the poor that circulated in English public culture during the years 1830 to 1860; it then looks at the welfare system built by the poor law commission-ers in their efforts to put public consensus into practice. The residualist wel-fare state of earlier times was renegotiated into a far harsher form by a middle- and upper-class public determined to combat the "pauperization" of the social body, at the same time as they defended their pocketbooks.

New Knowledge

When the Society for the Diffusion of Useful Knowledge evaluated the New Poor Law for the readers of the *Penny Cyclopaedia,* it proclaimed it a "suc-cess." By conducting detailed inquiries throughout the country, the "actual condition of the labouring class in every parish was ascertained with the view of showing the evils of the existing practice." And the editors felt confident that, "upon a careful review of all the facts which have been ascertained be-fore and since its enactment, [the statute] may be said to have answered the ends proposed. . . . It has been found adapted to nearly every emergency that has occurred."[4]

Much of the "knowledge" about the destitute captured by the Royal Com-mission had to be newly created because very little written evidence specifi-

[3] Peter Mandler, "The Making of the New Poor Law *Redivivus,*" *Past and Present,* 117 (Nov., 1987), 131–57.

[4] Society for the Diffusion of Useful Knowledge, *Penny Cyclopaedia* (London: Charles Knight, 1840), vol. 17, 328–9.

cally on the dependent poor was available in 1832. Each parish or township kept its own records, which were unpublished, and Parliament collected only limited information from local officials after 1800. For the most part, the shape of destitution was described in terms of its increasing cost to the tax-payers. In 1802 and then annually after 1811, the central government tabu-lated and published the amounts English and Welsh parishes spent each year on poor relief. The only detailed survey of the characteristics of people re-ceiving relief was done in 1802 and 1803, when Parliament asked officials to count the numbers of elderly and "able-bodied" people relieved. A few sim-ple calculations would have shown that the elderly, along with the ill and dis-abled people, comprised only about 16 percent of the total; the rest were sup-posedly healthy people capable of work.[5]

The other contemporary window into the operation of the poor laws came through the decisions of justices of the peace and their administrative prac-tices, which were codified in handbooks for magistrates. Richard Burn's *The Justice of the Peace and Parish Officer,* first published in 1755, had gone through 24 editions by 1825 and expanded into several massive volumes.[6] Emphasis lay on the correctness of administrative procedures and recent legal decisions that could be invoked to guide decisions. How to react to the poor occupied several hundred pages, whereas the poor themselves appeared only as claimants whose rights had to be adjudicated. In Burn's work and other similar handbooks, poverty and dependency emerged as problems of liability and jurisdiction. The knowledge that counted was a precise rendering of com-mon law and Parliamentary statutes, not the effects of public policies. In these books, which informed the activities of the magistrates and overseers, the "right" to relief rested on entitlement, rather than need.

To supplement this quite meager haul of information, the commissioners decided to contact poor law administrators directly. They sent out a list of questions to parish officials and then hired assistant commissioners to tour the country collecting answers. These men made a grand tour, talking with vicars, magistrates, and overseers. Despite the geographic breadth of their ef-forts, their inquiry was sociologically limited and intellectually quite narrow. Pauperism, rather than poverty, was its focus, and entire groups of dependent people got virtually no attention. In 1834, local reports, along with answers

---

[5] *Abstract of Returns Relative to the Expenses and Maintenance of the Poor, PP* 1803–4: XIII; and Karel Williams, *From Pauperism to Poverty* (London: Routledge, 1981), 149–50.

[6] Richard Burn, *The Justice of the Peace and Parish Officer,* 24th ed. by Sir George Chetwynd (London: T. Eadell, 1825).

to the commission's questions, were published in massive volumes and effectively consigned to oblivion, except for a few pithy quotes preserved in radically abridged editions. But Nassau Senior, the Oxford political economist, and Edwin Chadwick, Jeremy Bentham's former secretary and a leading philosophic radical, summarized the group's attitudes and recommendations in a relatively short report that got wide circulation.

The questions asked by the commission focused on limited themes, particularly on the operation of local labor markets. Primary attention went to rural parishes, where they concentrated on the issues of employment and family incomes. Overseers were asked to estimate workers' weekly wages, rents, and employment prospects at different times of the year. How many more agricultural laborers lived in the parish than could be employed regularly? Were there migrant Irish and Scots? Did they think that families could subsist on their yearly earnings? Did laborers save? In other words, could thrifty individuals avoid dependence on the parish? Other questions concerned current relief practices. Officials had to report the numbers in the workhouse and those getting parish allowances, as well as the amounts spent. If the parish assigned the unemployed to local taxpayers or subsidized their incomes, details were to be included.[7] The commissioners regarded rural parishes as labor markets and residents as either employers or workers. In their analytical framework, poverty resulted primarily from unemployment, the maldistribution of labor, and the misuse of wages, whereas pauperism – the real problem – arose from individual immorality and fecklessness encouraged by public policy.

Towns were treated similarly although more superficially, there being no detailed inquiries into urban employment and living costs. Moreover, the issues of seasonal unemployment and excess labor were ignored, as was the problem of immigration. The commissioners asked, however, about the types of workers most "subject to distress," and about the availability of jobs for women and children. They wanted estimates of average yearly earnings and their adequacy. Also, city officials had to explain their administrative procedures, the numbers and types of people relieved, and the cost of welfare. Suspicions about workers' characters led commissioners to ask if workers ever quit their jobs to go on parish relief.[8]

The assistant commissioners had considerable freedom in their analysis of

---

[7] Answers to queries were printed in *Report from His Majesty's Commissioners for Inquiring into the Administration and Practical Operation of the Poor Laws*, Appendix B1, parts I–V, *PP* 1834 (44): xxx–xxxiv.

[8] Ibid., Appendix B2, *Answers to Town Questions*, parts I–V, *PP* 1834 (44): xxxv, xxxvi.

this data and generally embellished it with quotations from local worthies and their opinions of the functioning of the poor law machinery. What they did not do was to probe very deeply into the problem of destitution. D. O. P. Oke-den reported on Dunstew, Oxfordshire, a small parish of arable land, where in the fall of 1832 about 30 percent of the residents received outdoor relief and about 50 percent got grants in the winter. Nevertheless, Okeden did not mention unemployment, illegitimacy, or broken families. He was content to note the existence of "an orderly and satisfied race of paupers," the "excel-lent" cottages, and good gardens. He even implied that wages were more than adequate. In Dunstew, he found the poor law system producing great "evils" that were partly mitigated by the intelligence of the local clergy. To quote Okeden, "The poor live a life of expedients; to use their own phrase, 'they live from hand to mouth.' They are like children, they want constant help and ad-vice. The greatest blessing to them is a clergyman constantly living with them, who is not only their teacher in religion, but their friend and guide in their worldly affairs."[9] In Salisbury, where about a quarter of the inhabitants received relief in 1832, the assistant commissioner reported in great detail on the cost of welfare and the city's charities. He described the workhouse as a "disgusting scene of filth and misrule," and found its master incompetent. Of the poor themselves, he said little, other than commenting on the inability of the poor to do simple laboring jobs.[10] His suspicion that the poor created their own dependence lurked behind his usually bland prose.

Learning about poverty from these isolated observations was rather like envisaging a complete jigsaw puzzle from a few unconnected pieces. The reader could find facts aplenty, but what to do with them? Nassau Senior and Edwin Chadwick, the dominant personalities on the commission, lacked such uncertainties. They mixed classical economics and moral indignation in a de-nunciation of welfare practices that, they felt, contravened laws of nature and allowed "pauperism" to "flourish like the funguses that spring from corrup-tion".[11] Ignoring the mountains of numbers collected by the assistant com-missioners, Senior retreated to economic theory to explain why cutting down on relief would raise wages, lower taxes, and produce a happier, more honest and independent population. If parishes no longer subsidized wages, taxes could be reduced and employers would pay more for the workers they needed. Knowing they had to get jobs to support themselves, people would

---

[9] Ibid., Appendix A, *Reports of the Assistant Commissioners*, part I, *PP* 1834 (44): xxviii, 3–4.

[10] Ibid., 9.

[11] Ibid., parts I-IV, 1834 (44) xxvii, 44.

marry later and have fewer children, thus slowing the rate of growth of the labor supply. The knowledge he used to construct this model was not the mountain of facts gleaned by the assistant commissioners, but his assumptions about human character combined with economic "laws" as propounded by Malthus, Smith, and Ricardo. Senior assumed the destitute to be capable of making rational choices. When shown that they would be worse off under the care of the state than working as independent laborers, he assumed that they would immediately look for, and find, work.

Conversely, state generosity bred the dependence that it sought to cure: "Every penny bestowed, that tends to render the condition of the pauper more eligible than that of the independent labourer, is a bounty on indolence and vice."[12] Although he supported the principle that "no one need perish from want," most of the report's analysis centered on ways to reduce dependence on the poor laws. In order to build more deterrence into welfare systems, Senior recommended (1) the abolition of outdoor relief to the able-bodied; and (2) increased use of disciplinary workhouses for the dependent poor.[13]

The report was surprisingly general in its tone and style, as well as amazingly confident of the beneficial effects of simple changes in administration. Senior and Chadwick laid down the outlines of a policy in vague terms and then recommended that a new central board of control be designed to implement them. The commission's aim was to reform welfare not through legislation, but through a central bureaucracy that would standardize practice according to new norms. Both the report and its design had great appeal in Parliament. Not only did the cabinet solidly support it, but opposition within both houses was ineffectual. Indeed, large majorities passed the bill and rejected major amendments. The bill had evidently tapped into wide support in all parts of the political spectrum. Peter Mandler argues that the law spoke to Tory concerns as well as Whig ones and, in the form of a "Christian political economy," packaged a solution to the poverty problem that both traditionalists and reformers welcomed. Much of the support for the bill in fact came from liberal Tory landlords, who were to have a major say in the election of guardians to run the new poor law administrative districts (unions) and who could use their power to "educate squires, tenants, and labourers in the principles of the natural order."[14]

[12] Ibid., 127.

[13] Ibid., 146–7.

[14] J. R. Poynter, *Society and Pauperism: English Ideas on Poor Relief, 1795–1834* (London: Routledge, 1969), 319–23; Peter Mandler, *Aristocratic Government in the Age of Reform: Whigs and Liberals, 1830–1852* (Oxford: Oxford University Press, 1990), 136. See also idem, "To-

Learning about the poor moved into a new phase with the government's appointment of the Poor Law Commission. Its original three members – Thomas Frankland Lewis, George Nicholls, and John George Shaw-Lefevre – along with its secretary, Edwin Chadwick, had the unenviable task of building a comprehensive, uniform welfare system in the roughly fifteen thousand parishes of England and Wales. But what they knew about these units and their poor was neither uniform nor complete. The many volumes of the Royal Commission report were filled with anecdotal evidence treating each parish as a separate world, which was exactly the situation that they had been appointed to combat. With effort, the commissioners discovered the number of workhouses, but how many paupers would they hold? In any case, how many paupers were there who ought to be offered space in a workhouse? Implementing their basic objectives required data that the administrators did not have.

A major part of the early work of the Poor Law Commission became the creation of information in a new form about the dependent poor. Its members had, in effect, to reconstruct public knowledge about the destitute, who under the old poor laws had been treated as separate cases of legal entitlement. Now this specificity had to be brought under control and disciplined into uniformity. Rules were to be used, and a typology constructed. In order for the New Poor Law to work, welfare clients had to lose their individual stories and be treated according to fixed principles. But how to do this if each applicant remained an individual who gained relief according to local knowledge of their needs and history? How could the central administration, which lacked such knowledge, control the actions of local officials, who would then have a monopoly of the relevant facts? The solution lay in the redefinition of knowledge about the poor, and the means – social statistics – lay ready to hand.

During the years when the Royal Commission on the Poor Laws did its work and the Poor Law Commission began to reorganize relief procedures throughout England and Wales, a particular kind of data – statistics about the poor – multiplied at a dizzying rate. When confronted with the human tragedies and environmental decay of the early industrial era, governments chose to confront them through the device of the investigating committee, which assembled witnesses, collected testimony on the problem as the committee had defined it, and then wrote a short report on what needed to be done. Dickens described their work as toil at "the national cinder-heap,"

ries and Paupers: Christian Political Economy and the Making of the New Poor Law," *Historical Journal* 33:1 (1990): 81–103.

where a member of Parliament could be found "sifting for the odds and ends he wanted, and . . . throwing the dust about into the eyes of other people who wanted other odds and ends."[15] But he was atypical in his ridicule of the seemingly endless line of Blue Books replete with numbers poured forth from Her Majesty's Stationery Office, many of which sold widely.

Royal Commissions and Select Committees presented readers with more than enough material to induce intellectual indigestion. Much was in anecdotal form, as each supposedly expert witness – usually an adult, Protestant, middle- or upper-class Englishman – recounted what he had seen when walking through a particular town or factory or what he had learned in the course of his work. Yet they laced their accounts with numbers and with specific details; empiricism reigned supreme. John Liddle, a doctor employed by the Whitechapel poor law union in London, spoke about his district to the Royal Commission on the State of Large Towns and Populous Districts. He began by submitting a chart that classified the 2,303 deaths in Whitechapel in 1838 and divided them by age group and occupation. Then he proceeded to discuss overcrowding in the area, mentioning that an average of five people lived in each room, which measured twelve feet by eight feet by eight feet and which rented for between one shilling and 6 pence and two shillings per week. Numbers substituted for adjectives. A computation, even if irrelevant, seems to have increased credibility.[16]

But what were these numbers thought to be? Michael Cullen argues that the meaning of the word "statistics" and, indeed, the identification of it with quantification remained in doubt through the early 1830s. Some early statisticians remembered its derivation from the German *Statistik* and regarded their work as the collecting of data in many forms about the condition of a state. Others wanted to distance their inquiries from politics and claimed they were presenting neutral "facts" about their society. By the later 1830s and 1840s, however, statistics became more closely identified with numbers, and the numbers acquired an aura of neutrality. Rawson Rawson, a leading member of the Statistical Society of London, touted the group's *Journal* as "an important instrument for developing and diffusing the knowledge of truth, and for detecting and removing error and prejudice."[17] Victorians had a strongly

---

[15] Charles Dickens, *Hard Times* (London: Chapman & Hall, n.d.), 471.

[16] *First Report of the Royal Commission on the State of Large Towns and Populous Districts*, PP 1844 (572), XVII: Q5669–81.

[17] Rawson Rawson, Introductory Statement, *Journal of the Statistical Society of London* [later *Journal of the Royal Statistical Society*], 1 May 1838, 1–2.

positivist faith in numbers, because they supposedly brought certainty into a world of difficult choices and intractable problems.

The work of the early statisticians had one other notable characteristic: It collapsed individual variations into categories. Influenced by the Belgian statistician, Adolphe Quetelet, who used the concept of the "average man" to stress similarities in human behavior, English demographers began to compute average ages of death and average rates of illegitimacy or marriage in order to chart what they considered to be normal human behavior. Behind these efforts lay the notion that the deepest structures of society could be discovered through quantitative analyses.[18]

Yet behind statisticians' claims of objectivity lay clear political agendas. Not only did their distrust of theory conceal multiple theories, but, as Mary Poovey has argued, statistical "facts" had many fictive qualities.[19] The early statistical inquiries formulated deep-seated social fears. In 1836, W. Felkin investigated a central London district where seventeen hundred people lived. He first tabulated the number of streets, houses, and families, but he soon strayed from simple headcounts. His readers learned about the numbers of "shops open on the Lord's Day" and the numbers who "neglect Public Worship entirely." He counted the "Houses of Ill-Fame" and the "Public Houses, all of which are open during the Sabbath." His study jumped quickly from physical description to a moral survey: "Little or no social feeling is exhibited amongst the neighbors; they seldom speak except to quarrel; cruelty, revenge and oppression are frequently practiced upon each other. Sickness, sorrow and death occur, and often no one heeds the sufferer; the widow and the fatherless may weep as in the solitude of a desert."[20] Clearly he was appalled by what he saw, and he tried hard to find standard categories for his indignation. Yet his numbers could not capture his message, so he shifted partially to a lyrical prose. Nevertheless, the rather mixed result was still presented as fact, as "moral statistics," to enlist support for legislation and social reform.

Public claims about numbers grew by leaps and bounds. By 1839, William Cooke Taylor called statistics a science and asserted confidently on behalf of the Statistical Society of London that "principles are valid for application

---

[18] Theodore M. Porter, *The Rise of Statistical Thinking, 1820–1900* (Princeton: Princeton University Press, 1986), 25–6, 40–54.

[19] Mary Poovey, "Figures of Arithmetic, Figures of Speech: The Discourse of Statistics in the 1830's," *Critical Inquiry*, 19 (1993): 256–76.

[20] W. Felkin, "Moral Statistics of a District near Gray's Inn, London in 1836," *Journal of the Statistical Society*, vol. 1 (1839): 541–2.

only inasmuch as they are legitimate induction from facts, accurately observed and methodologically classified." In other words, public policy needed to be based upon numbers.[21] During the 1830s, the English invented a host of new groups and offices to collect statistics about their society. The Statistical Office of the Board of Trade was founded in 1832, and the General Register Office opened in 1837 to collect and to analyze official returns of births, marriages, and deaths. The British Association for the Advancement of Science set up a statistical section in 1833, the same year as the founding of Manchester's Statistical Society. London enthusiasts followed suit in 1834. Both of these early groups helped to define the theory and the methodology of statistical research, while they carried out the inquiries that, to quote Michael Cullen, "disguised propaganda as facts."[22]

Many of the practicing statisticians in early Victorian Britain were also working to design or to administrate the poor laws. Both Nassau Senior and E. C. Tufnell, an assistant poor law commissioner, were among the first members of the Statistical Society of London. Overseers of the poor had the responsibility for choosing the Registrars of Births and Deaths in their districts, about half of whom by 1840 were either medical officers or paid administrators of poor law unions. When John Rickman, who supervised the taking of the 1831 census, was commissioned by Parliament to do a survey of primary education, he asked local overseers of the poor to provide the information. In the later 1830s, Edwin Chadwick used poor law medical officers and other doctors on his staff to collect early data on the health of towns, which then stimulated Parliament to order the Poor Law Commission to survey sanitary conditions throughout Britain.[23] Poor law officials had a corner on a newly invented knowledge market, and they slowly began to use the machinery of the New Poor Law to collect statistics that reduced the dependent poor to standard categories of their choice.

The slowly evolving numerical profile of poor law clients indicates what the commission wanted to know about the destitute. Until 1839, paupers were represented only in terms of money. What did it cost to support them? Thereafter, guardians decided to collect information about the people they aided. In the first national report on the operation of the poor laws, published in

---

[21] "Fourth Annual Report of the Council of the Statistical Society of London," *Journal of the Statistical Society of London*, vol. 1 (1839): 8; quoted in Poovey, "Figures," 261.

[22] Michael Cullen, *The Statistical Movement in Early Victorian Britain* (Hassocks: Harvester, 1975), 135, 139, 146.

[23] Ibid., 30, 54–5, 92.

1840, the basic units of analysis were the forms of relief: indoor versus out-door aid. This fixation on the method of granting aid dominated poor law re-porting for the rest of the century. How and where people received help re-ceived more attention than personal characteristics, amounts, or duration of welfare payments. Demographic distinctions were made in a few tables, but they were very simple, amounting to merely dividing paupers into adult males, adult females, and children under sixteen.

Onto these categories were grafted the obsessions of the authors of the Royal Commission report. The dependent poor counted as (1) aged, infirm, or disabled; or (2) insane, lunatic, or idiot; or (3) able-bodied, the most prob-lematic group. (What ought to be considered as "able-bodied" or "lunatic" was left up to local officials to decide, and there is no reason to assume that their definitions agreed.) Those who could not work, those disabled in body or in mind, as well as orphans, foundlings, and illegitimate children, got short shrift: a head count. Apparently, the commission took their dependence for granted and relegated them quickly into the category of defectives. The able-bodied on outdoor relief, however, were a different matter. Their depen-dence had to be explained in terms of deviance and breakdown, in terms of fault. The commission asked that the able-bodied men be divided into those who got aid because "of want of work," "insufficiency of earnings", or "other causes not being sickness, accident, and infirmity."[24] The first reports gave the numbers of cases during a quarter of the year; latter ones counted paupers on 1 January and 1 July only, so that it was, and remained, impossible to com-pute what proportion of the English and Welsh populations received relief during a given year.

What would readers of a Poor Law Commission report have learned? They would have discovered mountains of administrative orders hiding a few scraps of information about what was being done to and for the destitute, who remained virtually invisible. Poor law officials were far better at describing themselves and newly invented regulations than they were at coming to terms with the issue of destitution and its elimination. The battle to organize poor law unions and to build workhouses took center stage during the later 1830s, as did the effort to blanket the country with amended rules and regulations. By pushing through to the back pages of lengthy reports, readers could learn that 989,347 people had been relieved in 577 poor law unions in England and

---

[24] See, for example, Poor Law Commission, *Sixth Annual Report* (London: HM Stationery Of-fice, 1840), 10–16.

Wales during the quarter year ending Lady Day, 1840; at least 200,000 others had probably gotten aid from areas not yet organized into unions or had not reported themselves to the commission.[25] Most had gotten outdoor relief. Those tallied in this quarter year account made up approximately 9 percent of the total population of England and Wales. A wealth of numbers whose meanings were imprecise could be recovered from voluminous appendices.

The commission clearly valued knowledge about process more than information about the destitute. Because the treatment of able-bodied men who could work was one of their major interests, the position of that group on relief lists had to be located in order to monitor policy toward them. Other people were tallied less systematically. For example, children and the elderly, who probably formed the bulk of those on welfare, appear in the records with minimal specificity. The Poor Law Commission and its successors wanted knowledge – not, however, about the poor and their problems, but about particular kinds of welfare clients whose access to the system they wished to regulate. Their statistics sprang from their desire to curb what they saw as an abuse. For them, destitution only in particular forms was problematic, and those forms rested on representations of dependence, class, and gender. Their categories created a set of meanings about "paupers" well before officials tallied their numbers.

Reimagining the Poor

The realism of early Victorian social reporting was draped around a scaffolding of fanciful imagery about the poor. These representations revealed not the outlines of the destitute but the imaginings and the fears of their producers. The lines of drawings, the words on the page pointed toward the grotesque, toward difference and separation. Indeed by the 1840s, portraits of destitution lay in a world of disease, deformity, and savagery.

The place to begin tracking the reimagining of the poor is with discussions of children, particularly those working in the factories. Discussions of deformity quickly leaped from physical weakness to moral deficiency and suggested that the health of the larger social body was menaced by runaway juvenile vice. John Lettsom, a medical doctor and a philanthropist, set forth the basic argument in 1804:

---

[25] See Poor Law Commission, *Eighth Annual Report* (London: HM Stationery Office, 1842), 350–1.

The youth, by improper divisions of labour, is stinted in growth; and the organs upon which health depend are obstructed, and become diseased. If life is dragged on to puberty, vices are increased by the means of multiplying them – without education, religion, or morals, what restraints remain to stay the most dangerous and disgusting propensities?[26]

Distrust of the factories encoded itself in the physical forms and psyches of child laborers, as imagined by outsiders. Yet calling for an end to such work was not a permissible alternative. Hugh Cunningham shows that many reformers had an active fear of "the idleness of children in the streets," which would introduce them to crime and other debaucheries. In 1835, James Mc-Culloch deplored the potential results of abolishing child labor in the factories: "Four-fifths of them would be thrown loose upon the streets, to acquire a taste for idleness, and to be early initiated in the vicious practices prevalent amongst the dregs of the populace, in Manchester, Glasgow, Leeds, and other great towns."[27] This vision of wild, uncontrolled urban children who could easily lapse into delinquency was popularized in the 1830s by the Children's Friend Society and in the 1840s by Lord Ashley. Religious groups used similar imagery in their appeals for help in evangelizing urban workers. Witnesses before the Royal Commission on Towns complained that poor children broke loose from parents as soon as they could in order to live on the streets and to steal. Savage, uncontrolled children became central symbols of danger in the new urban, industrial society, triggering hostility and fear among many middle-class people. But poor children were seen as only one of many infections that threatened the social body. Indeed, because children represented the next generation, they were particularly problematic. Their diseases and vices became a sign not only of their own problems, but also of the inheritability and communicability of the ills that afflicted society.

Such fears of contagion widened during the 1832 cholera epidemic. Because cholera outbreaks generally began in the foulest, dirtiest workers' neighborhoods, the destitute became harbingers of death for the rest of the society. Medical handbooks advised people to "avoid beggars, vagabonds, old clothes men, smugglers and all liable to bring infection."[28] Churchmen

---

[26] J. C. Lettsom, "Seventh Letter on Prisons," *Gentlemen's Magazine* (1804), 1:491; quoted in Hugh Cunningham, *The Children of the Poor* (Oxford: Blackwell, 1991), 68.

[27] James McCulloch, "History of the Cotton Manufacture in Great Britain," *Edinburgh Review*, vol. 61 (1835): 464–5; quoted in Cunningham, *Children*, 102.

[28] R. J. Morris, *Cholera 1832: The Social Response to an Epidemic* (London: Croom Helm, 1976), 118.

charged that the first victims were the dissolute and the depraved, and news reports of the disease left no doubts about their social and physical locations.[29] The poor were the people to be avoided, to quarantine so they would not spread their evil ways and their infections to the respectable.

In 1842, Edwin Chadwick worked to establish explicit connections between dirt, disease, and immorality in his *Report on the Sanitary Condition of the Labouring Population.* He concluded: "Defective town cleansing fosters habits of the most abject degradation." On the basis of dozens of local reports, he announced "[t]hat these adverse circumstances [inadequate sanitation and derelict housing] tend to produce an adult population short-lived, improvident, reckless, and intemperate, and with habitual avidity for sensual gratifications."[30] His informants, many of whom were doctors, confidently accused the poor of infecting the wider society with their diseases and moral lapses. A witness from Tiverton marked out a block of houses where applications for poor law aid were particularly frequent and where the medical officer regularly had to attend patients sick from fever and other diseases. In his opinion, both the people and the bad air in that district threatened the entire town.[31] The medical officer in the Chelsea area of London in 1834 thought that overcrowding in workers' districts produced a series of "social ills." In particular, he alleged: "These abodes of wretchedness, overcrowded with inhabitants, are not only the hot-beds of pestilence and the haunts of famine with all its attendant ills, but from thence come the applicants for parochial aid."[32] Miasmatic theories of contagion allowed easy connections to be made between the dirt of the poor and an infectious "pauperism." Medical uncertainty about the origins of disease permitted a looseness of language that slid easily from description to correlation to causation.

Social reporting, too, slid quickly from description to blame and fear. Journalists used the tropes of race and empire to build portraits of difference. In extreme forms of the argument, the poor lived in another country; they made up a separate nation, a separate race. Missionary societies from the early nineteenth century used similar language for those they wished to save, both at home and abroad. According to the guiding spirits of Headingly Hill Con-

---

[29] Michael Durey, *The Return of the Plague: British Society and the Cholera, 1831–2* (Dublin: Gill & McMillan, 1979), 149–50.

[30] Edwin Chadwick, *Report on the Sanitary Condition of the Labouring Population of Great Britain, 1842,* M. W. Flinn, ed. (Edinburgh: Edinburgh University Press, 1965), 423.

[31] Ibid., 80.

[32] A. W. Barclay, *General Report upon the Sanitary Condition of the Parish of St. Luke, Chelsea During the year 1856* (Chelsea: Vestry of St. Luke, Chelsea, 1857), 4–5.

gregational Church in Yorkshire, workers were "as heathen and barbaric as the natives of darkest Africa."[33] By the 1830s, the poor had been marked out as the opposites of the respectable, Protestant, Anglo-Saxon middle-class population.[34]

Few commentators did more for this process than Charles Dickens, who began publishing short descriptions of the metropolis in 1834. Later collected as *Sketches by Boz,* his essays gave his many readers a sense of the vaguely sinister, lower-class London where they never went. In Seven Dials, the people matched their repellent environment: The wayfarer "traverses streets of dirty, straggling houses, with now and then an unexpected court composed of buildings as ill-proportioned and deformed as the half-naked children that wallow in the kennels."[35] He described his reaction to Seven Dials: "What wild visions of prodigies of wickedness, want, and beggary arose in my mind out of that place."[36] His understanding of space and place forged a link between poverty and depravity.

Descriptions of the poor asserted both moral and physical distance between them and respectable British. James Grant, whose essays on London appeared in multiple editions and forms during this period, described the metropolitan middle classes as "benefactors of their species," but he wrote of the lower classes: "In the case of thousands indeed, all traces of morality are utterly effaced from their minds. They are as demoralized in their thoughts and habits . . . as if they were living in the most heathen parts of the world."[37] Lord Ashley, in an 1846 article in the *Quarterly Review,* wrote of street children as a "reckless race" inhabiting hidden courts and alleyways. He remarked on their "wild" appearance and their "barbarian freedom."[38] These were people outside of civilized society, a group so morally distant from the middle-class majority that they needed missionaries to defeat their pagan

---

[33] Quoted by Susan E. Thorne, "Race, Reform and the Victorian Working Class: A Social History of the Missionary Encounter," unpublished paper presented at the Social Science History Association Conference (Chicago, 1992), 3.

[34] Gertrude Himmelfarb, *The Idea of Poverty* (New York: Knopf, 1984), 326.

[35] Charles Dickens, *Sketches by Boz* (London: Chapman & Hall, n.d.), 82. With illustrations by Cruikshank, his descriptions appeared in collected form in 1836 and went through four editions by the end of 1837; see Edgar Johnson, *Charles Dickens,* rev. and abridged ed., (London: Allen Lane, 1977), 78, 83–4.

[36] Quoted in Philip Collins, "Dickens and London," in H. J. Dyos and Michael Wolff, eds., *The Victorian City* (London: Routledge, 1973) 2:538.

[37] James Grant, *The Great Metropolis,* (London, 1837; reprinted New York: Garland, 1985), 275, 294.

[38] Quoted in Himmelfarb, *Poverty,* 375.

ways and to bring them into a Christian community. George Godwin, editor of the London architectural magazine, *The Builder,* used a mixed imagery of race, distance, and depravity to introduce his exposure of substandard housing in the metropolis. Announcing that he had dared to risk the "contact of men and women often as lawless as the Arab or the Kaffir," he boasted of his ability to penetrate the largely unknown neighborhoods of the poor.[39]

Henry Mayhew took this racial imagery a step farther in his analysis of London's "wandering tribes," the street sellers of the metropolis. His vocabulary, heavily laced with references to race, gave his generally sympathetic accounts of London workers a hostile cast. He told his readers that they lived surrounded by "nomadic predators" whom he identified as "paupers, beggars, and outcasts." He pointed to their protruding jaws, high cheekbones, and low foreheads, which to him signaled a love of cruelty, an "utter want of religion," improvidence, "lax ideas of property," and a "disregard of female honour."[40] Gertrude Himmelfarb argues that Mayhew made "poverty a form of social pathology, a cultural rather than an economic condition."[41] Mayhew's representation of poverty rested more on Victorian ideas of physiognomy and anthropology than it did on economics. Illustrations of strange-looking people with heavy jaws, low foreheads, and odd costumes supported the notion that the poor were indeed members of another race. Mayhew drove this point home by including in the 1861 edition drawings of a "Hindoo tract seller."[42]

Artists, particularly those who worked in the print media, took these tropes of difference and disorder and turned them into threatening shapes indeed. In the illustrated magazines during the 1840s, hostility to the poor was common. Comic cartoons of workers reveal stock responses. In 1848, *Punch* published a cartoon of poor workers bent upon destruction. Fortunately, a tall, handsome policeman arrives and nabs the short, ugly ringleader. His followers slink away.[43] Dirt, raggedness, and disorder went together in pictures of urban poverty. The *Illustrated Times* presented in the mid-1850s a print titled "Our Archaeologist discovers certain unpleasant odors in Cowgate," in which a pudgy well-dressed scientist holds his nose and runs away from groups of skeletal, wizened people.[44] In the iconography of the middle-class press,

---

[39] George Godwin, *London Shadows,* (London, 1854; reprinted New York: Garland, 1985), 1.

[40] Henry Mayhew, *London Labour and the London Poor* (London, 1861–2; reprinted New York: Dover, 1968), 1:xv, 2–3.

[41] Himmelfarb, *Poverty,* 366.

[42] Mayhew, *London Labour,* 1:197, 239.

[43] *Punch,* vol. 14 (1848), 108.

[44] *Illustrated Times,* vol. 3 (1856), 105.

workers were dirty, smelly, and skinny. They took on the characteristics of their slum environments. Artists depicted multiple fears in their images of the poor, who lurked in rubbish-filled streets ready to burst out into public squares when provoked.

The impulse to turn the poor into grotesques ran amok when the subjects drawn were paupers, people who had accepted public relief. Those who had lapsed into dependence forfeited all rights to respect and respectability. Hablot Browne, who in 1840 under the pen name Phiz drew the inmates of a London workhouse, turned paupers into leering wild men.[45] Their distorted features and sharply angled limbs told a story of discipline denied, of convention flaunted. They menaced one another and, by extension, the society from which they had been so wisely excluded. Because he assumed that character could be read through physical appearance, Phiz was asserting the "reduced humanity" of the poor through their shrunken and distorted bodies.[46] In 1846 and 1847, the *Pictorial Times* ran a series on the treatment of paupers. In "Poor Law Imprisonment: The Union Windows always looking inwards, country prospects exchanged for expansive views of the walls," the artist shows a group of pauper women who look more like skeletons than people.[47] The plant on the windowsill is dead, and the birdcage empty. The static lines of the composition reinforce the sense of death, literally of entombment within the workhouse walls. The artist, despite his hostility toward the amended poor law, still depicted the dependent poor as subhuman characters. That convention had spread far beyond conservative writers and artists. The aesthetics of destitution communicated revulsion and rejection.

After 1850, graphic artists retreated from caricature as a style and drew more explicitly on the conventions of phrenology and craniology. James Redfield's popular text, *Comparative Physiognomy,* published in 1852, confidently linked skull shapes and temperament.[48] Mary Cowling argues in her recent study, *The Artist as Anthropologist,* that mid-Victorian artists and writers simply assumed that clear, observable connections existed between facial form and character.[49] The popularity of such conventions gave mid-Victorian

---

[45] Phiz was Hablot K. Browne, an illustrator of Dickens's novels. The caricature of workhouse inmates was done for James Grant's work of 1840, *Sketches in London.*

[46] Michael Wolff and Celina Fox, "Pictures from the Magazines," in Dyos and Wolff, eds., *Victorian City,* 2:569.

[47] *Pictorial Times,* vol. 8 (1846), 136–7.

[48] Mary Cowling, *The Artist as Anthropologist* (Cambridge: Cambridge University Press, 1989), 22, 37.

[49] Ibid., 37, 106.

Figure 4.1. "The Police and the Poor." *Punch*, 1848

Figure 4.2. "A workhouse Dinner," Phiz (Hablot K. Browne). In James Grant, *Sketches in London*, 1837. Courtesy Philadelphia Athenaeum collection.

Figure 4.3. "Poor Law Imprisonment," *Pictorial Times*, 29 August 1845. Courtesy of the Boston Athenaeum

artists a new visual vocabulary with which to express assumptions about social roles and personal morality. High status and virtue were assigned to Caucasian features, especially those that approximated the idealized proportions of Greek statues. Foreheads and skull height corresponded to intelligence because they supposedly derived from brain size. A flat head and narrow forehead therefore were signs both of stupidity and vice. Large jaws signaled an excess of animal sensuality: The more developed were the lower parts of the skull, the lower the life form. Noses, too, sent messages through their length, angle with the skull, and general shape.

By the 1860s, the poor had turned from skeletal caricatures to exemplars of craniological catalogues of human weakness. In the 1861 edition of Henry Mayhew's *London Labour and the London Poor,* the "Able-Bodied Pauper Street Sweeper" has a short turned-up nose and heavy jaws, whereas his forehead disappears under his cap.[50] The "Vagrant from the Refuge in Playhouse Yard Cripplegate"slouches in his rags and tatters. Unruly sideburns accentuate his square jaws, and a battered top hat flattens his head, minimizing the size of his brow. His criminal propensities were there for all to see. In Matt Mor-

[50] Mayhew, *London Labour,* 2:263.

gan's drawing from the *Illustrated Times* in 1866, men applying for relief tickets at a police station shrink away from a tall, strong policeman. The irregular features, small eyes, and bulbous noses signal multiple defects of body and character, contrasting sharply with the policeman's well-proportioned, handsome face.[51] (See Figures 4.4, 4.5.) Gustave Doré sketched London street people, using similar images. Whereas his upper-class subjects had classically oval faces, high foreheads, and long, straight noses, the homeless had square jaws and heavy mouths and cheekbones.[52] For Doré, low status and ugliness went together. His poor are truly marginal people, festering in the shadows and enlightened only through their contact with the upper classes.

Readers of British illustrated papers and novels were bombarded with many messages about the nature of their society and its leaders, but a clear subtext united both the friends and the foes of welfare policy: The poor were different and menacing. The flagrant inconsistency of identifying the poor as "The Other Nation," as residents of an unknown country, at a time when readers were being bombarded with empirical studies of low-wage workers and their neighborhoods seems not to have struck novelists like Benjamin Disraeli or journalists like Henry Mayhew. The problem was not that the life of the poor was unknown, but that the poor were being represented as dangerous to know. Particularly from 1830 through the 1850s, they were portrayed as outcasts because of assumed differences. Their faces and bodies proclaimed them to be grotesques, criminals, deviants – as members of another race entirely. How could a respectable person "know" someone of that sort? How could they be granted status within the English community? And the more strange and different they appeared to be, the more explainable their destitution and dependence on the state and the more justifiable the deterrence enacted in 1834.

Gender, Family, and Work

The authors of the 1834 report on the poor laws presented their readers with a powerful vision of vice and virtue. The disease of pauperism had invaded society and was destroying individuals and family relationships. Those poisoned by it fell into idleness, became corrupted, and infected others with their

---

[51] *Illustrated Times,* vol. 7 (1866), 117.

[52] See, for example, Gustave Doré and Blanchard Jerrold, *London: A Pilgrimage* (London, 1872; reprinted New York: Dover, 1970), 143.

Figure 4.4. "Able-bodied Pauper Street Sweeper," In *London Labour and the London Poor,* Henry Mayhew, 1862

wicked ways. At stake, ultimately, were the prosperity and health of the economy, as well as its citizens. Current practices threatened to repeal laws of nature, to sever the links between individual action and responsibility. In their opinion, the self-respect of "the English peasantry" was being destroyed by an infectious pauperism. To counteract its poison, they offered the antidotes of hard work and discipline, which would return sick citizens to a healthy virtue and would remove "the debasing influences" that afflicted much of the

Figure 4.5. "Distress in London: Applicants for Relief getting Tickets at the Police Station," *Illustrated Times,* Matt Morgan, 1867. Courtesy of the Yale University Library

"Labouring Population."[53] At that point, education and religious training could be used to improve workers' moral sensitivities and behavior.

This vision of creeping infection rested on contemporary ideas about gender and family organization. When the Royal Commission of 1834 conceptualized the problem of pauperism, they identified it with the figure of the able-bodied laborer, who for them was a man and a household head. It was primarily his morality that was being destroyed, his lack of virtue that corrupted his family and community. The commission denounced current administrators of the poor laws for attempting to repeal "that law of nature by which the effects of each man's improvidence or misconduct are bourne by

[53] *Report . . . on the Poor Laws, PP* 1834 (44), XXVII, 205.

himself and his family."[54] They announced that "no man's principles can be corrupted without injury to the society in general," leaving open the possibility that similar lapses by females were irrelevant. When they described the corrosive effects of pauperism on family life, they usually chose men as their targets. They had the decision-making power that tore apart households. Their readers were asked to imagine the horror of hearing "the pauper threaten to abandon his wife and family unless more money is allowed him – threaten to abandon an aged bed-ridden mother, to turn her out of his house and lay her down at the overseer's door, unless he is paid for giving her shelter."[55] Importunate male paupers destroyed families and broke the links between generations. Men deserted their dependents; men harassed welfare officials. They were the people who demanded relief without being willing to work for it. "The poor man of twenty years ago, who tried to earn his money, and was thankful for it, is now converted into an insolvent, discontented, surly, thoughtless pauper, who talks of 'right and income' and who will soon fight for these supposed rights and income, unless some step is taken to arrest his progress to open violence."[56] For the Royal Commission and its investigators, problematic pauperism was male.

This gendered vision of the dependent poor arose not from a look at welfare applicants, but from the commission's views on men, women, and the world of work. They took middle-class notions of masculinity and femininity and applied them to the poor without change. They endowed each sex with opposite, but complementary, sets of social roles – the one set aggressive, active, and public, the other set passive and private. In the words of one anonymous poet, "Man is the rugged lofty pine / That frowns on many a wavebeat shore; / Woman the graceful slender vine / Whose curling tendrils round it twine, and deck its rough bark sweetly o'er."[57] Men determined the basic shapes of family relationships. Their position situated a couple within society, fixing its social location and providing the framework upon which women constructed their lives.

Masculinity had many attributes, but they centered around a commitment to work. Among the middle classes, men were seen as the producers: They manufactured things, ran businesses, had mechanical skills. Although women

---

[54] Ibid., 44.

[55] Ibid., 54.

[56] Ibid., 49.

[57] Anonymous, 1828; quoted in Lenore Davidoff and Catherine Hall, *Family Fortunes* (London: Hutchinson, 1987), 397.

could do, and in fact did, all of these things, production was defined as a masculine activity. One potent image of the Victorian middle class was that of the "Manchester Man," the factory owner and entrepreneur. But this identification of males and labor stretched much more widely over English and Welsh society. Lenore Davidoff and Catherine Hall have argued that, since early in the nineteenth century, "[w]hat men did was defined as man's work; because they did it they were men."[58] Victorians expected men to enter the labor market and to work hard, earning wages proportionate to their efforts and skills. Those who did not had lost the defining characteristic of masculinity and forfeited their right to be treated as adult citizens.

This commitment to work became by the mid-nineteenth century a central aspect of fatherhood, which became identified with a man's ability to support dependents. Respectable men delayed marriage until they had sufficient property or income to provide for a wife and children. The good father was the breadwinner; the fact that this activity removed him from his home and distanced him from his family was judged of secondary importance.[59] The British state also accepted this economic definition of fatherhood. According to a law of 1733 reenacted in 1809, justices of the peace had the power to order a man accused by a woman of impregnating her to pay the cost of child support. His obligation to her and to the child was strictly an economic one.[60]

These concepts of masculinity and fatherhood led the Royal Commission to view male pauperism in terms of work and wages. Moreover, their information about the rural labor market pointed them to the figure of the male laborer and to his employment problems. Witnesses before the commission concentrated on the issue of male employment in their parishes. They talked of the differences between the wages of married and unmarried men and about the ways in which their parish allocated the labor of unemployed males. Indeed, they talked as if female laborers did not exist on the farms of southern counties. In parish after parish, informants said there was no, or little, local employment for women, even at harvest. This presented a problem primarily for men, they concluded, because they now had to feed their entire families.

---

[58] Davidoff and Hall, *Family Fortunes*, 270–1.

[59] John Gillis, "Gender and Fertility Decline Among the British Middle Classes," in John R. Gillis, Louise A. Tilly, and David Levine, eds., *The Quiet Revolution* (Cambridge, MA: Basil Blackwell, 1992), 43.

[60] *Report . . . on the Poor Laws,* PP 1834 (44) XXVII, 92; see also Michael Nolan, *A Treatise of the Laws for the Relief and Settlement of the Poor* (London, 1805; reprinted New York: Garland, 1978), 2:288–9.

It was only a short step from the notion that men were being forced to support all of their dependents to the conviction that they ought to support them – without the aid of the poor laws. The moral man would "rather starve than apply" for parish help, relying on thrift and self-denial to see him through difficult periods. Like the lofty pine, he would jealously guard his independence. And the Royal Commission knew that such people existed. The Royal Commission identified agricultural workers who had accounts in savings banks as male household heads who had learned the lesson that hard work and thrift could keep them independent, given the current state of the British economy. They proved that self-support and independence were possible among male laborers. The commission represented decisions about saving and spending as exclusively male choices: "[N]o body of men save money whilst they are in want of what they deem absolute necessities. No common man will put by a shilling whilst he is in need of a loaf or will save whilst he has a pressing need unsatisfied."[61] Because some men had learned how to keep themselves and their families from pauperism, they assumed that all could and should do so.

Women, on the other hand, were seen primarily as daughters and wives. Their responsibilities were domestic and nurturing. The commission located their work as largely within the household, rather than the formal labor market. In this scenario of women as the clinging vines, wives derived their morality from the choices of their husbands and fathers. Overseers complained of paupers' daughters who demanded extra payments for nursing elderly parents and remarried widows who under their new husbands' prodding refused to care for children unless parish allowance money was increased. The assistant overseer of Windsor compared the households of paupers with those of independent laborers. "The wives of paupers are dirty, and nasty, and indolent; and the children generally neglected, and dirty, and vagrants, and immoral." On the other hand, he thought that among independent laborers, "the wife is a very different person; she and her children are clean, and her cottage tidy. . . . The difference is so striking to me, that in passing along a row of cottages I could tell, in nine instances out of ten, which were paupers' cottages, and which were the cottages of the independent labourers."[62] Women, their homes, and their behavior demonstrated the moral choices of male household heads. The wife communicated in her dress, her housekeeping, and her child-rearing practices the level of discipline exemplified by her

---

[61] *Report . . . on the Poor Laws,* PP 1834(44) XXVII. 229.

[62] Ibid., 50, 54.

husband, and the daughter by that of her father. She reflected his sins and his fecklessness (or his virtue) and was treated as dependent upon his will.

Single women could menace their communities independently, however, through their sexuality and reproductive powers. The image of women producing multiple bastards for profit haunted the commissioners. Witnesses before the Poor Law Commission pictured single women as willing to exploit their sexuality in order to live well on the public purse. They feared that once a pregnant female discovered that she could live and eat well in the workhouse at parish expense, she would continue to do so. The commission announced, "To the woman, a single illegitimate child is seldom any expense, and two or three are a source of positive profit."[63] A vestry clerk in Cornwall knew "from long and serious observations and facts occurring, that continued illicit intercourse has, in almost all cases, originated with the females" who used the allowances from their multiple bastards to support the household. They supposedly lied about the identity of fathers and shamelessly pursued men both for fun and for cash.[64] One Berkshire justice of the peace told the Royal Commission that because women knew they could get parish support for their children, they felt no "checks to irregular intercourse."[65] Women supposedly had no shame. One of the assistant overseers recounted the "horror" of seeing "mothers coming to receive the reward of their daughters' ignominy, and [witnessing] women in cottages quietly pointing out, without even the question being asked, which are their children by their husband, and which by other men previous to marriage."[66]

Women therefore became paupers in two ways: first, through the weakness of husbands and fathers; and second, through their own unrestricted sexuality and greed. Neither of these paths led through the world of work or took into account the hazards of the life cycle to which females were exposed. The problems of orphanhood, of old age, of sickness, of disability, and of widowhood were generally ignored by the Royal Commission; of course, they also ignored these issues as they affected men. In a report of over two hundred pages, the commission devoted only about five of them to the problems of the impotent poor – those who could not work to support themselves.

According to the Royal Commission, the disease of pauperism came in gender-specific varieties, which women and men caught in different ways.

---

[63] Ibid., 93.
[64] Ibid., 94.
[65] Ibid.
[66] Ibid., 54.

Some of the treatments for it were also gender specific. Whether work was to be exacted from women in return for aid proved to be the major issue. Overseers in Hatfield, Hertfordshire, outlined for the Royal Commission their response to adult, able-bodied welfare applicants: "All persons, except women, . . . shall be employed in task work." The nearby parish of Welwyn followed a similar rule: Unemployed men were given jobs at below market rates; women did not have to work for their relief. In St. Mary, Nottingham, overseers claimed that they invariably took "every applicant for relief and the whole of his family, however large, entirely on the parish, and [set] him to work of some sort or other without any view to profit, or to any principle but that it should be more irksome than ordinary labour."[67]

When, after 1834, the Poor Law Commission worked out its rules for dealing with able-bodied paupers, it regularly differentiated men from women. Healthy, adult male paupers could not have their rents or wages subsidized, and they could not continue receiving nonresident relief; women were not covered by those regulations.[68] The earliest series of orders that regulated outdoor relief called for a labor test in return for aid; the test applied only to able-bodied adult males, leaving authorities a free hand in their policy toward women. Heavy outdoor labor in return for relief was thought appropriate only for men. A second set of regulations issued in 1836 for urban unions, which by 1847 covered most of the country, prohibited outdoor relief to able-bodied men and women, but it exempted widows, deserted wives, and the wives of husbands in military service, jails, asylums, or overseas. The rule was intended to apply only to independent women, particularly mothers of illegitimate children. They, like men, were to be taken into the workhouse for disciplinary treatment in return for aid.[69] Women whose conduct was "deserving" could still get outdoor relief without having to work for it. Distinctions relating to conduct and, supposedly, character shaped policies toward women; for men, the relevant issues for a welfare official were only health and age. Work therefore was a male duty and a female punishment.

Another set of gender-specific distinctions operated within workhouses. By dividing paupers into groups according to sex and age, the Poor Law Commission could then dictate different ways of dealing with each. When they entered the workhouses, men and women were to be separated and kept

[67] Ibid., 230.

[68] Poor Law Commission, *First Annual Report* (London: HM Stationery Office, 1835), Appendix A, 52.

[69] See Sidney Webb and Beatrice Webb, *English Poor Law Policy* (London: Longmans, 1910), 36, 40–1.

within their own groups. They received different amounts of food and were assigned different jobs within the house. Women served as nurses, mended clothes, and worked in the kitchens and laundries, whereas men maintained gardens, repaired, painted, and carried. Adolescent boys went to a training ship to learn about the navy or studied music to prepare them to play in military bands. In the district schools, adolescent boys took classes in industrial skills, whereas the girls learned about domestic service.[70]

Official sensitivity to gender differences among paupers increased during the 1840s and 1850s, when clerks began to compile statistical data on the people relieved in each union. People getting outdoor relief had to be divided into categories according to the reasons for their entitlement. Initially, men and women were treated similarly, in ways that contradicted common notions of gender differences. Reports distinguished the able-bodied from the infirm and then divided each group according to sex, marital status, and parenthood. Surprisingly, both males and females could be "in want of work"; they could have "insufficient earnings" or they could have other, unspecified problems. In addition, women earned entitlement because of desertion, illegitimate children, or jailed husbands. This relatively evenhanded treatment disappeared by 1851, when the official linkages between labor markets and female poverty disappeared from the official reports. Thereafter, guardians offering outdoor relief to women used their family status and health to justify entitlement for welfare. Aid went to widows, to the deserted, to the wives of jailed or transported men, to the mothers of illegitimate children, to the sick, and to the insane. The lack of a male protector or physical problems were sufficient reasons for welfare aid to women, whereas the issue of their employment was ignored. In contrast, official statistics gave men's family status only limited attention. Guardians labeled able-bodied men on relief as (1) in "want of work"; (2) sick, injured or infirm; (3) insane; (4) having a family member who was sick, injured, infirm, or dead and needing burial; or (5) destitute because of "sudden or urgent necessity."[71] Not only were entitlement categories different for men and women, but women had several more paths to aid than men did. A female qualified for poor law help both as the spouse of an unemployed or otherwise distressed male and under categories that applied to her in her own right. In contrast, males who were single parents or widowers had no direct claim on the poor law as a result of their demographic status. The rules of welfare entitlement worked out by the Poor Law Commission

---

[70] M. A. Crowther, *The Workhouse System, 1834–1929* (London: Methuen, 1983), 199, 204–5.

[71] Poor Law Board, *Third Annual Report, 1850* (London: HM Stationery Office, 1851), 150–65.

and its successor, the Poor Law Board, were shaped by attitudes toward gender. Men worked and took care of families; women cared for children and needed help if they lacked a husband.

The extent to which local welfare administrators made decisions on the basis of official categories remained problematic, of course. Yet it seems clear that both guardians and welfare recipients explained entitlement in terms that differed by gender. After applicants told their stories to relieving officers and magistrates, a document called an examination was produced to show where they were officially settled and to give information about their cases. I have analyzed a sample of these examinations drawn from records of eight poor law unions – two in London and six from county towns scattered around England – for the years around 1848.[72] In those areas, clerks recorded for male and female applicants substantially different grounds for entitlement. They identified a large share of the men examined as out of work, whereas they almost never labeled females in this way. Women's justifications for grants came primarily from their family status or from pregnancy. Similar proportions of men and women were recorded as elderly or ill. Another example of local perceptions about welfare needs can be found in Huddersfield listings of the poor who got allowances from the poor law union. Clerks listed a reason for aiding every person or household they named. Men got temporary grants because they were out of work or sick; women received money because they were deserted, pregnant, sick or destitute.[73] Not even one woman was listed as lacking work in this West Riding textile town with its many female factory employees, even in bad years. In the eyes of poor law guardians, demographic events, rather than depressions brought women into welfare offices, while men were victimized by the business cycle.

As the interpreters of the New Poor Law tried to reform local welfare policies, they were guided by attitudes toward gender, work, and family common among the English middle classes. The image that they kept before them was of the male-headed household, supported by male wages and female domestic labor. To keep these units operating among the destitute, they hoped to discipline men into working and women into docile acceptance of a domestic role. This drew the male administrators of the law into an aggressively paternalist stance vis-à-vis the poor. They stood in for the fathers of poor children – arranging for their care by women and educating and apprenticing them. They contributed money to female-headed households in the parishes where

---

[72] For more information on these sources and the sample, see Appendix A.

[73] See Huddersfield, Poor Law Guardians, "List of Paupers Relieved in Huddersfield District, 1881" (Huddersfield Public Library), 1–28.

husbands and fathers had settlement rights. For those who transgressed gender norms – the unemployed, able-bodied male and the single mother – they tried to apply discipline to teach them the error of their ways, like a good father. Their attempts at social engineering rested on a familial model of strictly defined gender roles, where the state was the Big Daddy ordering about its children.

Implementing the New Regime

After the passage of the Poor Law Amendment Act in 1834, the newly appointed Poor Law Commission and its zealous secretary, Edwin Chadwick, began in earnest to reform local practices of dealing with the destitute. Circulars went out to parish officers and magistrates, informing them of the scope of the new law and its implications. Chadwick announced that they had to continue relieving the poor, but they should remember "the necessity of vigilance and strict economy." The law, he said, did not end their obligations to the indigent but was intended to prevent "various illegal and injurious practices" that the commission hoped to stop in the longer run. While the commission developed new rules and new administrative structures, he offered several suggestions for short-run changes, which he was sure would be to their advantage. They ought to put the able-bodied unemployed to work in return for wages less than those offered locally to laborers. If they had a workhouse, they could offer support within it to able-bodied paupers, and if they refused, the parish's obligation to the pauper was ended. If neither of these policies could be followed and they had to offer relief to the unemployed, they should give at least half of it in kind, not money.[74] The supposedly free lunch that laborers ate at the parish expense was to end; they could expect, at most, bread in return for hard labor.

As the commission organized poor law unions in some southern counties during the later 1830s, more precise instructions went out to newly elected guardians and relieving officers. The tone was hostile and prohibitory: no relief in money to employed male laborers and their families except in cases of sickness or accident, no relief in the form of rent payments for able-bodied males, no relief to new cases of the nonresident poor. Any grants to able-bodied males and their families were to be considered as loans and were recoverable by law.[75] Officials gave as little as possible under as tight controls as could be managed.

[74] Poor Law Commission, *First Annual Report*, Appendix A, nos. 3 and 4, 43–4.

[75] Ibid., no. 8, 52.

The Royal Commission had presented work as the best tactic for punishing welfare cheats: "All labour is irksome to those who are unaccustomed to labour; and what is generally meant by the expression 'rendering the pauper's situation irksome', is rendering it labourious."[76] To follow this dictum, the commission, in the Outdoor Labour Test Order of 1842 and the Outdoor Relief Regulation Order of 1852, forbade aiding able-bodied men and their families outside the workhouse except in return for work.[77] In 1847, about 20 percent of the poor law unions in England and Wales were covered by the orders, and they remained in force through the rest of the century, with their coverage expanding during the 1850s to include most of Lancashire, East Anglia, and the south-west. By 1871, in about half of the poor law unions of England and Wales, men could only get outdoor relief if they were prepared to break stones, dig ditches, grind corn by hand, or do similar tasks designed to be difficult and nasty. In Norfolk after 1834, men worked on the roads in exchange for welfare aid. In the Romford union in Essex, the guardians opened a stone yard and paid poor men according to the amount of rock they were able to break.[78] Although outdoor relief had not been prohibited in Leicester, guardians there refused to grant it to male laborers unless they passed a labor test, which was generally stone breaking or grinding grain by hand. The practice lasted at least through the 1850s, despite protests and occasional riots by the unemployed, who deeply resented the practice.[79] In 1862 and 1863, during the cotton famine, men were sent to work in Lancashire quarries in return for modest wages.[80] Even when thousands lacked work for clearly understood reasons and towns had no way of usefully employing them, the fear of subsidizing idleness led guardians to invent labor tests. The prevailing wisdom held that work brought discipline, whereas handouts bred pauperism. The fact that not enough jobs were available at certain times was conveniently ignored.

The alternative path for reforming adult paupers led through the work-

---

[76] *The Poor Law Report of 1834*, S.G. and E.O.A. Checkland, eds. (Harmondsworth: Penguin, 1974), 338.

[77] See Webb and Webb, *English Poor Law Policy*, 26–8.

[78] Felix Driver, *Power and Pauperism: The Workhouse System, 1834–1884* (New York: Cambridge University Press, 1993), 275; Anne Digby, *Pauper Palaces* (London: Routledge, 1978), 114; P. J. H. Burditt, "Philanthropy and the Poor Law: A Study of the Relief of Poverty in the Romford Union, 1795–1914," Master's thesis, University of London, 1979, 84–5.

[79] Kathryn M. Thompson, "The Leicester Poor Law Union, 1836–1871," Ph.D. thesis, Leicester University, 1988, 158–69; Board of Guardians, Leicester Poor Law Union, "Minute Book" (December 1857–June 1860), entry for 11 December 1857.

[80] See *Illustrated London News*, November 1862.

house, which the commission hoped would be offered routinely to applicants. The early regulations announced by the commission indicate the means of transformation proposed for people who chose to enter workhouses. First came disinfection and a bath. After paupers gave up their clothes for fumigation, they were washed by an attendant and inspected by a doctor. An ill-fitting, ugly uniform and a standard haircut began a process of homogenization that continued until they left the house. Workhouse attendants were ordered to confiscate all personal possessions and then to separate paupers into groups according to sex and age, each of which was supposed to have its own spaces, jobs, and special diet. Bells announced the hours for sleep, work, meals, and religious services, dividing time according to official, uniform schedules. All over the country, paupers were to rise at 7:00 a.m. in winter, and 5:00 a.m. in summer, put in a nine- or a ten-hour workday, and go to bed at eight in the evening. They ate together silently, worked and slept together, rigidly separated by sex and age.[81] The ideal workhouse regulated every minute of the paupers' day, trying to teach discipline through regimentation.

Using the model of a "total institution," M. A. Crowther stresses how officials designed rules and practices calculated to rob inmates of their individuality and independence.[82] When a person, or a family, entered a workhouse, normal routines and associations were broken. Inmates could not drink, and sometimes smoking was forbidden; all became quasi-children ordered into silent obedience. Inside workhouse walls, packages, visitors, and even speech were to be monitored to exclude the unacceptable. Proscribed behavior included swearing, insulting others, talking when silence was ordered, and refusing to work. By separating families, the poor law replaced familial hierarchies of power with institutional ones and blocked normal expressions of sexuality and nurturance. Karel Williams characterizes the strategy recommended by the 1834 report as "a blind and repressive discipline."[83]

Although historians dispute the effectiveness of these regulations, there is little controversy over the aims of the administrators, who wrote quite explicitly about their hopes and fears. E. C. Tufnell, an assistant poor law commissioner, announced his support for the strict confinement of paupers in the workhouse because the main object of poor law reform was to keep paupers from being too comfortable. He added, "At present, their [the workhouses'] prison-like appearance, and the notion that they are intended to torment the

---

[81] Poor Law Commission, *First Annual Report*, Appendix A, no. 9, 59–61.

[82] Crowther, *Workhouse*, 193–4.

[83] Karel Williams, *From Pauperism to Poverty* (London: Routledge, 1981) 58.

poor, inspires a salutary dread of them." Moreover, he quoted with approval a Kent official's complaint that the "confinement leads the labourers to call the workhouses prisons and excites strong feelings in their minds against them."[84]

The workhouse and its discipline were not distant threats for the poor. By 1839, 331 poor law unions, or about 44 percent of the total, had built new workhouses or had begun their construction; most of these were in the south and east. Twenty years later, about 60 percent of the unions had new workhouses. Building in this second phase reached the industrial north, Wales, the West Country, and the London area. Each workhouse held on average 250 to 300 inmates, the largest houses being the major cities.[85] Not only did most unions have a workhouse, but the commissioners worked tirelessly to encourage enforcement of their classifications and rules, as well as to pressure officials to use their workhouses. In 1844, they forbade the vast majority of poor law unions outside of Lancashire and Yorkshire to offer outdoor relief to able-bodied laborers and their families except in cases of sickness or sudden necessity. Over the next thirty years, the areas where this prohibition on outdoor relief to healthy adult males and females remained in force contracted in size, but they still comprised about half the unions in Wales, the south, the Midlands, and the northeast.[86] In large parts of the country, poor law guardians were supposed to offer the workhouse to healthy, adult applicants for welfare.

Fortunately for paupers, there was much slippage in the workhouse between theory and practice.[87] During the 1840s, most unions refused to build on the large scale recommended and so put all types of paupers into one mixed workhouse. Without elaborate facilities and staff, they found it difficult to enforce the discipline demanded by the New Poor Law. In any case, some conservatives balked at punishing the poor through semimilitary regulations and did what they could to thwart Chadwick and the assistant commissioners. Shropshire guardians tended to ignore the peremptory orders sent out by the central board; in Wales and Cornwall, existing workhouses tended to be squalid and badly administered, reflecting the worst of pre-1834 practice.

---

[84] Poor Law Commission, *Second Annual Report* (London: H.M. Stationery Office, 1836), Appendix C, 452.

[85] Williams, *Pauperism*, 77; Felix Driver, "The Historical Geography of the Workhouse System in England and Wales, 1834–1883," *Journal of Historical Geography* 15:3 (1989): 272, 280.

[86] Ibid. 274–5.

[87] Crowther, *Workhouse*, 52.

In Lancashire and Yorkshire, where local resistance to the New Poor Law was intense, commissioners did not order poor law officials to apply the workhouse test and permitted the continuation of outdoor relief. Even where workhouses were used, their operation could be quite different from the rigid order recommended by the commission. During the 1840s the master of the Rochdale workhouse described in his journal how paupers crawled out over the wall or bolted out through the gate and came back drunk. Teenage boys and female prostitutes refused to work. Paupers, he said, "think they can disobey, insult, or abuse us with impunity; and that the only consequence will be, our removal: a consummation which some of them, I dare say, heartily wish."[88] Not until the 1850s did unions in northern, industrial areas agree to reform and expand their workhouses.[89]

On the other hand, by 1834, many parishes and townships, in the northeast for example, had already refused to grant outdoor relief and had introduced deterrent workhouses without much conflict. In Durham during the 1840s, the commission found guardians who decided to be more frugal and harsh in their administration than the rules dictated.[90] In Braintree, Essex, welfare officials attempted to follow the commission's plan. The union opened its new workhouse half a mile out of town in 1838. Paupers wore uniforms and lost the right to go out to church on Sundays if they drank or returned late. During the rest of the week, they ground grain by hand or picked oakum between 6:00 a.m. and 6:00 p.m., and those who refused found themselves on a diet of bread and water.[91] In Leicestershire workhouses, paupers who insulted the master or matron, refused work, or became disorderly found themselves put in solitary confinement and fed on bread and water.[92] Officials of the St. Marylebone workhouse in London also adopted the rules of a deterrent workhouse. They cleansed and classified newcomers, fitting treatment to their age and sex. Activities and hours were rigidly controlled. As was intended, paupers found the regime harsh. Excessive zeal, rather than laxity, was the St. Marylebone problem. When the master and the porters in 1856 caned at least three teenage girls who had disturbed the house, the girls complained to a

---

[88] John Cole, *Down Poorhouse Lane* (Littleborough, Lancashire: George Kelsall, 1984), 100–2.

[89] Crowther, *Workhouse*, 45–50.

[90] Ibid., 48.

[91] Michael Barker, *The Poor in Georgian and Victorian Braintree* (Braintree, Essex: Beals-Cadwallader Litho., 1976), 23–36.

[92] Billesdon Union, Leicestershire, "Workhouse Punishment Book, 1854–1886"; Market Harborough Union, "Offenses and Punishment Book"; Lutterworth Union, "Offences and Punishment Book, 1879–1932," Leicestershire Record Office.

magistrate who took their side and forced the officials to resign.[93] The larger London unions adapted easily to the spirit of the New Poor Law, even though they guarded their local independence from the commission. Their paid staffs believed in cleanliness, punctuality, and order, and they tried to force paupers to conform.

Yet, no doubt, the reality of life in the workhouse fell short of Chadwick's disciplinary ideal. Even where large new workhouses had been built and where administrators attempted to follow the dictates of the commission, the result was not the Brave New World of Chadwick's dreams. Anne Digby judges that men found life in new Norfolk workhouses "tedious," not "arduous or uncomfortable." Guardians often could not provide ten hours of work a day for them, and both diet and living conditions were better than among laborers on the outside. Pressures remained psychological, rather than physical.[94] When Thomas Archer visited a large London workhouse around 1865, he found the building dreary, rather than oppressive. Paupers lived in "bare wards, where the long rows of low bedsteads, each covered with the same pattern of counterpane, [made] even the dull walls more monotonous." But there was a garden with flowers, shrubs, a fountain, and an aviary where paupers could sit. Play equipment for the younger children occupied one corner. The master chose not to enforce the rigid separations ordered by the Poor Law Commission, and Archer thought both the old and the young were gently treated.[95]

Yet what actually happened in workhouses was largely irrelevant. After all, the most important official tactic was to scare the destitute into not entering them. The myth of the workhouse defeated its more mundane reality. Popularly known as "bastilles," the workhouse inspired lurid stories and rumors for generations. One poor law inspector in Kent reported in 1839: "A short time back, it was circulated in this county that the children in the workhouses were killed to make pies with, while the old when dead were employed to manure the guardians' fields, in order to save the expense of coffins."[96] Because Parliament, after 1831, permitted the bodies of people dying in the workhouse to be sent to anatomists for dissection, popular hostility to workhouses was fed by poor law treatment of the dead. Ruth Richardson claims that well

---

[93] A. R. Neate, *The St. Marylebone Workhouse and Institution, 1730–1965* (London: St. Marylebone Society, 1967), 18–21.

[94] Digby, *Pauper Palaces*, 145–6.

[95] Thomas Archer, *The Pauper, the Thief, and the Convict* (London, 1865; reprinted New York: Garland, 1985), 69, 79–80.

[96] E. C. Tufnell, 10 January, 1839; PRO MH32/70; quoted in Crowther, *Workhouse*, 31.

into the nineteenth century, people circulated stories of "Nattomy Soup" and human body parts being used for workhouse dinners. She argues that a "desperate fear of death on the parish infected and afflicted the entire working class in the Victorian era," in part because of the threat of dissection.[97]

Broadsheet ballads pictured paupers ground into skeletal remains by the workhouse machine.[98] Respectable reporters also lashed out at the so-called bastilles. David Roberts has labeled *The Times* between 1837 and 1842 a "compendium of poor law crimes," which titillated the rich and terrified the poor. Tales of Andover workhouse inmates eating the bones they were ordered to crush took their place in a long saga of starvations, floggings, and mindless cruelties.[99] In an infamous pamphlet of 1838, "Marcus" called for "painless extinction" of the surplus poor, perhaps by gassing infants. Charging that one of the poor law commissioners or Henry Brougham, the Whig supporter of the New Poor Law, had written it, radicals pilloried both the legislation and the pamphlet for their design of "crushing, starving, and murdering the poor."[100] People fantasized about confinement within the workhouse, endowing it with superhuman powers of repression. It was a symbol of enormous weight and resonance in the dialogues over power and class that convulsed Victorian Britain.

The New Poor Law worked effectively to enforce social distance between paupers and the rest of Victorian society. Those who came to it for aid had to acknowledge the power of guardians over them and to signal their own subordination in multiple ways. Inspectors had to be admitted into their apartments upon demand and be shown the contents of closets and cupboards; they had to sell or pawn possessions that signified property and respectability. If they could not afford to bury a family member, they had to suffer the indignity of a pauper funeral, which Tom Laqueur argues signified "their absolute exclusion from the social body." In a society where increasingly elaborate funerals served to commemorate wealth and social standing, the message of a shroudless body in a thin pine box was clear. Moreover, coffins dumped without ceremony into mass, unmarked graves on workhouse land meant permanent anonymity and exclusion from the local community.[101]

---

[97] Ruth Richardson, *Death, Dissection and the Destitute* (London: Routledge, 1987), 222, 279.

[98] See illustration of 1836 broadside, PRO MH32/60; reprinted in Jerry Crowley and Andy Reid, *The Poor Law in Norfolk, 1700–1850* (Ely: EARO Resource and Technical Center, 1983), 121.

[99] David Roberts, "How Cruel Was the Victorian Poor Law?" *Historical Journal* 6 (1963): 97–107.

[100] Richardson, *Death*, 268.

[101] Tom Laqueur, "Bodies, Death, and Pauper Funerals," *Representations* 1:1 (1983): 109, 115, 117.

The New Poor Law was a problematic, divisive arena within which culturally important ideas and symbols were put into practice on the bodies of the poor. To combat what they felt was the creeping disease of pauperism, the commissioners wanted uniformity of treatment and certainty of outcomes, based on knowledge of the poor and of the individual case. Yet their demonstrated knowledge of the poor extended only to a few simple demographic distinctions, which were constructed using a heavily gendered model of responsibility and social functions. What they knew about destitution came less from investigating the poor than from their vision of a self-equilibrating labor market.

5

"THOUGH POOR, I'M A GENTLEMAN STILL"

When I left home some years ago old folks had lots of trade.
Some right good jobs came tumbling in and every one were paid.
We had good roast beef and pudding and of ale some decent swig
In fact they lived like fighting cocks and got as fat as pigs.
But know egad ther's no such stuff, poor folks have empty tripes.
They've no roast beef to stuff their ribs but poor law soup and swipes.
An honest working man's no chance, grim death on him doth frown.
I never thought things would come to this since I left our town.

Our Merry Town, c. 1870

The Poor Law Commission built the New Poor Law with the bricks of classical economics held together by the mortar of disdain for the dependent. The walls of the workhouse were to send out messages of shame to all who entered it. But for the most part, the poor rejected such lessons even if they sometimes ate parish bread and put on the garb of the pauper. When workers thought about the issues of poverty and of entitlement to relief, their views sharply contradicted the views of middle-class reformers, journalists, and administrators. They used different words and imagery from those of the middle class to discuss poverty, and they argued from different assumptions about labor. Those who worked were in principle worthy; therefore, the public's obligation to provide support outweighed its interest in deterrence. Against the triumph of the New Poor Law, workers defended the legitimacy of the Elizabethan relief system, which they saw as one of the fundamental rights of the English. Even though workers disagreed about whom to blame for hard times, they most definitely did not blame themselves. They entered into negotiations with welfare administrators using divergent assumptions about destitution and its origins. Conversations about dependence were dialogues of the deaf, in which each side refused to listen to the rhetoric of the opposition.

Why Am I Poor?

The impulse to testify, to persuade, or to entertain with the subject of poverty was not limited to social elites; ordinary people also wrote and remembered their own and their neighbors' stories of deprivation. They sang on street-corners, shouted at meetings, and scrawled slogans on walls. A few produced autobiographies; others talked to reporters. Some wrote or talked back to relieving officers. They told their families about childhood suffering and adult perseverance, morality tales of virtue and character for the next gener-ation. The respectability of the dependent and the destitute was a lyric sung loud and clear in the workers' neighborhoods, and it needs to be incorporated into analyses of the meaning of poverty in English public culture. Workers' narratives, which directly challenged Chadwickian orthodoxy, gave welfare applicants an independent position from which to ask for aid, a different vocabulary in which to sue for help.

The immense ballad literature that remained alive into at least the 1870s opens a window into the mental world of those who bought and sang it. On the borderline between a written and a declining oral culture, ballads fixed in everyday language images of deprivation and the right responses to them. Patrick Joyce, who has examined northern popular literature in the mid- and later Victorian period, sees in it social commentary mixed with messages of a popular morality.[1] Ballads that circulated in the Ashton area during the 1840s used stoicism, pride, and sometimes comedy to express their con-sciousness of poverty. The hero of "Days When I Was Hard Up," piously explains, "I've found a good old maxim, and this shall be my plan / Altho' I wear a ragged coat, I'll wear it like a man."[2] The troubles of the "Poor Mar-ried Man" made those of ordinary folk seem small: He lived on "sodgers, rashers, and faggots," chancing "the maggots." Too poor for a funeral or a proper coffin, he expected the "parish egg chest" to be his final resting place![3] Good humor, rather than class resentments, was the dominant tone of much popular literature.

During the Lancashire cotton famine, the unemployed both sold and sang ballads on the street. Martha Vicinus describes their tone as that of cheerful solidarity with the unemployed and of hope for improvement. In "Hard Toimes or the Weaver Speaks to his Wife," a starving man talks of his love for his wife and child, regretting his poverty mainly for their sake. Although he

[1] Patrick Joyce, *Visions of the People* (New York: Cambridge University Press, 1991), 232, 236.

[2] Quoted in ibid., 249.

[3] Quoted in ibid.

wants food and work, he blames only far-off quarrels in America for his problems. When workers looked at themselves and measured their incomes
against those of the rich or the merely comfortable, they had a strong con-
sciousness of difference and deprivation, but that awareness did not translate
automatically into guilt about their own condition. In the words of one bal-
ladeer, "poverty's no sin."[4] Rather, it was a hurdle to surmount, a test of
endurance and strength.

More complex reflections on poverty can be found in workers' autobiographies. Between 1790 and 1850, well over a hundred, albeit atypical,
British workers composed life stories, many of which were intended to be
printed and sold. Drawing on the rich oral tradition of popular culture and the
genre of spiritual autobiography, they struggled to explain their own lives and
personal development using an often biblical vocabulary of virtue and
endurance.[5] Working-class autobiographers, however, are difficult to call representative. Not only were they atypical participants in a print culture, but
they sought a wide audience, a kind of public self-justification foreign to
most of their peers. Moreover, many workers' autobiographies were constructed as morality tales by people who during the course of their lives distanced themselves from the circumstances and sometimes the beliefs with
which they began. Those who climbed into the middle class and those who
became important trade unionists or radical politicians were particularly
drawn to publishing their histories. For both of these groups, episodes of
early deprivation set the stage for later triumphs, providing an object lesson
about conditions that had to be surmounted. Like Josiah Bounderby, they
gained in stature in relation to the lowness of their start. Yet even those men
accepted deprivation as normal in the world they would in later life reject; it
came with unemployment, illness, bad weather. Poverty was branded as
undesirable, something to be defeated, but its existence helped them to
demonstrate their own worthiness and self-respect.

Their narratives regularly included vivid memories of poverty during
childhood or the years when they struggled to support small children. Joseph
Barker, born in 1806, one of eleven children, told of a period of seven weeks
when their father left the family without resources. He and a brother had to
beg on the roads to feed themselves.[6] Joseph Gutteridge, born in 1816 into a

---

[4] Crampton Ballad Collection, vol. 2, 99, British Library.

[5] For an evaluation of this literature, see David Vincent, *Bread, Knowledge, and Freedom* (London: Europa Publications, 1981), 1–39.

[6] Joseph Barker, *The History and Confessions of a Man, as Put Forth by Himself* (London: Chapman Brothers, 1846), 68.

Coventry weaver's family, described one severe winter when his father had been unemployed for four months. Frost had ruined their family supply of potatoes, and bread prices were high. He wrote of "bitter" experiences, of "suffering not easily forgotten" during a time when he and his brothers "scarcely knew where to look for the means to satisfy our hunger."[7] Joseph Terry, the son of a northern waterman, wrote of a time around 1821 when he said that, for a period of two or three years, there was often no fire and little food. He stole turnips and gathered wild fruit and roots to eat.[8]

What Terry, Gutteridge, and Barker did not do was to blame themselves for their condition or to express feelings of shame. To the contrary, pride in their family's ability to handle adversity was a more common response. Parents were praised for being honest and independent, despite their temptations and sufferings. To quote Joseph Barker, "Poverty is not a crime. . . . It is in reality no disgrace."[9] Guilt was accepted in workers' tales of deprivation primarily in cases where they or a parent drank. Thomas Carter, a Colchester tailor, accused his father of "imprudence" and "intemperance," both of which led him to spend money on indulging his "sensual appetite," rather than caring for his family.[10] Carter firmly rejected such behavior and identified virtue with temperance and self-discipline. Shame came from responses to poverty, rather than from the condition itself. John Castle's mother got poor law aid after his father died at some point in the 1820s. Once during Castle's adolescence, he entered a workhouse. Although he found the experience unpleasant, his main complaint was that officials did not provide enough relief to support him in the style he wished.[11] He mentions neither shame nor humiliation. For him, accepting relief was a fact of life compatible with his self-image as an industrious, respectable person. Josiah Bassett spent five years in the St. George, Southwark, workhouse as a child. His series of commitments and escapes ended at age seventeen, when he notes that because he was "wearied of staying in the workhouse, and desirous of seeing strange places," he ran away for the last time. He ended his life as a professed Christian, teetotaler, and Sunday School teacher. Looking backward, he condemned his

---

[7] Joseph Gutteridge, "The Autobiography of Joseph Gutteridge," in Valerie E. Chancellor, ed., *Master and Artisan in Victorian England.* (London: Evelyn, Adams & MacKay, 1969; originally published 1893) 99–100.

[8] John Burnett, ed., *Destiny Obscure: Autobiographies of Childhood, Education, and Family from the 1820's to the 1920's* (London: Penguin, 1984), 70–7.

[9] Barker, *History,* 60.

[10] Thomas Carter, *Memoirs of a Working Man* (London: Charles Knight & Co., 1845), 16.

[11] Burnett, *Destiny,* 262–6.

occasional lies and other moral lapses, but paid little attention to his begging and periods of workhouse residence. He faulted overseers for not teaching him a trade.[12] It seems to have been possible in the early nineteenth century to accept poor law aid without self-recrimination and apology because many workers thought that poverty arose not from individual failings but from circumstances not under a person's control.

Greater ambivalence about poor law aid surfaced later in the century, particularly as men looked backward from the vantage point of decades of exposure to the New Poor Law, but worker autobiographers still spoke up for the poor's right to relief. Joseph Arch defended the entitlement of the destitute to public charity, to early marriage if they chose, and to relief when needy. Yet he also lauded his family's independence from all outside help. His parents, he said, remained both "honest and independent. They had a long tough fight of it, but they kept their heads up bravely; they stole from no man, nor did they take alms from anyone; they never sank down to the level of the thief and the pauper."[13] From the vantage point of the 1870s, Thomas Cooper, the Chartist, praised his widowed mother for avoiding the workhouse and parish relief when he was a child.[14] Although he maintained a sense of superiority over those who applied to their parishes, he also defended the right of Leicester workers to support under humane conditions. For Cooper, belief in the entitlement of the poor to generous relief was compatible with rejection of pauper status for oneself. His disdain for dependence indicates that some of the lessons that the New Poor Law sought to teach were absorbed by workers, but Cooper put those lessons to a very different use than supporters of the 1834 reform intended.

Although poverty seemed virtually unavoidable in the life stories of low-paid workers, analyses of its origins varied substantially. Some commentators, particularly women, used a religious vocabulary to link divine intentions and human outcomes. Elizabeth Browett, a penniless Quaker seamstress in London, wrote in her diary during the 1830s that she would "endeavour to be Content with my Lot, which it has pleased Providence to put me in."[15]

[12] Josiah Bassett, *The Life of a Vagrant, or the Testimony of an Outcast to the Values and Truth of the Gospel* (New York: Robert Carter & Brothers, 1852), 15, 17, 24.

[13] Joseph Arch, *Joseph Arch; The Story of His Life Told by Himself* (London: Hutchinson & Co., 1898), 14–15.

[14] Thomas Cooper, *The Life of Thomas Cooper. Written by Himself* (London: Hodder & Stoughton, 1872), 9–10.

[15] Elizabeth Browett, "Diary of a Seamstress," 29 Nov., 1833; Quaker Collection, Haverford College Library. I wish to thank Trudi Abel for this reference and transcription, from her article

Poverty, as well as riches, came from God, and she saw her duty as being one of acceptance. Others were less passive in the face of hardship, but still linked their fate to supernatural design. Mrs. Sullivan, a Roman Catholic resident of a central London slum, told a City Mission visitor during the 1860s, "God don't willingly afflict any of his creatures without some good purpose, and I know my afflictions have brought me nearer to God, but sometimes I think that God deals very hard with me."[16] As these women worked to endure poverty, religion gave them a partial framework of explanation, one that removed responsibility from their shoulders and connected them to a moral universe with a rational design.

In contrast, many workers preferred secular explanations that showed an awareness of economic theory, politics, and social stratification. Radical trade unionists and political activists like Joseph Arch, Samuel Bamford, William Lovett, and Thomas Cooper offered wide-ranging analyses of poverty, blaming it on a variety of corrupt social groups and institutions. Arch identified rich landlords and traders who refused to sell grain to the poor at a reasonable price, and who "did their best – or worst – to keep them [the people] in a state of poverty and serfdom."[17] Cooper linked his mother's economic struggles to "rent and taxes, bad harvests and dear bread," and he took pains to note how around 1840 some of the Leicester unemployed rejected on the grounds of disbelief the suggestion that God would soon relieve their sufferings.[18] In his autobiography, Lovett, author of the People's Charter, linked destitution to government policies: "Exclusive legislators, having their own interest to secure, rather than the general happiness of society, have, by their corrupt enactments, ruinous wars, extravagant expenditure, taxation and monopoly, generated great poverty amongst the people."[19]

The view that poverty originated in the selfishness of elites and wrong-headed government policies circulated widely among workers and radical political groups during the first half of the nineteenth century. Patricia Hollis notes that writers in the working-class press around 1820 commonly identified corrupt aristocrats and rich landlords as the chief social villains. By the early 1830s, when England was flooded by editions of cheap unstamped

"Needles and Penury in 19th Century London: The Diary of a Poor Quaker Seamstress," *Quaker History* (Fall 1986): 102–14.

[16] J. M. Oppenheim, "Visitor's Book, 1862," 99, St. Giles in the Fields, London.

[17] Arch, *Joseph Arch*, 10–12.

[18] Cooper, *Life*, 25–6, 173.

[19] William Lovett, *Life and Struggles of William Lovett in His Pursuit of Bread, Knowledge and Freedom* (London: Trubner & Co., 1876), 184–5.

newspapers, this imagery had shifted blame more to factory owners and middle-class capitalists. Commercial, more than landed, wealth ground down the face of the poor.[20] Through the 1830s and 1840s, newspapers such as *The Poor Man's Guardian* and *The Northern Star* linked poverty to the institution of private property and to the unjust system of political representation. Yet in all of these cases, poverty stemmed from causes that operated on the level of the entire society, not the individual. Although it is not clear how many people read such papers and how well they understood their messages, dozens of these papers circulated widely in British towns and were available in pubs and coffee houses. Dorothy Thompson credits the unstamped press, along with broadsides and pamphlets, with much of the political education fostered within the Chartist movement, which included thousands of workers in the cities. *The Northern Star* at its peak year of circulation in 1839 printed an average of 36,000 copies weekly, each of which would have been read by several people. Supplemented by hundreds of other short-lived journals selling for one pence or less an issue, the radical press during the 1830s and 1840s had a vast audience at least among the politically conscious workers of the towns.[21] Despite the multiplicity of political criticisms expressed in the unstamped papers, there was a party line on poverty: It was not the workers' fault. It also was a normal part of life at that time. The papers used interchangeably the terms "the poor" and "the labouring man" to describe their readers.

Similar ideas were expressed in ballads hawked on city streets and sold by peddlers door to door. The countless thousands who bought "Jone o'Grinfilt, Jr." – an immensely popular ballad for at least fifty years after its composition around 1818 – learned of a "poor cotton weaver," who had "nowt to eat" and had "worn out [his] cloas." Jone, who could not compete with the power loom, told of eating nettles and losing his furniture and loom to the bailiff. Despair, however, quickly changed to social protest against parsons, shopkeepers, landlords, and employers, who did nothing to help and much to worsen his condition. In the end, Jone and his wife talked of appealing for justice to the king.[22] Poverty came out of a wider world over which individuals had no control. The powerful who could have shown compassion did not, and therefore they earned the contempt Jone offered them.

A radical critique of the idle and the propertied occupied a secure place in

[20] Patricia Hollis, *Pauper Press* (New York: Oxford University Press, 1970), 205, 219, 227.

[21] Dorothy Thompson, *The Chartists* (New York: Pantheon, 1984), 45, 51–2.

[22] The ballad is reprinted in Martha Vicinus, *The Industrial Muse* (London: Routledge, 1974), 49–51.

ballad literature. In a song that pleads for work and fair treatment, the author brands the "lordlings of Belgravia" and the "coroneted vagabonds" for robbing the poor of their land and of wages. The ballad continues:

> They store ill-gotten thousands,
> These lords of wealth and rank,
> While some are daily starving,
> On the doorsteps of the bank.
> The weapon of starvation,
> Does dozens daily kill,
> And that's the reason England, boys,
> Is going down the hill.[23]

The ballad world was one of good and evil, of struggling workers sinned against by manipulative and callous aristocrats. In this universe, both Christian and social morality demanded charity, fair wages, and aid to the poor. Although the economy as it functioned during the early nineteenth century was clearly not moral, balladeers wished that it were. Although the political views of workers varied, many of them agreed on a displacement of the blame for poverty from the individual to starkly defined social enemies – the aristocracy and the mill owners.

Part of the belief in their own virtue came to workers through their acceptance of a labor theory of value. A modified version of Ricardian economics in which capitalists, landlords, church, and state deprived laborers of their fair share of the produce of their work circulated in the *Poor Man's Guardian* and other radical papers, as well as in the writings of economic theorists such as T. Hodgskin, W. Thompson, and J. Gray.[24] Defended strongly in the unstamped press and in Chartist speeches, the notion that the value of a commodity came from the amount of labor taken to produce it was common among English workers in the early nineteenth century. In the *Poor Man's Guardian* in 1834, Bronterre O'Brien argued: "Since all wealth is the produce of industry, and as the privileged fraction produce nothing themselves, it is plain that they must live on the labours of the rest." He then went on to charge the propertied with the use of fraud and force to seize the produce of workers via rents, taxes, tithes, interest, and profits.[25]

William Cobbett presented his views on labor both in print and in person

---

[23] Crampton Collection, vol. 2, 161.

[24] Hollis, *Pauper Press,* 221–2.

[25] Quoted in ibid.

during his long career. In *A Legacy to Laborers,* written in 1834, he reacted directly to the New Poor Law and Malthusian analyses of economics and population. Cobbett thundered: "Without the labourer the land is nothing worth. . . . Without his labour there can be no tillage, no enclosure of fields, no tending of flocks, no breeding of animals. . . . It is the labourer that causes the rents."[26] Cobbett eloquently defended workers' right to relief partly on the basis of the labor theory of value. Their contribution earned them maintenance from the produce of the land: "[T]he laborers have a right to subsistence out of the land, in all cases of inability to labour; . . . all those who are able to labour have a right to subsistence out of the land in exchange for their labour."[27]

The extent to which the labor theory of value was absorbed by ordinary people is uncertain; yet there are echoes of such views in workers' autobiographies, in street ballads, and in the public images presented by English trade unions. In his autobiography, William Lovett quoted with approval a statement circulated by the National Union of the Working Classes: "Labour is the source of wealth."[28] Work songs firmly located virtue and productivity among the miners and weavers of the region.[29] In "The Collier Lass," a young woman defends her occupation and social worth:

And what would you do, were it not for our labour?
In wretched starvation your days they would pass.
While we can provide you with life's greatest blessing,
O do not despise a poor collier lass.[30]

The Scottish ballad, "The Wark of the Weaver," which dates from the later eighteenth century, argues: "If it were nee for the weavers, what would we do?" and asks all to "drink to the health of the weavers!"[31] The London ballad, "A Labouring Woman," makes the point that wives work harder than husbands and are therefore as socially useful. "Work, Boys, Work and Be Contented" proclaims "labour leads to wealth."[32] Labor took on mystical qualities

---

[26] William Cobbett, *A Legacy to Labourers,* new ed. (London: Charles Griffin & Co., 1872), 109.

[27] Ibid., 110–1.

[28] Lovett, *Life,* 72.

[29] Martha Vicinus argues that these songs "reflected and rarely led or manipulated popular attitudes." Vicinus, *Industrial Muse,* 13.

[30] Louis James, *English Popular Literature, 1819–1851* (New York: Columbia University Press, 1976), 108.

[31] Ewan MacColl and Peggy Seeger, *Steam Whistle Ballads* (London: Topic Records), selection 1.

[32] Crampton Ballad Collection, vol. 1, 128, 62.

for Samuel Bamford, a Lancashire handloom weaver, who mused about the sources of English greatness: "First, labour and its reward, from which follow plenty, peace, reverence, obedience, order, security, opulence; and, as a consequence of these, encouragement to continued exertion."[33] The notion that manual labor was the source of value was both familiar and powerful in the oral culture of the industrial north and in the world of working-class radicalism during the first half of the nineteenth century. As workers defended the way they spent time, they also defended their stake in the nation.

A Right to Relief

If labor was the primary source of value, but laboring entailed poverty, then by definition workers were both poor and worthy, entitled to help in cases of need from the society that benefited from their toil. The right to charity and relief thus formed part of an integrated view of the position of workers in an insecure capitalist society. Although there were many ambivalences expressed by articulate workers by the early nineteenth century about dependence on public support, the notion of the legitimacy of charity and relief was an important part of popular culture through the first half of the nineteenth century.

In many workers' autobiographies, charitable aid is portrayed as the moral course of action by the rich. Joseph Arch bitterly recalled the decision of a local parson's wife not to give his parents the coal, soup, and other gifts regularly dispensed to villagers; he branded this action an "unfair deprivation," despite his vigorous defense of his own family's independence.[34] Joseph Gutteridge included in his life history a song written by a Coventry compositor and sung during the 1860s by groups of impoverished weavers. It recounts with irony a poor weaver's attempt to survive in the face of market forces and ends:

> Take no heed of the precept, "Love one another,"
> A Weaver's a weaver, don't think him a brother;
> And to do unto others as they should do unto us
> Is a figure of speech that requires no fuss.
> All should be selfish – they need not bestow
> A thought on the duties to others they owe;

---

[33] Samuel Bamford, *Passages in the Life of a Radical* (London: T. Fisher Unwin, 1893; first published 1841), 210–11.

[34] Arch, *Joseph Arch*, 7–8.

Need not strive to assist their poor fellow-man,
but endeavour to get for themselves all they can.[35]

The assertion of the wealthy's social duty to aid the poor became, in the context of debate over the poor laws, a conviction of the legitimacy of relief. Workers' discussions of the poor laws during the 1830s were infused by a strong defense of their social rights. Chelsea inspectors of the poor found themselves confronted by people who challenged the amounts of grants, saying that they deserved more; others complained of having to wait in line for payment or travel to the relief offices. Local inhabitants claimed pensions for parents on the grounds that they had been ratepayers. Applicants had a keen sense of their rights and of acceptable forms and levels of relief. Nonresident paupers regularly wrote the overseer of Kirkby Lonsdale during the 1820s to complain of delays in the dispatch of "their" money, their pay.[36] In his recent study of the agricultural economy in southern counties, Keith Snell argues that "the poor themselves regarded parish settlement and the right to relief as their birthright."[37]

When workers' sang in the mid-nineteenth century about the good old days, they made them vanish with the New Poor Law. At some point in a mythical past, there had been roast beef, ale, and jobs for all. Then, there had been plenty and openhanded kindness; but now, poverty, cruelty, and oppression. Workers conjuring visions of "traditional" welfare clothed them in the beautiful dress of a caring, paternalist community, not the rough gray garb of laissez-faire. Such songs were sticks with which to bludgeon reluctant overseers.

Consider the ballad, "The State of Great Britain, or, a Touch of the Times for 1841." Its narrator sings of unwelcome changes that were disrupting the natural harmony of the nation:

As old John Bull was walking
One morning free from pain,
He heard the rose, the shamrock,
and thistle to complain;
An alternation must take place,
Together they did sing

---

[35] Gutteridge, "Autobiography," 180–2.

[36] St. Luke's, Chelsea, Middlesex, "Inspectors' Reports on Paupers, 1833–1834," P74/Luk 30; Greater London Council Archive; Kirkby Lonsdale, "Township Letters, 1809–1836," Cumbria Record Office.

[37] K. D. M. Snell, *Annals of the Labouring Poor: Social Change and Agrarian England, 1660–1900* (New York: Cambridge University Press, 1985), 112.

In the Corn Laws, and the Poor Law Bill,
And many other things.

. . . .

The Poor Law Bill, now many say,
Are arbitrary laws,
But they are quickly going to alter,
Now the first and second clause,
The ninth and tenth, and thirty-first;
But the forty-third does say,
Give old men and women beer and tea
And a half-a-crown a day.[38]

Parliament could, and indeed would, bring back an earlier harmony by whole-sale revision of the New Poor Law. In the proper order of things, the elderly would be indulged and supported, and the people would ratify changes in the law. In the meantime, they had the right to protest.

In the Yorkshire Anti-Poor Law meetings of 1837 and 1838, speakers echoed William Cobbett's well-known defense of the Elizabethan poor laws as a social compact, which guaranteed support for those who worked the land. Demonstrators proclaimed: "The poor have a claim on the soil, and ver-ily they shall be fed"; "The poor have a right to subsistence from the land."[39] Yorkshire men and women also demanded that relief be offered under accept-able conditions. "God, Nature, and the Laws have said that men shall not die of want in the midst of plenty," they pronounced. They attacked the New Poor Law because of its form, not its function of support: "Can the Christian Man Bastille the poor? The people answer, 'No'"; "The men of Lockwood will not be separated in a bastille, nor will our children be emigrant slaves." Speakers at a Huddersfield rally in 1837 invoked the Magna Carta to prove that the New Poor Law had broken some of the fundamental laws of England, which guaranteed that no man should be imprisoned or dispossessed of lands with-out the judgment of his peers. A Bradford factory worker, J. Dowthwaite, charged, "[T]he Whigs are the only *real* destructives, and the object of their attack was the rights and liberties of the people of England," clearly imply-ing that these rights had persisted into recent times.[40]

The widespread hostility to the New Poor Law after its introduction sup-ports the notion that similar attitudes were pervasive in both southern and northern counties. John Lowerson, who has studied the Anti-Poor Law move-

---

[38] Baring-Gould Ballad Collection, vol. 1, 75, British Library.

[39] *The Times,* 18 May 1837, 5–6.

[40] *The Times,* 18 May 1837, 5–6.

ment in Kent and Sussex, found ninety-three reported incidents of protest in those counties in 1835. People marched and demonstrated against the law in dozens of villages and market towns. Hated poor law officials were forced into wagons and carted out of town in Battle and Eastbourne. A group of laborers with blackened faces, flags, and clubs paraded around Sittingbourne and blockaded magistrates in the local workhouse until the army forced them to scatter. In Ringmer, thirty men marched into an overseer's office and demanded "money or blood," and then left when he agreed to pay their relief in cash, not in kind. When he retreated to pre-1834 practices, they considered themselves satisfied. They defended "tradition," which meant money payments to the destitute, who could continue to live at home.[41] Anne Digby has discovered dozens of similar incidents in Norfolk, east Suffolk, and northern Essex between 1835 and 1837. People attacked guardians' meetings, torched workhouses, or went after the property of relieving officers and guardians. They petitioned against the law, sent threatening letters, and demonstrated against its introduction. At issue was the survival of customary forms of relief, which they were prepared to defend actively.[42]

How were these popular rights defined in the 1830s? Workers in northern towns seemed to be using the standard of eighteenth-century radicals, as defined by E. P. Thompson. They equated the "rights of Englishmen" with freedom from intrusion by the state and with the maintenance of local customs.[43] And one of these customs was outdoor relief in the parish of one's settlement. When the law of 1834 mandated entry into union workhouses and separated spouses, parents, and children, it infringed local rights of self-government, as well as the independence of individual families. Demonstrators pronounced through their banners, "England, home, and liberty: local rights, wholesome food, and no separation in bastilles!"[44] Workers rejected the idea of a disciplinary poor law and confinement in the workhouse, not outdoor relief as it was usually practiced during the eighteenth century. Historians who argue that workers hated the poor laws and found pauperism repugnant need to distinguish between the rejection by the poor of specific welfare institutions and their adamant insistence upon their own entitlement to parish relief.

---

[41] John Lowerson, "Anti-Poor Law Movements and Rural Trade Unionism in the South-East, 1835," in Andrew Charlesworth, *An Atlas of Rural Protest in Britain, 1548–1900,* (Philadelphia: University of Pennsylvania Press, 1983), 156–7.

[42] Anne Digby, "Protest in East Anglia Against the Imposition of the New Poor Law," in Charlesworth, *Atlas,* 160–1.

[43] E. P. Thompson, *The Making of the English Working Class* (New York: Pantheon, 1964), 80, 82.

[44] *The Times,* 9 June 1837, 6.

Popular Greetings to the Overseers

By the early nineteenth century, the world of generous relief freely given had a more mythic than real status. Surely one of the reasons that the right to relief was asserted so vociferously was its tenuousness. Consider the case of emigrants from the township of Kirkby Lonsdale in Westmorland, who had traveled throughout the north looking for work. Many of the applicants were skilled workers, people who had been apprenticed or who worked in the mills and foundries of the northwest. When they wrote back to their township asking for help – letters survive for the years 1809–36 – many knew that it would be difficult to obtain. They therefore had to present a good case and had to appear in the most favorable light. Most letters struck a deferential tone, although insisting at the same time on undeniable need. Writer after writer began appeals with the phrases, "I am sorry to be under the *necessity* of *troubling* you. . . ." Again and again, applicants apologized for troubling the overseer, for forcing him to deal with their problems. Self-support was "no longer in their power," and they cited long strings of economic problems that blocked independence. Both men and women described their frantic, but unsuccessful, efforts to earn, frustrated by illness, accidents, and unemployment. Using a language of deference and humility, they asked the "gentlemen" of the board to consider their requests and promised that, when trade got better and they became stronger, they would again be independent. James Wilson wrote in 1822: "It was my earnest wish, and fond expectation after your late kindness for which accept my sincere thanks to you, and the taxpayers, to be able to support my family without becoming any more troublesome to you, but alas my hopes are again for a wile [sic] all vanished – having had the Misfortune to have my leg break again."[45] Normality was self-support, but petitioners claimed that the functioning of the economy or their physical condition made this goal impossible. They asserted not only a "need" for relief, but its necessity in a world where accident, illness, unemployment, and low wages undermined independence.

The people of Kirkby Lonsdale approached Stephen Garnett, long-time overseer and later guardian of the poor, hat in hand. They used a rhetoric of lowly status and traditionalist deference. He was addressed as "Sir," by those who announced themselves as "your humble servant" or even "your ever humble servant and well wisher." People appealed to his "goodness," and asked him to be "kind." Those given help expressed their "sincere thanks." John Loftus, in 1816, began his request by expressing his "greatful thanks to

---

[45] Kirkby Lonsdale, "Township Letters," 8 October 1822, no. 641.

you and through you to the principal Inhabitants of your Township for the assistance you afforded me last February." He then went on to say that he was "rather hurt" to have to again write for aid. Garnett sent him ten shillings to help him clothe his six children.[46] Evelyn Carr, a widow with four children, asked for an increased weekly allowance in April of 1813. She "presumes humbly to request your worship will take her case into consideration . . . and as in duty bound she will ever pray for your worship."[47] Charlotte Beck announced that "I dow [sic] feel myself as long as I shall live duty bound to pray with you and yours for all past faveurs [sic]."[48] Writers whose major aim was to persuade him to give them money were scrupulously polite and usually obsequious. Whether any of this was heartfelt is impossible to determine; its style was adopted easily by claimants, however, indicating widespread popular knowledge of overseers' expectations and modes of acceptable self-presentation.

Petitioners stressed their own frugality and needs but also sometimes exhibited a creative flair for making precise requests that would help them reestablish an acceptable life. Most of the letters to overseers in Kirkby Lonsdale asked for rent money or for a few shillings for food and medicine. The authors often described naked, barefooted children who needed warm winter clothing. They cried for subsistence, but were prepared to make do with the few shillings in temporary aid Garnett was willing to advance. Their precise requests struck a practical tone: Wives needed travel money to move families to where husbands had found work; adolescent children wanted an outfit of clothes so that a would-be employer would take them on; families requested back rent paid so that their household goods would not be seized and sold. Margaret Addison asked for money to go and live in Lancaster with her daughter, who would "use every Lawful means to make me happy."[49] One applicant for relief to the Hammersmith guardians in 1848 claimed to be out of work and "not strong, not able to carry things on my head. I wish the Guardians to advance me money to purchase a donkey with."[50] Subsistence needs for food, shelter, and continued employment were the order of the day, but applicants were not embarrassed to make, and indeed sometimes succeeded in obtaining, special requests tailored to a family's needs. Their sense

---

[46] Ibid., 27 November 1816, no. 118.

[47] Ibid., 7 April 1813, no. 204.

[48] Ibid., 21 March 1836, no. 64.

[49] Ibid., n.d. (c. August, 1817) No. 42.

[50] Hammersmith Board of Guardians, "Settlement Examinations, 1848," no. 94, Greater London Council Archive.

of entitlement stretched to specific amounts, specific objects that they claimed would reestablish normality in their lives, even after the passage of the New Poor Law.

The bow-and-scrape mode of presentation seems to have been necessary in some areas. Not only the poor of Kirkby Lonsdale used this approach, but those in the parish of Atcham, Shropshire, clearly abandoned it at their peril. In 1849, several elderly women with low incomes who were legally settled in the parish requested outdoor relief. Inspectors' reports on their condition granted that all were rather feeble and incapable of complete self-support. All got their pensions, except for seventy-five-year-old Elizabeth Keary, who was offered the workhouse instead, when she would not answer questions about her income. Moreover, she and her daughter had talked back to the overseer, who noted that the daughter "had become so violent in her language that he had to turn her out of the house."[51] In Chelsea, too, the language and tone of appeals for help influenced outcomes. The inspector there in the mid-1830s clearly favored polite paupers in his decisions about amounts and types of aid. In a report explaining his actions, he noted: "It has invariably occurred that he has left all those whom he has visited grateful to the Board for such amount of Relief to be awarded to them; except only those persons who are the least worthy or, comparatively, the least necessitous of its receivers."[52] Without the proper approach, authorities, who had in practice the right to determine eligibility, as well as the amount and the form of aid, proved reluctant to grant relief in congenial forms. The poor knew this, and many bowed and scraped appropriately in front of the overseers in order to maximize their chances of gaining outdoor relief.

That responses were not consistently humble can be seen in many of the Kirkby Lonsdale letters, where thinly veiled threats sometimes crept into appeals. John Pearson, an unemployed worker in Whitehaven, announced to Stephen Garnett that "if I do not gett [sic] some support I cannot last on . . . but I will be obliged to come to you which I am shewre [sic] will be a greater expense to you than [showing] me a little here."[53] Rachaell Boothman, a widow with two small children, threatened to get herself removed back to Kirkby Lonsdale, adding, "If I am forced to come . . . I will be found to be but a heavy burden."[54] Mary Grime, whose husband had deserted her and a five-year-old son, asked for nonresident relief in 1835. The alternative she

[51] Shrewsbury Incorporation, "Applications for Relief, 1849–1851," 83/221–2, no. 440.

[52] St. Luke's, Chelsea, Middlesex, "Inspectors' Reports on Paupers, 1833–1834," P74/Luk30.

[53] Kirkby Lonsdale, "Township Letters," 25 April 1813, no. 202.

[54] Ibid., 30 May 1835, no. 47.

posed to Garnett was: "You will send a cart for me as quick as possible . . . or I shall be obliged to apply to the Overseers of Langcliffe for Reliefe. Gentlemen, I leave this to your candid consideration."[55] Applicant after applicant threatened to return to Kirkby Lonsdale and throw their entire cost of maintenance on the township if their request for temporary help or a partial income subsidy was not met. They wrote to ask about the whereabouts of "their" pay, noting that Garnett was late in arranging it. Ruth Nelson sent a note saying curtly: "Gentlemen, you will be so kind as to send my pay by the 13th May as it is my rent day. Your compliance will oblige your Parishioner."[56] Poor law inspectors in Chelsea met occasional paupers who challenged their rulings and attempted to manipulate outcomes. Anne Roberts, married and the mother of seven children, refused the relieving officer's suggestion that she was lucky to get four shillings a week. When he suggested a possible reduction in her pension, he reported that she became angry and threatened that "if any of her money were to be taken off, she knew how to proceed."[57]

In the encounters between paupers and relieving officers during the first half of the nineteenth century, humble deference seems to have been the most common stance taken by applicants for aid, but it was tempered by firm assertions of need and entitlement, as well as occasional threats to cause trouble if they were not satisfied. They invoked religious duty and tried to induce guilt in the case of refusal. One Kirkby Lonsdale expatriate suggested: "It is the duty of every overseer in the sight of god and his own [conscience] to do for the poor and [aid those] that can not assist themselves."[58] The poor used whatever weapons were at hand to try to produce the desired outcome. Even if their bargaining position was weak, applicants had vocabularies of Christian virtue, human compassion, and self-interest that could be brought to bear on reluctant overseers.

Circles of Obligation

The judgments that workers had to make in hard times included not only whether and how to apply for relief, but what sorts of obligation they felt for kin outside the nuclear family – elderly parents, grandchildren, or siblings

---

[55] Ibid., 17 May 1835, no. 53.

[56] Ibid., 4 May 1833, no. A36.

[57] St. Luke's, Chelsea, Middlesex, "Inspectors' Reports on Paupers, 1833–34," P74 Luk30, no. 216.

[58] Kirkby Lonsdale, "Township Letters," November, 1809, no. 57.

and their families, for example. Intergenerational support, particularly when residences were nearby, was taken for granted by many. Daughters nursed elderly relatives or cleaned their homes. Widows minded grandchildren; gifts of food and clothing circulated among relatives and neighbors as needs arose. Difficult to document but impossible to ignore, the voluntary contributions of relatives and friends helped the poor to survive and supplemented the meager handouts from parish officers. Welfare strategies were often collective strategies, balancing out collective resources by individual appeals. Just as workers had family work and wage economies that helped them survive, there was a family economy of welfare and of welfare entitlement.

The shape of this family economy of welfare intersected with the moral obligations and the demographics of family life. Fertility rates did not begin a steady decline until around 1870, so that large family sizes went along with high urban death rates, and a substantial proportion of marriages were broken by either death or desertion. The resulting population included large numbers of orphans and elderly widows and widowers who could not support themselves; family, poor law, and charity were the obvious alternative sources of income. But, as Peter Laslett and Richard Wall point out, at any given moment, there were relatively few three-generation households in England and Wales. They argue against any socially sanctioned expectation of coresidence of kin beyond the boundaries of a nuclear family.[59] Many elderly chose and managed to live alone, either with or without the help of their children. To what extent and under what terms did they use poor law resources to supplement their own? The law gives some answers; custom dictates others. Pat Thane suggests that the poor law provided some, but probably not the major means of, support. Instead she sees multiple close, but voluntary, forms of aid from independent to dependent kin, which poor law officials often supplemented in order to encourage. In her opinion, family support and poor relief complemented one another in varying proportions as part of a larger "makeshift economy" of the poor.[60]

According to the poor law of 1601, the obligation to maintain was narrowly defined. Husbands had to support their wives, parents their children, and grandparents their grandchildren. Tight lines of responsibility ran downward

---

[59] Peter Laslett, *Family Life and Illicit Love in Earlier Generations* (New York: Cambridge University Press, 1972), 176–7; Peter Laslett, "Family, Kinship and Collectivity as Systems of Support in Preindustrial Europe: A Consideration of the 'Nuclear-Hardship' Hypothesis," *Continuity and Change* 3 (1988): 153–76; Richard M. Smith, "Some Issues Concerning Families and Their Property in Rural England, 1250–1800," in Richard M. Smith, ed., *Land, Kinship, and Life-Cycle* (New York: Cambridge University Press, 1984), 1–87.

[60] Pat Thane, "Old People and Their Families in the English Past," unpublished paper, 1995, 27.

through three generations of nuclear families, but not to wider sets of kin. They also stretched to households of origin, because unmarried adults and married males were obligated to maintain elderly parents. Women's responsibilities were somewhat less than those of their brothers and husbands, but after 1834 unmarried mothers were liable for the care of their illegitimate children.[61] During three centuries of remarkable social and economic changes, these legal obligations remained virtually constant, marking out a narrow circle of welfare liability among kin. Moreover, even these liabilities vanished if a household head was too poor to contribute to a destitute person's support. Those who could not relieve and maintain were very rarely even asked to do so.

These narrow legal obligations seem to have been less extensive than a wider and flexible set of moral obligations. In practice, families made their own decisions about whom to support and whom to try to shift onto the poor laws. Even if the law identified a three-generation chain of responsibility, popular notions of direct obligation to provide support marked out a tight circle – that of the nuclear family – and a wider circle of those to help as circumstances allowed. Those who applied for poor law aid privileged the units of husband/wife and parent/child, reserving for those groups a first claim on resources. Others – stepchildren, grandchildren, siblings, elderly parents – even if coresident, were placed beyond this inner circle and given a secondary claim. When income was not sufficient for all, or even when it was, those in the outer circle could be shifted to parish or union support. English law seemed to support this distinction, as did popular practice.

As long as relief meant a pension, many people seemed willing to apply for state funds for parents. After study of several parishes in Norfolk during the seventeenth century, Tim Wales concludes that aid was given to elderly people who had adult children alive. He found very few cases where justices ordered close kin to provide financial support.[62] Richard Smith states that "there is no doubt that many poor spent their old age as dependents of the parish whether they had adult children or not," and he suggests that this welfare pattern showed "remarkable continuity" from the late sixteenth into the early nineteenth century.[63] Dependence, however, is not a straightforward concept. Because outdoor relief did not give full support, the poor had to

---

[61] M. A. Crowther, "Family Responsibility and State Responsibility in Britain Before the Welfare State," *Historical Journal* 25:1(1982): 132.

[62] Tim Wales, "Poverty, Poor Relief and the Life-Cycle: Some Evidence from Seventeenth-Century Norfolk," in Smith, ed., *Land*, 383–4.

[63] Richard M. Smith, "Fertility, Economy, and Household Formation in England over Three Centuries," *Population and Development Review* 7:4 (1981): 608.

combine it with other resources, kin being the obvious other contributor. The issue was usually one of amounts and proportions of aid, rather than of alternative sources of help:

In the nonresident relief applications by Kirkby Lonsdale migrants, many of the poor tried to shift the support of the elderly more fully onto the community. They made the case that children were too poor to provide full support; therefore, the parish ought to supplement families' efforts. Sarah Battersby asked for an allowance in 1831 from Kirkby Lonsdale. Although she lived with her married son and his four children in Huddersfield, she said that he could only allow her "house room," and that if she were to stay with him, she had to have money to pay for her food.[64] Eleanor Beck, a sixty-three-year-old woman who lived with her frequently unemployed son and his family, appealed to Garnett in 1833 for money because her son's grant was "not enough to find them their bread."[65] In 1833, the overseer in Littleborough claimed that Betty Waddington had trouble with her daughter and son-in-law, who threatened to evict her if parish money was not forthcoming.[66] When her coresident mother fell ill, Margaret Redhead nursed her and bought extra food and "necessaries unknown to my husband." Nudged by the grocer's demand for payment, she wrote to Kirby Lonsdale for aid, rather than confront her husband and include debts for her mother's needs in their household budget. (Garnett, however, refused her request, perhaps reasoning that sufficient family resources were available.)[67] In 1820, Isabella Kirby asked Kirkby Lonsdale to increase her mother's pension. She reasoned:

My mother Isabella Pratt . . . has been in such a state for some weeks back to be an entire burden to us. Altho one's desire be ever so strong and duty to a Parent ever so binding yet she is, and has been, so ill . . . as to be all my work to take care of her wants to the neglect of my own large family and the small pension of 2s. per week does not suffice for her little necessary comforts at this time. . . . I beg with every degree of respect that you'l loose [sic] no time as what with the great trouble she occasions to a Poor working family and having in part to support into the Bargain is an inconvenience we can not any longer do with.[68]

In each of these cases, the elderly parent had been taken into the household of a low-income worker, who then attempted to get state aid on grounds of

[64] Kirkby Lonsdale "Township Letters," 23 September 1831, no. 3.

[65] Ibid., 4 January 1833, no. 21.

[66] Ibid., 27 May 1833, no. 52.

[67] Ibid., 5 September 1817, nos. 335–6.

[68] Ibid., 27 September 1820, nos. 537–8.

poverty. Both the parent and the overseers seemed to recognize that nuclear families had the first claims on resources and elderly parents a secondary one. When choices had to be made, the elderly could turn to their communities for partial support.

Similar distinctions between obligations to parents and to one's own children appear in poor law documents in the later nineteenth and early twentieth centuries. C. E. Wells wrote to the Cheltenham union in 1909, saying that he could no longer pay one shilling and six pence per week toward the support of his mother because he had been on short time at work for the past eighteen months. He noted that his weekly wages could scarcely cover food and rent for his wife and three children. His sense of obligation went first to them and then to his mother.[69] No doubt his income did not stretch far enough to support six people; yet he conceptualized the problem as a lack of money for his mother.

People interviewed by Paul Thompson in the 1960s and early 1970s, although professing great aversion to acceptance of relief by either their parents or themselves, saw poor law aid as inevitable for the elderly, and they invested this use of welfare with a kind of legitimacy denied to that given to the unemployed. The daughter of a building laborer spoke of her early life in London around 1900. Her family sometimes "got help" from the parish, although her father "didn't believe in charity." She added, however, "although my grandmother was different to us. She had to go on the parish, of course, she was too old."[70] Others told of elderly relatives who had to go into the workhouse when their children could no longer stay and nurse them because of obligations in other towns. In the English kinship system, welfare obligations toward the elderly became attenuated once children had married and formed households of their own.

This reluctance to support the elderly sometimes conflicted with the wishes of guardians of the poor to force adult children to maintain their parents. Although overseers in the eighteenth and early nineteenth centuries had rarely tried to coerce kin to support elderly paupers, many guardians moved aggressively to do so, particularly after 1870.[71] Although the vast majority of people in England and Wales lived in households composed of nuclear fam-

---

[69] Cheltenham Union, "Register of Maintenance and Recovery of Relief, 1905–1922," 6 July 1909.

[70] Family Life and Work Experience Archive, University of Essex. #124:33.

[71] Mary Barker-Read, "The Treatment of the Aged Poor in Five Selected West Kent Parishes from Settlement to Speenhamland," Ph.D. thesis, Open University, 1986; Marguerite Dupree, *Family Structure in the Staffordshire Potteries, 1840–1880* (Oxford: Oxford University Press, 1994) 309–10.

ilies, during the mid-nineteenth century increasing numbers of households took in relatives beyond the nuclear unit, for varying, but often brief, periods of time.[72] It is noteworthy that this change took place just at the time when guardians put maximum pressure on adult children to provide pensions for low-income elderly. This increase in the incidence of extended families was much more common among middle- and upper-class households, however, than among the poor, who had little space or income to spare. Nevertheless in workers' communities, too, the coresidence of elderly people and their married children rose during the last quarter of the nineteenth century, probably for economic reasons.[73]

Stepchildren and illegitimate children were another group whose rights to support in a coresidential family were secondary to those of the core couple and their offspring. In the applications for nonresident aid sent to the overseer of Kirkby Lonsdale, husbands sometimes sought to shift to the parish the cost of rearing their wives' children by earlier marriages or liaisons. John Hirst sent several letters to Stephen Garnett in 1831 and 1832 shortly after his marriage, prodding Garnett to send the quarterly parish allowance to him for Hannah Nelson, daughter of his wife, Sarah Nelson. Hirst threatened not to continue to rear Hannah if the full sum were not sent, and he reacted angrily to any delay in receiving the grant. "I expected it [the allowance] at the time. If I do not receive an answer in a week from this letter, the child will be sent by an order from the poorhouse. We are both out of employ and the town will not keep other town poor."[74] In London, in 1834, Elizabeth Bryant and her husband tried to get a parish allowance for her two children from a former marriage, reasoning that if she were still a widow, overseers would have given

---

[72] Steven Ruggles, *Prolonged Connections: The Rise of the Extended Family in Nineteenth-Century England and America* (Madison: University of Wisconsin Press, 1987). Ruggles shows that the frequency of coresident, extended families rose sharply between 1750 and 1900 to hit a peak of about 20 percent in the later nineteenth century. He argues against economic reasons for this shift, pointing toward the relatively high frequency of extended families among the more affluent. As in past times, richer folk had larger families as well as larger households. See also, Dupree, *Family Structure.*

[73] Steve Ruggles argues against the notion that economic necessity triggered these changes in residential patterns, and he documents the more substantial shift to extended families among people of higher status and incomes. Nevertheless, in studies of working-class communities, both Sonya Rose and Jean Robin show that parents moved into children's households in higher proportions during decades when employment dropped and when guardians began to sue paupers' kin for support payments. See Ruggles, *Prolonged Connections;* Jean Robin, "Family Care of the Elderly in a Nineteenth-Century Devonshire Parish," *Ageing and Society* 4:4 (1984): 505–16; Sonya O. Rose, "The Varying Household Arrangements of the Elderly in Three English Villages: Nottinghamshire, 1851–1881," *Continuity and Change* 3:1 (1988): 101–122.

[74] Kirkby Lonsdale, "Township Letters," 3 March 1832, no. 15.

her the money. She asserted entitlement, rather than need; however, her tactic did not work.[75] Several Chelsea householders in the parish of St. Luke's in 1834 received grants for grandchildren, illegitimate children, and children of former marriages; in each case, the inspector noted the special status of these children within their households, justifying the grant because of it.[76] At a time when family allowances were under attack as corrupting and unnecessary, children whose kinship status within families was different from that of a child born to a lawful marriage of the head and his wife seem to have had a greater entitlement to relief from the parish and a lesser one to the resources of their households. Stepney workhouse files from the 1890s include cases where stepchildren were placed in workhouses, whereas those of the head of the household remained at home. For example, John and George Kersey were sent by their stepfather into a London poor law school after their mother's death. He told authorities that he had six other children to support and was not legally liable for his stepchildren; therefore, he wanted them to be taken under state care.[77]

In practice, only blood relatives within a very narrow range offered to shelter orphans or abandoned children. David Vincent notes how, in workers' autobiographies written during the nineteenth century, the people outside the immediate household who stepped in during a time of family crisis to offer care included only the siblings or the parents of the mother and father, and, he adds, this obligation only continued during periods when they had the resources to permit aid. Their duty was seen as both contingent and limited.[78]

Over the long run, the English poor law helped to reinforce the dominance of the nuclear family, patriarchal lines of responsibility, and the relative shallowness of English kinship networks. The predominant direction of responsibility went from male adult to child or grandchild. Husbands had to support wives, children, and grandchildren; women's obligations were less because it was generally acknowledged that they could not support a family given existing wage levels, and poor law authorities were regularly willing to take into workhouses the children of impoverished females. Moreover, an individual had no legal right to aid from siblings, step-kin, aunts, uncles, and cousins. Such aid as occurred was voluntary, contingent on resources and inclination.

---

[75] St. Luke's, Chelsea, Middlesex, "Inspector's Reports on Paupers, 1833–1834," August 1834, no. 483.

[76] St. Luke's, Chelsea, Middlesex, "Inspector's Report for 1833–1834," see nos. 198, 441, 598.

[77] Booth Collection, B-82/162, case no. 43, British Library of Political and Economic Science.

[78] Vincent, *Bread,* 66.

The willingness of the state, albeit grudging, to support the elderly reduced pressures on couples to take in members of their parents' generation.

The lesson that, in England, communities would help to maintain their dependent members was one that had been learned by low-income workers. Although they strongly denounced the cultural construction of "pauperism" as defined in the report of 1834, they did not distance themselves during the eighteenth century and the first two-thirds of the nineteenth century from the selective use of poor law services. As citizens, they claimed a right to relief from the communities in which they lived and had worked. Christian compassion, "natural rights," and common sense all dictated collective responsibility for the poor, and it was the atypical worker who could afford to reject on principle an extra resource in hard times.

6

"PAUPERISM" IN PRACTICE, 1834–70

Eliza Patterson, age 70, single, Needlewoman. Relief: 12 shillings/month; has received for 6 years.

Benjamin Farmer, age 41, married with 7 children, Smith out of work. Relief: Bread, value 1 shilling.

    St. Giles Union, 1869

Hannah Donovan, Aged 66. In England 33 years, in House 3 years. This woman has great objection to go and pretends she does not know where born, but is recommended to be sent [to Ireland].

    St. Olave's Union, 1854

The rhetorical storms unleashed against pauperism and the flurry of central regulations to contain it have distracted attention away from the day-to-day relief work of local authorities. Fixation upon rules has crowded out attention to what actually happened when a destitute person applied for welfare. State aid brought certain practical benefits, quite obvious to the destitute, whatever representations of pauperism circulated in print and in polite conversation. Despite their hearty dislike of the workhouse, destitute people came in droves to relieving officers in the winter and when they were sick or unemployed. Widows asked for help after the death of a spouse, and the elderly applied for pensions when they could no longer support themselves. Recourse to the community was a common action by English and Welsh workers well past the mid-nineteenth century. The poor law after 1834 offered aid in multiple forms that proved important for family economies just as it had before 1834. Understanding the meaning of welfare requires looking beyond abstract pronouncements and lurid exposés to the routine encounters of applicant and overseer, where communal aid was negotiated.

Unfortunately, the actual practice of local administrators is far less easy to track than are the policies of the Poor Law Commission or Poor Law Board. A complete survey of actions taken under the Poor Law Amendment Act would require looking at dozens and dozens of volumes of records for each of the more than six hundred poor law unions of England and Wales. Moreover, local sources reveal only limited amounts about the people aided. Guardians of the poor gave central authorities only a skeletal account of their activities. Some of what they did on a day-to-day basis was undocumented, as was much of what they learned about applicants.

English welfare records that deal with the poor, rather than with procedures, are primarily of two kinds: (1) centrally collected and published statistics of numbers of paupers and the cost of their maintenance; and (2) local records of individuals who received relief and of their treatment. The published, national sources merely count and classify people according to quite narrow and uniform categories; local sources named the poor, often adding demographic or personal details that shaped policy decisions. Local records are clearly the more interesting, but they pose serious problems of interpretation, as well as questions about aggregation. The most common types are the settlement examinations, statements sworn before justices of the peace, which were designed to establish entitlement, and registers of cases, which gave data on the institutionalized poor and on those in receipt of outrelief. In both sets of records, we meet the destitute as described by clerks and relieving officers in terms of familiar categories. What we see, however, are not photographs of the poor, but simplified sketches of images contrived by welfare applicants to magnify their needs and their entitlements. But real people with recognizable problems existed behind these representations, and they have left clues to their identities and their wants in the written records. Certain details are almost universally recorded and recognizable in some types of local records: sex, age, ethnicity, family structure and size, common types of disability, and treatment by the officials. Although these descriptive categories say little about the particular events that led a person to apply for relief, they help to identify need as it was understood by welfare administrators in the nineteenth century.

Using a variety of local records from a widely drawn sample of poor law unions throughout England, supplemented by national reports, I have investigated two major questions: What sorts of people received poor law aid, and what were they given? Answers to these basic questions permit both a quantitative and a qualitative assessment of the mid-nineteenth century welfare state as it operated in England and Wales. My data show clearly that not all destitution was equal. Welfare officials used their notions of gender, age, and ethnicity to shape welfare provision. As the scale of local communities increased because of population growth and urbanization, the intimate knowledge of poor individuals that had guided overseers of the poor in earlier centuries vanished and had to be replaced by more abstract rules pertaining to eligibility and entitlement. Gender, age, and ethnicity offered easily ascertainable guides to "appropriate" policy. Officials tried unsuccessfully to exclude both healthy, adult males and Irish migrants from benefits, whereas they more willingly gave income subsidies to women, children, and the elderly. But they gave meager aid at best: the poor laws provided only partial support to those whose entitlements were clear. As a result, they encouraged the destitute to remain in local, low-wage jobs. Relief commonly operated as an income subsidy to low-skilled workers, tying them to the local economy and shifting the wage cost onto the taxpayer. This pressure operated more clearly in the case of women than of men.

It is a mistake, however, to think of the poor laws as touching only a small minority of the English and Welsh population in early and mid-Victorian times. Workers commonly used the poor laws in times of life-cycle crisis, illness, and old age. Asking the community for support was a familiar tactic in the battle to survive, one that, as I have argued in Chapters 2 and 5, did not bring disgrace but was considered a right. Negotiations over welfare aid continued to define the meaning of social citizenship in the parishes of England and Wales during much of the nineteenth century. Recourse to the community for support was an acceptable action for workers, one made necessary by economic and demographic pressures. Not until late in the century did the experience of "pauperism" become one that touched relatively few workers, dividing them from their more respectable neighbors.

Numbers of Paupers

If the reports of the Poor Law Commission and Poor Law Board are to be believed, pauperism was not a serious problem in England and Wales after the mid-nineteenth century, but their statistics need to be examined with care, for they are misleading. According to national records, only 6.2 percent of the total population received relief in 1849, and the rate supposedly declined steadily from that point until 1920, when it reached 1.5 percent, undisturbed by cyclical downturns in the economy. After rising sharply during the mid-1920s and early 1930s, the rate fell again to 3.0 percent at the beginning of the Second World War.[1] (See Table 6.1, column 2.) Levels such as these

---

[1] Karel Williams, *From Pauperism to Poverty* (London: Routledge, 1981), 158–62.

Table 6.1. *Estimated population on relief in England and Wales, 1840–1939*

Date	Mean number	Rate/1,000 Pop.	Corrected Number[a]	Estimated rate/1,000[a]
1840[b]	1,200,000	77	2,688,000	172
1845[b]	1,471,000	88	3,295,000	197
1850	1,009,000	57	2,260,000	129
1855	898,000	48	2,012,000	108
1860	845,000	43	1,893,000	96
1865	951,000	46	2,130,000	102
1870	1,033,000	47	2,314,000	104
1875	801,000	34	1,794,000	76
1880	808,000	32	1,810,000	71
1885	769,000	29	1,723,000	64
1890	775,000	27	1,736,000	61
1895	797,000	27	1,785,000	59
1900	797,000	25	1,785,000	56
1905	879,000	26	1,890,000	56
1910	916,000	26	1,969,000	56
1914	748,000	20	1,608,000	44
1920	563,000	15	1,210,000	32
1925	1,229,000	32	2,642,000	68
1930	1,183,000	30	2,543,000	64
1935	1,529,000	39	3,287,000	81
1939	1,208,000	30	2,597,000	63

[a]In order to take account of paupers aided but not relieved on the two days a year when their numbers were officially counted, I have inflated the number of applicants by a factor of 2.24 for the period 1840–1900 and by 2.15 for the years 1905–39. For an explanation of the ratio between the recorded applicants and the estimated total number of cases, see Sidney Webb and Beatrice Webb, *English Local Government*, part 2, *The Last Hundred Years* (London: Longmans, 1929), vol. 2, p. 1051.

[b]For the years 1840 and 1845, the data represent paupers aided during a quarter year, not the average of the 1 January and 1 July figures that were reported after 1849. Because there still would have been a substantial turnover of paupers during these years, I have also inflated these figures by the estimated ratio of 2.24.

Sources: Karel Williams, *From Pauperism to Poverty* (London: Routledge, 1981), pp. 158–62; *Royal Commission on the Poor Laws and Relief of Distress* (London: H. M. Stationery Office, 1911), Statistical Appendix, vol. 25, table 2, p. 24.

would bring joy to the hearts of welfare officials today, who would consider the poverty problem solved.

Unfortunately, these figures ought to be treated as only a rough guide to reliance on poor relief, and they say nothing at all about the incidence of either destitution or poverty. The mean figures are averages of the number of paupers recorded as receiving relief on 1 January and the total figure for 1 July of the same year. The calculations exclude those who applied for, but were denied, aid as well as those who got relief on any of the other 363 days, but not on the selected two. In addition, they neglect cases where local officials found means other than the poor rate to finance payments to the destitute. When times were really bad, special funds and charities leapt into action, becoming short-term substitutes for the poor laws. The official record offers minimum figures for, rather than an accurate accounting of, the population on relief.

Part of the difficulty stems from the fluctuating levels of temporary pauperism, about which centrally collected statistics are virtually silent. Although the elderly and widows with small children could receive aid throughout a year, others got help for only limited periods of time, and there was a rapid turnover of paupers given short-term grants during a few weeks of sickness or family emergency. When poor law authorities began to keep case records on applicants, they discovered a pattern of irregular welfare use among low-income workers. Illness or an accident could send someone to a relieving officer for a few weeks in one year; death in the family, or unemployment, could force a trip a year or two later. Husbands would leave to find work, expecting families to fend as best they could. Each of these situations could lead to an application for relief, only some of which would be captured in the centralized records. Unfortunately, we have little consistent information on the issue of temporary relief, its duration, or its frequency.

In 1892 and again in 1907, poor law authorities tested the relation between average numbers of people relieved and the total numbers aided. They required local officials to count all the people given welfare during a year, subtracting cases where individuals had taken grants more than once. Results suggested that in 1892, 2.24 times more people got welfare help during the year than had been aided on any given day; in 1907, the ratio dropped to 2.15. If the ratio for 1892, which emerged during a period of relatively low use of the poor laws, is applied to figures for the period 1850–1900 that count only people aided on the two sampled days, figures for total pauperism can be estimated. (See Table 6.1, columns 3 and 4.) It seems reasonable to assume that from 1850 to 1870, between 10 and 13 percent of the total English and Welsh populations received poor law aid each year. Thereafter, the rate of total pauperism declined slowly to about 6 percent around 1910.

These revised figures also seriously underestimate use of the poor laws by the English and Welsh populations because of the pattern of irregular application that existed. Most paupers got outrelief, and few had rights to a permanent pension. Others had grants only for a few weeks intermittently during illness, pregnancy, or unemployment. Over a period of a few years, many more families and individuals used the poor laws than applied to them in a single year. Assume that half of the people counted as being on relief at mid-century had only temporary grants and that each received aid on average only once every three years; then the proportion of the total population that used the poor laws during a period of three years would be about 25 percent. If people applied on average once every four years, the proportion by the end of that period would rise to 32 percent, a rate high enough to include all the laborers' families in England and Wales. If a similar calculation is done for 1900, as much as 11 percent of the population would have used the poor laws during a three-year cycle and 14 percent over a period of four years. This suggests that low-income workers not only were familiar with the poor laws, but that they used them regularly in the early and mid-nineteenth century. It seems reasonable to assume that during the first three-quarters of the nineteenth century a high proportion of workers' families would have applied for poor law aid at least once and probably more often during their adult lives, and that in any given year, some of their friends and neighbors would have done so. Although some had the resources to avoid the poor law permanently, I believe that most did not. Until late in the nineteenth century, workers knew about the poor laws because they had used them for support. They feared potential dependence on their parishes because they had experienced it themselves.

The incidence of recourse to the poor law most probably declined during the last quarter of the nineteenth century and the early years of the twentieth century. At that time, paupers constituted a far smaller proportion of the population than they had in early Victorian times, and there was less turnover among paupers applying. Being a pauper became a much less familiar status, which helps to account for a rising hostility toward pauperism and the poor laws visible in workers' communities.

Recourse to the poor laws was more frequent in some parts of the country than in others. The industrialized and heavily urbanized counties normally had far lower proportions of their population supported by the poor laws than did the agricultural areas of the west, south, and east. (See Map 6.1.) In the early years of the New Poor Law, rates of pauperism in southern counties were about double and, in extreme cases triple, those in the industrial Midlands and the north. To be sure, these differences reflect relief policies as well as destitution levels. Northern administrators and officials in the big towns knew that multiple employment opportunities existed nearby. Moreover, the rapid pace of urbanization meant that employers had ample labor supplies. Therefore, they had little incentive to be generous to the poor. In southern

LEGEND:

20–59

60–89

90–120

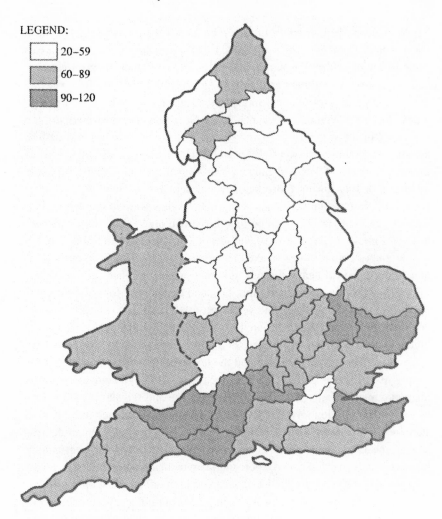

Map 6.1. Regional Incidence of Pauperism, 1 January 1850.
(Paupers per 1000 total population.)

rural parishes, however, employers had a greater need to encourage laborers
to remain. They could both discourage migration and save their own money
by shifting some of the cost of maintaining their workers onto the poor laws.[2]

The numbers on relief also varied according to the season. Agricultural

---

[2] George R. Boyer, *An Economic History of the English Poor Law, 1750–1850* (New York: Cambridge University Press, 1990).

employment dipped sharply in the winter, as did work on the docks and in construction. But many urban, artisanal trades flourished when upper classes came to towns during the winter and then declined when they retreated to country houses in summer and fall. In general, relief needs followed the unemployment cycles of local industries. Using the dates at which magistrates examined welfare applicants, Keith Snell has demonstrated striking variations in the monthly levels of recorded cases in southern and eastern agricultural counties between 1835 and 1860.[3] For men, the incidence of applicants in December and January was over three times higher than the incidence in July during those years; relief demands by women were over twice as high in the late fall and early winter as they were in the spring. Patterns of seasonal variation can be found in urban unions, too, although they differed somewhat. Around 1850, numbers of examinations in London and in my sample of county towns peaked in January and then again in early summer, both periods of heavy seasonal unemployment, and then decreased during the spring and again in early fall. Demand by the poor for public support operated according to seasonal cycles, but these differed according to local economic cycles and the sex of applicants; 1 January and 1 July were not the high and the low points of demand for aid in every region.

Cyclical depressions also changed the levels of demand for relief, but the supply of aid seems to have varied much less. Although rates of reported unemployment among trade union members rose and fell sharply according to the state of the economy, official rates of pauperism remained roughly constant, declining slowly over the century.[4] During the so-called great depression of the late nineteenth century, when registered unemployment among trade unionists reached over 10 percent, paupers made up under 3 percent of the total population. Clearly, the poor law did not adjust the supply of relief automatically to the demand for it. During times of high unemployment, poor law officials often asked local charities to shoulder much of the added burden, and civic authorities collected special funds for the poor, but their clients would not have appeared in poor law records. Guardians seem to have regarded their own resources as roughly fixed in size. The poor law officials themselves were responsible for limiting the scope of their commitment to relieve destitution.

---

[3] K. D. M. Snell, *Annals of the Labouring Poor* (New York: Cambridge University Press, 1985), 20–1.

[4] Williams, *Pauperism*, 191.

Guardians supplied relief in two major ways: People either had to enter an institution – such as a workhouse, asylum, or boarding school – in order to gain complete support; or they remained in their own homes and were given grants of money, food, or medicines. The former strategy of "indoor relief" was the one, of course, recommended by the Royal Commission on the Poor Laws and by the Poor Law Commission for able-bodied adults and their families and for the insane. The latter could be adopted for the elderly, for widows with dependent children, and for the sick and disabled. But guardians had some discretion in their choice of policy, and official orders, in any case, contained major loopholes. Centrally kept records of the numbers on indoor and outdoor relief on two sampled days per year show that, between 1849 and 1939, the vast majority of paupers received aid outside institutions. The institutionalized poor never exceeded 1 percent of the English and Welsh populations during that period, whereas the percentage of the population getting outdoor relief ranged from a high of 7 percent to a low of about 3 percent.[5] A "crusade against outrelief," implemented in 1870, produced a sharp drop in the numbers relieved at home during the last third of the nineteenth century, but it did not eliminate the practice. Despite continued efforts by central administrators to curb allowances to the poor, most people on relief got weekly grants of money and food, not the workhouse.[6]

Amounts of Aid

While taxpayers and administrators worried about the high cost of relief, they knew that they could manipulate the total spent by shifting types and amounts of aid. Workhouses cost a great deal of money to build and to run, despite continued efforts to make them as unattractive and as harsh as possible. Although the budgets of local unions varied considerably, most spent twice as much per year on paupers supported in the workhouse as they did upon those to whom they gave pensions. (In 1854, Lancashire and West Riding unions spent on average £5 10s. 5d. per pauper in the workhouse, but only £3 11s. 5d. per head on their pensioners; in eastern counties around 1860, workhouse charges per year ran about £9 per head, whereas an average yearly pension cost only £4 11s.) Local officials knew these differences in

---

[5] Ibid., 160–4.

[6] Michael E. Rose, "The Allowance System Under the New Poor Law," *Economic History Review* 19:3 (1966): 607–20.

cost well, and some thought it "ruinous" to shift families into institutions where they would have to provide the destitute not only with food and shelter, but also with clothes, medical care, education, work, and supervision.[7] In contrast, paupers who remained at home could earn money on the side, perhaps grow some of their own food, and supervise each other. Best of all, they paid their own rent. Michael Rose argues that few boards of guardians gave grants large enough to maintain a person without additional sources of income. In 1869, Holborn guardians admitted to the Poor Law Board that the pensions they offered were inadequate for full support; paupers had to supplement them in order to survive. Other poor law officials made similar statements. Outdoor relief topped off other resources; it did not substitute for them.[8]

Both central and local records confirm this verdict on the size of poor law pensions. Using figures for poor law unions' yearly expenditures on outdoor relief and the average number of paupers, Karel Williams has calculated the average weekly allowance given, assuming that all paupers got aid throughout the year. Grants ran about 1s. per head per week in the 1840s, rose to 1s. 6d. in the mid 1850s, and then slowly climbed to a level of 2s. per head per week in 1900.[9] Finally, in the 1920s and 1930s, poor law allowances increased sharply to between 5s. and 6s. a head weekly. Williams's figures are confirmed by local records of the actual sums transferred in weekly grants to the poor.

Pensions usually varied within a narrow range, although some unions were stingy and others were more generous. Some rewarded pious widows or the elderly, while penalizing the unemployed. Most gave more freely to familiar faces than to strangers. Who you were and where you were mattered, but not a lot. The elderly clearly received preferential treatment. David Thomson found that during the later 1830s, guardians in rural areas of Bedfordshire, Norfolk, and Suffolk gave single, elderly people 3s. a week on average. In 1863, medical officers reporting on laborers' incomes judged that elderly people got grants of about 3s. a week in a variety of urban and rural unions.[10] The strictest unions, however, used a lower standard: In Atcham, a rural union

---

[7] Ibid., 613.

[8] Ibid., 613–14.

[9] Williams overestimates the duration of aid but underestimates the numbers of recipients; the errors counterbalance each other; Williams, *Pauperism*, 169–72.

[10] David Thomson, "The Decline of Social Welfare: Falling State Support for the Elderly Since Early Victorian Times," *Ageing and Society* 4:4 (1984): 451–82.

near Shrewsbury where officials were especially miserly, elderly people on outrelief received only 1s. 6d. a week around 1850.[11]

Thomson's figures for pensions in rural areas are somewhat higher than recorded relief payments in the larger cities. Scattered figures for London unions, for example, show that they were less generous to their pensioners. St. Marylebone in London offered elderly couples on outrelief only 4s. a week, or 2s. per head. Single people over age sixty received either 2s. 6d. or 3s. a week. Those who were known to be working and earning some money got less.[12] In Chelsea, in 1834, payments to the elderly were 2s. or 3s. per person per week.[13] St. Giles in the Fields gave the elderly 2s. 6d. or 3s. per head per week; others usually were given only bread and relief in kind amounting to less than 1s. per head per week.[14] Pensions for the single elderly in Lambeth, as well as in the northern unions of Bradford and Huddersfield, ran around 2s. 6d. or 3s. a week during the 1880s.[15]

Figures of pension rates for younger people in London both around 1834 and in the later 1840s indicate that they had to be content with less than the elderly received. Widows with children in St. Marylebone got on average 1s. per head per person. In Chelsea, grants to female-headed households usually ran between 1s. and 1s. 6d. per head per week. Guardians in St. Giles in the Fields supported women at a similar level.[16] In towns outside the capital, grants were just as small. Bedford guardians gave women and families at most 1s. 6d. per head per week.[17] In Cambridge, in 1840, Charlotte Mott, a widow with three children, had a weekly pension of 3s. to support all of them;

---

[11] Shrewsbury Incorporation, "Applications for Relief; Atcham," B10-A, 83/221, Shropshire County Record Office.

[12] St. Marylebone, Board of Guardians, "Persons Receiving Outdoor Relief," St. Marylebone, 1847.

[13] St. Luke's, Chelsea, Middlesex, "Poor Relief Lists and Examinations, 1833–1846," Genealogical Society Archive, film no. 3585469.

[14] St. Giles in the Fields and St. George, Bloomsbury, "Application and Report Book, 1869," Ho. B.G. 509/1, Greater London Record Office.

[15] Lambeth, Board of Guardians, "A List of Persons Chargeable to the Parish in January, 1888" (London, 1888) La. B.G. 152/3, Greater London Archive; Huddersfield, Poor Law Guardians, "Lists of Paupers Relieved in Huddersfield District, 1881," Huddersfield Public Library; Bradford Poor Law Union, "Outdoor Relief Recipients, 1878," B362-53, Bradford; I would like to thank Karl Ittmann for this reference and material.

[16] St. Marylebone, Board of Guardians, "Outdoor Relief, 1847," Greater London Archive; St. Luke's Chelsea, "Poor Relief Lists and Examinations, 1833–1846," Genealogical Society Archive, no. 3585469.

[17] Amthill Union, Board of Guardians, "Early Application and Report Books, 1840–1841," PUAR 5/2, Bedfordshire Record Office.

Alice Coulson got the same amount.[18] Keith Snell has calculated a rate of 1.78 s. per week as an average cash payment for single-parent households in Yorkshire in the early 1830s during the final years of the old poor laws.[19] Listings from Lambeth, York, Bradford, and Huddersfield in the 1870s and 1880s show little change from earlier in the century: Female-headed households got between 1s. and 1s. 6d. per person per week.[20] Evidence from both urban and rural unions points to pension levels for adults below the age of sixty of 1s. to 2s. per head per week for the years between 1834 and 1890. Only the elderly got as much as 3s. per person per week, and these grants did not change much in size over the century.

What would this amount of money have purchased and what proportion of a subsistence income did it provide? The standard against which it is measured obviously makes a difference. David Thomson argues that pension provisions for the elderly were quite generous, perhaps 80 percent of a male laborer's weekly wage, but he uses a misleading standard based on agricultural wages in Bedfordshire, Norfolk, and Suffolk.[21] Agricultural laborers in the south and east could not have supported themselves on the amounts (3s. 6d. to 4s. 4d.) that he calculates as a weekly wage for the early and mid-Victorian period, and laborers elsewhere earned much more. In any case, by 1850, an agricultural laborer was no longer a typical English worker. England and south Wales were urbanizing at a rapid rate, and urban wages exceeded rural ones. A fairer comparison would be between pension levels and the weekly wages of an urban laborer. In addition, calculations should consider household incomes; low-wage people pooled resources in order to survive.

Poor law pensions for the elderly do not look generous when measured against recent calculations for the weekly wages of urban laborers in the first half of the nineteenth century. Payments to single-parent families or unemployed workers' households, which amounted to only a half or two-thirds of grants to the elderly, appear even more meager, when compared to family incomes during the same period. Jeffrey Williamson estimates that male unskilled laborers earned 15s. per week around 1835; a poor law pension for

---

[18] Cambridge Union, "A List of Paupers Who Have Been Relieved in This Union During the Quarter Ending Midsummer, 1840," P28/19/7, Cambridge Record Office.

[19] I have eliminated the sum he added for rent and miscellaneous payments that the New Poor Law eliminated. See K. D. M. Snell and J. Millar, "Lone-Parent Families and the Welfare State: Past and Present," *Continuity and Change* 2:3 (1987): 405.

[20] Lambeth, Board of Guardians, "A List of Persons"; York, Board of Guardians, "Application and Report Book for 1871," BG/YK Acc#2; Bradford Poor Law Union, "Outdoor Relief Recipients; Relief Arrangements, 1878," B362-53: Huddersfield Poor Law Guardians, "Lists of Paupers."

[21] Thomson. "Decline," 453, 457, 477.

an elderly person amounts to only 20 percent of that figure. Using wage figures for both agricultural and industrial jobs, Sara Horrell and Jane Humphries have calculated both average male earnings and family incomes in Britain for the period 1836–40; their figures translate into a male weekly wage of 7s. to 8s. per week and to a family income of 12s. per week for the households both of agricultural workers and of casual laborers.[22] Given those standards, an elderly person's grant amounted to between 37 percent and 42 percent of a male wage, and payments to a family of five calculated at a level of 1s. per head brought in 42 percent of a weekly family income among agricultural or urban laborers. Even in the early years of the New Poor Law, outrelief grants did not replace regular incomes. Later in the century, when money wage levels rose but relief grants did not, pensions gave paupers an even smaller share of the weekly incomes of employed workers. Outrelief under the New Poor Law did not replace either male wages or family earnings.

Another measure of the adequacy of outdoor relief would be to compare pensions with actual costs of living, using family budgets of low-skilled urban workers. In 1849, Henry Mayhew reported the weekly expenditures of an Irish streetsellers' family of five living in London. Because they lived in a slum and ate lots of potatoes rather than a proper English diet that included some meat and cheese, their living costs were close to rock bottom. Still, weekly expenditure amounted to 15s. 6d.: food 11s.; rent 2s.; fuel, clothes, and miscellany, 2s. 6d. per week. A second budget estimate for a lower-paid, unskilled urban laborer's family in 1860 also pegged living costs at 15s. 6d. per week. With this amount to spend, an adult male could buy food that would give him 2,900 calories a day, about the caloric level provided in English convict prisons around 1857.[23] Single people could have lived more cheaply, but they still required much more than the 1s. to 3s. provided weekly by the poor laws. Beds in the sleaziest London lodging house cost about 1s. per week, and even a diet of potatoes, bread, and tea enlivened by a few herrings cost almost 3s. per week. As part of his study of poverty in York, Benjamin Seebohm Rowntree in 1900 estimated the cost of a plain, subsistence level diet for an adult male, using data provided by the Local Government Board for

---

[22] Jeffrey G. Williamson, *Did British Capitalism Breed Inequality?* (Boston: Allen & Unwin, 1985), 12. Sara Horrell and Jane Humphries, "Old Questions, New Data and Alternative Perspectives: Families' Living Standards in the Industrial Revolution," *Journal of Economic History* 52:2 (1992), 871.

[23] W. A. MacKenzie, "Changes in the Standard of Living in the United Kingdom, 1860–1914," *Economica* 1:3 (1921): 228–9; Valerie J. Johnston, *Diet in Workhouses and Prisons, 1835–1895* (New York: Garland Press, 1985), 211.

workhouse inmates – scarcely a model of fine dining. In 1849, that diet could be purchased in Manchester for 4s. 3d.; its cost in York in 1899 was 3s. 3d. Note that both sums were substantially higher than the average weekly allowance for people other than the elderly.[24] When set against the cost of living, it is clear that poor law pensions did not even provide a subsistence diet for an adult male. Welfare grants would have paid the rent and perhaps a pittance for fuel or clothes. But if living on a poor law pension, recipients had to choose between food and shelter. Their relief money would not provide both.

Clearly some variation existed between regions and over time. People in Cumberland or north Wales probably fared better than their counterparts in London. In particular, those who could grow some of their own food had a substantial advantage over people who bought everything in the market. Rents were lower in rural areas than in the large cities. Moreover, the real value of poor law pensions changed over time because of fluctuations in price levels. Periods of deflation raised the real value of what people were given. The poor clearly benefited during the depression years of 1874–96, when food prices dropped sharply and remained lower than their 1870 levels until the beginning of the First World War.[25] Nevertheless, paupers still lived on very short rations. Outrelief was intended to be merely an income subsidy, not an income substitute. Neither at mid-century nor in late Victorian times did it provide complete support. For that, people had to enter the workhouse.

Targets of Relief in the Cities

Anyone with charity or relief to dispense soon discovered that needs were far greater than their resources. In an era when few of the elderly had private pensions, when rates of industrial accidents, adult mortality, and tuberculosis remained high, when families were large and many jobs insecure, the poor were not hard to find. The difficulty for administrators lay in choosing among them and in deciding what sort of support to offer. Who would be helped under what conditions? Although poor law guardians had the legal responsibility to offer aid to destitute people in cases of "sudden and urgent neces-

---

[24] John Foster, *Class Struggle and the Industrial Revolution* (London: Methuen, 1974), 255–6.

[25] Sauerbeck-Statist Price Index, in Brian Mitchell and Phyllis Deane, *Abstract of British Historical Statistics,* 474–5; see also P. Lindert and J. G. Williamson, "English Workers' Real Wages: A Reply to Crafts," *Journal of Economic History* 45 (March 1985): 145–53; and N. F. R. Crafts, "English Workers' Real Wages During the Industrial Revolution: Some Remaining Problems," *Journal of Economic History* 45 (March 1985): 139–44.

sity," they were free to determine not only the form, but also the targets of aid and its duration. By quibbling over entitlements, denying responsibility, and threatening removal of a person to another parish, administrators had many weapons to use to coerce applicants to withdraw. They could, and did, use these weapons selectively, privileging some groups and penalizing others. Applicants could, and did, challenge their decisions, and of course they had the right to refuse an offer and abort the relief process. One result of doing so, if their decision was made at an early stage of negotiations, might well have been the disappearance of their case from the public record. The destitute people we know about are those who chose to deal with administrators and who pressed their cases vigorously enough to create a paper trail.

Who were the people relieved under the New Poor Law? The idiosyncratic preoccupations of early administrators make it difficult to create a profile that makes sense in twentieth-century terms, but the statistics collected can be reworked to delineate sex, age, and household structure of those aided on sampled days around 1850. In the middle of the century, about 20 percent of the people listed as being on relief were adult males, 40 percent were adult females, and 40 percent were children. As the century progressed, the proportion of adult males slowly rose to 25 percent of the total in 1901, whereas the proportion of children shrank to 30 percent. Guardians acknowledged the support of twice as many adult women as adult men. Over time, children claimed a smaller share of aid, probably because of declining adult mortality rates and the decreased use of the poor law by working-class families, whose real incomes rose sharply during the second half of the century.

The people tallied can be distributed into groups that give information on age and physical condition. Karel Williams has divided paupers into (1) aged and infirm adults; (2) fatherless families; (3) the insane; (4) unemployed men; and (5) others, a category dominated by children (orphans, abandoned children, children of non-able-bodied adults) but also including vagrants and single women on relief. I have tabulated male heads of household and their dependents relieved on account of illness, accident, or sudden necessity and removed them from the category of "other" in order to give a more complete picture of families' use of the poor laws and create a category for male-headed households. (See Table 6.2.)

Dependence on the state, at least as reflected in the official records, arose from old age, illness, disability, and broken families. Even if the rhetoric of pauperism stressed moral decay, its statistics documented physical weakness and the results of high mortality. During the second half of the nineteenth century, the elderly and the infirm accounted for between 42 percent and 48

Table 6.2. *Changing composition of state support: Age and general health,*
1803–1911 (% of all paupers)

	1803	1851	1872	1891	1911	1931
Elderly and infirm						
Adults	16	42	44	47	41	31
Fatherless families		25	25	21	21	12
Unemployed men	84	1	1	1	2	4
Insane		2	5	10	13	10
Others		31	25	22	23	43

Source: Karel Williams, *From Pauperism to Poverty* (London: Routledge, 1981), p. 231.

percent of all the people relieved, whereas fatherless families – which comprised the households of widows, deserted wives, women with husbands in jail or in the military, as well as single women with children – made up between 19 percent and 25 percent of the total. People classified as insane, who were a group of negligible importance in 1851, amounted to over 12 percent of the total by 1901. As the medical services offered by the poor laws expanded, so did the group institutionalized in asylums. In contrast, official records list very few cases of unemployed males given aid. They are notable by their virtual absence from national tallies.

Local records can be used, however, to supplement this sketchy picture of the pauper host. In the larger towns, where most applicants would not have been known personally by welfare officials, documents to establish a person's legal settlement were collected both for people with local entitlements to relief and for those whose right to relief lay elsewhere. Normally, the person considered the head of a household unit was queried about his or her past work and family history, and the results were often checked against other sources and then sworn to in front of a magistrate. Because the questions asked by authorities followed quite similar patterns, the examinations provide comparable data on parishes and poor law unions across England for long periods of time.

In order to give a more complete profile of the pauper population, I collected a sample of examinations from several English towns for the years around 1820 and 1850.[26] The places I have chosen – three London parishes

---

[26] See Appendix for details on the sample and its coding.

(Hammersmith, St. Pancras, and St. Giles in the Fields, supplemented by material from St. Martin, Vintry, in 1820 only) and six towns (Bedford, Cambridge, Cheltenham, Shrewsbury, Southampton, and York) – represent the population of both the largest and the medium-sized towns. It includes data from north and south, and east and west England. I was, however, unable to find suitable records from a northern manufacturing center. Nevertheless, I would like to make the case that the sampled paupers represent the urban population that applied for welfare in the early and mid-nineteenth century.[27] About half of this group established their settlement in their parish of application; about half did not. These were people whose combination of needs, reputation, and probable entitlement induced poor law officials to take them seriously and check their stories, rather than frightening them away early in the welfare process. Although not all of them gained long-term public support, most were given temporary aid during the process of investigation. Many, however, would not have been included in the yearly tallies of paupers because their cases were not in process on either 1 January or 1 July of the year they applied.

The people examined by poor law officials in the towns at mid-century differed in three important ways from the population described in central poor law records. First, they include a wider group than those who were counted on sampled days. Second, they record information on kinship units. Because examinations covered people who applied together, they give us a glimpse of the households of the very poor, at points of maximum need. In the third place, they give some information on entitlements and outcomes, giving a clearer profile of public policies.

In the towns around the middle of the century, men and women applied for aid in roughly equal proportions. (See Table 6.3.) Most were adults between the ages of twenty and sixty. Indeed, few children or adolescents came to urban welfare offices on their own; most remained part of family units, spoken for by adults. About a quarter of the examined population was over sixty-five years of age. Although many more of the elderly applied for relief than their proportion of the population warranted, their dominance among paupers was less marked than at the end of the century.

The picture of paupers obtained from examinations directs attention away

---

[27] The demographic characteristics of the sampled paupers have been compared with those of the town in which they lived. Although they differed in some ways (age distribution, occupational profile) they were statistically representative of the whole in others–for example, sex ratios. I would like to thank Miriam King for her coding and analysis of this data.

Table 6.3 *Poor law applicants in English towns, c.1850*

	London (%)	Six county towns[a] (%)
Sex		
Females	43	52
Males	57	48
Ages		
<20	15	6
20–44	42	52
45–60	19	19
>60	24	23
Household structure		
Solitary	42	26
Married couple	27	35
Single parent	22	30
Other combination	9	9
Life-cycle stage[b]		
Young	62	42
Middle	23	34
Old	15	24
Coresident children under 16		
0	60	41
1	19	15
2	9	16
>2	12	28

[a]The London distributions and those of the six county towns have been compared using chi-square tests; in each case, the distributions are statistically different; $p < 0.001$.
[b]Percentages refer only to households of single parents or married couples. Solitaries, groups of siblings, and nonrelated people are excluded.
Source: Sampled poor law examinations from three London parishes (Hammersmith, St. Giles in the Fields, St. Pancras, $N = 274$) and six county towns (Bedford, Cambridge, Cheltenham, Shrewsbury, Southampton, York, $N = 316$). See Appendix for details.

from children and the elderly to the middle stages of the life cycle and to families, both female-headed and those of the two-parent variety. (See Table 6.3.) Although, in London, significant numbers of people applied individually for relief, most applicants who were examined by magistrates in the county towns were either couples or widows with dependent children.[28] Married

[28] The only way that these results can be made compatible with the tabulations of the Poor Law Commission is to assume that the category "aged and infirm" included large numbers of men under the age of sixty who were ill or injured and who were listed in that category, rather than as unemployed. Also, many adult males were given only small and temporary forms of outre-

couples, either with or without children, and single-parent families constituted about 65 percent of the examined applicants in the county towns and 49
percent in the metropolis. Most were in the young (wife under age forty-five;
all coresident children under the age of ten) or middle stages of the life cycle
(wife under age forty-five; at least one coresident child over the age of ten).

Unlike typical English families, which Peter Laslett calculates had a mean
size of roughly 4.75 people, pauper households were relatively small, having
on average only 2.89 people in them, in part because of the relatively high
proportion of single-parent families.[29] (Over 25 percent of the people examined were widowed, and an additional 9 percent claimed to be deserted by
their spouses.) London households of the very poor were particularly small.
Only 12 percent of the examined pauper households in London had more
than two resident children under the age of seventeen; the figure was 28 percent for the county towns. Unlike the often large middle-class families of
mid-Victorian times, the urban poor had few resident children. Many of their
children died in infancy or left in early adolescence to work elsewhere; others lived with relatives in difficult times. When the poor knocked on the
relieving officer's door, they came with kin, but in relatively small numbers.
Recourse to the poor law was a family matter, but that family was a truncated
unit, not representative of the households of the English population at the
time. Destitution acted to dissolve households, just as the dissolution of
households led to destitution.

Most paupers in my sample worked in relatively few occupations. Urban
male paupers were typically laborers, working on the docks or in construction. Some sold goods on the streets or processed food. If they were artisans,
as many of the poor were in London, they usually made clothing or simple
objects from wood or leather. Artisans were far more likely to have applied
for relief in the period around 1815 than at mid-century. Women for whom an
occupation was recorded worked in the needle trades or in domestic service.[30] Many had jobs as laundresses or charwomen; some hawked food on
the streets or sold flowers. Only rarely did a clerk, a shop worker, or a teacher
have to resort to the poor laws. Apparently, people with a toehold in the middle class could draw on enough other resources to avoid pauperism. Paupers
typically held low-skilled, low-paying jobs to which access was easy and in

---

lief – money for the burial of a child or a medical order for themselves or family. I suspect that
all of these brief encounters with welfare officials were not captured in official statistics.

[29] Peter Laslett and Richard Wall, *Household and Family in Past Time* (New York: Cambridge
University Press, 1972).

[30] For a description of such women, see Eileen Yeo and E. P. Thompson, *The Unknown Mayhew*
(London: Merlin, 1971), 120–6, 168–78.

which security was minimal. Not only were such trades overcrowded, but most were either not unionized or had large, nonunionized sectors in the mid-nineteenth century. In London and the county towns, the destitute worked in the least secure, worst-paying jobs. Because of an underrepresentation of artisans, people with factory jobs, clerks, and shop workers, they were not a cross-section of the urban labor force.

What had changed since early in the century? Those seeking welfare in the county towns around 1850 differed in several significant ways from the group under the old poor laws around 1815. (See Table 6.4.) In the earlier period, more applicants were male; moreover they were younger. More were married and had young children, and a significantly higher proportion followed skilled trades. They resembled more closely the working population of the town than did welfare applicants around 1850.

Women and Welfare

Most of the adults who received welfare aid after 1834 were women. The Poor Law Board reported on 1 January 1850, that 350,446 of 528,514 adults on relief were females, a rate of 66.3 percent.[31] These numbers represent recorded cases of paupers living in workhouses or asylums in addition to people receiving medical or other forms of outdoor relief from their parish or union on one sampled day. (The figures exclude vagrants, but they were a quite small proportion of the total.) This heavy feminization of welfare continued virtually unchanged during the rest of the century: About two-thirds of all adult paupers (excluding those in lunatic asylums) in both 1871 and 1900 were females.[32]

Women were prime candidates for poor relief. A depressingly long list of familiar problems – widowhood, longevity, desertion by husbands, child-rearing responsibilities, poor diets, and low wages – led them into welfare offices.[33] Nevertheless, the well-known weaknesses of women's social and economic position in Victorian England do not suffice to explain female pauperism for three reasons. First, the incidence of pauperism in England and Wales after 1834 was relatively low, much lower than rates of widowhood, desertion, and female unemployment, for example. Among those who lacked

---

[31] Poor Law Board, *Third Annual Report, 1850* (London: HM Stationery Office, 1851), 122–125.

[32] *Royal Commission on the Poor Laws and Poor Relief,* 1910, vol. LIII, 22–3.

[33] Pat Thane, "Women and the Poor Law in Victorian and Edwardian England," *History Workshop* 6 (1978): 33–5.

Table 6.4. *Occupational structure of welfare applicants, county towns,*
1815 and 1850

Trade	1815 (%)	1850 (%)
Laborer, building trades, transportation	15	44
Manufacture	41	22
Commerce, food sales	4	3
Service	29	22
Agriculture, gardening	12	9

(N = 339; chi–square = 33.008; $p < 0.001$.)

an adequate income, only a small share in any given year were granted parish aid. Second, rates of female pauperism varied substantially throughout England and Wales. A satisfactory explanation of female pauperism should take into account the contrast between the spatial distribution of females at risk of poverty and the uneven rates at which poor law authorities supported such women. Third, the status of the pauper was a contested, negotiated one, granted only after a process of application, discussion, and acceptance. The poor had to ask for aid from their union or parish, and then they had to convince inspectors and guardians of their inability to support themselves, as well as their right to relief. Before a woman received support, her story of destitution and entitlement had to be found acceptable; her demands had to be reconciled with local public policy.

In 1851, rates of pauperism for adult women varied substantially among the counties of England and Wales, when measured using the 1851 census and average figures for pauperism on the two sampled days of that year. Whereas only 3.6 percent of the women over age fifteen residing in Lancashire received poor relief in 1851, 11.9 percent of those in Wiltshire did![34] Heaviest in Wales, East Anglia, and most of the southern agricultural counties, female pauperism dipped sharply in the London area and in the industrial and urban counties of the Midlands and the north. (See Map 6.2 and Table 6.5.) At mid-century, pauperism among women showed a high degree of regional concentration.

In contrast, several of the conditions commonly blamed for women's pauperism – specifically widowhood, incidence of desertion, mean overall fertility – varied only slightly at the county level. County populations, whether in

[34] Poor Law Board, *Third Annual Report, 1850; Census of Great Britain,* 1851.

LEGEND:

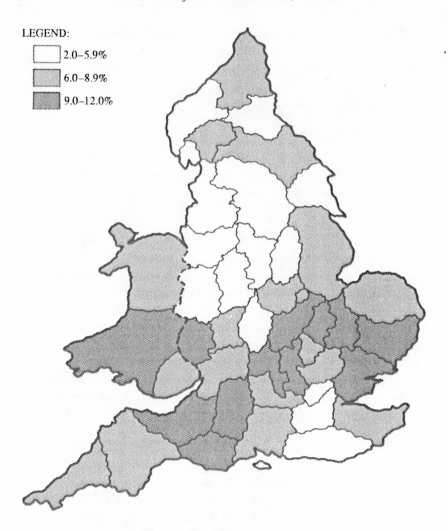

Map 6.2. Rates of Female Pauperism in English and Welsh Counties, 1851 (% of female population age 16 and over receiving relief, average of 1 January and 1 July 1851).

the northern pastoral areas, the grain-growing regions, or the industrialized districts had about the same proportions of widows and deserted wives, and similar overall fertility rates. In terms of these demographic measurements, the women of every county faced similar risks of pauperism. Other factors account for the clear regional differences in women's dependence upon public support.

Counties that were highly urbanized had the lowest proportion of adult

Table 6.5. *Female Pauperism in England and Wales, 1851–6*

County	Ratio of female to male paupers	Rate of female pauperism*	County	Ratio of female to male paupers	Rate of female pauperism*
Bedford	1.89	7.3%	Norfolk	1.94	7.7%
Berks	1.63	8.5	Northampton	2.15	9.0
Buckingham	2.03	11.2	Northumberland	3.09	8.3
Cambridge	1.89	9.8	Nottingham	1.94	5.2
Chester	2.17	4.2	Oxford	1.74	9.1
Cornwall	2.82	7.0	Rutland	2.09	6.7
Cumberland	2.46	5.8	Salop	1.82	5.2
Derby	2.10	3.7	Somerset	2.00	9.9
Devon	1.99	7.1	Southampton	1.92	7.6
Dorset	2.05	11.0	Stafford	2.12	3.4
Durham	2.79	5.9	Suffolk	1.63	9.6
Essex	1.62	9.3	Surrey	1.82	2.6
Gloucester	2.04	6.2	Sussex	1.48	5.8
Hereford	1.83	10.9	Warwick	2.26	4.6
Hertford	1.75	8.7	Westmorland	2.08	6.0
Huntingdon	1.88	9.9	Wilts	1.93	11.9
Kent	1.92	6.4	Worcester	1.99	8.5
Lancaster	2.00	3.6	West Riding, Yorkshire	2.75	3.9
Leicester	1.76	7.2	North Riding, Yorkshire	2.50	6.5
Lincoln	2.06	6.7	East Riding, Yorkshire	2.25	6.5
Middlesex	2.36	2.6	South Wales	2.80	11.6
Monmouth	2.16	6.4	North Wales	2.47	8.4

*Proportion of a county's female population age sixteen are over on indoor or outdoor relief, average figures for 1 January and 1 July, 1851.
Sources: Census of Great Britain, 1851; Poor Law Board, *Third Annual Report,* 1850.

females on poor relief. In 1851, there was a strong negative correlation between female pauperism and county rates of urbanization, as well as a positive correlation between female pauperism and the proportion of the county labor force employed in agriculture. Moreover, in districts where male wage levels were relatively high – in other words, the industrial and urban areas – women also faced a lower risk of becoming paupers. A county's economic base, therefore, would seem to have had a strong influence on the likelihood of pauperism among women.

Migration patterns also shaped local profiles of women's dependence. Districts that had a relatively high proportion of women age fifty-five and over also tended, not surprisingly, to have relatively high rates of female pauperism. Because the towns attracted young female migrants from the countryside, rural areas had an excess of women who were elderly. The linkage between poverty and old age helped to increase the rates of female pauperism in the largely rural counties of the west and south.

Rates of female pauperism also varied according to local poor law policies. Where authorities tended to use workhouses more frequently for their paupers, fewer women went on relief. Because towns had the most elaborate networks of welfare institutions, this inverse correlation of rates of pauperism and proportions of paupers in workhouses reflects local levels of urbanization. But it also captures the strong aversion of many paupers to the workhouse. If guardians forced a relatively high proportion of the destitute to use the workhouse, they were likely to have a lower rate of pauperism than did areas where outrelief was generously given.[35]

Local poor law authorities received only limited guidance from central authorities about the treatment of adult females. Clearly, the 1834 New Poor Law mandated welfare aid to women, but at what level and under what conditions? Sidney and Beatrice Webb called the intentions of the Poor Law Commissioners "indeterminate" on the issue of outdoor relief for able-bodied women, and they criticized the Poor Law Report of 1834 on the grounds that

the single independent woman is nowhere mentioned. The wife is throughout treated exactly as is the child; and it is assumed that she follows her husband. . . . With regard to the really baffling problems presented by the widow, the deserted wife, the wife of the absentee soldier or sailor, the wife of a husband resident in another parish or another country – in each case whether with or without dependent children – the Report is silent.[36]

Local authorities clearly had much independence during the 1830s in formulating policies toward female applicants. They were slowly constrained by regulations sent from London, but large loopholes remained. A House of Commons Select Committee in 1838 recommended that local guardians continue outdoor relief to widows with young, dependent children, as long as they considered carefully the character of the parties involved. By 1847, most

[35] See also Mary MacKinnon, "English Poor Law Policy and the Crusade Against Outrelief," *Journal of Economic History* 47:3 (1987): 603–26.

[36] Sidney Webb and Beatrice Webb, *English Poor Law Policy* (New York: Longmans, Green, 1910), 6.

poor law unions were covered by the Outdoor Relief Prohibitory Orders, which required the elimination of outdoor relief to able-bodied independent women but then listed several exceptions: (1) sudden or urgent necessity; (2) sickness, accident or infirmity in the family; (3) death in the family; (4) widows for six months and for an indeterminate time if they had dependent children and had not given birth to an illegitimate child after the death of a husband.[37] Because much destitution could be seen as deriving from these exceptions or from conditions that permitted a woman to be defined as not able-bodied, central regulations did not impose much constraint on local boards of guardians in the mid-nineteenth century. They did, however, set the parameters for thinking about female pauperism and establish the legitimacy of certain claims for outdoor relief. Widowhood, medical needs, child support, and physical debility, which could be interpreted to include old age, were privileged conditions, whereas unemployment was not.

The rules of settlement disadvantaged women in comparison with men. Females had fewer avenues to secure entitlement in the place where they lived and worked. Largely excluded from apprenticeship and officeholding and infrequently registered as renting houses or paying taxes in their own names, women usually had to prove their settlements indirectly through the rights of fathers and husbands. They therefore had to accumulate a store of family information about apprenticeships, jobs, migration, and house rentals in order to make a plausible case. That so many were able to do this effectively testifies both to the power of family oral histories and to women's awareness of the relevant legal categories. Commonly, they had to use information, rather than an apprenticeship certificate or a tax receipt, to establish eligibility. Virtually all the women applying for aid in county towns during the later 1840s claimed settlements on the basis of marriage or inheritance. Fewer than 10 percent had gained independent settlement through either apprenticeships or the rental of property; about 15 percent had worked for a year as a servant, usually as an adolescent, and had not acquired any subsequent right of residence. Only in London did a significant proportion of female relief applicants (30 percent) acquire settlement in their own right through the rental of property: The combination of high London rents and relatively high wages there gave widows and single women in the capital the chance to acquire local rights of relief.

Rose, Ashforth, and Boyer all argue that females living outside the parish of their fathers' or husbands' settlements were a population at relatively high

---

[37] Ibid., 36–7.

risk of removal. Rose mentions pregnant women and female-headed households as especially easy targets for officials eager to save money on welfare costs.[38] Female-headed households, orphans, and domestic servants, most of whom were women, comprised about 29 percent of the English paupers removed from Lancashire and 26 percent of those removed from West Riding parishes in the year 1841–2.[39] About 25 percent of the paupers removed from Bradford between 1840 and 1843 were unattached women.[40] Yet women comprised about two-thirds of all adult relief recipients; the figures suggest that women were removed less frequently than their numbers would warrant.

When face to face with the destitute, guardians had a range of determinations to make: eligibility, deportability, and the type of need. In each of these areas, concepts of gender interacted with law and administrative regulations to shape outcomes. Because poverty was endemic in the society around them and administrative regulations were ambiguous and weakly enforced, decision makers had some latitude for choice. Urged by the New Poor Law to discourage male pauperism, they had ample justification for discriminating against men in the provision of welfare.

There were, however, large regional differences in the willingness of guardians to slant aid toward females. The sex ratios among adult paupers in the counties of England and Wales in 1851 show a wide variance: Authorities in East Anglia and most of the south reported relieving, on average, 1.70 females for every male, whereas the ratio was about 2.50 per male in Yorkshire, Cumberland, Northumberland, and Wales, and around 2.10 in Lancashire, Staffordshire, Warwick, Cheshire, and Middlesex. (See Table 6.5.) In counties where there was a relatively high demand for female labor – in the dairying and pastoral economies of the north and Wales, as well as industrial and urbanized areas – guardians channeled relatively more welfare aid to women than did officials in the grain-growing counties. In the agricultural counties of the east and south, where opportunities for women's work had declined in the early nineteenth century, poor law guardians paid relatively more attention to male welfare needs than did their counterparts in the west

---

[38] Michael E. Rose, "Settlement, Removal and the New Poor Law," in Derek Fraser, ed., *The New Poor Law in the Nineteenth Century* (New York: St. Martin's Press, 1976), 39.

[39] George R. Boyer, *An Economic History of the New Poor Law, 1750–1850* (New York: Cambridge University Press, 1990), 251.

[40] David Ashforth, "Settlement and Removal in Urban Areas: Bradford, 1834–1871," in Michael Rose, ed., *The Poor and the City: The English Poor Law in Its Urban Context, 1834–1914* (New York: St. Martin's, 1985), 70–1.

and north. Their interest in retaining the male laborers needed for the harvest continued into the period of the New Poor Law.[41] Relative desirability in the labor market appears to have shaped the allocations of aid to men and to women. Those needed were those aided.

Yet a direct connection between unemployment and poor law aid to adult women is difficult to discover in poor law records. After 1834, entitlement for women rested on other conditions, both in the minds of officials and among applicants. During the later 1830s, women listed as "out of work" still constituted one of the groups recognized by the welfare bureaucracy; they remained so through the 1840s. But, after 1851, the out-of-work female disappears from central poor law records. The official reasons for aiding women shrank to include only their family status, physical and mental health, or the health of family members.

If local poor law records are surveyed for the years around 1850, it is clear that single women continued to apply to the poor law and to be investigated, but most of them had a claim on welfare funds based on problems other than unemployment. In a 10 percent sample of poor law examinations from six towns in selected years during the decade of 1840–50, single women between the ages of twenty and sixty formed one-fourth of the females investigated.[42] Yet in none of their examinations was loss of work noted by officials. Examiners mentioned illness, disability, and pregnancy, but did not probe current employment history. In the rural union of Atcham near Shrewsbury, case histories from 1849 and 1850 mention a few young and single women with local settlements, but all were listed as either sick or disabled, rather than out of work. A few unemployed, single domestic servants appear in Southampton records for the period 1845–50, but they, too, were recorded as sick or pregnant.[43] Destitute, single women seem to have been investigated by poor law officials when they could claim aid because of a physical problem or when they needed child support.

Of course, women continued to be out of work. Ellen Jordan argues for "endemic female unemployment" between 1851 and 1911 in most parts of England and Wales.[44] She points to the high proportion of teenage girls (ages

---

[41] George R. Boyer, *An Economic History of the New Poor Law, 1750–1850* (New York: Cambridge University Press, 1990).

[42] See Appendix for more information.

[43] Southampton, Board of Guardians, "Register of Examinations, 1845–1858," SC/A9, Southampton City Archive.

[44] Ellen Jordan, "Female Unemployment in England and Wales, 1851–1911: An Examination of the Census Figures for 15–19 Year Olds," *Social History* 13:2 (May 1988): 175–90.

fifteen to nineteen) who were recorded in the census as having no occupation, although few were married at that age and most were expected to contribute to their own support.[45] Rather than attributing teenagers' low employment rates outside the textile districts to either underrecording or voluntary absence from the labor force, she believes that large amounts of structural unemployment for women were built into British labor markets and remained unacknowledged in the census.

Occasionally during periods of high unemployment, charities and welfare officials recognized women's need for work. During the Lancashire cotton famine in 1862–3 when many of the mills closed and others went on short time, thousands of female workers lost their jobs. Initially, guardians concentrated on married men, offering them work on the roads or stone breaking for a small daily wage. But by the fall of 1862, churches in several of the Lancashire towns ran sewing schools for women. One in Blackburn paid women eight pence a day for up to three days a week to produce clothing.[46] Several others operated in the smaller towns of Leicestershire for three months during the winter of 1863, until they closed for lack of funds.[47] This kind of public recognition of female unemployment was rare, however.

Even the women who went to the relief offices usually told stories about family and life-cycle crises, rather than unemployment. In my sample of examinations drawn from London and from six county towns in the 1840s, most females explained their situations in terms of widowhood, desertion, pregnancy, sickness, or old age. They told overseers the stories that would be most likely to produce help; on the other hand, there might well have been gender differences in the way that the destitute conceptualized the reasons for need. In the long correspondence carried on by Stephen Garnett, overseer and later guardian of the poor in Kirkby Lonsdale, Westmorland, with people wanting nonresident relief, men and women told different sorts of stories.[48] His male correspondents, scattered through the industrial towns of Lancashire and West Riding, usually recounted tales of layoffs, short time, injuries, and eviction. During the mid-1830s, women recounted family woes,

---

[45] Ellen Jordan, "The Exclusion of Women from Industry in Nineteenth-Century Britain," *Comparative Studies in Society and History* 31:2 (April 1989): 273–96.

[46] Webb Local Government Collection, Part 2, The Poor Law, vol. 310, British Library of Political and Economic Science, London School of Economics.

[47] Ibid., vol. 311.

[48] Although the Poor Law Commission restricted its use drastically, prohibiting it to able-bodied males between sixteen and sixty except in cases of sickness, accident, and urgent necessity and blocking new cases under all but temporary emergencies, people already receiving it could continue to do so; see Webb and Webb, *English Poor Law Policy*, 53.

alternating between stridency and obsequiousness. Rachaell Boothman, writing from Carlisle in May 1835, had for some years received an allowance from Kirkby Lonsdale, which supplemented her and her children's earnings as bobbin winders. Her husband had died in 1827, leaving her with two small children. After spending about six weeks in a Cumberland workhouse in 1828, she discharged herself and went back to work. At some later date, she left the parish and succeeded in getting a nonresident's allowance from Kirkby Lonsdale, which she claimed as necessary for child support.[49] Mary Grime sounded a similar note in May of 1835 and successfully arranged for a weekly grant of five shillings per week for herself and her young "very delicate" son. After informing Garnett of her husband's desertion, she continued, "I wish to know whether you will consider to allow me Something towards maintaining me and my son or you will send a cart for me as I am not able to come of myself. You will please to be as quick as possible as I have nothing to take to or otherwise I shall be obliged to apply to the Overseers of Langcliffe for Reliefe. Gentlemen, I leave this to your candid consideration."[50]

Poor law records for the port city of Southampton recount many female demands for aid, most of which were linked to particular family problems. Sarah Burnett, a widow with three children, asked for welfare at least five times during the later 1830s and 1840s. In these encounters, she clearly negotiated about the types of aid needed and timed requests effectively. Although she had an acknowledged settlement via marriage in the Hampshire market town of Beaulieu, she had to support herself and her family there after her husband's death. After she was widowed, Beaulieu overseers granted her a small allowance and apprenticed her son to a ship's captain. One daughter was put in the workhouse, where she remained for unknown reasons; a second daughter was kept by Burnett.

Southampton records trace a series of encounters between Burnett and both Hampshire and Dorset poor law guardians, which illustrate the ways in which welfare aid was intermittently claimed and manipulated by Burnett in order to maintain herself and her household. Two years after her husband's death, Burnett moved to Southampton, the nearest large town, where she worked as a laundress and a lodging housekeeper. Meanwhile, her income continued to be subsidized by a weekly grant from Beaulieu. After six years,

---

[49] Kirkby Lonsdale Township letters, 30 May 1835, no. 47, 1 June 1835, no. 46, (CRO/K); I wish to thank James Stephen Taylor for allowing me to use his microfilms of this collection from the Cumberland Record Office.

[50] Ibid., 17 May 1835, no. 53.

she moved to a small port town in Dorset with one of her male lodgers, remaining there for one year and bearing an illegitimate child. During a period of illness, she asked Dorset guardians for temporary outrelief and medical aid, which they granted for three months; by this point, her partner had disappeared, and she seems to have concluded that she would be better off back in Hampshire, where she had greater claims on local authorities. Soon Burnett asked for and received a grant to allow her to return to Southampton, where she promptly asked local guardians for passage to Beaulieu. Once back in her husband's parish, she entered its workhouse with at least one child; there seem to have been no local relatives willing to support her. After six months in the workhouse, she discharged herself and her family, returning to Southampton, where she got work and reestablished an independent household. When, four years later, she again had financial troubles and applied for relief, Southampton authorities granted her a small pension, but soon began proceedings to have her removed to Beaulieu, where authorities were still legally obligated to maintain her. For a period of about fifteen years, Burnett headed a single-parent household, obtained welfare grants to supplement a low income, and raised two of her children herself, migrating from time to time to try to improve her circumstances.[51] She advanced successful claims for aid on the basis of widowhood, sickness, and a lack of local settlement. Her low wages must have been taken into account, but they seem a secondary consideration in her negotiations with poor law officials.

Like Burnett, many widows with young children found themselves in need of parish assistance.[52] Few workers' families had savings, and private insurance benefits were small. As a result, widows and their children normally found themselves thrown on their own resources soon after a spouse's death. Because the law clearly recognized their rights to a weekly pension and other services, turning to the poor laws was an obvious way of supplementing meager incomes. Nevertheless, application was a bit like a lottery with familiar, but shoddy prizes. You could never be sure you would win anything that would be of use.

To those who asked and were judged to be entitled, the poor laws offered pensions, medical services, vaccinations, funerals, legal help against absent

---

[51] Southampton, "Register of Examinations," 1850, 206.

[52] During the early 1840s and 1850s, widows with children under the age of sixteen who received poor law aid on the days when statistics were collected represented between 35 percent and 39 percent of all widows in England and Wales between the ages of twenty and forty-five; the proportion aided during an entire year would have been much higher. See Williams, *Pauperism,* 199.

husbands, foster homes, apprenticeships, and schooling for children, as well as complete care in institutions. Some unions had better facilities than others, of course, and guardians differed in their willingness to take on custodial care. Welfare in practice, therefore, lacked the uniformity and predictability of an insurance system. Outcomes could differ for members of the same household, and they certainly varied across England and Wales.

A look at the outcomes of welfare applications shows the range of possible treatments. In the six county towns whose applications I sampled for the period around 1850, 9 percent of the adult females applying were offered medical relief or burial payments only, 57 percent were granted allowances in money and in kind, and 33 percent were offered care in an institution. Welfare aid was linked most commonly to a workhouse or infirmary for pregnant women, the more seriously ill, and the elderly who could no longer live independently and had no kin willing or able to care for them. The workhouse also offered a temporary refuge for female-headed households when the women could no longer pay rent or found themselves homeless for other reasons. During a period of several years, women like Sarah Burnett used a variety of poor law services as their needs dictated. I suspect that they ignored offers of welfare aid that they did not find useful in the short run. The poor were consumers in a welfare marketplace, and they could and did refuse services that did not meet minimum criteria for acceptability.

Although allowances and workhouse care were the main forms of relief on offer, poor law authorities quickly developed other options, which they offered selectively to applicants. A look at the treatment of female paupers in a rural union well known for its strictness shows how aid was administered there. Around 1850, the Atcham guardians investigated several households of poor widows with young children whose members were settled in the union. Because those families were clearly entitled to welfare, the generous solution would have been to offer a weekly cash grant. But this is not what happened in most cases. Guardians granted medical help to all who claimed sickness, but other forms of outrelief were hard to come by. For one family, the guardians offered to vaccinate the children. For another, they said they would support one child in the workhouse, so that the mother would have fewer mouths to feed. In other cases, they paid for a burial and then a temporary grant, which would be followed by the workhouse if the widow did not quickly become self-supporting.[53]

In urban areas by the later 1840s, authorities had a longer list of options.

---

[53] Shrewsbury Union, Atcham, "Applications for Relief, 1849–1851," B10-A, (Shropshire Record Office).

After building asylums, schools, dispensaries, and hospitals, they worked to fill them. London and Manchester guardians sent children to large boarding schools, and staffs of doctors attached to the larger unions attended the sick in their homes, as well as in the sick wards. Poor women gave birth in workhouse infirmaries, and their children got free vaccinations in the local dispensary. London guardians offered institutional care most freely, in large part because of the wide range of facilities in the capital. In 1850, 22 percent of all paupers recorded on 1 January in the metropolis received some form of indoor relief; the rate was only 13.2 percent for England and Wales as a whole. In Wales, only 4 percent of all paupers on that date went into an institution.[54]

In most parts of England, women with dependent children typically received a weekly allowance, which functioned as an income supplement. In the six county towns I sampled, 40 percent of the female household heads who applied for welfare received pensions in the period around 1850, some temporarily and some for relatively long periods. Virtually all the female household heads applying in Southampton between 1846 and 1850 got weekly payments in cash and in kind.[55] Although London authorities led the drive to institutionalize paupers, even there, over two-thirds of the adult women drawing welfare on sampled days in the 1860s got outrelief grants.[56]

Local records show how the system worked in the county towns. In Bedford, authorities offered young unmarried women medical help and 2s.–3s. a week during a short period after childbirth. Several female lace makers about forty years old who lived with dependent children got allowances of between 1s. 6d. and 2s. 6d. when ill and out of work.[57] Female household heads under age sixty with dependent children made up about 14 percent of the welfare cases registered by Cambridge guardians in the midsummer quarter of 1840. Those who were recorded as "infirm" and one woman with an illegitimate child were offered workhouse relief; the rest – 10 percent of the total – received small pensions, on average 2s. per week. The typical subsidy for a female-headed household was less than 1s. per head per week.[58] Those who asked for more found themselves either denied or removed from the city, if

---

[54] Poor Law Board, *Third Annual Report, 1850,* 124–7.

[55] Southampton, Board of Guardians, "Register of Examinations," 1846–50, SC/A9.

[56] *Royal Commission on the Poor Laws,* PP 1910, LIII, 14.

[57] Amthill Union, "Application Books, 1840–1841," vol. 2.,

[58] Cambridge Union, "A List of Paupers Who Have Been Relieved in This Union in the Quarter Ending Midsummer, 1840," P28/19/7, Cambridgeshire Record Office.

their entitlements were not secure.[59] These pensions should be seen as modest income subsidies. They did, however, give women an incentive to remain in places where they could add welfare aid to the income of low-wage jobs. By pooling the family's incomes and adding a welfare grant, they could survive. The outrelief system helped to tie women into the labor markets of areas where they were legally settled. It was an insurance policy against destitution that restricted their mobility.

Elderly women were somewhat better off, except in unions determined to hold down relief costs. But under the New Poor Law, they too had to pull together an income from a variety of sources in order to survive. The records of the rural union of Atcham give a rare look at the makeshift economy of elderly paupers in a union that practiced the deterrence that all preached. Elderly women made up the lion's share of new cases between 1849 and 1851; 36 percent of the households investigated were headed by women over age sixty and an additional 10 percent included a wife over age sixty. Guardians offered most of the single, elderly women who had some resources of their own only 1s. 6d. per week to supplement their resources; a few elderly married couples had pensions of 2s. a week. But even in Atcham, such grants did not stretch very far. Because a cottage plus garden rented for £2–£5 per year, a typical poor law pension barely paid for housing. If a pauper wanted to maintain an independent household, other income was needed. In Atcham, elderly women worked in the fields earning about 8d. a day. Others knit, dyed stockings, or took in washing. One old woman collected manure on the roads and sold it for fertilizer. These rural women worked as much as they were able to well into their seventies.

Jane Tudor, a single woman of eighty-two who had lived in the union all her life, could earn 8d. a day from time to time as a field laborer, and she took care of a lodger in her cottage. For food, she grew potatoes in her garden, and sometimes neighbors gave her small gifts or aid. In 1849, local guardians offered her medical relief during an illness, but at that time she was offered nothing else.[60] Another elderly widow lived with a son's family, and they supported her because she was too weak to work. After the son's death, her daughter-in-law continued to provide housing but not clothing or food. Because the woman's other married sons each had eight children, guardians realized the futility of pursuing them for their mother's support. In this case, they offered an allowance of 1s. 6d. per week. The rather flinty Atcham

[59] Cambridge Union, Guardians of the Poor, G/C/As26, 39, no. 18, 8 April 1847.

[60] Shrewsbury Incorporation, "Applications for Relief," B10a, 83/221–2, 14 May 1849, 39, no. 10.

guardians assumed that elderly women would work as long as they were able, and they knew enough about local employment opportunities and family resources to estimate incomes and living costs. For the most part, they gave allowances only to those women who had kin or neighbors with whom they could live. Others who needed more help were offered the workhouse.

Under the New Poor Law, women kept their entitlement to outrelief, although it could be grudgingly given and painfully inadequate. Trapped in a low-wage, limited labor market, they had to draw on multiple sources of support and be flexible in the face of personal disasters and hard times. Piecing together their private resources with some public aid kept them and their families alive. When measured against the insecurities inherent in the early capitalist economy, this looks like scant protection. But it was better than nothing at all.

The Dubious Entitlement of Males

The Poor Law Commission wanted to deny just that sort of minimal protection and support to men. In their orders to local authorities, they tried to stop wage subsidies and family allowances to employed males. But just how effective was their attempt to cut off welfare to male workers after 1834? Because adult males made up about one-fifth of the people officially recorded as receiving aid around 1850, they were not totally ignored by welfare officials. Yet total amounts of welfare to men would seem to have dropped in comparison to the Speenhamland years of the later eighteenth century and early nineteenth century. Under the New Poor Law, the labor market problems of men got less attention than they had earlier in the century. Karel Williams argues that by the early 1850s, "a line of exclusion was drawn against able-bodied men," who were effectively barred from gaining relief until after World War I.[61] Certainly, guardians did not report to central poor law authorities the granting of outdoor relief to many able-bodied males out of work. Reports of the Poor Law Board count unemployed males as being 1 percent or less of the entire group relieved outside the workhouse.[62] But, as Williams notes, unemployed males could have been relieved in the workhouse and recorded under other headings or not listed at all; yet he discounts these possibilities. William Apfel and Peter Dunkley agree. Using data for rural Bedfordshire in the 1830s and 1840s, they find that guardians offered able-bodied males the workhouse and did not continue to give them outdoor

---

[61] Williams, *Pauperism,* 75.

[62] Ibid., 231.

relief. But few healthy males entered the workhouses; they preferred to take their chances in the labor market just as the Royal Commission predicted.[63]

Poor law records do indicate aid to able-bodied males for reasons other than unemployment. For example, in 1850, about thirty-one thousand able-bodied men officially got outrelief because of illness in the family or because of unexplained emergencies; they accounted for 3.6 percent of the total number of paupers, which does not represent a major share of welfare cases.[64] The official records no doubt misrepresented some recipients, but they do not register in any form substantial numbers of adult males.

Some unions adopted the New Poor Law with a vengeance, making it almost impossible for adult males to get aid. In the rural parish of Atcham, where officials were known for their enthusiastic adoption of deterrent principles, adult male household heads got almost no relief during the later 1840s. In records for the years 1849–51, the only male household heads under the age of sixty who got outrelief were listed as blind, rheumatic, dying of lung disease, or injured on the job. One destitute, asthmatic itinerant peddler was offered the workhouse.[65]

Using sources from a different region, where less rigid officials made welfare decisions, Anne Digby disputes this cutoff of aid to unemployed men. She explains that guardians in East Anglia listed unemployed workers as being sick or as having a sick family member in order to give them outrelief without violating Poor Law Commission directives.[66] The assistant commissioner for Wales charged that the orders prohibiting outdoor relief were so frequently evaded that they were hardly worth the paper they were printed on![67] George Boyer's recent analyses of the economics of the agricultural labor market during the 1830s and 1840s show how it was in farmers' economic interest to continue to employ laborers seasonally and to offer outrelief during the winters, but he sees this practice decreasing where central administrators succeeded in imposing the workhouse test.[68]

---

[63] William Apfel and Peter Dunkley, "English Rural Society and the New Poor Law: Bedfordshire, 1834–1847," *Social History* 10 (1985): 41–6; see also Boyer, *Economic History,* 204.

[64] Williams, *Pauperism,* 190; and Poor Law Board, *Annual Reports,* 1858–61 (London: HM Stationery Office, 1859–62).

[65] Shrewsbury, "Applications," 5 November 1849, 56.

[66] Anne Digby, "The Rural Poor Law," in Derek Fraser, ed., *The New Poor Law in the Nineteenth Century* (London: St. Martin's, 1976), 158; idem, *Pauper Palaces* (London: Routledge, 1978) 110–14.

[67] Quoted in John V. Mosley, "Poor Law Administration in England and Wales, 1834–1850, with Special Reference to the Problem of Able-Bodied Pauperism," Ph.D. diss., University of London, 1975, 307–9.

[68] Boyer, *Economic History,* 216, 231–2.

Unemployed men certainly went to welfare officials and claimed support. In Hammersmith in May of 1848, William Vernum asked for relief for himself, his wife, and an infant daughter. Claiming "want of employment," he told officials that he had been working in local market gardens and also in a ginger beer factory. Because he had been in the parish only for seven or eight months and was legally settled in Clapham, Hammersmith guardians checked his story and gave responsibility for him to that union, which acknowledged his settlement. Neither Hammersmith nor Clapham authorities ignored him.[69] Daniel Watts, a thirty-three-year-old sawyer who was also a migrant into the parish, applied for relief for himself and his family in 1848 "because I have nothing to do." Because he had lived in the parish for about twelve years, he was not removable, and Hammersmith had to grant relief.[70]

Local records show that in many places large numbers of men continued to apply to welfare offices, at least through the 1840s. During 1840 and 1841, 70 percent of the applicants for aid in the Bedford Poor Law Union were men. In the quarterly totals reported for the winter of 1839 to the Poor Law Commission, men made up 50 percent of the adults relieved, a rate significantly higher than the average for the country as a whole.[71] In the six county towns whose examinations I sampled, about half of the people applying for relief in selected years during the 1840s were male. Moreover, the large majority of them were married and between the ages of thirty and sixty. Most headed households that included children under the age of sixteen. If they are compared with the women who went to relief offices in these same towns, many more of them lived with a spouse. Then, just as today, single-parent families on welfare were headed by women. (See Table 6.6.) Although the men and women examined by welfare authorities had similar age structures, their family lives were quite different. Male-headed households included more children; they were larger on average and were more likely to be in a middle phase of the life cycle.[72]

The men on welfare in the county towns were the same sorts of people who had gotten family allowances and income subsidies under the old poor laws but were supposed to be denied under the amendments of 1834. Young

---

[69] Hammersmith Union, Board of Guardians, "Settlement Examinations, 22 April 1848–21 February 1851," P80/P pau/15, 194, Greater London Record Office.

[70] Ibid., 199.

[71] Poor Law Commission, *Sixth Annual Report*, Appendix. (London, 1840); idem, *Seventh Annual Report*, (London, 1841). See also Amthill Union, "Application Books, 1840–1841."

[72] I have defined the middle stage of the life cycle as a wife under the age of forty-five and at least one coresident child age ten or over.

Table 6.6. *Welfare applicants' households: County towns, 1840–50*

	Females (%)	Males (%)
Solitary	26	26
Married couple	6	62
Single parent	55	6
Other combinations*	13	6

(N = 313; chi–square = 140.316; $p < 0.001$.)
*grandparent and child, siblings, and unrelated individuals

unmarried men did not use the poor laws to any great degree, but in the later stages of the life cycle, recourse to welfare was much more common. In these six towns, 77 percent of the male applicants were given some sort of relief – 35 percent went into an institution, 15 percent got medical aid or funeral payments, and 50 percent were given outrelief, generally of a temporary sort. The examinations of 10 percent of the men listed them as being out of work. For example, St. Botolph, Cambridge, gave one middle-aged railway worker and his family outrelief and medical aid in 1847 for several months when he lost his job after becoming ill. Although he did not have a settlement in the parish, he had married in the city eight years earlier and had been living there since 1839. They noted that he had "bad legs," as well as a liver complaint, and they were prepared to support him for an extended period.[73]

A similar set of examinations sampled for London in 1849 and 1850 show that adult male family heads made up about half of the male applicants.[74] About a third had more than one child. They received much less generous treatment than men in the county towns, however. Among those for whom officials recorded their decisions, 61 percent had to enter an institution and 20 percent got no aid or were passed to another union; only 7 percent got outrelief or medical aid. About 10 percent were treated as vagrants and given a night in the workhouse and then pushed out. Both in the capital and in the county towns, men were somewhat less likely to be given outrelief than were female applicants, but similar proportions of each group were offered care in

[73] St. Botolph, Cambridge, Overseers of the Poor, "Settlement Papers, 1840–1849," P26/13/3, G/C/As 22, 20 December 1847, Cambridgeshire Record Office.

[74] Hammersmith, Board of Guardians, "Sworn Examinations, 1848–51;" St Giles in the Fields, Holborn, "Examinations of Paupers, 1849"; St Pancras, Board of Guardians, "Sworn Examinations, 1850–1."

an institution. Differences in the profiles of the types of relief offered to men and to women during the 1840s were not statistically significant.

These results are clearly at variance with the portrait of poor law aid found in national records. Because local officials had few poor law inspectors looking over their shoulders, they had considerable freedom over their welfare decisions and controlled the tabulations reported to London. No doubt there was much regional and local variation in policies toward men, but I suspect that a high proportion of the unemployed married men with families who got poor relief simply did not make it into national records. Those who refused to enter the workhouse could be ignored; migrants just passing through the parish did not need to be listed. Inefficiency probably led to the undercounting of the many requests for medical aid and short-term grants, which the relieving officer or doctor could decide upon on the spot.

It is also plausible to suggest that local guardians manipulated their records and treatment of the unemployed in order to avoid trouble with the Poor Law Board and Poor Law Commission. John Mosley, who argues that outdoor relief to able-bodied males remained high at least until 1850, maintains that parishes used the highway rate to raise funds for public employment. Because proceeds were under the control of overseers but not subject to central review, funds could be used freely to provide jobs for surplus labor without accountability. Parishes also sponsored private rates or special subscriptions to fund soup kitchens or outdoor relief during depressions or harsh winters, and he cites cases of parishes using such evasive techniques to continue outdoor relief in Sussex, Dorset, East Anglia, Oxfordshire, Gloucestershire, Wales, Lincolnshire, Shropshire, Staffordshire, Worcester, and Warwick. In his opinion, the support for unemployed laborers did not change radically during the early years of the poor law although it was clearly funded and administered in a different way.[75] The Poor Law Commission may not have succeeded in cutting off aid to the unemployed, but it did manage to force support for this group outside the normal administrative procedures for the poor law.

This hypothesis of continuing public support for the unemployed – albeit at an unknown level – gains plausibility when policies toward them in the period 1875–1905 are examined. During the depression at the end of the century, aid for the unemployed regained political legitimacy, but the mechanisms for implementing it remained separate from the poor law. Particularly in the cities, special funds were collected to provide public works jobs for

[75] Mosley, "Poor Law Administration in England and Wales," 207, 305–9.

unemployed laborers. The Unemployed Workman's Act of 1905 codified practices that had been used in bad times since the 1830s.[76]

Soup kitchens and a few public works jobs on the roads offered cold comfort to the high proportion of unemployed British workers who were skilled and had been decently paid. For them, the poor law and its offshoots did not compensate adequately for their losses of income and status. Their recourse lay elsewhere. Many unemployed men simply traveled during depressions to look for work. Eric Hobsbawm has described the cultural practice of tramping by artisans.[77] Particularly during the early and mid-nineteenth century, when the economies of regions within Britain were not tightly linked, a migrant could escape recession in one district by moving to a more prosperous community. Trade societies encouraged members to move by offering relief payments at "houses of call" in towns across the country if work could not be obtained there. Migration was a standard means of escaping unemployment. Using the records of the Steam Engine Maker's Society between 1835 and 1846, Humphrey Southall argues for the "remarkable" mobility of its members, of whom 17 percent moved in the depression year of 1840. For those who belonged to the union six years or more, 64 percent moved at least once and 21 percent moved four or more times during a period of ten years, with the bulk of the moves concentrated in times of recession. Southall presents a picture of English skilled workers as people in motion; long-term stability of residence was the exception rather than the rule. Drawing on census data, he shows that the rates and distances traveled by artisans were not all that different from those of unskilled workers. Migration rates among workers have probably been seriously underestimated.[78]

Poor law records indirectly confirm men's migratory habits. Deserted wives regularly applied for poor law aid after their husbands disappeared. George Grigg walked out on his wife and three children in September of 1846. Soon after, Mary Ann Grigg became destitute and applied for poor law aid in the parish of St. Martin in the Fields, London, where the family was living. Overseers took the family into the workhouse, although they did not have a local settlement and had been in the parish for only six months. Five months later, when Grigg had not reappeared, guardians established that the legal settlement of the family was in Margate, Kent, and began efforts to

---

[76] See José Harris, *Unemployment and Politics* (Oxford: Oxford University Press, 1972).

[77] E. J. Hobsbawm, "The Tramping Artisan," *Economic History Review* 3 (1951): 299–320.

[78] Humphrey R. Southall, "The Tramping Artisan Revisits: Labour Mobility and Economic Distress in Early Victorian England," *Economic History Review* 44:2 (1991): 283, 286, 294.

remove them.[79] Guardians sometimes complained that periods of high unemployment brought higher numbers of abandoned families into their offices.[80]

Artisans also left Britain for North America. Arthur Redford claims that all the major trades joined in the rush overseas during the depression years of the 1840s. Local commentators in Bolton mentioned the departure of iron founders, engineers, millwrights, and machine makers – the sort of men who rarely applied to the poor laws for help but still ran a major risk of unemployment. During 1840 and 1841, people left the wool-manufacturing areas of West Riding at a yearly rate of 62 per thousand.[81] Later in the century, British trade unions mounted extensive campaigns to encourage and finance emigration by members in periods of depression. Because many accepted the predictions of the classical economists, the notion that the exodus of some would raise the wages of those who remained found a ready audience. During the Lancashire cotton famine of 1861–5 and the lockout of iron workers of 1865, workers and union officials repeatedly called for assistance in emigrating. They linked the wish to move to North America with a desire to escape pauperism. In fact, during the 1860s, many northern unions offered an emigration benefit, or a subsidy for migration, as a standard payment available to members, and a variety of such groups spent several hundred pounds each assisting unionists to move across the Atlantic between 1860 and 1880. The Colonial Land and Emigration Commissioners counted over 500,000 skilled workers leaving the United Kingdom between 1862 and 1885.[82] Whatever the attraction of starting a new life in Canada or the United States, part of the emigrants' impetus was certainly dissatisfaction with conditions at home and with their options in periods of depression.

British men faced with unemployment and the hated workhouse had clear alternatives: They could remain in their community of origin waiting for better times and rely on kin, past savings, charity, casual earnings, and possibly small amounts of help from the poor law. Many obviously took this route. Nevertheless, the scare tactics of welfare bureaucrats worked to make this solution unappealing. Migrating remained an attractive option, given the

---

[79] St. Martin in the Fields, Board of Guardians, "Sworn Examinations, 1840–1870," 2 March 1847, Greater London Record Office.

[80] Webb and Webb, *Policy*, 175; Thane, "Women," 33.

[81] Arthur Redford, *Labour Migration in England*, 2nd ed. (Manchester: Manchester University Press, 1964), 123; E. H. Hunt, *Regional Wage Variations in Britain, 1850–1914* (Oxford: Oxford University Press, 1973).

[82] Charlotte Erickson, "The Encouragement of Emigration by British Trade Unions, 1850–1900," *Population Studies* 3:3 (1949): 264.

multiple opportunities to be found in the several industrializing regions of both North America and the British Isles. Information about other cities and regions was easily accessible. Friends and kin who had followed a chain of migrants elsewhere beckoned, while welfare officials and trade unionists waved goodbye.

No Irish Need Apply

Because poor law officials paid more attention to entitlement than they did to destitution, the welfare claims of Irish migrants often fell on deaf ears. Although their potent combination of poverty, dirt, and disease could not be completely ignored, the rules of the poor law game allowed many of them to be shunted aside or removed to Ireland. As recognizable outsiders in the parishes where they lived, they were easy targets for administrators eager to save money and curry favor with angry taxpayers. Largely without political clout or local defenders, the Irish poor got the leavings at the already scanty poor law table until late in the nineteenth century, when changed conditions of access to welfare aid forced local officials to deal more seriously with their problems.

Dislike of the Irish, especially destitute ones, ran rampant in England. Blamed for their poverty and choice of housing, Irish were widely targeted as social menaces out to exploit the English welfare system. In 1834, George Cornewall Lewis, who later became one of the English poor law commissioners, completed a study of the Irish poor in Great Britain for which he interviewed employers and local officials in major British towns. After several months of research, he concluded that the average Irish migrant came to Britain hoping to get rich, but failed miserably. As a result, he said, they applied to public and private charities, as well as the poor law, which had "a very hurtful effect on them." With money in their pockets, they could indulge "vicious appetites" and revel in "mischievous luxuries." The provisions of the poor laws supposedly led them into deceit and violent, abusive behavior. Lewis quoted a Manchester overseer's complaints: "[T]hey are always plaguing us; they expect us to find everything, bedding, clogs, clothing, food, physic, and medical attendance; and they will be saucy beside."[83]

Sympathy for the needs of Irish migrants was in short supply during the 1830s among English poor law officials, who worried about public liability

---

[83] George Cornewall Lewis, "Report on the State of the Irish Poor in Great Britain," PP 1836, XXXIV, vi, xviii, xxiv, xlviii.

for their support. By 1841, about 290,000 Irish-born lived in England and Wales, and another 125,000 in Scotland. Few had skilled, secure jobs, and unemployment rates for laborers were high. Because Irish migrants could legally reside where they wished in England, local officials could do nothing about their movement into a parish. Not only were they British citizens, but after 1795, they could only be removed if they applied for and accepted relief. Moreover, English law required that destitute wayfarers, casuals, and those lacking settlements be given short-term aid in the place where they applied until such time as they could travel to the parish of their legal settlement. Because the cost of removing a pauper to Ireland was relatively high in terms of money, time, and trouble, officials wanted to use that particular weapon sparingly. But their other options were limited.

Moreover, overseers and guardians assumed that virtually no Irish-born migrants had a clear, legal entitlement to relief in England. In 1836, Lewis concluded that few had earned legal settlements because few had been apprenticed in England or been hired on a yearly contract. Moreover, settlement through property ownership or parish officeholding was out of reach for the Irish poor. Welfare rights came to second-generation Irish because of birth in England and to women who married an English man with a secure settlement, but these numbers were not large during the first half of the nineteenth century. Virtually the only easy way for an Irish-born person to secure settlement was through the rental of property for at least a year at a rate of over ten pounds a year or four shillings a week. In cities where both rents and wages were relatively high, such as London, this path could be followed by those with secure jobs. Another, more chancy route to settlement came via long-term residence. Lewis claimed that in both Liverpool and Manchester, authorities treated ten years' residence in a parish or township as the equivalent of settlement, although they were not legally liable to do so.[84] Yet such practices depended upon the good will of administrators, who were responsible to local taxpayers. Irish entitlement to welfare in England was precarious at best.

English law treated families as units and made women and children share whatever fate poor law authorities decreed for husbands and fathers, but when families headed by Irish males broke up, English law granted independent rights to their English-born dependents. The children of migrants acquired settlements in the parishes where they were born that became operative after they reached the age of sixteen.[85] Such children, if deserted, had to

---

[84] Ibid., xxiii.

[85] *Report from the Select Committee on Poor Removal*, PP 1854, XVII. 32.

be relieved in England in their parish of settlement. Migrants' English-born wives, if deserted, were treated as single women; they reacquired their maiden settlement rights and were sent back to that parish if they required relief.[86]

The claim of Irish migrants on the English poor laws became stronger after the Poor Removal Act of 1846, which outlined the status of "irremovability" protecting long-term residents of a parish from expulsion if they accepted relief under the poor laws. Five years' continuous residence brought a pauper freedom from removal and a presumptive right to local relief; later acts of 1861 and 1866 lowered the requirement to one year's residence.[87] And to make the changed rules of liability more palatable, Parliament decreed in 1847 that relief costs for nonsettled, nonremovable paupers were to be shared among all the parishes of poor law unions, rather than being assessed to the specific district in which they resided.[88]

But the group covered by the poor removal acts was not clearly defined, nor was the concept of "residence." Did Parliament intend it to protect the Irish? Legal disputes began almost immediately. An act of 1845 specifically provided that people born in Ireland, Scotland, and the Channel Islands could be removed to their birthplaces, if they had no legal settlement in England and if they became chargeable to the poor laws.[89] Did the later acts supplement or supersede it? Moreover, the Poor Removal Act of 1861 implied that the Irish were to be treated differently from the English. Migrants who had left Ireland within the previous twelve months could be removed to any parish mandated by justices of the peace, whereas those who had been in England longer had to be sent to the most convenient Irish port. Because the major thrust of the law was to protect destitute English people from being removed at all from places where they had resided for a year, Parliament seemed to be differentiating the status of the Irish-born from that of the English. Herbert Davey argues that Irish rights under the laws remained vague for years; only after 1900 was a residence requirement of five years specified for the Irish-born, which guaranteed their irremovability.[90] But legal irremovability by itself did not put food on the tables of the Irish poor. They still had to persuade local officials of their destitution and their local entitlement.

---

[86] Herbert Davey, *Poor Law Settlement and Removal*, 3rd. ed. (London, 1925), 256–8.

[87] 9 & 10 Victoria, c. 66; 24 & 25 Victoria, c. 76.

[88] *Report from the Select Committee on the Irremovable Poor*, PP 1860, XVII, 2.

[89] 8 & 9 Victoria, c. 117.

[90] *Report from the Select Committee on the Irremovable Poor*, PP 1858, XIII, 1, 3–4. Davey, *Settlement*, 255.

After 1846, the Poor Law Commission brought pressure to bear on local officials to treat settled and irremovable paupers equally, although many resisted.[91] Several parishes complained to the Poor Law Commission that their relief costs had doubled after 1846, once nonremovable paupers had to be aided; others simply ignored the act. In 1847, J. T. Rowsell, Clerk of the City of London Union, protested against "our being called upon to give relief to those cases which really do not belong to us."[92] A poor law official from Manchester feared that English towns would be "inundated" by the Irish as a result of changes in legal liability.[93] Because the central Poor Law Commission was short on personnel and enforcement mechanisms, they could do little to force resistant officials to aid the Irish-born who had resident rights. Moreover, Irish paupers continued to be removed to Ireland in large numbers; they surface in local welfare records primarily when guardians took measures to get rid of them.

Just how heavy a welfare burden was produced in England and Wales by the Irish-born is difficult to determine with precision. It differed widely from place to place. Early in the nineteenth century, Irish use of the poor law in most provincial towns was minimal. But, around 1815, they made up 30 percent of the applicants examined in St. Giles in the Fields and the Liberty of Saffron Hill, Holborn; by 1850, in those same areas, their proportion had increased to about 50 percent of relief applicants. Most of the settlement examinations for Lancashire and other northern areas of heavy Irish residence have long since been destroyed, making an estimate impossible for those regions. Parliament, however, collected data on the numbers of paupers removed to Ireland until late in the century, when officials turned their attention to other problems and began to ignore the question of paupers' birthplaces.

The point at which to begin a more systematic survey of Irish paupers in England is 1834, when the Royal Commission on the Poor Laws asked local officials to specify the numbers and ethnicities of people in their parishes who lacked settlement rights. Hundreds of parishes replied. At that date in southern and eastern rural areas, the Irish welfare problem was nonexistent. Few lived permanently in rural areas of the Midlands, the north, or Wales. Although Irish harvesters came seasonally into the Isle of Ely, the Isle of

---

[91] Bermondsey, St. Olave's Union, "Signed Minutes," vol. 5 (4 July 1844–28 January 1847), 569, 612; (5 October 1846; 10 December 1846), Greater London Record Office.

[92] *First Report from the Select Committee on Settlement and Poor Removal:* 19 February 1847, PP 1847, XI, 7–10, 18–21.

[93] *Sixth Report from the Select Committee on Settlement and Poor Removal,* PP 1847, XI, 100–104.

Thanet in Kent, and a few parts of Lincolnshire and Northumberland, no rural parish complained of a permanent Irish influx. Only where there was industry – railway construction in Cumberland, a vitriol works in Newton Borough, Lancaster, for example – had more than a handful of Irish moved in. Around 1834, welfare officials in agricultural areas had nothing to complain about.[94] Of course, overseers had helped to produce this result through their treatment of the migrants who passed through their areas. As one man from a Yorkshire parish near Wakefield told the Royal Commission, "Irish and Scotch in Stanley cum Wrenthorpe find no rest for the soles of their feet."[95]

By the mid-1830s, large numbers of Irish poor had settled into a relatively small number of British towns. Moved across the Irish Sea by steamboat, they were most numerous in the largest ports and from those places had moved inland. Poor law officials in Oldham, Preston, Wigan, and Barnsley reported that several hundred Irish poor lived in their towns. Overseers in Chatham, Kent, claimed, "[W]e are overrun with Irish!"[96] One Birmingham official reported "very numerous Irish," but he did not seem worried. "Were it not that we remove all who become chargeable, I have no doubt that they would greatly increase," he added frankly.[97] Some of the largest settlements of Irish poor were in London, where they had gathered by the thousands in the back alleys along the river and in central districts.[98] Hundreds of Irish asked for welfare every year in St. Giles in the Fields and Holborn; moreover, many had clear entitlements because they could document their rental of local property at rates of more than ten pounds per year. Yet few London overseers complained to the Royal Commission in 1834; officials implied they had the Irish problem under control. Consider the report from St. Leonard, Shoreditch:

The Irish are very numerous, and in my opinion would be more so, and certainly be still more troublesome to the Parish were they not deterred by the fear of being passed. If by any means they could be fixed upon the Parishes, they would not only increase by importation in myriads, but struggle less by hard work, & etc., to keep from the Parish.[99]

As a statement of policy, the St. Leonard assessment was probably typical.

---

[94] *Report from Her Majesty's Commissioners for Inquiring into the Administration and Practical Operation of the Poor Laws,* Appendix B1, Answers to Rural Queries, part 1, London: House of Commons, 1834, 30–625.

[95] Ibid., 630.

[96] Ibid., Appendix B2, part 4, 57–77.

[97] Ibid., 239.

[98] Lynn Hollen Lees, *Exiles of Erin* (Manchester: Manchester University Press, 1979).

[99] *Report . . . on the Poor Laws, 1834,* Appendix B2, part 4, 174.

Each year around 1830, Middlesex parishes sent about 1,500 Irish-born back home, more than enough to show that poor law authorities frowned on Irish welfare applications. Liverpool passed back to Ireland over 2,700 paupers per year around 1830, and other Lancashire towns together sent around 3,300.[100] The practice of sending home Irish paupers was well established; for the price of £1 10s. per head a contractor would transport a destitute Irish pauper from the metropolis back across the Irish Sea, and the cost was certainly less from towns on the west coast.[101]

The Irish shifted from being a minor welfare nuisance to a major expense and problem during the 1840s, when migration intensified and the potato famine turned the act of repatriation from an inconvenience into a possible death sentence. The size of the Irish welfare burden in England during the famine years cannot be determined, but it is clear that the number of applications for relief skyrocketed in the towns of heavy Irish settlement. The Irish-born accounted for 25 percent of the settlement cases included in my sample of London welfare applicants in 1849, at a time when the Irish-born made up at most 5 percent of the total population.

London authorities reacted to this intensified welfare burden with hostility, as well as decisive action. More and more Irish were spirited back to Ireland and dumped at the major ports. The guardians of the poor of Cork Union complained in 1842 to the Lord Lieutenant of Ireland that "[f]or the last two years it has been the practice of the parochial authorities in London and its adjacent districts to send over weekly by the steam packets plying between London and the port of Cork all persons born in Ireland who were alleged to have become chargeable . . . and had not obtained a settlement in England." Apparently people from all over Ireland found themselves dumped in Cork with no means of getting home.[102] Both London and Lancashire parishes continued to repatriate Irish paupers in significant numbers during the potato famine. Between 1845 and 1849, over 26,000 Irish-born were removed from Lancashire towns.[103] Comparable figures for the metropolis are not available,

---

[100] *An Account of the Number of Paupers Removed to Ireland in the Years 1823–1831*, PP 1837–8, XXXII, 353.

[101] *Report . . . Respecting the Regulations for the Removal of Scotch, Irish, and Other Paupers, 1850*, H.O. 45/ O.S. 3040, Public Record Office.

[102] "Memorial of the Chairman and the Guardians of the Poor of Cork Union to His Excellency Thomas Earl de Grey, Lord Lieutenant and General Governor of Ireland, Jan. 29. 1842," H.O. 45/360, Public Record Office.

[103] *Return of the Numbers of Orders of Removal . . . in England and Wales for Each of the Last Five Years, Specifying the Number of These Who Were Irish and Scotch Paupers . . .*, PP 1850, L, 31.

but J. Rankley, one of several contractors who shipped Irish paupers back home from London, reports that he sent back over 5,000 from 1847 through 1849. And both London and Liverpool continued to export paupers at a rapid clip through the early 1850s.[104] For the most part, guardians in Chelsea sent back young women who had recently arrived, but they also sent older men who had lived in England for substantial periods of time.[105] Although the number of Irish passed home represents a small fraction of the Irish-born residing in central London, they indicate that the Irish faced a continuing risk of deportation if they dared to ask for welfare.

At least in London, local guardians perceived the Irish as a major welfare problem. In January of 1847, the relieving officer of Bermondsey Union apologized to the Board of Guardians for not having his weekly report finished; at least two hundred cases had not been entered in the books because of "the unprecedented pressure of the Irish for relief and their very riotous conduct during the past, the preceding, and the present weeks." He claimed to have been putting in fourteen-hour days, six days a week in the welfare office attending to business, and had called out the parish constables to defend the workhouse from attack.[106] In 1850, guardians in Marylebone, Westminster, Fulham, and Clerkenwell protested the financial burden of Irish poverty, given the new irremovability of long-term residents. The parish clerk in Fulham told of the Irish laborers who worked on local market gardens during the summer but were discharged in the winter and applied for relief. The board felt it could not afford to remove them to Ireland, nor could it support all of them in the off-season.[107] Whitechapel guardians accused Irish steamship companies of dumping Irish paupers in the metropolis in order to extort high fares for their return trips and complained bitterly of the "serious and increasing evil" of Irish pauperism in their midst. Although they seemed willing to provide for long-term residents, they saw recent Irish migrants as interlopers who unfairly burdened taxpayers.[108] The St. Olave, Southwark, response to

---

[104] *Report from the Select Committee on the Removal of Irish Poor,* PP 1854, XVII, 547; *Return of the Number of Paupers Removed to Ireland in 1849–1854 from Parishes or Unions Within the Metropolitan District of the Registrar General,* PP 1854, LV, 305, 327.

[105] St. Luke's, Chelsea, Board of Guardians, "Orders of Removal, Scotch and Irish Paupers, 1842–1850," Greater London Record Office.

[106] Bermondsey, St. Olave's Union, Board of Guardians, "Signed Minutes," vol. 4 (5 November 1845–27 September 1848), 645–7.

[107] *Report . . . on Removal of Scotch, Irish and Other Paupers 1850,* H.O. 45/ O.S. 3040.

[108] Stepney, Whitechapel Union, Board of Guardians, "Signed Minutes," vol. 12, (March 1850–April 1851), 15 April 1851, 481, Greater London Record Office.

many Irish claimants was to give a bit of short-term relief, followed by the offer of either passage to Ireland or their withdrawal of claims for aid.[109]

But whatever response they faced, many Irish managed to get relief during the later 1840s and early 1850s. The Irish were strongly overrepresented in most metropolitan workhouses in 1851. Over 20 percent of the adult inmates in the Whitechapel and St. Giles workhouses in 1851 were Irish born, whereas the rate was over 10 percent in Kensington, Marylebone, St. James Westminster, St. Olave's Southwark, Greenwich, and East London.[110]

Even if guardians tried to ignore destitute migrants fleeing the Irish famine, they had to cope with the Irish during the cholera epidemic of 1849. In Southwark and Stepney, cholera erupted first in areas heavily settled by Irish migrants. Irish homes and neighborhoods quickly became major targets for attention from parishes' medical officers; the sick were whisked away into cholera wards at the workhouse or into special fever hospitals; the dead got parish funerals, while cleaning crews whitewashed walls and scraped up muck and refuse. Guardians in Stepney had to ask local priests to assure the Irish poor that the quarantines and cleansing were for their benefit and to "recommend habits of personal and domestic cleanliness."[111] Self-interest clearly led parish officials to expand their aid to the Irish during the epidemic; yet suspicion of Irish migrants continued. Doctors and poor law personnel, who believed that dirt caused disease, fastened on the Irish as the producers of the afflictions under which they suffered. Pointing to the filth and over-crowding of Irish neighborhoods, George Cornewall Lewis flatly announced that "they are frequently the means of generating and communicating infec-tious disease."[112] The medical officer in St. Olave's Union, Bermondsey, tar-geted Irish laborers as a local medical and relief problem. He added: "The imperfect drainage, the accumulation of Filth, the uncleanly habits of the Poor and the crowded state in which they live are general causes operating in the production of these diseases."[113] Although he credited the important con-tributions of the open sewers and dirty privies, he pointed his finger first at the dirty Irish.

[109] See Bermondsey, St. Olave's Union, "Signed Minutes," vol. 4, passim.

[110] Census manuscript schedules: H.O. 107/1468; H.O. 107/1485; H.O. 107/1488; H.O. 107/1559; H.O. 107/1526; H.O. 107/1580; H.O. 107/1508; H.O. 107/1587; H.O. 107/1545, Public Record Office.

[111] Stepney, Whitechapel Union, Board of Guardians, "Signed Minutes," vol. 10 (December 1848–February 1849), 604.

[112] Lewis, "Irish Poor," xi.

[113] Bermondsey, St Olave's Union, "Signed Minutes," vol 2., 30 April 1838, 211.

Yet if welfare records for areas outside of Lancashire and London are examined, the burden of Irish destitution during the 1840s and early 1850s seems to have been moderate. Most of the counties of England and Wales sent back to Ireland fewer than thirty paupers during the entire famine period.[114] In Bristol in 1851, the Irish-born constituted 3.4 percent of the population, but only 2 percent of the paupers in workhouses or on outdoor relief. A few local charities, such as St. Peter's Hospital, the Royal Infirmary, the Mendicity Society, and the Refuge for the Homeless, served a much more heavily Irish clientele, but apparently poor law officials had managed to limit their support.[115] In my sample of relief applicants drawn from six county towns during the 1840s, the Irish-born constituted only 5 percent of the people whose settlements were formally examined, most of whom were granted relief. Because the Irish-born comprised less than 5 percent of local populations in Bedford, Cambridge, Cheltenham, Shrewsbury, and Southampton, they might well have been overrepresented on welfare rolls in those towns; yet in no sense did they overwhelm local ability to deal with their destitution. Moreover, authorities in the county towns sent back virtually no Irish paupers to Ireland during the famine. They apparently did not feel a strong need to move destitute Irish out of their cities in order to keep them from becoming a welfare burden.[116] In York in 1851, a smaller percentage of the Irish-born showed up on relief lists (6.4 percent) than among the total population (7.2 percent), despite the presence in the city of hundreds of Irish with insecure jobs and low incomes. Poverty did not bring automatic entitlement.[117] In much of England and Wales, the Irish were not a serious burden on the poor laws during the first half of the nineteenth century, an astonishing conclusion given the lurid pictures of Irish poverty and dependency circulated in the popular press as well as public opinion.

In the longer run, however, acute need diminished, but entitlement rose. Families with local employment histories replaced the half-starved wanderers of the 1840s. The numbers of migrants deported from the country dropped

---

[114] The only counties that sent more were Chester, Lancaster, Middlesex, Stafford, Warwick, the West Riding, Gloucester, and Glamorgan, all areas that offered atypical amounts of industrial employment. *Return of the Number of Orders of Removal . . . in England and Wales for Each of the Last Five Years,* PP 1850, L, 43.

[115] David Large, "The Irish in Bristol in 1851: A Census Enumeration," in Roger Swift and Sheridan Gilley, eds., *The Irish in the Victorian City* (London: Croom Helm, 1985), 38, 55–6.

[116] *Return of the Number of Orders of Removal,* PP 1850, L, 31.

[117] Frances Finnegan, *Poverty and Prejudice: A Study of Irish Immigrants in York, 1840–1875* (Cork: Cork University Press, 1982), 111; see also Frances Finnegan, "The Irish in York," in Swift and Gilley, *Irish,* 59–84.

sharply during the 1860s, signaling a more relaxed attitude to Irish welfare claims. Then, too, Irish access to welfare eased because of irremovability. In York, 35 percent of all welfare applicants were Irish-born by 1861 and they made up 43 percent by 1871, years in which they made up about 8 percent of the city's population.[118] These figures exaggerate somewhat the financial drain on the city, for most of the Irish made claims because of sickness or pregnancy, which brought only short-term aid.[119] Nevertheless, the York Irish represented the city's most visible welfare problem in the two decades after the famine.

In London in 1861, the Irish could still be found in metropolitan work-houses far more frequently than their proportion of the total population war-ranted, and even in 1881, when only 2 percent of all Londoners were Irish-born, Irish migrants accounted for 20 percent of workhouse inmates in St. Giles and Holborn and over 6 percent in Shoreditch and Camberwell.[120] Their London-born children also received substantial amounts of poor law aid. The district and industrial training schools had hundreds of Irish children in them, as did the workhouses.[121] The issue of whether to give such children Roman Catholic or Church of England religious instruction agitated many on both sides of the issue, but the children's entitlements to relief was not debated. The Irish constituted a major burden on English welfare institutions in the second half of the nineteenth century in the towns where they settled and established residence rights.

The issue of ethnicity in the allocation of welfare raises the question of equality, as well as quantity of service. What treatment was meted out to the destitute Irish? Many guardians and overseers went out of their way to announce their unwillingness to deal with Irish destitution as a legitimate claim on the poor laws. In 1858, a Wolverhampton guardian claimed "that it was well known that the Irish poor would have parish pay if possible," and he attacked proposed changes in removal rules that would make it more difficult to send the Irish home.[122] That some guardians continued to bend the law to

---

[118] Finnegan, *Poverty,* 111.

[119] Ibid., 111–14.

[120] In 1861 Irish-born made up about 14 percent of the inmates in the St. Pancras and West London workhouses; see census manuscript schedules, R.G. 9/216; R.G. 9/118; they were 13 percent of the inmates in the Marylebone Workhouse (R.G. 9/76), 11 percent in Lambeth (R.G.9/347), and 8 percent in Greenwich (R.G. 9/403). For data on workhouse populations in 1881, see R.G. 111 324; R.G. 11/409, Public Record Office.

[121] H.O. 45/6840, June 1859, Public Record Office.

[122] *Wolverhampton Chronicle,* 6 June 1858.

the detriment of Irish paupers is clear from the number of cases of illegal removals reported to the Poor Law Board and investigated by it during the 1850s and early 1860s. Limerick authorities complained in 1853 that Bridget Garrey, three English-born children, and a grandchild were forcibly put onto a London steamship by guardians of St. Luke, Middlesex, and then deposited in their midst, even though she had no claim on Limerick and had not only lived in St. Luke for sixteen years but had gotten relief from them at two earlier dates after her husband died. Garrey had apparently gone into the workhouse briefly and then asked to be discharged when she was hustled down to the port. In its defense, St. Luke's guardians said that they had gotten a legal deportation order some weeks before and told Garrey that any additional requests for support would mean removal. When she appeared again, they pounced.[123] In the fall and winter of 1861, forty-six cases of illegal removals and irregular procedures were reported by Irish authorities to the Home Office in England. Several London unions merely gave paupers a ticket for deck passage on a steamer to Cork or Dublin, plus a little money to pay for their transportation home when they landed. Marylebone sent the Breen family of five to Limerick, although they had lived in London for twenty-three years and originally had been residents of Cashel. The Poor Law Board claimed it could do little to enforce the law when local magistrates would not. Generous, humane treatment for the Irish poor was not high on the list of priorities of London poor law officials.[124]

Yet such qualities did not characterize treatment of the English poor either. I have compared samples of English and Irish relief recipients in St. Giles in the Fields, London, during the years 1830–3, testing to see whether the populations and the decisions taken by poor law officials in their cases were statistically different or not. (See Table 6.7.) In demographic terms, the two groups resembled one another: They had similar household structures and numbers of coresident children, although more Irish paupers were elderly, male, and widowed than among the English group. The destitute Irish were more likely to work as street traders or unskilled laborers than their English counterparts; therefore, they were more economically vulnerable. Around 1830, the St. Giles overseers recommended different sorts of policies toward the two groups: Most of the English applicants got outrelief or were given a

---

[123] *Correspondence Between the Poor Law Board, Whitehall, the Poor Law Commissioners in Dublin, and the Guardians of the Parish of St. Luke, Middlesex, relative to the Removal of a Pauper family of the Name of Garrey from the Port of London to the Port of Limerick,* PP 1852–1853, LXXXIV, 1–5.

[124] "Removal of Irish Paupers from England, 1861," H.O. 45/O.S. 7253, Public Record Office.

Table 6.7. *Ethnic differences in treatment of paupers, St. Giles in the Fields, London, 1830–3*

Policy	Irish-born (%)	Non-Irish (%)
Passed\denied aid	30	0
Outrelief	15	5
Workhouse	48	7
Pension	0	29
Casual relief	6	58
Duration of relief		
Under 1 year	78	4
1–5 years	22	29
Over 5 years	0	67

(N = 88; chi–square = 58.315; $p < 0.001$. Sample comprised one-tenth of the total cases.)

pension, whereas if the Irish did not go into the workhouse for aid or accept passage to Ireland, their claims were denied.[125] In addition, Irish paupers were given aid for much shorter periods. Before 1834, therefore, welfare authorities in central London turned a different face to English and Irish.

If a similar comparison is made for the period around 1850 in London using data from St. Giles, St. Pancras, and Hammersmith, the results are strikingly different. At that time, English and Irish got essentially equal treatment. Similar proportions of each group had to enter the workhouse; similar proportions were turned away or passed out of the union. About the same number got temporary outrelief or medical care.[126] Irremovability meant that more of the Irish had to be given aid locally, whereas the provisions of the New Poor Law streamed more away from outrelief into the workhouses. In other words, after 1834, treatment of English paupers in St. Giles declined to the point where it resembled that given earlier to the Irish. Equality had come at a price.[127]

---

[125] This data relates to a 10 percent sample (N = 98) drawn from St. Giles in the Fields, Holborn, "Examinations of Paupers, 1831–1833," Holborn Public Library. The distributions of relief given to the Irish and non-Irish are statistically different; chi square value = 58.315; $p < 0.001$.

[126] These data relate to the London 1850 sample described in Appendix (N = 274). The distributions of the type of relief given were not statistically different for English and Irish applicants. The figures are as follows: Institutionalization – E. 66 percent, I. 56 percent; outrelief – E. 22 percent, I. 23 percent; passed or denied – E. 13 percent, I. 21 percent.

[127] Although policy choices in London do not represent those of the entire country, they show how the poor laws were interpreted in one important area of Irish residence.

Applying for welfare aid under the New Poor Law resembled the purchase of a raffle ticket for a set of not-very-desirable prizes. Although the prizes warranted an expenditure of time and effort, they did not solve the problems of the destitute, and no one expected them to do so. At most, welfare provided an additional resource for fragile family economies. But by applying for aid under the poor laws, people asserted their membership in a local community and, usually, present or past participation in a local labor market. They signaled belonging, a sense of entitlement. Relief, both in the giving and in the receiving, solidified relationships of interdependence. Whatever the public rhetoric of "pauperism" and the spirit in which relief was dispensed, the poor laws transferred income and services from the propertied to the propertyless.

PART THREE

RESIDUALISM REEVALUATED AND REJECTED, 1860–1948

B Y THE TIME the gears of the New Poor Law were fully engaged, its cumbersome machinery faced multiple tasks for which it was not designed, and shifts in political power brought increasing conflict into normal procedures. Largely a response to rural poverty and seasonal underemployment among unenfranchised male farm laborers, the New Poor Law had to cope during the second half of the nineteenth century with an urbanized, mobile labor force and with cyclical changes in employment, rapid shifts in technology, and increasingly powerful and organized groups of trade unionists. Social engineering recipes from the 1830s, which ordered deterrent workhouses and strict limits on outdoor relief, quite obviously could not cure widespread pauperism during an industrial depression, such as that of the Lancashire cotton famine, nor did they sit well with workers elected to either national or local governments.

Nevertheless, workhouses had a bright future; when reconfigured into hospitals, hospices, orphanages, and old age homes by social workers and medical personnel, they became the sites for massive efforts of rehabilitation. In the eyes of its practitioners, welfare came to mean therapeutic intervention to save the destitute from themselves, rather than subsidies for incomes. Administrators, reformers, and social theorists modified aid to the destitute in the interests of efficiency and community benefits. Less wary of state action than their early Victorian predecessors and energized by a positivist faith in social science, they aspired to control poverty and the poor scientifically, using institutions to compensate for defects in the social environment.

They did so within a changing intellectual and political context, in which the deprived became more demanding and more powerful. The growth of a populist liberalism brought legitimacy to workers' claims for active citizenship. Then, as growing numbers of male workers gained the vote, those men also gained a public voice on welfare issues. When elected to boards of guardians or to Parliament, they acquired both an audience and legitimacy for the interests they represented. Women's voices added to the chorus through charitable groups, boards of guardians, and local lobbying efforts. The unemployed marched in the streets, while the poor brought discussions of benefits and entitlement into welfare offices and social theorists pushed for reforms.

Welfare theory and welfare practice in the later nineteenth century encompassed an extraordinary range of positions and styles. Welfare was a contested arena both in its analysis and its implementation. Contradictions abounded. Less was defended as more; discipline was said to bring freedom. The same people would be offered medical care freely but denied outdoor relief that could be used to buy food for the sick. A town during one winter might provide public works jobs for unemployed male adults – and nothing for women out of work – whereas the next year only the workhouse or a few pennies for smashing stones would be on offer. Welfare theory and practice embodied multiple, and inconsistent, Victorian attitudes and rejections, as well as an unstable balance of power. Karel Williams quite correctly rejects portrayals of the New Poor Law after 1870 as either oppressive or progressive, describing the law as "an apparatus that intertwined repression, classification, special treatment, and surveillance . . . it is more like a Barthesian text than a Foucauldian institution."[1] Variance was built into the system because it was contested, locally administered by elected guardians, and built on inconsistent and fluctuating attitudes toward poverty. As the nature of social theory and the political communities that put ideas into practice changed, welfare policies shifted away from their early Victorian form.

In the longer run, the Victorian poor law atrophied. First Liberal, then Conservative politicians chose to remedy destitution with social insurance, circumventing its rickety, resented structures. The shift was not inevitable, but once begun, it offered a popular alternative to the poor law, which brought British welfare practices much closer to those of continental Europe and which politicians operating in a democracy could not reject.

[1] Karel Williams, *From Pauperism to Poverty* (London: Routledge, 1981), p. 144.

7

REEVALUATING THE URBAN
POOR, 1860–90

Aw've sowd until aw've nowt to sell,
An' hew we'n clemm'd 'is past o' belief;
An' wheer to goo aw could no tell,
Except to th' 'Board' to get relief.
Ther wur no wark, for th' mill wur stopt;
Mi childher could no dee, yo known;
Aw'm neaw a pauper, cose aw've dhropt
To this low state o' breakin' stone.

       Joseph Ramsbottom, *Philip Clough's Tale*

The virulent hatred of pauperism that prompted passage of the New Poor Law
had derived strength from faith in an ethic of self-help and individual responsibility, coupled with a refusal to admit the impact of social or biological constraints on individual action. But in a post-Darwinian world, the logic of constraints became more widely accepted. After theorists of evolution and
idealist philosophers popularized analyses of society as a living organism
governed by processes and institutions, many people saw individual responsibility as operating within a relatively narrow compass. Poverty became a
problem to be attacked, rather than a sign of moral failure. As a result, pauperism looked much different in 1890 than it had in 1850. Moreover, in times
of industrial depression, theories of pauperism received a public test: Was it
character or the market that cost men and women their jobs?

The Lancashire Cotton Famine, 1861–5

The neat and tidy theory of the deterrent workhouse met an unruly, intransi-
gent reality in Lancashire during the American Civil War. When naval blockades cut off cotton supplies, thousands of people found themselves out of

work or on short time through no fault of their own. Moreover, shopowners, artisans, and landlords saw their incomes drop because textile workers could not pay their bills. As the county's major industry shut down, so did the local economy. During December of 1862, at the peak of the famine, almost five hundred thousand people, representing about one-quarter of the county's population, were getting aid from the poor law or from local relief committees. Not only the intensity but the longevity of the distress created problems: Only in the spring of 1865 did the numbers on relief decline below one hundred thousand and stay there.[1] The notion that the tens of thousands of unemployed could find work locally if they would only look harder for it was patently absurd, as was the prediction that fear of the workhouse would keep them off relief rolls.

The resulting spectacle of destitution and despair could not be contained within local communities. Soon the cotton famine became a preoccupation all over the country and, indeed, over the English-speaking world as responses to slavery, to British foreign policy, and to the issue of public behavior in adversity became intermixed with welfare questions. Particularly for those who approved of British neutrality in the war or who objected to the defense of slavery, it seemed short sighted to restrict relief to the unemployed. But what could legitimately be provided, and who should pay? For over three years, the question of how to treat the destitute during an industrial depression remained in the spotlight. The *Illustrated London News* sent reporters and artists to Lancashire to chronicle relief efforts. The *Times* broadcast its concerns via lead articles and readers' letters, whereas newspapers all over the north printed descriptions of the unemployed and their activities. As poor law authorities leapt into action, dragging out their stock remedies, they had to operate in a glare of publicity in which the amounts and types of relief offered were closely scrutinized by the outside world.

Although not forbidden to grant outdoor relief to the able-bodied, Lancashire boards of guardians had instructions from the central administration to force male applicants to perform a labor test before giving them money. This meant that daily work had to be provided for thousands of people, with attention paid to the thorny problems of supervision and equity. Because the Poor Law Board refused to suspend the labor requirement, Lancashire guardians also had to run labor yards, in addition to their efforts to feed, clothe, and support the destitute. The thousands of unemployed women and children had to be dealt with, too. Although the principles of 1834 mandated

---

[1] Poor Law Board, *Annual Reports* (London: H M Stationery Office, 1862–1866). See in particular "Appendix to the Fifteenth Annual Report," (1862–1863), p. 206–207.

different treatment according to the sex, age, and physical condition of paupers, the repertoire of available policies was pitifully small and the demand for aid gargantuan.

From the early stages of the famine, extraordinary efforts that went beyond the hallowed "principles of 1834" were made to deal with destitution. The central Poor Law Board sent H. B. Farnall to Lancashire as a special commissioner to report on conditions and help plan local strategies. Parliament changed the rules for poor law finance to allow heavily burdened parishes to spread costs among other parishes in the union or in the county. Meanwhile, special relief committees multiplied, and extra money was collected. London's Lord Mayor set up a fund that drew contributions from all over Britain and the Empire, whereas the Mayor of Manchester appealed for money to aid unemployed cotton workers. Lord Derby and a host of other Lancastrian notables formed a Central Relief Committee that both collected money and made decisions about how it should be spent. Working through district committees, it financed a multitude of local efforts that functioned alongside the poor laws.[2]

Although most of what was done merely repeated the conventional tactics of earlier decades, the scope of the distress and the number of players in the relief game encouraged innovation and competition. Provident societies distributed clothing, coal, and money; soup kitchens fed the hungry; emigrant aid societies financed movement to Australia and Canada. Under pressure to deal effectively with unemployed men, the Poor Law Board sent its chief engineer, Robert Rawlinson, to Lancashire in the spring of 1863 to plan projects that might be carried out under the direction of local governments. When he calculated that money could easily be spent on building new roads, sewers, and parks, thereby employing thousands of local people, Parliament quickly passed a public works act, offering low-interest loans to towns in the manufacturing districts. Within a year, over ninety local authorities had borrowed money for construction projects. In Wigan, the Board of Health and the Voluntary Distress Committee hired men to fix the streets, and in Rochdale, the town council voted to hire several hundred men to work on the roads.[3] Although the numbers employed represented only a small fraction of those on relief, the principle that the government should provide useful work

[2] Norman Longmate, *The Hungry Mills,* (London: Temple Smith, 1978), 84–7, 128–30; W. O. Henderson, *The Lancashire Cotton Famine, 1861–1865* (Manchester: Manchester University Press, 1934).

[3] Longmate, 206, 282–3; *Manchester Guardian,* 10 April 1862; Webb Local Government Collection, part 2, The Poor Law, vol. 310: Rochdale, Lancashire, 1862, British Library of Political and Economic Science; see also Henderson, *Cotton Famine,* 61–5.

instead of punishment was an important one, and it was accepted by national and local administrators, as well as by the Poor Law Board.

In another departure from standard practice, charities financed schools for the unemployed. After workers protested the continuation of the labor test as a requirement for relief and suggested classes as a substitute, poor law authorities changed their policy. Tens of thousands of new scholars poured into makeshift classrooms in reading rooms, churches, and closed factories for the period of the famine. Instruction in manual trades for men, in sewing for women, and in basic education for all was financed by grants from the Central Relief Committee. They, as well as the boards of guardians, paid pauper children's school fees so they could continue in their normal classes. In Rochdale, a Committee for Instruction of the Unemployed set up a school to teach reading, writing, arithmetic, and geography, with additional lectures by "gentlemen" on specialized subjects. Guardians in Oldham offered to pay costs if mill owners would provide space in their factories for an adult school and appoint an overlooker or manager as the teacher. The demand for places in the schools seems to have been high: Warmth, company, and free tea added to the attractions of payment for attendance. Moreover, after work in the sewing schools, women could buy the clothing they produced at cost or reduced prices. In Blackburn, local churches ran such schools for about nine hundred women in the fall of 1862. Artists for the *Illustrated London News* sketched rows of diligent male readers and needlewomen hard at work as typical scenes of the Lancashire unemployed.[4]

From the early stages of the famine, many guardians and charitable workers refused to hold to a strict enforcement of the poor law. Guardians in Rochdale, Ashton-under-Lyne, and Oldham asked permission from the central Poor Law Board in 1862 to dispense with a labor test. Although their requests were refused, Oldham guardians granted relief without it anyway and voted to defy the board's instructions. The Central Relief Committee, worried that the relation of operatives and capitalists would be "deranged," wanted regular, manual work offered to the unemployed, not punitive tasks. Their support of schools and local public works projects helped to provide alternatives to normal poor law practices.[5]

The willingness of the propertied to funnel cash and work directly to the

[4] John Watts, *The Facts of the Cotton Famine* (London, 1866), 201–2, 210–11; Frank Smith, *The Life and Work of Sir James Kay-Shuttleworth;* Webb Local Government Collection, Part 3, vol. 310: Rochdale, Lancashire, 1862–3, Oldham, 1862; vol. 308: Blackburn, Lancashire, 1862; *The Illustrated London News,* 29 November 1862.

[5] *Manchester Guardian,* 24 February 1863.

unemployed in defiance of cherished laissez-faire precepts was fostered by public images of the Lancashire poor. In the early stages of the famine, "A Lancashire Lad" described for readers of the *Times* a humble, suffering population: "[S]ome others of these fathers turn out in the morning with long besoms as street sweepers, while others again go to breaking stones, in the town's yard or open roadside, where they are unprotected from the keen east winds. . . . Our factory women and girls have had to turn out; and plodding a weary way from door to door beg a bit of bread or a stray copper that they may eke out the scanty supply at home."[6] Edwin Waugh visited homes of the unemployed in Preston, Wigan, and Blackburn and concluded that Lancashire workers were made of "noble stuff" because they chose to suffer silently rather than complain or apply for relief.[7] In contrast to the imagery of predatory, depraved paupers that circulated but the 1830s and 1840s, many observers in Lancashire saw the destitute as stoic people bitten by the iron teeth of poverty but not defeated. In the rhetoric of radicals and Liberals, the unemployed operative merged into the larger-than-life figure of the "Rochdale Man," a self-educated, hard-working artisan who represented the aspirations of organized labor in the region. Rather than fears of "dangerous classes," reporters and politicians offered a vision of harmonious social relations based upon common interest in respectability and the return of prosperity.[8] The lack of serious social unrest in the county gave credibility to these comforting visions of community.

The cotton famine was a severe test for the mid-Victorian poor law and one that, in a certain sense, it passed. Guardians proved active and flexible enough to cope with thousands of extra applicants. Charitable efforts supplemented, rather than supplanted, the official machinery. On the other hand, the famine had exposed for all to see the inadequacy of conventional strategies and institutions. Only by redefining the labor test and by encouraging public employment could work be made a requirement of relief to the unemployed. Only by massive, voluntary efforts could industrial poverty be dampened during a depression. The famine taught the lesson that prevention of pauperism required early and creative intervention, rather than a stint in the workhouse, and it cast doubt on the automatic connection between destitution and crimi-

---

[6] *The Times*, 14 April 1862.

[7] Longmate, *Hungry Mills*, 110.

[8] M. E. Rose, "Rochdale Man and the Stalybridge Riot: Poor Relief During the Lancashire Cotton Famine, 1861–1865," in A. P. Donajgrodzki, ed., *Social Control in Nineteenth-Century Britain* (London: Croom Helm, 1977); Patrick Joyce, *Visions of the People* (New York: Cambridge University Press, 1991), 57–8.

nality often made by middle-class writers. The principles of 1834 had been dealt a body blow by the strong fists of industrial, urban poverty.

Reconstructed Communities

When Hippolyte Taine neared Manchester in 1871, he first glimpsed a "strangely-shaped cloud [hanging] over the plain; under this motionless covering are hundreds of bristling chimneys, as tall as obelisks; a huge and black mass is next distinguishable, then endless rows of buildings, and we enter the Babel of bricks."[9] England became a country of city dwellers during the second half of the nineteenth century. By 1871, over 65 percent and by 1900 over 80 percent of the English population lived in towns of more than two thousand people, and places as diverse as Birkenhead, Bradford, Stoke-on-Trent, Nottingham, and Portsmouth had more than one hundred thousand residents. Well over a million people moved into English cities and towns during the the 1850s and 1860s, into settlements ill equipped to receive them.[10] The typical citizen no longer lived in a village where green fields lay a short walk from a parish church whose spire dominated the horizon. To quote Charles Masterman writing in 1901: "The England of the past has been an England of reserved, silent men, dispersed in small towns, villages, and country homes. The England of the future is an England packed tightly in such gigantic aggregations of population as the world has never before seen."[11]

Many found the potential social impact of urbanization truly frightening. Charles Trevelyan linked urban growth to a "rising tide of pauperism and crime," and he depicted London as a "gigantic engine for depraving and degrading our population." Matthew Arnold warned of the "vast, miserable, unmanageable masses" entombed in London's East End. In marked contrast to the rhetoric of northern writers during the cotton famine, London journalists, such as James Greenwood and Thomas Archer, made their reputations with lurid portrayals of metropolitan lowlife, weaving together anecdotes of paupers, thieves, and beggars against slum backdrops.[12] During the 1860s

---

[9] Hippolyte Taine, *Notes on England* (New York: Holt & Williams, 1872), 273.

[10] B. R. Mitchell, *Abstract of British Historical Statistics* (New York: Cambridge University Press, 1962), 20, 24–7; Jeffrey G. Williamson, *Coping with City Growth During the British Industrial Revolution* (New York: Cambridge University Press, 1990), 19, 23, 88.

[11] C. F. G. Masterman, *The Heart of the Empire: Discussions of Problems of Modern City Life in England* (New York: Harper & Row, 1973; originally published, 1901), 7.

[12] Sir Charles Trevelyan, *Seven Articles on London Pauperism and Its Relations with the Labour Market* (London: Bell & Daldy, 1870), 6–7; Matthew Arnold, *Culture and Anarchy* (London: Dover Wilson, 1966; originally published 1869) 193; James Greenwood, *The Wilds of London*

and 1870s, a host of social commentators warned of the "demoralization" of the poor triggered by the segregation of classes in the capital. In the 1880s, many writers focussed on chronic poverty and on the supposedly degenerative effects on the minds and bodies of big city environments, which they blamed for creating explosive social conditions.[13]

Ironically, these heightened fears came at a time when both skilled and unskilled workers found their real incomes rising and their standard of living markedly improving. As workers shifted out of agriculture into service and commercial jobs in the towns, they earned higher wages. Moreover, declines in the cost of living produced by falling prices during the depression of 1873–96 were shared by all income groups. Cheap food from abroad flooded the British market, and all consumers benefited. On an upswing since at least the 1840s, real wages rose on average by about 75 percent in the last forty years of the century.[14] Family budgets collected by the United States Department of Labor from English textile and steel workers around 1890 show substantial spending on things other than food and rent. The better-paid industrial workers found themselves able to afford holidays, newspapers, and insurance, while drinking more milk and eating more meat.[15] As cheap consumer goods multiplied, many workers acquired the trappings of respectability. Moreover, family sizes became smaller after 1871. As a result, adults of working age had fewer dependents to support.

Between 1850 and 1873, the English economy boomed, although its gains were distributed unevenly, and individual industries had occasional setbacks. Workers benefited directly through more secure jobs and higher wages and then, indirectly, because governments invested some of their increased revenues in the cities. During the last thirty years of the century, expenditures on human capital took a great leap forward: national schools after 1870, compulsory appointment of medical officers of health after 1872, municipal

(London: Chatto & Windus, 1874); Thomas Archer, *The Pauper, the Thief, and the Convict* (London: Goombridge & Sons, 1865).

[13] Andrew Lees, *Cities Perceived* (Manchester: Manchester University Press, 1985); see also Gareth Stedman Jones, *Outcast London* (Oxford: Oxford University Press, 1971), 261, 286–7.

[14] Ian Gazeley, "The Cost of Living for Urban Workers in Late Victorian and Edwardian Britain," *Economic History Review,* 2nd ser. XII, 2 (1989): 207–21; Roderick Floud and Donald McCloskey, eds., *The Economic History of Britain Since 1700,* vol 2., *1860 to the 1970's* (New York: Cambridge University Press, 1981), 1, 128–9, 131; C. H. Feinstein, *National Income, Expenditure and Output of the United Kingdom, 1855–1965* (New York: Cambridge University Press, 1972).

[15] Lynn Hollen Lees, "Getting and Spending: The Family Budgets of English Industrial Workers in 1890," in John M. Merriman, ed., *Consciousness and Class Experience in Nineteenth-Century Europe* (New York: Holmes & Meier, 1979), 169–87.

sewage and water systems at varying dates during the second half of the century. By 1885, local governments spent just about as much of their budgets on education, housing, hospitals, and care of the insane as they did on poor relief, and by 1914, they spent three times as much.[16] The incidence of death by infectious diseases, such as cholera, typhus, typhoid, and tuberculosis, dropped sharply. The social investments of the state during the late Victorian period brought solid gains to workers, but poverty was still endemic among the lowest paid.[17] The years of depression (1873–96) at the end of the century meant rising real wages for those with work, but hard times for the unemployed and for many agricultural laborers. The song, "Poverty Knock," in which a power-loom weaver complains, "I wonder that we keep alive," was still being sung with feeling in Lancashire around 1900.[18] A sense of insecurity haunted workers in late Victorian Britain.

Along with the economic reshuffling brought by industrial growth and urbanization came marked political changes. In 1867, Parliament granted the right to vote in national elections to male householders who paid taxes on property in the boroughs; the electorate almost doubled immediately. Skilled workers found themselves courted by Liberal and Conservative politicians and brought into local party organizations. Supported by their unions and Liberal clubs, a handful of workers contested and won places in the House of Commons. Many others ran successfully for local office, where they brought new points of view into town governments. After 1894, all ratepayers, women as well as men, could run for positions on town councils, boards of guardians and boards of education, whose seats were often hotly contested. Growth in the numbers and sizes of trades unions magnified the power of new voters because organized labor could bring lobbying energies and demonstrative strength into the public area.

During the second half of the nineteenth century, local balances of power adjusted to a populist liberalism and burgeoning numbers of new organizations.[19] Cooperatives, unions, temperance groups, trades councils, and suffrage societies, among others, jostled for a place in the public eye. Socialists and feminists contested familiar conceptions of state action. Changing rules of the political game, which produced a mass electorate protected by the

[16] Anthony S. Wohl, *Endangered Lives: Public Health in Victorian Britain* (Cambridge: Harvard University Press, 1983), 124, 127, 181; Floud and McCloskey, *History of Britain*, vol. 2, 228.

[17] Ibid., 7, 461.

[18] Roy Palmer, ed., *Poverty Knock* (New York: Cambridge University Press, 1974), 15.

[19] Eugenio F. Biagini, *Liberty, Retrenchment, and Reform* (New York: Cambridge University Press, 1992).

secret ballot, brought easy entry into town politics. Even if policies changed by only a small amount, political culture and rhetoric were transformed by the legitimizing power of the vote. As William Gladstone proclaimed in the mid-1860s, workers had become, "our fellow-subjects, our fellow Christians, our own flesh and blood."[20] By the 1880s, the patron saints of the new Liberalism proclaimed tolerance and respect for the masses. Arnold Toynbee announced in 1884: "Not only has the law given to workmen and employers equality of rights, but education bids fair to give them equality of culture. We are now, workmen as well as employers, inhabitants of a larger world; no longer members of a single class, but fellow citizens of one great people."[21]

Organization, especially when combined with a widened suffrage, brought recognition. Groups of working men could announce a position on the opening of a local park or a change in rates by the municipal gas works and send a deputation to the mayor, who would receive them with courtesy. Trades councils intervened in local strikes or discussed poor law policies. In the opinion of John Gerrard, groups well below the elite in English industrial cities could shape local affairs. Working men, even if rather low in a hierarchy of power, could force conciliation and sometimes have "significant influence" upon municipal politics. Rochdale workers helped to defeat Tory guardians who supported using the labor test during the cotton famine, whereas during the later 1860s Bolton workers successfully petitioned the town to get city parks opened on Sunday mornings.[22] Representatives of friendly societies, cooperative stores, and trades unions participated in civic ceremonies alongside church groups, temperance societies, and town councilors. Newspapers in northern cities reported benefit balls thrown by drapers' assistants and evening lectures sponsored by working men's clubs with almost the same enthusiasm as they showed for the social life of the gentry.

In the second half of the nineteenth century, civic communities widened to include regular participation by respectable male workers – as voters, as ratepaying residents, as members of voluntary societies, and occasionally as elected officials. Neighborhood, church, job, and trade, as well as political loyalty, produced occasions for entry into public life. Whether a class model stressing conflict or a populist model emphasizing a larger more complex set of loyalties is used, the important point remains the rise of participation and

---

[20] Quoted in Harold Perkin, *The Origins of Modern English Society, 1780–1880* (London: Routledge, 1969), 319.

[21] Jones, *Outcast London,* 9–10.

[22] John Gerrard, *Leadership and Power in Victorian Industrial Towns, 1830–1880* (Manchester: Manchester University Press, 1983), 152, 202, 222.

recognition. In a political world where the Liberal party triumphed by building a cross-class coalition of skilled workers, professionals, entrepreneurs, and employees, and where factory owners sought to depict their firms as families, rhetorical stances toward workers were unstable formations. Mass education and mass culture blurred social lines in Britain during the 1870s and 1880s.[23] Even when scholars stress the hardening of class lines among the groups jostling for local position, they depict a process of interaction between interests.[24]

By the late nineteenth century, therefore, the poor laws operated in a rather different world than that of the 1830s. Because of economic growth, rising incomes, and declining incidence of infectious diseases, a smaller share of the population was at risk of pauperism. Moreover, many more adult male workers had joined friendly societies, benefit clubs, and trade unions. By organizing, male workers had chosen to use the private sector to insure themselves against risks, thereby diminishing the likelihood that they would need poor relief if their incomes declined. Collectively and privately, they had created alternatives to a state welfare system that disadvantaged them.

Reconstructed Knowledge

As workers' economic and political status rose during the second half of the century, the images of the poor circulating in print became more diverse. Public discourse could draw on a potpourri of philosophical and religious principles and statistical, scientific, and pseudoscientific lore; the result was a portrait sketched in multiple, but basically still unflattering, colors.

Arguments that built a harmonious social and moral order on personal responsibility and character were in retreat by the 1860s, after Darwin, Spencer, and their interpreters had spread faith in evolutionary theory. Moreover, the lessons of statistics, psychiatry, and medicine combined to shift causal explanations away from the human will to more deterministic models. Agency lay not in volition but in society, mass phenomena, and biology. Changing conceptions of human nature, individualism, and collectivism pushed social theory and ideas about welfare in new directions.[25] Henry

[23] John Vincent, *The Formation of the Liberal Party* (London: Constable, 1966); Patrick Joyce, *Work, Society, and Politics* (Brighton: Harvester, 1980); José Harris, *Private Lives, Public Spirit* (New York: Oxford University Press, 1993), 252.

[24] Dennis Smith, *Conflict and Compromise: Class Formation in English Society, 1830–1914* (London: Routledge, 1982).

[25] Harris, *Private Lives;* Martin Wiener, *Reconstructing the Criminal* (New York: Cambridge University Press, 1990) 159–60, 162, 166.

Maudsley, a leading English psychologist in the 1870s, thought that much human action was shaped by the activity of the spinal cord and the functioning of nerve centers. In *The Physiology and Pathology of the Mind*, he proclaimed: "No one can escape the tyranny of his organization; no one can elude the destiny that is innate in him, and which unconsciously and irresistibly shapes his ends, even when he believes that he is determining them with consummate foresight and skill."[26] This determinism, which received reinforcement from a variety of fields, directed attention along chains of causation outside the individual.

Doctors and statisticians, in particular, helped to popularize physical determinism as an explanation for poverty. Their investigations of public health brought wide publicity to social conditions among workers and substituted images of physical and biological decay for moral weakness. William Farr, the guiding spirit at the Registrar General's office after 1839, chose to use his yearly reports on mortality and morbidity to focus attention on urban sanitary problems. Moreover, he blamed the state, rather than the poor, for problems of sanitation that, he argued, destroyed the lives of workers in the city slums.[27] The poor were victims rather than offenders. During the 1850s and 1860s, the Statistical Society of London and the Social Science Association heard many similar reports, which shifted attention away from the poor to the malignant environments in which they lived. John Simon, who headed the medical department of the Privy Council after 1858 and later the Local Government Board, sent inspectors to comb and sniff through the towns looking for nuisances and pollution.[28] In the language of sanitary reformers, pollution and sickness came from the failure of society to cleanse and drain cities effectively. Individuals, surrounded by noxious vapors and impure water and food, sickened and died, their poverty an indirect result of their weakness.

Doctors and journalists also popularized environmental explanations for poverty. Dr. Hector Gavin, a lecturer on forensic medicine and public health at Charing Cross Hospital, wrote and spoke extensively in London at mid-century on links between sanitation and destitution. Drawing his information largely from official statistical and sanitary reports, he described a puny, stunted population, whose residence in the slums produced physical and moral collapse. As young migrants moved into filthy, ramshackle housing, he

---

[26] Quoted in Wiener, *Reconstructing*, 168–9.

[27] Wohl, *Endangered*, 143.

[28] Ibid., 157–61.

saw "poverty overtaking and overcoming [them] like an armed man."[29] John Morgan, a doctor in Salford and secretary of the Manchester and Salford Sanitary Association, warned in 1865 of the "danger of deterioration of race" stemming from rapid migration into the cities. Bad air, congenital syphilis, and drink turned urban workers into physical wrecks and made them incapable of hard labor. His theory of decline began with physical factors, but then quickly moved to more general predictions of decline.[30]

By the 1880s, environmental explanations for poverty grew into a full-blown theory of hereditary urban degeneration, which was applied primarily to workers. James Cantlie wrote of "urbomorbus," the city disease, which produced weak people with weak brains who, after several generations, were incapable of reproduction.[31] Dr. John Fothergill bluntly declared that people born in cities who chose to remain there were "a dying race."[32] Such ideas spread far beyond the medical community and surfaced repeatedly in analyses of the London poor published in the 1880s and 1890s by Charles Booth, William Llewellyn Smith, and G. B. Longstaff. Royal commissions, charitable committees, and meetings of the Royal Statistical Society were told about the physical collapse of native Londoners.[33]

Poor law officials throughout the country could attach this statistical portrait of disease and death to paupers in their care. Guardians of the poor in York included a judgment about the complaints of people applying to them for relief. In a 10 percent sample of the cases they recorded in the fall and early winter of 1871, all the adult males were classified as needing aid because of sickness or a death in the family. One man had injured his back; others had dropsy, rheumatism, or phthisis; still others got aid for sick children. Female applicants had a wider range of problems, but the guardians considered that about half of them were ill and needed medical care.[34] In the second half of the century, representations of the poor, whether derived from direct study or statisticians' abstracts, centered on their physical weakness. If nature decreed that only the most fit survived, the urban poor were in trouble.

[29] Hector Gavin, *The Habitations of the Industrious Classes* (London: Society for Improving the Condition of the Labouring Classes, 1850), 65, 70–1.

[30] John Edward Morgan, *The Danger of Deterioration of Race* (London: Longmans, Green, 1866), 3–4, 49–50.

[31] James Cantlie, *Degeneration Among Londoners* (London: Field & Tuer, 1885), 23–4.

[32] J. Milner Fothergill, *The Town Dweller: His Needs and Wants* (London: H. K. Lewis, 1889) 109.

[33] Jones, *Outcast London*, 128–33, 286–7.

[34] York Union, Board of Guardians, "Application and Report Book for the Quarter Ending December, 1871," BG\YK Acc. no. 2–837.

When the opinions of evolutionary anthropologists were added into the simmering stew of medical and biological analyses being served to the Victorian middle classes, the images of the poor they ingested became more sinister. Because many biologists and anthropologists believed in the inheritance of acquired characteristics, they feared an automatic transfer from parent to child of environmentally produced inadequacy. Moreover, many anthropologists argued that the psychological impact of degraded living conditions also could be passed on to the next generation. Both Darwin and Spencer had discussed the inheritance of moral characteristics, so an easy leap could be made between spiritual decline and its transmission to a wider population.[35] Although evolution operated to put England in the forefront of the race to ever-higher planes of civilization and progress, some of its citizens were being left farther and farther behind, creating massive problems for their society in the process.

This line of argument removed blame from individuals, but it also branded them as hopelessly degenerate. Gareth Stedman Jones has shown how this combination of fear and pseudoscience produced pictures of a brutish population that threatened the physically and morally fit. The spotlight of social scientific attention turned from the poor to the very poor and called for increasingly coercive measures to block their ability to corrupt and threaten respectable workers and citizens.[36] Increasingly, threatening poverty was identified not with the ordinary laborer but with an urban underclass formed from the unemployed and the criminal population. This shift, dramatized by Jones as the fear of "outcast London," hinged upon differentiation between the respectable and the "residuum."[37] In these collective representations, poverty took on several shapes.

The disjunction between representations of urban workers in medical and anthropological literature on the one hand and in liberal publications on the other hand must have been confusing. Where one set of messages signaled inferiority and decline, another touted equality and progress. How to reconcile these blatant inconsistencies? On a larger scale, how could the supposedly iron laws of social evolution and anthropological difference be tamed by moral commitments to the collective good? Idealist philosophy, whose influence was rising, identified ways in which evolutionary theory and ethical norms could be harmonized through the collective will. Activists such as Sir

---

[35] Henrika Kuklick, *The Savage Within* (New York: Cambridge University Press, 1991), 81–2.

[36] Jones, *Outcast London*, 286–7, 303.

[37] Ibid., 1, 16.

John Simon and William Beveridge believed that enlightened social policies could point the evolutionary process toward the common good; much of the late-Victorian world of social reform was fueled by such ideas.[38] The heady mixture of Lamarckian biology and Neo-Hegelian philosophy pushed dozens of reformers toward collective solutions to social problems. Even if biology was destiny, it could be reshaped by creative intervention. With vision and statesmanship, the wounded social body could be healed.

Interest in the ideas of Auguste Comte also contributed to a social scientific zeal for reform. Through observation and experimentation, scholars could discover the truth about human affairs and could shape policies accordingly. By 1873, when the second edition of Comte's *Positive Philosophy* appeared in English, positivism had acquired a respectable following in England among statisticians, scientists, and reformers. Charles Booth praised both the method and the underlying philosophy of positivism, which offered the potential for discovering "the true welfare and right progress of the human race." By the mid-1880s Booth had articulated a belief in social laws that could be discovered. For Booth, the path to social knowledge led through numbers. He and other members of the Statistical Society saw statistics as a "science" that could reveal "the structure of human society." In the longer run, the collection of social statistics could offer guides for legislation and good government.[39]

During the last quarter of the nineteenth century, statistics became an even more important component of social knowledge than they had been in the 1830s and 1840s. Then as now, numbers carried authority. When Andrew Mearns wrote *The Bitter Cry of Outcast London* in 1883, his sensationalist call for action against a "terrible flood of sin and misery," he moved quickly from diatribe to what he called "plain facts," a recitation of the low proportion of residents who attended church in a variety of inner-city neighborhoods. Readers were invited to shiver in horror when confronted by the 39 out of 4,235 people in one section of St. George-in-the-East who attended worship. His depiction of immorality in the slums rested heavily on the numbers of prostitutes, public houses, and gin palaces he counted in particular areas. Although the bulk of his evidence lay in anecdotes of the urban poor and their squalid housing, he regularly anchored his descriptions in an arithmetic of woe to give it weight and verisimilitude.[40] Amid the resulting furor

[38] Harris, *Private Lives,* 228–31.

[39] Gertrude Himmelfarb, *Poverty and Compassion* (New York: Knopf, 1991), 82–3, 92.

[40] Andrew Mearns, *The Bitter Cry of Outcast London,* ed. Anthony S. Wohl (New York: Humanities Press, 1970), 56–7, 61–2.

over his charges, Queen Victoria contacted Gladstone and called for "more precise information as to the true state of affairs in these overcrowded, unhealthy and squalid abodes." Lord Salisbury, then leader of the Conservative party, in a speech to Parliament called for a government inquiry to collect data on London housing. Soon thereafter, the Royal Commission on the Housing of the Working Classes was appointed.[41] In the 1880s, statistics were an important ingredient in debates about public policy toward the poor. Indeed, multitudes of social fears seemed to require a numerical scaffolding for containment. The hard edges of a statistical representation brought fictive limits to the potentially contagious problems of the urban poor.

By the mid-1880s, Charles Booth was a member of the Statistical Society and was hard at work classifying and counting the occupations of the London population. He had read Robert Giffen's 1886 essay for the Statistical Society on the "progress of the working classes," which gave an optimistic reading of workers' incomes and standards of living. On the other hand, he was well aware of horrific pictures of London slum life sketched by Mearns and others and had posed for himself the question of proportion. How were workers distributed among the respectable, intermediate, and lowest classes? Because Booth thought London contained both the richest and the most destitute population in the country, he considered it the proper site for assessing the dimensions of the poverty problem.[42] As a wealthy owner of a shipping company and an import–export merchant, Booth had the means, and he made the time, to launch an investigation into what seemed the most pressing social question of the 1880s.[43]

His study, eventually published in 1902 in seventeen volumes entitled *Life and Labour of the People of London,* began modestly in 1886, targeting the East End at first but eventually covering the entire metropolis. Booth employed a few assistants to investigate special topics and to work with the school board visitors, whose judgments about family income, character, and living conditions constituted the basic data of the survey. The project, aptly described by Clara Collet, who worked on it, as "a statistical record of

---

[41] Wohl, "Introduction," in Mearns, ibid., 33.

[42] Charles Booth, "The Inhabitants of Tower Hamlets (school board division): Their Condition and Occupation," *Journal of the Royal Statistical Society* 49 (1886): 374; quoted in E. P. Hennock, "The Measurement of Poverty: From the Metropolis to the Nation," *Economic History Review,* 2nd ser., 40:2 (May 1987): 210.

[43] Quoted in Himmelfarb, *Poverty,* 84. The story spread by H. M. Hyndman that Booth undertook his famous London survey to refute an earlier study done by the Social Democratic Federation has been discredited both by E. P. Hennock in "Poverty and Social Theory in England: The Experience of the Eighteen-Eighties," *Social History* 1 (January 1976): 70–1, as well as by Himmelfarb, *Poverty,* 90–2.

impressions of degrees of poverty," had a wide evidentiary base, but one vastly different from that of surveys of poverty in the 1990s. The staff lived for a time in the areas surveyed; they interviewed local clergy, government inspectors, school board visitors, and welfare officials, and they used school board records, as well as the census, for demographic information. What they did not do was to interview their subjects or to create a representative sample of the East End population. Their information was only partly statistical, and virtually all was obtained indirectly and filtered through the eyes of a group of middle-class social engineers who had profoundly ambiguous attitudes toward their subjects.

Although the survey presents elaborate descriptions of London industries, streets, and religious life, contemporaries, as well as later readers, fastened on Booth's classification of households into a hierarchy of groups. On the basis of estimated earnings, Booth divided the London population into eight units (A–H). Each was identified in several other ways – through descriptions of their social position and households, their relation to the labor market, and their moral character. Booth saw these categories as varying jointly; deficiency in one index implied deficiency in all the others. For example, the category of the "lowest class, which consists of some occasional labourers, street sellers, loafers, criminals, and semi-criminals," got the worst marks on every scale. Its members were judged to have little family life, incomes too irregular to permit estimation, and the character of "barbarians." As he ascended the rungs of the social ladder, Booth progressed through the casual laborers, the poor, and the comfortable workers to the middle class, finding that each group earned more and gained in respectability. To the social portrait of each, he added numbers and a percentage, quantifying in great detail for the first time the social pyramid of the metropolis.[44]

E. P. Hennock sees Booth as a "systematizer," someone who reasserted the relevance of familiar categories, but at the same time made them more specific.[45] Booth's contribution to the debate on poverty was twofold: First, he estimated the lowest class and the very poor as being only 12.4 percent of the East End population; second, he portrayed the remainder of London's workers in guardedly optimistic terms. They ranged from the poor, who were "not 'in want'" and "neither ill-nourished nor ill clad," to the comfortable working

[44] Charles Booth, *Life and Labour of the People of London*, 1st Ser., *Poverty*, vol. 1, rev. ed. (New York: Augustus M. Kelley, 1969; originally published 1902), 36–9.

[45] E. P. Hennock, "Poverty and Social Theory," 69; see Karel Williams, *From Pauperism to Poverty* (London: Routledge, 1981), 324.

class, who lived "in plenty." His divisions, moreover, undermined the social-ists' image of a unified proletariat, just as they confirmed the liberal's view of most workers as respectable citizens who were enjoying a share of national prosperity.[46] Although Booth's assertion that 30.7 percent of the London pop-ulation lived in poverty was widely quoted by contemporaries (as well as by social scientists ever since), his division of this group into units posing very different social problems and challenges was his major contribution to social policy. Responsible social engineering meant multiple responses to social problems, each of which was cut down to size by Booth's categories.

While the gargantuan dissection of London poverty continued, Booth undertook in the early 1890s to study the relationship of pauperism and old age. An early advocate of pensions, he realized that it was impossible to quantify the dependence of the elderly on relief because of the form of poor law records. To strengthen his argument for a shift in relief policies, he turned first to the records of Stepney poor law inspectors and later to newly produced statistics from each poor law union on the numbers of people on relief, which included information on sex, age, and need for medical care. He published his analyses in two books: *Pauperism: a Picture and the Endowment of Old Age* and *The Aged Poor in England and Wales.*[47] Booth's work directly under-mined some of the most cherished Victorian beliefs about paupers. Stepney records indicated that old age and sickness were the principal causes for the granting of relief. Because many writers discussing pauperism around 1890 continued to blame pauperism on the corrupting effects of welfare and to identify paupers with "the idle" and "the improvident," Booth's statistics had a devastating effect on common arguments.[48] Moreover, by showing that in 1892 about 30 percent of the English and Welsh populations over age sixty-five and 37 percent of residents in the metropolis over age sixty-five were in receipt of relief, he identified pauperism as a major social problem among the elderly. Even if the rate of dependence on welfare within the total population had declined to insignificance, this was certainly not the case among those over age sixty-five. Thus provided with statistical ammunition, Booth fired away at poor law policy. "Indoor relief lacks humanity and outdoor encour-ages improvidence," he announced. He suggested that universal, tax-financed

[46] See Hennock, "Poverty and Social Theory," 73.

[47] Charles Booth, *Pauperism, A Picture and the Endowment of Old Age, an Argument* (London: Macmillan, 1892); idem *The Aged Poor in England and Wales* (London: Macmillan, 1894).

[48] See, for example, Francis Peek, *The Workless, the Thriftless, and the Worthless: The Problem* (London: William Isbister, 1888): and Thomas MacKay, *Methods of Social Reform: Essays Critical and Constructive* (London: John Murray, 1896).

pensions were a far better solution to the need to provide greater security and a higher standard of life for the elderly.[49]

By 1895, Booth had brought into public discourse a set of familiar classifications for urban poverty and had attached numbers to them. His conclusions were comforting: Neither the poor nor the decently paid worker posed a problem for the state, which should concentrate on removing from the regular labor market the casual workers and the disorderly. Paupers, too, posed a smaller threat than before, because their ranks were dominated by the elderly and the sick. His numbers gave Liberal and Socialist reformers strong sticks with which to flog the poor laws. In a culture where empirical research and biological theory dominated the sciences, statistics proved to be a powerful weapon in debates over public policy. When the poor could be counted and divided into manageable groups, policies toward them could be tailored to specific problems and needs. Social scientists could take W. S. Gilbert's advice and try to make the punishment fit the crime.

Reconstructed Images

People with long lives and good memories would have noticed that images of the poor in illustrated books and newspapers changed dramatically between mid- and late Victorian times. In *Punch*, John Leech's isolated, dwarfish creatures were replaced by John Tenniel's muscular renderings of politically active workmen. The most popular illustrators between the later 1850s and the mid-1890s found fame and fortune through idealized, romantic drawings whose conventions were similar to those of high art and academic painting, rather than through caricature. As comic visions faded in favor of sentimental ones, the poor acquired some of the lineaments of respectability. By 1890, artists brought the poor into much closer kinship with the middle classes.[50]

As the social hostilities of the 1840s receded in public memory, illustrators found it easier to portray even destitute workers as respectable, ordinary people. In the many sketches of Lancashire workers published during the cotton famine, relatively clean, docile people lined up in rows waiting for charity. Adult males, formerly the most likely to be shown in threatening poses, were

---

[49] Booth, *Aged Poor,* 14; idem, *Pauperism,* 235, 241.

[50] The shift away from caricature in book illustration became noticeable after the appearance in 1855 of William Allingham's *The Music Master,* which popularized a Germanic, idealized style of drawing the human body. Caricaturists such as George Cruikshank and Hablot K. Browne began to have trouble getting commissions. Michael Steig, *Dickens and Steig,* (Bloomington: Indiana University Press, 1978), 11; John Buchanan-Brown, *Phiz!* (Newton Abbot: David & Charles, 1978), 23.

drawn studying or collecting food and clothing for their families.[51] In an illustration from 6 December 1862, dozens of clean, smiling men sit quietly in rows, sipping tea, reading, and talking; they seem contented with the minimal provisions and austere environment. Although they lack individuality, they reek with respectability and good intentions. Indeed, copies of the *Illustrated Times* lie on the table next to spectacles and multiple books. A handful of caretakers and tea givers manage the scene.

The drift away from caricature in artists' work was accelerated by the arrival of an illustrated magazine, the *Graphic*, in 1869. W. L. Thomas, who was dissatisfied with the low standards of current pictorial journalism, set out to produce a paper with high-quality illustrations, many of which he commissioned and engraved himself. He allowed artists to choose their own subjects and was prepared to print explicit scenes of contemporary poverty, many of which were featured in large, full-page treatments.

Throughout the 1870s, the pages of the *Graphic* contained dozens of illustrations by Luke Fildes, Frank Holl, and Hubert von Herkomer, a relatively young group of artists, who had absorbed many of the Pre-Raphaelites' lessons in realistic observation.[52] Although low foreheads, snub noses, and relatively coarse features mark these representations, they were not unsympathetic toward the poor. The *Graphic* presented its audience with pictures of urban poverty contained. Francis Walker's "Young Ravens" from 1874 shows a charity dinner for poor children. As a crowd, they are controlled by their middle-class benefactors, who dispense plates filled with hot food. But the interest in the drawing lies in the carefully drawn, lively faces of the children, who gossip and gorge themselves with a good dinner. The girls' bare arms and heads and disorderly dress and hair suggest eroticism and energy. Indeed, their numbers suggest the large dimensions of the poverty problem. Like young ravens, they are scavengers, half-wild but tamed in the cage-like hall. But the drawing is not unsympathetic. In it, the social problem of the poor is "solved" by a modest amount of middle-class charity.

Over time, more and more of the *Graphic's* artists took their subjects off the streets and put them into public or charitable institutions.[53] They added policemen, public officials, and social workers to their compositions and separated the poor into the respectable and the suspect. In Frank Holl's "The Foundling," printed in 1873, a policeman rescues an abandoned baby and cradles it lovingly in his arms. A family of workers clings to one another

---

[51] See *Illustrated London News*, 29 November 1862; *Illustrated Times*, 6 December 1862.

[52] Julian Treuherz, *Hard Times: Social Realism in Art* (London: Lund Humphries, 1987).

[53] The *Graphic*, 21 December 1872, 585; 25 December 1876, 30.

Figure 7.1. "Men's Tearoom at the Institute, City Road, Manchester," *Illustrated Times,* 6 December 1862. Courtesy of Yale University Library

and watches with dismay; meanwhile, a woman – presumably the mother – crouches to one side, clutching the stones of the bridge. She seemingly gives up her maternal role, abandoning it to the state, which takes it on effectively. At the same time, unnatural actions lead to isolation and exclusion.

On the pages of the *Graphic,* hostility to the poor was muted and secondary to a message of redemption. Von Herkomer's "Christmas in the Workhouse" (1876) identifies pauperism with elderly women, who sit in rows and require help even to collect their small treats. The benign hand of the state supports them both literally and figuratively, and they look profoundly grateful. A wall motto announces: "God bless Master and Matron." Paupers in this rendition had become dependent on society and could no longer make any contribution to it.

By the century's end, the host of books surveying urban social conditions had moved far away from the conventions of caricature and physiognomy. Both women and men appear rough but redeemed by the helping hand of charities, religion, and the state. In the famous series of photographs commissioned by Dr. Barnardo of the children he "rescued" from the streets,

Figure 7.2. "The Young Ravens: A Friday Dinner at Great Queen Street," *The Graphic,* 21 December 1872

many were built on the contrast of before and after: rags into respectability, dirt replaced by cleanliness. Whatever the threatening potential of the unwashed, the photographer portrays them as salvageable by the joint efforts of charities and the state.[54] L. Raven-Hill's drawing of an East End night refuge, "Bridge of Hope," which appeared in Walter Besant's *East London,* published in 1901, shows the process in action. A matron tends a fire, which lights up a dark bedroom. Women lie in coffin-like beds, but some rise, drawn by the light and heat. A religious motto can be glimpsed on the wall.

In 1895, Hugh Thompson selected adult males, the most socially problematic category of the poor, for his illustrations in *The Poor in Great Cities.*[55] He juxtaposed the unemployed and the homeless against the backdrop of the Salvation Army. In his drawings, some listen transfixed to a preacher; others make bundles of kindling, transformed from isolated individuals into a group. Although their irregular features and disorderly clothing

---

[54] Seth Koven, "Dr. Barnardo's Artistic Fictions," unpublished paper presented at the North American Conference on British Studies (Washington, D.C., December 1995).

[55] Robert A. Woods, et al., *The Poor in Great Cities* (New York: Scribner, 1895).

Figure 7.3. "The Foundling," *The Graphic*, 26 April 1873. Frank Holl

mark them as lower class, they have moved into an environment where ideas and activities have begun to do the work of redemption. They are no longer an active threat to society.

Illustrations of poverty became more sanitized with the shift from wood-cuts and lithographs to photographs, which became increasingly common in the press and in books after the 1890s. Text and image worked together to depict urban "realities" as seen by journalist-explorers. Readers as con-sumers were given a product that supposedly was identical with a slice of a larger social world. When George Sims edited an elaborate work of urban description, *Living London,* published in 1901, it was profusely illustrated with contemporary photographs, as well as lithographs. Celebratory in tone, authors reported on visits to such uncommon sights as lunatic asylums and shelters, thereby introducing readers to those unaccustomed worlds. J. Wilkinson presented a benign picture of the St. Marylebone workhouse, which he called the "last refuge of civilization's superfluities and failures." Yet he conjured friendly images of the "veritable dear old creatures" he found within, noting how "pleasing" they looked as they "hobnobbed over their

Figure 7.4. "Christmas in a Workhouse," *The Graphic*, 25 December 1876, Hubert von Herkomer

tea."[56] The accompanying photos stressed the good, professional care obtainable within and presented the destitute inmates as completely harmless. In the eye of the photographer, the poor had been successfully disciplined by the routines and rules of the workhouse. The tone is one of a boring order; rows and rows of paupers who lack individuality and vitality, and who have

[56] George Sims, *Living London*, 3 vols. (London: Cassell, 1902–3).

Figure 7.5. "Bridge of Hope," by L. Raven-Hill, in *East London*, Walter Besant, 1903

become known through their contact with the state. The photographer's gaze fixes them in the routine of the workhouse, and he speaks for them in a language of uniformity.

By the 1870s, photography had become a tool of the state and of social reformers for representing and surveying the poor. Visual "likenesses" of prisoners, lunatics, and orphans became part of a public record by which knowledge of the poor was communicated and kept for multiple uses. John Tagg

Figure 7.6. "Dinner at St. Marylebone Workhouse," in *Living London*, George Sims, 1902

argues that such photographs operated in a "realist" mode of representation, one in which the viewer is presented with an image supposedly identical to one part of a larger social world. Manipulations of setting, dress, lighting, and expression remain hidden and unacknowledged because the photographic image is seen as a transparent reflection of the scene it captures. In Tagg's view, realist photography acquired its power through repetition: A limited range of variations led viewers through familiarity to acknowledge the "truth" of the representation.[57] Seth Koven reminds us, however, of the complexity of late nineteenth-century photographic images of the poor, which combined disparagement, titillation, and heavy-handed moral lessons. Photographs necessarily interpret what they depict. They function as "artistic fictions," rather than as mirrors of "reality." Dr. Barnardo's manipulations of the dress and poses of orphan children he had photographed as part of his fund-raising activities, which led to widespread demands for truth in advertising, were egregious but by no means unique examples of photographic interpretation.[58] Not only Dr. Barnardo's images but also the photographs that appeared in *Living London* and elsewhere, captured particular visions of the destitute and fixed them in the public mind. Those representations encoded late Victorian ideas of poverty, in which state and voluntary organizations took the inferior and successfully disciplined them in the public interest.

---

[57] John Tagg, *The Burden of Representation* (Amherst: University of Massachusetts Press, 1988), 5, 11, 99.

[58] Barnardo quickly retreated to the claim of literalness – and presumably stopped tearing the clothes of his street Arabs to dramatize their poverty. See Seth Koven, "Dr. Barnardo."

8

THE MULTICAMPAIGN WAR ON
PAUPERISM, 1870–1906

[Considering] in what direction progress toward improved administration
may be immediately practicable it may, I hope, be considered not pre-
sumptuous or visionary to suggest that, for the present at least, . . . in-door
relief shall be the rule and out-relief the exception.

> Henry Longley, 1873

Indoor relief lacks humanity and outdoor encourages improvidence. We
are therefore justified in seeking some better plan. . . . It is not insurance
we require, but the endowment of old age.

> Charles Booth, 1892

The destitute in late Victorian Britain could find help in multiple places: Families, charities, and the state combined to provide support. Philanthropy flourished, probably raising and dispensing more money per year than did the poor
law; trade unions and friendly societies provided a venue for group insurance.
Using the framework of 1834, guardians investigated applicants and dispensed modest pensions to those who passed muster. Yet the rules of the poor
law game changed yet again in the 1870s, as officials tried once more to
restrict outdoor relief. Meanwhile, charities transformed themselves into professional organizations with more rigid aims and procedures. Activist women
redoubled their efforts to visit the poor and to redeem them through personal
contacts and individually tailored assistance, whereas charity administrators
fretting about waste and fraud worked to tighten procedures. What Jane
Lewis has termed a "mixed economy of welfare" was unstable, shifting along
with attitudes to the poor and to their dependence.[1]

[1] F. K. Prochaska, *Women and Philanthrophy in Nineteenth-Century England* (Oxford: Oxford
University Press, 1980); Jane Lewis, *The Voluntary Sector, the State and Social Work in Britain*
(London: Edward Elgar, 1995).

The role of the state in this period was threefold: Its administrators helped to determine the clientele for the philanthropists by setting the ground rules for poor law aid, and it pushed families to extend their financial support for the elderly by more aggressively pursuing adult sons in the courts. At the same time, the reworking of poor law institutions under the pressures of female reformers and health care professionals transformed the workhouse from "bastille" to hospital and orphanage. Social engineers reconfigured the Victorian poor law under the impetus of multiple agendas.

Discipline and Efficiency, 1870–90

The Poor Law Board thought that to make informed decisions about relief, guardians needed extensive knowledge about individual paupers. But how was that to be achieved in growing cities amid their mobile populations? In most of urban England, the face-to-face knowledge of the poor gained in a community through decades of coresidence had long since vanished, but guardians hoped to recapture it with modern methods. Relieving officers were instructed to visit homes, to judge applicants' health and ability to work, and to make inquiries into the families and their means. But overburdened inspectors cut corners, listed only the obvious, and ignored the demand to investigate relatives. Neither they nor the guardians normally had time to build the nuanced portraits of households called for by zealous welfare reformers. Edmond H. Wodehouse, who surveyed London, found many local officials unable to check effectively the information that paupers gave them, and he painted a picture of sloppy procedures that shocked London officials.[2]

The fruits of investigators' efforts went into the Application and Report books. Clerks inscribed into large, heavy ledgers demographic information on the pauper's household, adding details on disabilities, health, wages, length of residence in the union, resources, and claims for aid. They recorded the bare bones of destitution, fast facts about the poor. In theory, these books were to give officials what they required to make an appropriate decision. But how could a thin line of demographic description be translated into the Solomonic judgments about character, spending habits, and association called for by the rules on outdoor relief? Guardians had to twist actuarial categories and tallies of shillings and pence into criteria of virtue. Assumptions about age and gender, embellished by visual impressions and informal com-

---

[2] Edmond H. Wodehouse, "Report on Outrelief in the Metropolitan District," in Poor Law Board, *Twenty-Third Annual Report, 1870–71,* Appendix. (London: HM Stationery Office 1871), 32–42.

mentary from the pauper and the inspector, were all they had to supplement demographic profiles. Although the logic of their classification schemes pushed them to economic and physical criteria for destitution, their prejudices turned them toward the intangibles of character.

What then gave solid knowledge of the poor? What set of criteria to trust? Henry Longley, a poor law inspector for London, proposed in 1873 multiple reforms of welfare rules, which were designed to increase the efficiency of the system. His analysis of the deficiencies of the poor laws hinged upon the issue of information: Officials had to have exact and full details about lives and incomes in order to make sure that relief was adequate, but not excessive. Also, the poor needed to know exactly what was on offer and for whom so that they would not organize fishing expeditions into the public purse. But in his opinion, the knowledge necessary for efficient outdoor relief was never available. Only in institutions could officials calibrate exactly the balance between need and support. Longley recommended, therefore, that indoor relief become the rule, and outdoor relief, the exception.[3]

Longley, whose report was widely circulated by the Local Government Board during the 1870s as a statement of sound policies, argued that institutions could improve welfare administration in several ways. He pointed out that guardians deliberately set levels of outdoor relief to be less than full maintenance, which for the destitute he termed "inadequate." This practice he found disastrous: It encouraged paupers to lie and beg for more; it gave guardians of the poor a cheap, easy way to fob off applicants; and it did not effectively support those who were truly destitute. Only in institutions could relief be adequate, but not excessive. Longley also defended the positive impact of institutions on the children of the poor; they would "rescue" such children from their families and put them in a better environment where they would have "exceptional opportunities of becoming ultimately independent."[4] Workhouses would also reaffirm the principle of deterrent forms of welfare. By offering "discipline," as well as "disgrace," workhouses would push applicants away from welfare and back to habits of self-reliance. Longley saw state institutions as redemptive in both positive and negative ways. They would discourage pauperism among those who with a bit more effort could help themselves, and they would redeem those who came within their walls.

[3] Henry Longley, "Report to the Local Government Board on Poor Law Administration in London," Appendix to the *Third Annual Report of the Local Government Board, 1873–1874* (London: HM Stationery Office, 1874), 168–9.

[4] Ibid., 169, 170–1.

Longley outlined a series of precise rules for granting outdoor relief, far more specific than those of the 1834 report. Rather than prohibit outdoor relief, he proposed to construct a series of high hurdles that an applicant would have to leap over before obtaining it. If a person had a bad character, had no suitable home, had not saved, had refused a job offer, or had relatives who could contribute to his or her support and would not to do so, he or she would be disqualified and would be offered aid only through an institution. Longley explained that his rules would encourage thrift among the poor, as well as habits of independence. In Karel Williams's opinion, Longley defined a "strategy" for the "crusade against outrelief" that dominated the Local Government Board's policy in the 1870s. Different from the principles of 1834, it proposed educating the poor by clarifying for them precisely what the state had on offer and what they had to do to obtain it. "Knowledge by the poor" would reform welfare, according to Longley.[5]

Local officials interpreted Longley's ideas in their own fashion, however, and it is not clear whether they equated reform of the poor with draconian measures. Workhouse practices, in particular, varied from place to place. In Salford, for example, the master and matron of the workhouse held to the notion of discipline, but retreated from that of disgrace and minimum standards. Workhouse dormitories had walls lined with pictures; inmates celebrated the fall season's Harvest Home in a chapel decorated with flowers and encouraging homilies. (See Figures 8.1, 8.2.)

Although Longley's elaborate scheme for educating the poor fell by the wayside, his and the Local Government Board's call for reform was heeded by local officials, who pursued an intermittent campaign against outrelief, while ignoring the more subtle changes in policy they recommended. (See Table 8.1.) Indeed, between 1871 and 1876, the number of people receiving outrelief fell by 33 percent to 567,000; it then declined and remained low, averaging only 538,000 per year between 1877 and 1896, when the Local Government Board again accepted the principle of outdoor relief for the deserving poor. The number of paupers on outrelief, when measured per 1,000 of national population, declined sharply from 37.7 per 1,000 people in 1870 to 23.6 per 1,000 in 1876 and then to 17.1 per 1,000 in 1897. Meanwhile, the numbers of paupers in institutions rose slowly. As a proportion of the total population in institutions, they accounted for 5.2 per 1,000 people in 1876, rising slowly to 6.1 per 1,000 in 1896 and 7.1 per 1,000 in 1905.[6] Despite the

---

[5] Karel Williams, *From Pauperism to Poverty* (London: Routledge, 1981), 98–9.

[6] Ibid., Table 4.5, 159–61.

Figure 8.1. "Boy's Dormitory, Salford Workhouse," c. 1890. Courtesy of the City of Salford, Arts & Leisure Department

Figure 8.2. "Harvest Home Celebration, Salford Workhouse Chapel," c. 1890. Courtesy of the City of Salford, Arts & Leisure Department

Table 8.1 *Indoor and outdoor relief, 1860–1905*

Year	Indoor		Outdoor	
	No.	%	No.	%
1860	101,000	13	695,000	87
1865	118,000	13	783,000	87
1870	141,000	14	838,000	86
1875	129,000	17	616,000	83
1880	159,000	21	582,000	79
1885	162,000	23	533,000	77
1890	166,000	24	530,000	76
1895	184,000	26	523,000	74
1900	188,000	27	500,000	73
1905	240,000	30	547,000	70

Sources: Royal Commission on the Poor Laws and the Relief of Distress: Statistics Relating to England and Wales (London: H.M. Stationery Office, 1911), appendix, vol. 25, p. 26; Karel Williams, *From Pauperism to Poverty* (London: Routledge, 1981), p. 159–61.

major economic problems of the last quarter of the century, welfare officials chose to restrict relief, even in institutions, rather than expand it. Longley's faith in institutions was not adopted by those who had to pay the bills.

This "crusade against outrelief" affected several different types of paupers. In London, most unions targeted the able-bodied by offering them maintenance in the Poplar Workhouse, which in 1871 became a specialized institution where inmates had to perform particularly nasty jobs, such as oakum picking or stone breaking. The combination of the long tramp to the workhouse in the East End, strict discipline, and hard labor produced a massive refusal of relief – exactly what the guardians intended.[7] In the Basford union of Nottinghamshire, officials largely stopped subsidizing the wages of elderly workers, who either had to find other means of support or had to enter the workhouse. In addition, single, able-bodied women and widows found that their entitlement to pensions had decreased. Moreover, far fewer people classified as non-able-bodied, presumably the elderly and the disabled, got outdoor relief.[8] Using local records, David Thomson has documented a wide-

[7] Sidney Webb and Beatrice Webb, *English Poor Law History,* Part 2: *The Last Hundred Years,* vol. 1 (London: Longmans, 1929), 379, 445–7.

[8] Sonya O. Rose, "The Widowed Elderly in Nineteenth Century Nottinghamshire: Community, Kin and Household Strategies," unpublished paper presented at the Tenth International Economic History Conference, Leuven, 1990), 11–12.

spread cutback in outdoor relief to the elderly residing in southern and northern unions, both urban and rural, from 1870 to at least 1900.[9] The crusade
against outrelief therefore hit two groups of people traditionally labeled the
deserving poor.[10] Ironically, just as the wider society had begun to soften its
view of the poor, welfare officials hardened their attitudes.

The heartland of the crusade lay in London and in the large towns of the
Midlands and northwest. Most of the poor law unions in London cut back the
proportion of paupers on outdoor relief to below 30 percent of total paupers
relieved; Liverpool, Manchester, and Birmingham guardians did likewise, as
did those in Preston, Salford, Reading, and Oxford. A few predominantly
rural unions, Atcham near Shrewsbury and several districts in Berkshire and
Kent, were also known for their strict relief policies. Atcham officials, consistently among the most stingy in the country, in 1871 told the Local Government Board with pride that their union never gave long-term outrelief to
the unemployed, deserted wives and children, paupers living outside the
union, or people who rented over a half-acre of land. If applicants' cottages
were dirty, they were told to clean them up or risk losing relief.[11] In the rest
of the country, however, outdoor relief was easier to obtain; at the peak of
restrictive practices in the 1870s, 73 percent of all paupers still received aid
outside institutions.[12] As long as they lived outside the major cities and a few
atypical rural areas, paupers had to face broad-based cutbacks in outdoor
relief, but not its virtual elimination. Institutionalization of the poor was an
urban strategy, not a rural one, and one used extensively only in the largest
cities.

A look at Southampton, a southern port town, shows how local authorities
interested in economy but not draconian cutbacks responded to the call for
renewed use of the workhouse. Interest in reforming local poor law administration swelled in 1875, after the founding of the Southampton Charity Organization Society (C.O.S) by Richard W. W. Griffin, a poor law medical officer in the town. Articles in local papers, as well as the *Times*, warned readers
that pauperism in Southampton in 1874 had reached double the national average and that per capita expenditure on paupers was 50 percent higher than in

---

[9] David William Thomson, "Provision for the Elderly in England, 1830–1908," Ph.D. diss., Cambridge University, 1980, 204–41.

[10] Williams, *Pauperism*, 103, 161–2.

[11] Ibid., 105; Sir William Chance, *The Better Administration of the Poor Law* (London: Swan Son-
nenschein & Co., 1895), 95.

[12] See ibid., 159, Table 4.5.

the country as a whole. Griffin charged that most of those on relief were "unnecessary paupers" and recommended strict enforcement of poor law policies and a decrease in expenditure. Because the town had built a new workhouse in 1866, guardians had additional space and better facilities to offer applicants, and the Charity Organization Society offered to coordinate charitable giving to encourage the respectable poor to help themselves. During the winter of 1877, the board of guardians tightened the rules on the granting of medical relief and limited grants of outdoor aid to a period of three months. More information was to be collected about applicants, and even the sick poor had to have character references to demonstrate "worthiness." The screws were tightened in a variety of small ways as administrators resolved to give fewer people welfare. The results were dramatic: The number of people granted outdoor relief each year, which had averaged 4,300 between 1863 and 1872, plummeted, and from 1875 to 1900, the annual average remained under 2,000. Moreover, those stricken from the outdoor relief rolls, for the most part able-bodied adults, did not enter the workhouse. The group that entered state welfare institutions each year decreased in size after 1880 and remained below 1,000 for the rest of the century. This general shrinkage in the population on welfare cannot be explained by changing economic circumstances because the restrictive years coincided with the end-of-the-century depression.[13]

During the 1870s, residents in other cities saw even less extensive changes in relief policies. In Gateshead in the northeast, guardians ignored orders to enforce the workhouse test and continued to grant outdoor relief rather freely. Overall, towns in the northeast usually ignored orders from London and administered the poor law in line with the wishes of local property owners. This, for the most part, led to economy and limited innovation by the later nineteenth century.[14] In Leeds, welfare policies seem to have shifted according to whether Tories or Liberals controlled the board of guardians: The latter group cut back on outdoor relief and on beer in the workhouse, whereas the former one spent money much more freely.[15] Leicester, which had for

---

[13] Ruth Hutchinson Crocker, "The Victorian Poor Law in Crisis and Change: Southampton, 1870–1895," *Albion* 19:1 (Spring 1987): 23–7.

[14] Keith Gregson, "Poor Law and Organized Charity: The Relief of Exceptional Distress in North-East England, 1870–1910," in Michael Rose, ed., *The Poor and the City: The English Poor Law in Its Urban Context, 1834–1914* (New York: St. Martin's, 1985), 107; June Valerie Corrigan, "The Administration of the Poor Law in Tynemouth Union, 1830–1939," Master's thesis, University of London, 1985, 354–64.

[15] Webb Local Government Collection, Part 2, *The Poor Law*, vol. 344: Yorkshire, 1873–1884, London, British Library of Political and Economic Science.

some time used labor tests and workhouse tests to limit grants to the unemployed, continued that policy into the 1870s and 1880s, relying on charities and public works jobs to support men out of work during difficult years.[16] Able-bodied adults living in English towns found it much more difficult to get welfare outside an institution during the last quarter of the nineteenth century than they had around 1860.

Ground rules in the crusade against outrelief consisted of multiple circulars from boards of guardians that described the unworthy in lurid terms, definable in the eye of the beholder. The "immoral," "indolent," improvident, or vicious were to be denied outrelief, as were "habitual drunkards," "common beggars," and gamblers. It was not enough to notice age, sex, and physical condition; inspectors were also to check on the minutiae of private lives and sniff about for drink and the odors of impropriety. The Sheffield union calibrated four degrees of virtue for those chosen to receive outdoor relief: Class A merited 5s., whereas the less deserving got only 4s., 3s., and 2s. 6d., respectively, per week per adult. Some unions set niggling rules that condemned standard practices in poor communities. Visits to a pub, "insanitary or immoral surroundings," residence in a lodging house or in furnished rooms could debar applicants from a pension. At the same time, paying too much for rent or having spent excessively on a family funeral signified a lack of thrift and therefore signaled trouble. Conversely, those who had saved and owned a cottage or a farm animal, or those who had a savings account or a small pension were disqualified as not sufficiently poor.[17] Those on relief could not be disreputable according to middle-class standards, nor could they show any pretensions to comfort. Few could manage the precise blend of bland suffering and unsuccessful foresight demanded by the guardians. Standards for support had clearly risen late in the century, as guardians articulated a model of morality to which paupers were expected to conform.

Women had additional hurdles to leap. Having a husband in jail or overseas with the army, having borne an illegitimate child, or living in a dirty house could doom appeals for a pension. Some unions forbade outdoor relief to those who lived alone; others rejected those who shared houses. Women could not have male lodgers without permission, nor could they rent space to females with illegitimate children, in case the lodgers' immorality were to be contagious. Elderly applicants could not have a daughter older than age thirteen living with them who was not at work. Women who were heads of house-

[16] Ibid., vol. 311, Leicestershire, 1857, 1877–94.
[17] Webb and Webb, *English Poor Law History*, Part 2, vol. 1, 445–6, 450–1.

holds found that the poor law after 1870 did little to help them keep their families together. Guardians usually refused to aid deserted wives for a year after abandonment, fearing collusion between couples to get welfare outside the workhouse. Widows, too, found their rights to aid reduced. Many unions denied aid altogether to widows with one child, assuming that they could earn enough for the household. Others imposed strict time limits of a few months after which outdoor relief would cease. It was also common, the Webbs found, for many unions to offer workhouse support for children in larger female-headed families, expecting mothers to give them up and earn their own keep. On the other hand, guardians became more reluctant late in the century to subsidize normally low female wages for fear of undermining women's incentives to self-support.[18] In late Victorian times, female dependence combined with destitution no longer conferred automatic access to welfare. To deserve the care of the state outside a workhouse, women had to demonstrate not only extreme need but virtue, independence, and a lack of ties to people with suspect morality. Ironically, many of the family situations that necessitated their recourse to the poor laws also debarred them from it. Guardians coupled a calculated blindness to common female predicaments with intolerance of viable options for earning a living.

In practice, however, fewer and fewer people as a proportion of the population received welfare aid after 1870, and outdoor relief was denied to thousands who would have received it using midcentury criteria. Ironically, just as the wider society was softening its views of the destitute and incorporating workers more extensively in political structures, the poor law was tightening the screws on the poor. Charities therefore bore a greater burden, which was both practical and ideological in nature. What attitudes should be taken toward the destitute? The legacy of 1834 lived on in an atmosphere transformed by the analyses of Herbert Spencer, Charles Darwin, and T. H. Green.

The Charity Organization Society's Therapy for the Destitute

The front line in the war on poverty was staffed by multiple local groups. Daily, thousands of charities and church societies fed, clothed, and visited the poor. For many, however, fears of deception undermined the impulse to give. What if paupers collected twice? How could charities reform and redeem the poor, if they encouraged the poor to deceive in return for alms? A stock Victorian response to such common queries was to call for more information, more efficient superintendance.

[18] Ibid., 447–450.

Women led many of these efforts. The vast army of women visitors, who fanned out through the slums, questioning and encouraging, collected first-hand knowledge about day-to-day needs. Many of them, through their work with the Workhouse Visiting Society, the Reformatory and Refuge Union, the Waifs and Strays Society, or Jane Senior's Metropolitan Association for Befriending Young Servants, bridged the large gap between public and private welfare efforts. After 1875, elected female guardians brought their pragmatic concerns into the board rooms of the poor law.[19] Females were the foot soldiers in the Victorian attack upon destitution and pauperism, but as in many armies there was not perfect order in the ranks.

The vast numbers of private charities and evangelical reformist groups that ministered to the poor often worked at cross-purposes, and they offered the destitute multiple venues for assistance. Yet in a society obsessed with the morality of the poor and with exact knowledge of their condition and resources, the possibility of double- or even triple-dipping in the welfare coffers raised the hackles of many in the welfare establishment. The Charity Organization Society, after its founding in London in 1869, made solving this problem one of its aims. Agents for the C.O.S. would register all those who asked for aid in a given district and would record what they received. "Judicious and effectual assistance of all deserving cases" was to be combined with "the promotion of habits of providence and self-reliance." Meanwhile, they expected to repress "mendicity and imposture," diverting the undeserving into the heavy hands of the poor law.[20] To this end, the C.O.S. set up an elaborate machine for visiting and collecting information about the poor. Within three years, thirty-six district offices had been opened in the metropolis, and numerous local committees had been organized. Despite their grandiose hopes, only rarely did they succeed in disciplining the dozens of local charities run by rival churches and reforming groups to work under their direction. Moreover, local C.O.S. groups sometimes took an independent line from the central organization. Nevertheless, they popularized "scientific charity" and casework, their major stock in trade after schemes to coordinate charitable giving failed.[21]

The society, guided by its first two secretaries, Charles Bosanquet and Charles Stewart Loch, became an effective voice for the C.O.S. gospel, which

---

[19] Prochaska, *Philanthrophy*, 150–1; Patricia Hollis, *Ladies Elect* (Oxford: Oxford University Press, 1987).

[20] Charity Organization Society, *Fifth Annual Report* (London, 1875), 5–6, quoted in C. L. Mowat, *The Charity Organization Society, 1869–1913* (London: Methuen, 1961), 26.

[21] Lewis, *Voluntary Sector.*

linked altruistic voluntarism to the collective good. Charity for its members embodied the highest moral purpose. Indeed, they saw themselves simultaneously improving both individuals and society, bringing the poor into full citizenship by returning them to the paths of righteousness. Tracts and manuals detailed this message of elevated principle and pragmatic penny-pinching. Conferences and lectures brought together both amateur and professional charity workers to discuss and proselytize. Then, too, the social and intellectual stature of C.O.S. advocates such as Octavia Hill and Bernard Bosanquet ensured that the society's ideas got respectful attention and ample publicity in the public sphere. Not only did the C.O.S. activists have intellectually impeccable credentials, but they were aggressive and self-assured. Queen Victoria signed on as Patron, and the Archbishop of Canterbury and a long list of peers served as the society's president and vice-presidents. By the end of the century, its influence reached across the empire, as well as throughout Europe and the United States, as charitable activists elsewhere imitated its example. In the opinion of Geoffrey Finlayson, the society served as an important "weathervane of opinion" in the early twentieth century.[22]

In Britain, the C.O.S. quickly spawned affiliated societies around the country. Eighteen had been organized by 1879, twenty-five by 1893, and dozens of others generally allied themselves with C.O.S. doctrines.[23] In the northeast, C.O.S. societies existed in Newcastle upon Tyne, Sunderland, Darlington, Middlesbrough, South Shields, and West Hartlepool. Although these groups rarely managed the strict coordination of relief efforts that central policies demanded, several did introduce the principle of casework and the use of individual visitors during the 1880s. Throughout the region, charities moved to classify applicants more strictly, train officials, and work toward a more professional style of administration. Although "scientific" precision eluded them, they had adopted the notion that proper relief practices demanded knowledge and training.[24] The C.O.S. helped transform paupers into cases to be investigated and given an individualized response.

The ideal C.O.S. worker would be a "neighbor" to the poor, maintaining a respectful, friendly manner toward them and visiting at least once a month to maintain contacts. Charles Bosanquet compiled a list of helpful hints for visitors, whose chief function he defined as assisting "the poor with such information and advice as a person of education and comparative leisure has oppor-

---

[22] Geoffrey Finlayson, "A Moving Frontier: Voluntarism and the State in British Social Welfare," *Twentieth Century British History* 1:2 (1990): 199–200.

[23] Mowat, *Charity*, 92.

[24] Gregson, "Poor Law," 94–131.

tunities for obtaining and supplying." While discreetly collecting information about their families, the visitors should offer simple recipes, encourage membership in savings banks and friendly societies, and lend "interesting books and periodicals." They should concern themselves with the children, checking on choice of schools and their progress and suggesting appropriate jobs for older children. The elderly were to be disabused of the "horror of the workhouse" because its inmates got good food, medical care, and visits from the chaplain and "benevolent Christian ladies." Although advice was to be freely dispensed, Bosanquet discouraged visitors from distributing much relief. Help in finding a job was said to be more useful than a handout, a gift of cooked food better than money. In particular, he warned: "Great caution should be exercised . . . in assisting the wife and family of a drunken husband. . . . Beware of allowing importunity, or the excitement of a momentary sympathy, to obtain from you an aid which your conscience disapproves." More positively, however, he encouraged the visitors to be advocates for their families – to inform them of their rights vis-à-vis city institutions and to report sanitary problems in their neighborhoods to the Medical Officer of Health and to the Inspector of Nuisances. The families could be put in touch with labor exchanges and helped to join medical insurance clubs. Although the contacts suggested reeked of noblesse oblige and the condescension of patron toward client, the C.O.S., at least in theory, was prepared to work with families to improve their health, their incomes, and their education.[25]

But how effective was it? The best place to see the system in operation is to turn to the case records generated by C.O.S. investigators. As part of his investigation of local poverty, Charles Booth made an abstract of the judgments on eighty households that had asked for aid in January and June of 1890 from the Stepney committee of the London C.O.S. In each case, its district visitors gathered details about the demography of the applicant and coresident family, as well as of other members of the nuclear unit and other kin of the adults who supported the group. They inquired into work, wages, schooling, and physical conditions as part of their preliminary mapping of eligibility for aid. Usually they found ample reasons for poverty: Unemployment, accidents at work, illness, and large families figured prominently in the life stories they recorded. The C.O.S. constructed profiles of need and physical deprivation, whose authenticity it did not question. But economics was only a small part of entitlement to aid. Thomas Brown, a forty-seven-year-old bargeman with a wife and six young children, came down with bronchitis and

---

[25] Charles B. P. Bosanquet, *A Handy Book for Visitors of the Poor in London* (London: Longmans, 1874), 8, 15–24.

an abscessed leg. His wife was unable to work because of heart disease, and the family was said not to belong to a friendly society. Moreover, because of illness, Brown for several months had apparently not been working full time. A poor law doctor sent him to the sick asylum, but it was full and could not take him. Brown then asked the C.O.S. for food, nursing care, and money to feed his family. The society decided not to help because his "character [was] unsatisfactory." Brown apparently drank heavily and, at that time, was said to "ill-treat" his wife, although informants said he had reformed. The society attributed his poverty to drunkenness and dropped the case.[26] No suggestions of remedies or alternatives were recorded. Those who could not demonstrate good character forfeited their right to help. Margaret Lawless, a sixty-one-year-old widow, asked for a weekly allowance to pay her rent, claiming that she had never asked for money before. Neighbors apparently were support-ing her. When the society found out that she had applied for aid after her hus-band's death in the winter of 1883 and again 1887 and when the visitors learned that local people branded her "noisy," "eccentric," and a "nuisance," the C.O.S. decided that she should . . . go into the workhouse.[27] Those who drank, those who were dirty or uncongenial, and those who asked too often lost eligibility, even if their poverty was not in question.

The Stepney C.O.S., although it recognized economic, demographic, and physical origins for poverty, only engaged positively with people whom they judged to be worthy. In addition, needs had to be small and, ideally, tempo-rary. People with varicose veins got surgical stockings; the ill could be given time in a hospital or convalescent home; women trying to support themselves could be loaned the money to buy a sewing machine or a mangle. For the rest, a small loan or a temporary pension was the usual extent of C.O.S. aid. Despite their concern to define charity in terms of interclass contact that brought permanent improvement of the poor, the Stepney society restricted its contact with applicants to a superficial level. Concern for children's edu-cation, for housing, or for long-term care was not evident in the records. The Stepney C.O.S. focused on a quick fix for short-term problems and left to oth-ers the thorny issues of family instability, dysfunctional behavior, or long-term deprivation. Social work for its members had a quite limited meaning, one that shoved to the margins the vast majority of the urban poor whose con-dition was chronic and serious or whose character was sufficiently flawed to justify the denial of help.

---

[26] Charity Organization Society, Stepney Committee, "Abstract of Cases, January and June 1890"; Case 5610, no. 5, Booth Papers, British Library of Political and Economic Science.

[27] Ibid., Case 2409, no. 3.

The C.O.S. model of charity cum social work could be widened somewhat, although it was limited by the resources and the imagination of local inspectors. The Leicester C.O.S., which had operated from 1876 through 1902 along lines recommended by C. S. Loch and the London leadership, hired a new secretary in 1903. William Edwin Hincks then ran the group until 1937, helping it to spend more money and assist more people.[28] The C.O.S. quickly became more active, referring people to a range of local and regional institutions and visiting them repeatedly. They consulted doctors, employers, guardians, and clergy before they made a decision. Bible women were sent around to check on spiritual progress. Throughout the flurry of activity, the C.O.S. concentrated on investigation rather than friendship; judgments remained severe.

In February of 1904, Annie Greet asked the society to pay the train fare of her twenty-year-old son Ernest from London back to Leicester. He had a "weak spine" and could not walk. At age thirteen, he had been placed in a London home for cripples, but he did not like it there and wanted to come home. The C.O.S. sent a visitor to the Greets' apartment and to Harry Greet's employer, a shoe manufacturer, and it corresponded with Leicester poor law authorities and with London C.O.S. branches. The Society worked very little with the family, but primarily with professional charity workers and Mr. Greet's employer to decide Ernest's fate. The local poor law inspector was hostile to the Greets' request; he judged Mrs. Greet to be "drunken and dirty" and claimed that she had recently been warned about some unnamed offense by the National Society for the Prevention of Cruelty to Children. In fact, he thought it would be "a mercy" to put Ernest in the workhouse. Mr. Greet's boss agreed: He announced that Mr. Greet had been "dragged down by a drunken wife" who regularly got him into debt, and he did not want one of his reliable workmen to have someone else to support and worry about. Although the C.O.S. visitor made no complaints about Annie Greet and judged her home to be "fairly clean," he sided with the family's critics. Moreover, he noted that if Ernest were to return home, there would be eight people having to share two bedrooms. With all this information in hand, the C.O.S. declined to help the Greets, although a second inspector seems to have paid Ernest's train fare privately.[29]

The Leicester C.O.S. formed part of an elaborate network of charitable

---

[28] Zoe D. Oakleaf, "Poverty in Leicester at the Turn of the Century, 1904–1912," Ph.D. diss., University of Iowa, 1982, 40–2.

[29] Leicester Charity Organization Society Case Records, 1904, no. 64, Leicestershire County Record Office.

institutions functioning alongside the poor laws. The network of people and groups dealing with the Greet family was a fairly simple one, but the web of interconnecting charities could stretch much farther. In Leicester, King Charles's Charity gave money for coal and wood to several hundred poor at Christmas; the Blanket Lending Society passed out bedding, and two groups, the Police Aided Association and the Ladies' Charity, provided clothing. Six clubs housed or supported the elderly poor; there were seven refuges for young girls or women in distress, some of which provided job training. Orphan boys could go to a Church of England home, and the Institution for the Blind provided training, employment, and partial support for those who had lost their sight. In addition, local churches staffed a variety of groups for their own parishioners. The town's charities also included a long list of partly subsidized groups through which workers could ensure themselves against a variety of risks, in particular that of illness. With small weekly contributions to the General Infirmary, the People's Dispensary, or the Provident Dispensary, subscribers could get medical care and medicine as needed.[30] The C.O.S. served as an intermediary between these groups, referring people to them and to other charities within the county as needed. Its repertoire of solutions to the poverty problem closely resembled that of the town's list of official charities.

The C.O.S. style of "social work" in Leicester resembled that of poor law inspectors: narrow inquiries into income, character, and family resources, with a roving eye for alternatives to granting relief. The society's unit of analysis remained that of the individual and his or her nuclear family. Therefore, it worried about morals, health, and capacity for self-help, largely ignoring other determinants of need. The presence of character flaws, rather than economics, was its standard explanation for misfortune. For example, tuberculosis was treated as a given, rather than a communicable disease strongly linked to environment. The society dealt with acute physical problems far better than metaphysical ones and resolutely turned its eyes away from wider questions of causation and cure. Confronted daily by destitution and family breakdown, district visitors did a quick balance sheet of individuals' resources and defects before placing small Band-Aids upon the gaping wounds of social distress. Discrimination was their strong suit, as they attempted to separate those who could easily be returned to independence, leaving the hard cases to the poor laws.

[30] Oakleaf, "Poverty," 27–33.

The State's Specialized Treatment of the Poor

The invention of social work and the notion of specialized "treatment" reshaped poor law practices in this same period. Modernizing administrators reconfigured the poor law around specialized institutions catering to particular types of need. A range of more sophisticated concerns – education and medical care, for example – became important as professional staffs grew and as ideas about rehabilitation became more sophisticated. Particularly in the areas of medicine and child care, the poor law moved very far from the Elizabethan recipe of minimal work and alms. The elderly, too, shared in this shift. They became a separate category with particular rights and privileges, no longer merely part of the "impotent poor." Pauperism, a term applied to all the dependent destitute early in the century, became a more nuanced condition, one in which age, gender, and physical and mental condition warranted different responses.

Children were the group most clearly targeted by reformers' efforts. Because they comprised a substantial proportion of the population relieved – about 40 percent in 1849, which fell to 25 percent by 1907 – policies toward them accounted for substantial amounts of effort and cash.[31] In the first years of the New Poor Law, they were given little attention. But James Kay, an assistant commissioner, suggested in 1838 that they needed special treatment in order to eradicate "the germs of pauperism from the rising generation."[32] He and others pushed unions to build large, district schools where children admitted to workhouses could be trained efficiently away from their families and adult paupers. Nevertheless, the few that were built proved unpopular, expensive, and liable to outbreaks of contagious diseases. Nevertheless, education as a remedy for pauperism became official policy, leading to the organization of large numbers of workhouse schools.

During the 1850s and 1860s, criticisms of large, barrack-style schools multiplied, coming both from men charged with inspecting workhouse schools and from several female reformers. Revulsion against their size and rigid discipline led women such as Louisa Twining, founder of the Workhouse Visiting Society, and Mary Carpenter, leader of efforts to organize juvenile reformatories, to attack them publicly. In *Children of the State* (1868), Florence Davenport Hill asked that children be trained within family-

---

[31] Williams, *Pauperism*, 230.

[32] Poor Law Commission, *Fourth Annual Report* (London, 1838), 140; quoted in Felix Driver, *Power and Pauperism: The Workhouse System* (New York: Cambridge University Press, 1993), 96.

size units. She, Carpenter, and Twining thought moral reformation and train-ing would only be effective within settings where children received individ-ual attention and affection; hence their recommendations for "family princi-ples" for pauper children's education and housing. Calls for decentralized "cottage homes" for pauper children mounted during the 1870s after Jane Senior recommended such a solution to the Local Government Board. The institutional settings 'within which pauper children were educated soon shifted markedly. Although the principle of moral regulation had not been abandoned, authorities decided that it could be achieved more effectively out-side the workhouse.[33]

Between 1870 and 1914, most guardians made a conscious decision that children within their care required treatment different from that intended for adults. For them, the problem was not "less eligibility" but "dispauperiza-tion," which could be effected through carefully regulated, family-style care. About two hundred small, cottage residences were built by guardians throughout England and Wales. In Sheffield, these were scattered around the city, so that the children could attend local state schools in small groups; Whitechapel union in London adopted a similar plan, whereas Neath, Birm-ingham, Kensington, and Chelsea unions opted for grouped structures on a single site. Baths and laundries encouraged cleanliness; garden plots, work-shops, and band rooms allowed for training in various useful skills. Matrons, chaplains, and masters hovered over their charges to mold them into disci-plined, contented citizens. Other unions simply boarded out pauper children to foster families, so that they would grow up in ordinary working-class com-munities. After the Education Act of 1870 established both the expectation of, and the structures for, universal primary education, most unions shifted pau-per children into the local schools and shut down their separate workhouse establishments. Disabled children, blind children, and sometimes Roman Catholic children – all conceived as different and particularly needy – could be sent at public expense to various certified schools, each of which catered to a particular clientele. As Felix Driver argues, the concept of classification lay at the heart of treatment of paupers. Children who needed state care were separated out from the pauper host and trained for a life of labor according to their gender, age, religion, and physical capabilities.[34]

Old people, too, became a group marked for particular treatment. The cru-sade against outrelief had made no distinction between the elderly, the sick,

[33] Francis Duke, "Pauper Education," in Derek Fraser, ed., *The New Poor Law in the Nineteenth Century* (New York: St. Martin's, 1976), 71–82.

[34] Driver, *Power,* 95–105.

the widows, and the infirm: All were to go into the workhouse for support. But in 1895, the Royal Commission on the Aged Poor had recommended outdoor relief for the "respectable" elderly, insisting that they deserved more generous treatment. In 1896, the Local Government Board advised local guardians to

inquire with special care into the antecedents of destitute persons whose physical faculties have failed by reason of age and infirmity; and that outdoor relief in such cases should be given to those who are shown to have been of good character, thrifty according to their opportunities, and generally independent in early life, and who are not living under conditions of health or surrounding circumstances which make it evident that the relief given be indoor relief.

Moreover, relief was to be "adequate," although a specific standard was not defined.[35] In other words, elderly applicants were to be classified on the basis of age and character; they were cases to be investigated before their claims on the state could be resolved. Under this system, outrelief became a reward for an independent moral life, not an entitlement based solely on age or destitution. Character again emerged as a central focus for welfare policy.

The net result of renewed interest in elderly paupers was not, however, great generosity. After looking at local records in different parts of the country, the Webbs claimed that in the later 1890s, "only a few boards" increased allocations to elderly pensioners and that there was great variation among unions in the amounts they granted. David Thomson, who argues that social support for the elderly fell in England and Wales during the later nineteenth century, finds that by 1890 grants had declined both in absolute and relative size. Moreover, they were given for shorter periods of time, and in comparison with the 1830s and 1860s, far fewer people received them. Under the influence of the Charity Organization Society, communities abandoned their earlier commitment to support the elderly poor, insisting upon a character test and detailed knowledge of family resources so that kin could pay as much of the cost as possible.[36] To give only one example, the Loughborough union in Leicestershire in the early 1890s had an active collector who pursued in local courts the adult children of pensioners in order to gain repayment of pension costs. He located them and then calculated their liability, getting county justices of the peace to issue maintenance orders. The sons of Cather-

---

[35] Local Government Board, *Twenty-Sixth Annual Report* (London, 1896), 8–9; quoted in Sidney Webb and Beatrice Webb, *Poor Law Policy* (London: Longmans, 1910), 231.

[36] Webb and Webb, *Poor Law Policy*, 234; David Thomson, "The Decline of Social Welfare: Falling State Support for the Elderly Since Early Victorian Times," *Ageing and Society* 4:4 (1984): 451–82; idem, "Providing for Old Age: Public and Private in the English Experience," Michael Katz and Christopher Sachße, eds., *The Mixed Economy of Social Welfare* (Baden-Baden: NOMOS-Verlagsgesellschaft, 1996), 333–4.

ine Bowley, an eighty-one-year-old "poor, old, and impotent person," agreed after much pressure to pay six pence a week each toward her keep. When one of them, who worked as a farm laborer nearby, defaulted, the clerk of the union hauled him into court to force him to pay, even though he had low wages and a wife to support. In 1896, when Esther Kidger, a partly paralyzed elderly widow, could no longer maintain herself, the Loughborough board of guardians investigated her and her children, recording her comments that they were all "addicted to drink" and that "they ought to keep me off the parish." Although all were married, had low-wage jobs, and had made some voluntary contributions to the mother, the guardians pushed forward with legal proceedings against them. The guardians saw Mrs. Kidger's welfare needs not as a problem of entitlement but as an issue of family support for an elderly parent, which they would fight in the courts.[37]

Classification linked to appropriate action also became the hallmark of policies for dealing with the sick and the insane poor. From early in the century, medical opinion had isolated people in those categories as needing different sorts of treatment from the ordinary pauper. Illness brought entitlement to relief; in most unions, medical officers dispensed medicines and visited the sick poor in their homes. Unions in the cities and larger towns had infirmaries or dispensaries for the poor, whereas those judged to be foolish or lunatic were housed among ordinary paupers in the workhouse. Although such services were widespread, they were not well funded.[38]

By the later 1860s, however, poor law doctors were better organized, and they could point to revolutionary changes in the voluntary hospitals, where trained nurses served in the wards and antiseptic practices reduced infections. Slowly, both central administrators and local inspectors began to show more interest in providing the sick with more than bread and broth. In 1867, Gathorne Hardy, president of the Local Government Board, told the House of Commons that the sick "were not proper objects" for deterrent practices, and the Conservative government sponsored legislation that began the administrative separation of hospitals from workhouses.[39] The sick became yet another special variety of pauper, one for whom "reforms" could be claimed and to whom professional services could be offered. Slowly, administrators

---

[37] Guardians of the Poor, Loughborough Union, "Applications for Orders for Contributions Towards Pauper Maintenance, 1892–1903," G/7/51/10/3, G/7/51/7/8, Leicestershire County Record Office.

[38] M. A. Crowther, *The Workhouse System, 1834–1929* (London: Methuen, 1981), 156.

[39] M. W. Flinn, "Medical Services Under the New Poor Law," in Derek Fraser, *The New Poor Law in the Nineteenth Century* (New York: St. Martin's, 1976), 65.

allocated more resources to care of the sick: Wards were adapted to reflect advances in medical practice, trained nurses replaced pauper women as caretakers, new hospitals and wards were built. Between 1870 and 1914, poor law administrators authorized 384 new infirmaries; unions constructed 155 new sick wards and 156 fever wards between 1867 and 1883. Medical staffs became larger and larger, as poor law doctors succeeded in raising their professional status and widening their responsibilities.

Over time, the sick destitute were removed from the general wards of the workhouse and given specialized attention according to a doctor's diagnosis of their cases. Medical officers of health reinterpreted coughs and fevers as symptoms of tuberculosis, bronchitis, or pneumonia. And as the range of recognized diseases widened, so did the legitimacy of treatment within poor law institutions, which gained in public esteem. Workhouse infirmaries after 1867 became known as "state hospitals"; newly constructed ones occupied buildings separate from the main workhouse blocks. Then, after 1885, those who received medical relief retained their right to vote. In multiple ways, medical care for the poor became separated from relief for destitution. In consequence, workers began to use poor law infirmaries as if they were public hospitals, and the services provided, at least in the cities, came to mirror those of the larger charitable institutions.[40] Poor law doctors turned paupers into patients.

The poor "of unsound mind" underwent a similar transition in the realm of public policy. Andrew Scull argues that during the middle and later nineteenth-century medical opinion, using a rhetoric of humanitarian treatment, legitimized state custodial care for people with a wide range of mental conditions, going far beyond the "outrageous madness" that had counted as insanity around 1800.[41] In 1845, Parliament passed bills that required the building of county and borough asylums for "lunatic" paupers and created a national Lunacy Commission to set standards for care. Over the next half-century, local officials constructed an elaborate network of asylums in which to isolate the insane poor. By 1850, there were twenty-four such places, and by 1890, sixty-six of them, each of which, on average, housed several hundred people. In addition, forty-four special wards for imbeciles or for lunatics had been built in the workhouses by 1914.[42]

Diagnosis, incarceration, and separate treatment of "lunatics" became an

---

[40] Ibid.

[41] Andrew T. Scull, *Museums of Madness* (London: Allen Lane, 1979).

[42] Williams, *Pauperism*, 221; Driver, *Power*, 88; Scull, *Madness*, 198.

important activity of the poor law. In 1859, poor law clerks registered at least forty-eight different descriptions of insanity given to them by medical officers. People were sent into asylums for "cerebral excitement," dementia, melancholia, idiocy, imbecility, "head affection after fever," or simply being "silly."[43] As doctors and judges constructed the category of lunatic, the supply of people to fill it grew. While about 12 of every 10,000 people in England and Wales had counted as lunatics in 1844, the proportion rose to 29 of every 10,000 by 1890.[44] Unconvinced of this apparent explosion of insanity, Dr. John Bucknill, co-author of a popular text on psychological medicine and editor of the *Asylum Review,* argued that since 1845 "medical science has discovered whole realms of lunacy" and, through its classifications, shunted into asylums "a motley crowd of persons of weak minds or low spirits."[45] A medical model of management shaped handling of the poor with mental problems: Individuals judged to be defective in one respect or another were examined by professionals and then brought to state institutions – in theory for appropriate treatment, in practice for custodial care.

The classificatory style of managing paupers was mirrored in the physical form of workhouses. Karel Williams points out that an 1868 Poor Law Memorandum on construction prescribed "a new indoor strategy," calling for "a finer classification of paupers in general purpose and specialized institutions which were all now to be built on new architectural models."[46] In the designs for new construction, paupers were to be separated from one another, rather than rigidly divided from the outside world. The Holborn workhouse built outside London in the mid-1880s had an infirmary, a chapel, a receiving ward, a dining hall, administrative buildings, and residences for adult paupers – all surrounded by a low railing rather than a high wall. It looked like a cluster of large homes, not a prison. Men and women occupied different buildings, each of which had its own yards, exercise areas, and open walkways. Moreover, children, insane, and vagrants went to facilities elsewhere. Spatial segregation of the several classes of paupers gave emphasis to the differences in treatment mandated by the newly therapeutic poor law.

In addition, the "pavilion system" permitted variations in disciplinary regimes. The elderly judged to be deserving could be given tea, tobacco, and

---

[43] Driver, *Power,* 108.

[44] Scull, *Madness,* 243.

[45] J. C. Bucknill, *The Care of the Insane and Their Legal Control* (London: Macmillan, 1880), 3–4; quoted in Scull, *Madness,* 253.

[46] Williams, *Pauperism,* 116.

flexible hours without undermining the harsh schedules and punishments still in force for the disreputable.[47] Physical separation thus permitted moral discriminations of the sort called for by the C.O.S. and other critics of the workhouse system. Rebuilding the workhouse became an important tactic of late nineteenth-century reformers. Felix Driver argues that "classification thus occupied a privileged place in the discourse of workhouse policy. Its reinvention during the 1860s marks one of the most significant moments in the history of nineteenth-century social policy."[48] Despite ongoing conflicts among social scientists, philanthropists, and poor law officials over the design of particular welfare institutions, most operated within the same moral universe. They believed that poverty arose from a variety of causes, many of which were particular to the individual. An appropriate response therefore required discrimination and specific knowledge of the destitute. Social investigation and social work would provide cures for both pauperism and poverty.

Therapeutic Interventions

By the 1890s, poor law officials had refined their discriminations among several sorts of paupers and had rebuilt their institutions accordingly. Relieving officers slowly changed into therapists, who were expected to diagnose various social diseases and prescribe appropriate treatment. The gap, however, between visions and achievement remained immense. Not only were public means grossly inadequate to effect the transformations welfare administrators desired, but official contacts with the majority of paupers occurred when they were ill and/or elderly, unlikely candidates for behavioral reformation. What the poor law dispensed remained far distant from the hegemonic control desired by reformers and attacked by analysts today. Even if one grants the proposition that workhouses functioned as "total institutions," the life histories of most paupers indicate limited exposure to poor law discipline. Within the families of the poor, most individuals used poor law services for limited amounts of time, returning to kin and communities after short stints on relief or in institutions. The reformatory effect of state aid was probably short-lived.

Charles Booth's research into London pauperism proves the point. In 1889 and 1890, Booth gained access to the records of relieving officers in Stepney, who had compiled family histories of local people aided by the poor law

---

[47] Ibid., 118–21.

[48] Driver, *Power,* 72.

between 1876 and 1889. The records described 1,194 cases organized in terms of nuclear and extended families; most of the paupers had had extensive contact with the Stepney welfare bureaucracy over the thirteen years surveyed. Through the thickness of the files, the relieving officers demonstrated both extensive experience with, and detailed knowledge of, the working poor in their district. Stepney paupers had been visited, investigated, labeled, and aided repeatedly – but with few long-term effects. To use the language of the 1990s, Booth's records described an urban "underclass," whose unemployment, illnesses, and dysfunctional behavior sometimes extended into three generations. The people described in the Stepney records were not a cross-section of the working-class population. In a district where Booth estimated that approximately 17 percent of all residents in 1887 were "very poor" or living in a "state of chronic want," people aided by the poor law in Stepney on January 1, 1891, made up only 1.5 percent of the total population.[49] They were the most heavily dependent of the Stepney destitute, people whose experience with welfare was extensive enough to prompt officials to generate detailed records. Most were adults who had been admitted to either the Poplar or Bromley workhouses or who were being treated at a sick asylum or at a lunatic asylum. About 16 percent of all paupers aided in Stepney union on April 30, 1889, were children sent to district schools, and these were not investigated in their own right; another 12 percent were adults on outrelief, mostly receiving medical care or burial fees after a death in the family. Only a few elderly received pensions.[50] Stepney paupers were, and had been for some years, a largely institutionalized population subject to the therapies designed by welfare officials to "cure" the need for dependence on the state.

When Charles Booth investigated pauperism among the "aged poor" of the East End, he used these case books for evidence. Booth transformed the narratives into an official discourse on pauperism, which merged the concerns of the C.O.S. with more social explanations for destitution. Booth and his assistants isolated twenty-three reasons for dependence; most of the first twelve were high on the Victorian list of deadly sins (Crime, Vice, Drink, Laziness, Pauper Association, Heredity, Mental Disease, Temper, Incapacity, Early Marriage, Large Family, Extravagance). The state of the economy, life-cycle

[49] Charles Booth, *Life and Labour of the People in London, First Series: Poverty, 1. East, Central, and South London* (London: Macmillan, 1902), 33, 36; idem, *Pauperism: A Picture and the Endowment of Old Age* (London: Macmillan, 1892), 113.

[50] Booth, *Pauperism*, 6. Stepney Union had aggressively enforced the "crusade against out-relief," refusing after 1879 to grant new pensions. Those getting money grants were either legacies from the earlier period or the beneficiaries of short-term aid because of an emergency.

crises, and physical problems got less attention, but were part of the mix. In his introduction to *Pauperism and the Endowment of Old Age,* which was published in 1892, Booth chose to distance himself from lurid, moral explanations of poverty among the elderly, but his text highlights exactly these concerns.[51] Booth's transformations of local welfare records show the confusion of categories within which a reading public had to situate the destitute.

The tale of Michael Rooney, age eighty-six, begins his book. Its litany of miseries, worthy of a contemporary soap opera, would have been read with popular stereotypes of the Irish very much in mind. Members of Rooney's extended family had supposedly flitted in and out of local workhouses and sick asylums for years, laid low by multiple illnesses, jail terms, and bouts of unemployment. Booth made sure that readers came to appropriate conclusions by listing official diagnoses in the margins. Rooney and his family came to pauperism through "Desertion, Sickness, Blindness, Drink, Old Age, Unhealthy Work, Crime, Loss of Wife, Vice," and the list continues.[52] His other lead stories also wove together titillating tales of immorality and bad luck. The elderly paupers of Stepney needed therapy, institutionalization, and reformation – not merely the right to a pension for which Booth had begun to campaign. Booth's book offered readers scandalous narratives of class and danger. In them, paupers flaunted norms of upright behavior: Men deserted their families, hit commanding officers, and took up with prostitutes. Women cursed, fought, and bore illegitimate children. Some roamed the streets in a drunken stupor and slept on doorsteps. Both sexes constantly got into fights, injuring themselves and others. In Booth's presentation of the Stepney stories, the elderly poor regularly violated canons of civilized behavior and showed themselves incapable of self-help. The state needed to take them in hand for everyone's safety. Although Booth explicitly identified destitution with elderly people who could no longer work, his stories spread an alarmist message suggesting jail, rather than pensions, as a suitable response.

The case records themselves tell a somewhat different story. The run-of-the-mill pauper lacked the dramatic vices of Michael Rooney, and the state offered more limited and less restrictive forms of aid. At least a portion of Stepney's destitute in the 1890s regularly claimed short-term social services and support from the poor laws. They found poor law aid instrumentally useful and built it into their family economies.

Consider the case of Martha Dangerfield. A laundress around age fifty-five,

[51] Ibid., 9, 12.

[52] Ibid., 14–18.

she applied to poor law authorities when her husband got sick with bronchitis. Saying that she could "keep him no longer," she applied for his admission to the sick asylum, where he went in 1878 and died soon thereafter. She then went into service for a few years. At some point in her early sixties, she went to live with her sister, but she soon found that she could not earn enough to pay her own expenses. By 1883, she applied to the poor laws for help and was admitted to the workhouse, where she established a pattern of leaving and reentry after visits to her sister. After every exit, she returned, announcing, "I cannot remain out having no home or work."[53]

Ann Tanner, a widow with seven children, turned to the poor laws in 1886 for help with child rearing. She asked guardians to admit two sons, ages nine and eleven into workhouse schools, because they were "troublesome" and she could not feed them. With those two off her hands, she deputized a teenage daughter to care for siblings, while she and the oldest girl worked to support the remaining children and themselves. Mrs. Tanner brought the boys home occasionally when her earnings rose and then sent them back in harder times.[54]

Most of the people in Stepney institutions had come there by their own or their family's choice, given their general lack of other resources. The poor law offered needed services, even if the setting for them was unpalatable. Catherine Briggs, a twenty-nine-year-old factory worker, asked for medical help for her common law husband, Samuel Vincent, when he had a "paralytic fit." He was sent to the sick asylum in 1884 and later on to a lunatic asylum for long-term care when he did not recover. Pregnant with their fourth child, she was left alone to support the family. (Vincent's father and sister were living in Stepney workhouses and could not offer help.) Briggs went into a workhouse infirmary for the birth of William in September of 1884, applied for medicine for the child in October when he fell ill, and then asked for a parish burial when the infant died in November. By December, she decided that she could not raise three children on her own and therefore petitioned guardians to take her two younger children into workhouse schools, where they would be boarded and educated. Because she herself had been raised in a workhouse school, Briggs knew what to expect and how to request the service. We do not know what she or her children thought of this decision; its emotional cost may well have been heavy. But it permitted her to support herself and to keep her eldest daughter at home.[55]

---

[53] Booth Papers, Series C/164, case no. 582, 800, British Library of Political and Economic Science.

[54] Ibid., Series B, Book A/162, case no. 25, 61–2.

[55] Ibid., Book A/162, case no. 3, 11–12.

Stepney relieving officers regularly met with people who requested that their children or other relatives be taken into poor law institutions. After her husband's death in 1885, when much of the remaining family fell ill, Harriet Clough got one of her daughters into the fever hospital, sent one to her mother for care, and entered the sick asylum herself for a brief period. In 1886, Clough helped her older daughter find work as a servant, took a job herself, probably as a servant, and had her younger daughter "admitted to the schools."[56] Survival meant breaking up her nuclear family. Because her mother and other kin in London were apparently either unable or unwilling to provide long-term care for her youngest daughter, Clough turned to the poor law as her best alternative. William Roberts, a dock laborer, applied to Stepney authorities in 1877 on behalf of his seventeen-year-old son Thomas, who was described as having a "weak intellect." His father told relieving officers, "The boys made fun of him, and he threatened to kill himself." Thomas was admitted to the Leavenden asylum and lived there until his death in 1889. His father paid two shillings per week for his care for some years, until other children fell ill. Several members of the family also turned to Stepney institutions: Robert's older brother, an unemployed dock laborer in his mid-seventies, entered the workhouse in 1884, as did his sister, who died there.[57] The Bromley workhouse was filled with elderly people whose families would not or could not care for them. Illness and unemployment led them to apply for welfare aid, which in Stepney meant entry into an institution.

The majority of people living in Stepney workhouses or institutions remained in them for short periods of time, for less than three years. A few, however, spent most of their lives in them. Samuel Hardwick, the illegitimate son of a coffee house keeper, was born in 1850 in the Wapping workhouse, where he was raised after being abandoned by his parents. At age thirteen, when ill, he was struck in the eyes by an infirmary nurse, and he became partially blind as a result. Hardwick remained in the workhouse until age twenty-seven, when he took off for the countryside and spent several years earning his own living as an itinerant peddler. In 1884, alone and destitute, Hardwick returned to the East End. When his father refused to help him, he turned to the poor law; officials sent him to a school for the blind, where he presumably remained.[58] The poor law had supported him, but clearly had not provided either the skills or the resources to lead an independent life. Yet the

[56] Ibid., Book E/166, case no. 1,021, 1,222.

[57] Ibid., Book A/162, case no. 140, 222.

[58] Ibid., Book E/166, case no. 1,041, 1,237.

poor law had become his family of last resort. We do not know what he thought about the poor law, but he did return to it.

Only rarely did poor law officials take a more active stance vis-à-vis the local poor. They had the authority to remove children from their parents in cases of gross neglect or maltreatment and sometimes did so when forced to confront such a case. The Sullivan children, three boys and three girls, were discovered in a state of "deplorable neglect," probably during the 1860s, and were removed to workhouse schools. Their mother died soon thereafter, allegedly from "neglect." The father, clearly marked as the villain in the case, was refused custody of the children for several years. When she reached adolescence, the Stepney board of guardians arranged for the oldest girl to work as a servant, and they finally released the other children to their father's care. The boys got low-skilled jobs in the area and married. One of the daughters lived with her father for a time and then entered the sick asylum suffering from venereal disease; another daughter, Jane Sullivan, went to work at the Bryant and May match factory but had to enter the sick asylum in the mid-1880s when poisoned by phosphorus. She, as well as her father-in-law and mother-in-law, regularly requested – and received – medical care.[59]

Stepney households with multiple deprivations and few resources turned to the poor law for help, even if they disliked having to do so. The state offered them medical treatment and shelter for limited amounts of time. Those who were permanently disabled or incapacitated could get long-term care, if they were willing to accept it under the terms on which it was offered. These were not negligible benefits in a city of relatively high rents and high mortality and morbidity, although they were obviously inadequate to level the mountain of need that confronted welfare officials. Some of the poor turned the state's meager offerings to good account: pregnant women who found a hospital; the homeless who came in briefly from the cold; deserted children who gained an elementary education and some job training; families who sent troublesome relatives into public institutions; the sick who needed nursing. The obligation of the poor law to provide relief gave the destitute some space in which to maneuver for their own advantage. The weak could be shifted temporarily, or permanently in some cases, to the care of the state. The very poor used workhouse institutions as boarding schools, old-age homes, hospitals, and asylums, moving in and out of them as need dictated. This instrumental use of state reflected a pragmatic response to the poor law; it was one resource that could be tapped in a world that offered them little and

---

[59] Ibid., Book A/162, case no. 170, 261–2.

demanded much. There is no reason to assume that they enjoyed their dealings with guardians, but the dependent poor were not dragged kicking and
screaming into the arms of welfare officials; they chose to use state services
in the absence of more palatable alternatives. If pensions were not available,
then in certain circumstances, institutionalization would do.

Work for a Fraction of the Unemployed

Although the provision of work had been a central tenet of English welfare
policy since the sixteenth century, none of the official methods had ever
proved effective for more than a small number of the destitute. Overseers
managed to establish neither work for profit nor work for punishment. Until
the 1880s, social workers, welfare officials, and most politicians strove to
ignore the unemployed. Orthodox economists and social theorists had not yet
turned to the analysis of labor markets, and virtually no data were available
on those who lacked jobs. Poor law officials isolated a group, "able-bodied
men in want of work," into which they lumped fewer than 1 percent of all
paupers given outdoor relief between 1859 and 1890.[60] Despite awareness of
trade cycles and seasonal layoffs, they remained largely indifferent to the
contribution of unemployment to destitution, except in special cases such as
the cotton famine and particularly harsh winters. Because they saw the unemployed as a group of men – and "real men" were independent, self-reliant,
and competent – by definition, the unemployed were defective. Unemployed
able-bodied men became part of a "demoralized residuum," criminals and
deviants out of work by choice who should be shunted into a "test workhouse" for some redemptive oakum-picking or stone breaking.

By the mid-1880s, however, economic fears and international competition
redirected thinking about joblessness. The experience of the Lancashire cotton famine had shown that external events, rather than individual fecklessness, could produce unemployment. During the Great Depression, a Royal
Commission asked for theoretical analyses of trade cycles and empirical
studies of their results. Between 1886 and 1904, a wide variety of new policies were suggested, implemented locally, and for the most part, abandoned
when they did not work. Although contemporary discourse labeled the unemployed as a social problem, it did not settle on a particular response.

The notion that the unemployed could be scared and shamed back to work
remained alive. Its contemporary vitality owed a great deal to the Charity

[60] Williams, *Pauperism*, 182.

Organization Society. By 1895, the group acknowledged that policy toward the unemployed was "one of the great questions of today." But their position had scarcely shifted from their hard line of earlier decades. Because it was essential not to "pauperize" the destitute, those temporarily out of work should find help through charities or be taken into the workhouses for aid in a deterrent setting. Helen and Bernard Bosanquet argued that poverty from a wide range of causes could be cured by an act of will; character could triumph over circumstance. By fostering "character," the C.O.S. could effectively aid those victimized by economic forces such as unemployment.[61] William Chance, whose suggestions for improved administration of the poor law were circulated by the C.O.S., focused attention on the permanently unemployed. He branded such people "misfits," concluding, "[W]e can do nothing for this class, except by emigrating the most active and capable of them." He judged that the rest were "unsteady and unreliable, and . . . usually of low character, and more or less given to tippling, etc." He condemned efforts by local governments to offer them work, arguing that those whom a private employer would not hire could not do anything effective for the state. In his opinion, they should be left to their own devices.[62] Careful investigation could distinguish them from the temporarily unemployed and from workers of good character, so that resources were not wasted on them.

But dismissing the unemployed so curtly became politically impossible during the mid 1880s, when a depression combined with winter weather to keep thousands out of work. In London, in February of 1886, the unemployed marched on Trafalgar Square and rioted at Hyde Park Corner; in 1887, the homeless camped out in St. James Park and were forcibly ejected from Trafalgar Square by soldiers. Gareth Stedman Jones argues that during these years, fears of "outcast London" shifted middle-class attitudes toward the casual poor. In his view, London's "social crisis" triggered a reaction against C.O.S. theories. Attacks on a laissez-faire approach to what was seen as an urban underclass arose from both the political left and the political right, bringing calls for state intervention in the labor market.[63] The Reverend Samuel Barnett of Toynbee Hall asked the Whitechapel board of guardians to set up agricultural training centers, where the unemployed could be housed

---

[61] H. Bosanquet and B. Bosanquet, *Contemporary Review* (January 1897); quoted in José Harris, *Unemployment and Politics* (Oxford: Oxford University Press, 1972), 78.

[62] Chance, *Better Administration*, 174, 176, 178.

[63] Gareth Stedman Jones, *Outcast London* (Oxford: Oxford University Press, 1971), 296–7.

and trained for farming. In the longer run, he hoped that they could be provided with land at public expense, either at home or in the colonies.[64]

Another clear sign of the shifting winds of opinion came in March of 1886, when Joseph Chamberlain, president of the Local Government Board, sent a circular to local authorities pointing out the need to schedule public works during periods of depressions as a way of providing temporary jobs for the deserving unemployed, reversing his earlier hostility to just such actions.[65] Although it was intended to supplement, not supersede, the workhouse and labor tests for the unemployed, the Chamberlain circular remained part of Local Government Board policy through the mid-1890s. It legitimated local efforts to provide public works jobs for the unemployed, but its effectiveness seems doubtful. José Harris brands it "an almost complete failure" because the central government neither enforced it nor provided money to finance local projects. Moreover, the types of projects suggested were difficult to perform in the winter and did not employ the skilled workers whom public opinion wanted to keep out of the workhouse.[66] Nevertheless, the circular identified a mode of granting relief different from that of the C.O.S. and the poor laws and recommended it to local governments throughout England and Wales.

Slowly during the 1890s, intellectuals as well as politicians reconceptualized the loss of work. The shift from thinking about "the unemployed" – individuals with the normal human failings upon which joblessness could be blamed – to the abstract problem of "unemployment" came after Alfred Marshall first used the word in 1888, and J. A. Hobson formally defined the concept in 1895 in the *Contemporary Review*. By the mid-1890s it had spread among poor law officials and politicians, shifting attention from individual pathologies to labor markets, trade cycles, and the industrial system itself.[67] Enthusiasts for social imperialism linked expansion abroad and military security at home to the fate of the ordinary English worker. Strong armies depended on healthy citizens, who needed jobs, as well as decent housing, good food, and clean surroundings.[68] A discourse of economic structures and environmentalism supplemented, and to some extent supplanted, one that focused on individual character and moral reform.

---

[64] W. J. Fishman, *East End 1888* (Philadelphia: Temple University Press, 1988), 54–5.

[65] Local Government Board, *Sixteenth Annual Report* (London, 1886–7), 5–7.

[66] Harris, *Unemployment*, 76–7.

[67] Ibid., 4.

[68] Jones, *Outcast*, 308–12.

At the same time, town governments put some of these newer ideas into practice. Thirty-three local authorities within metropolitan London and sixty-three outside the capital took on extra workers during the depression years of the early 1890s.[69] Throughout the industrial north and the Midlands, city councils financed wintertime public works to employ the jobless. Blackburn employed men to paint and clean local bridges. After 1888, Leicester city officials organized systematic help for the unemployed. The corporation's highway and sewer boards hired extra men, and a Mayor's Committee for the Relief of Distress in Leicester collected funds to finance soup kitchens. Then, in 1892, the town established a registry for the unemployed and advertised it through the city. Men out of work were invited to sign up as a first step toward qualifying for public works positions. A committee recommended projects ranging from repainting the cattle market to excavations for new sewers, which could be undertaken if enough money were found. Within a few weeks, over seventeen hundred men had registered for work, although in the first year few were hired. But in later years, the city offered several hundred men unskilled laboring jobs leveling land, shoveling snow, and repaving streets. Both the Unemployed Labour Bureau and the public works gained the approval of organized workers; deputations from local trade unions suggested projects and supplied data on members out of work.[70]

Middlesbrough in Yorkshire also moved during the 1890s to set up a jobs registry. From 1893, the town organized a labor exchange, where lists were kept of the unemployed and individual job histories (which included judgments on drinking, striking, and the tendency to loaf on the job) were collected. Local employers used the registry when new positions became available, and the men who passed the various tests of character and energy set by the exchange got referrals to major firms in the area.[71] Bradford also tried a job registry to lessen unemployment. The town clerk asserted that it listed twelve hundred people during the winter of 1892–3. But apparently few local employers used it, and trade unionists distrusted it, too. Its failure prompted the town to provide some public works jobs by building a new tramway line and enlarging the electricity plant.[72] The register itself got mixed reviews:

[69] Harris, *Unemployment*, 84.

[70] "Unemployment in Leicester, 1888–1907," Webb Local Government Collection, Part 2, The Poor Law, vol. 311: Leicestershire, British Library of Political and Economic Science.

[71] "Unemployment in Middlesbrough, 1893–1903," Webb Local Government Collection, Part 2, The Poor Law, vol. 342: Yorkshire.

[72] William Thomas McGowan, "Report to the Local Government Board, 8 April 1893," Webb Local Government Collection, Part 2, The Poor Law, vol. 341: Bradford, Yorkshire.

During the following winter, an Unemployed Emergency Committee did a census of local joblessness and demanded the reopening of the register. But the town council refused. The town's newspaper called the register "useless." Instead of working to identify the unemployed, the town council hired extra men to work on the roads and to clear snow.[73] In each of these cases, job creation grew out of the mechanisms for providing charity. Soup kitchens and road work went together. Publicly collected funds financed them both, using a rhetoric of need and merit. Jobs were parceled out to the favored few, to those who had several children, to the sober, and to the deferential. They were treated as rewards, rather than as a cure for underconsumption.

Meanwhile, the unemployed and the political left kept the issue of joblessness in the public eye. In northern towns, distress committees, trades councils, and deputations to poor law guardians directed local attention to the unemployed. In London, from 1892 to 1895, demonstrations on Tower Hill by men out of work so alarmed police that they regularly patrolled such gatherings. Yet such demonstrations in some of the riverside districts effectively pressured local boards of guardians to provide wintertime work breaking stones. The Social Democratic Federation, the London Trades Council, and several other workers' groups set up the Unemployed Organization Committee in the fall of 1892 to investigate the extent of unemployment, to agitate for public works jobs, and to lobby for the right to meet publicly in Trafalgar Square, off limits since the violence of 1886–7. Their deputations to government departments asking for additional jobs kept a steady pressure on the central government, while James Keir Hardie of the Independent Labour Party called within the House of Commons for effective public policies to combat unemployment. He and other trades unionists suggested a wide range of policies – the eight-hour day, agricultural colonies, and public works funded nationally – intended to implement "the right to work," but with little success. José Harris argues that at the time, the Home Secretary saw unemployment primarily as "a threat to public order rather than as a source of social distress." Although parliamentary discussion of unemployment had increased exponentially, little had been done in practice to alleviate the problem. In Harris's opinion, the decade of agitation between the mid-1880s and mid-1890s achieved "virtually nothing."[74]

Both the aims and the style of early efforts to help the unemployed can be

---

[73] *The Bradford Observer,* 30 January 1894; 28 January 1895; 26 February 1895; Webb Local Government Collection, Part 2, The Poor Law, vol. 341: Bradford, Yorkshire.

[74] Harris, *Unemployment,* 80–9, 99–100.

seen in an East London project in force during the winter of 1892–3. The Mansion House Conference, a group representing several London charities and public authorities, deputized its East London subcommittee to investigate unemployment in that district. Deciding that abnormal numbers of dock and riverside laborers were out of work, it borrowed some land on the edge of the metropolis that needed to be leveled, prepared it for allotment gardens, and offered suitable applicants the chance to earn four shillings per eight-hour day doing spade work. The committee decided that the local unemployed were primarily casual workers, who had lost regular jobs as a result of the reorganization of dock labor after the strike of 1889 and for whom there was little chance of reemployment even in good times. The committee members had a mission: to locate men who could be turned into permanently employed workers outside London, either in Canada or in a rural part of Britain. Their technique was investigation and inquiry: Applicants were interviewed, references were checked, and "character" was judged. Over seven hundred men asked for work, and most were dismissed because they were too old, were single, lived in a disreputable common lodging house, or were defective in some other way. About two hundred and fifty got temporary jobs digging and then had to appear before the subcommittee to be grilled about future plans. The interviewers did not like the answers they got and quickly decided that "it was the failures in life who were being dealt with, . . . men who had lost character, or who were broken down in health and were unfit for continuous labour." After much effort, the subcommittee financed the emigration of thirteen families to Canada and three to the country; almost none of the workers wanted to leave the East End. Its members concluded reluctantly that "comparatively few of the men can be said to have been lifted out of the slough of despond," and that they could do virtually nothing to improve the position of unemployed dockworkers because such people were "unable to make any effort to alter their surroundings or to strike out on a line of their own."[75]

During the depression years of the next decade, authorities tried other temporary expedients to combat joblessness. Labor exchanges multiplied in manufacturing towns along with distress committees and mayors' funds for soup kitchens. Poor law guardians opened or expanded stone yards, and the Poplar union leased a farm in Essex to provide training and work for some of the East End poor. Small-scale experimentation was the order of the day, because the Local Government Board had refused to set a national policy or to provide effective support for the Chamberlain circular. The most repressive

---

[75] H. V. Toynbee, "A Winter's Experiment," *Macmillan's Magazine* 69 (1893–4): 54–8.

of these initiatives, the Salvation Army's detention colonies to reform the unemployed, got the most public attention. Outlined by General William Booth in his book, *In Darkest England and the Way Out,* the plan called for city workshops, rural farm settlements, and overseas labor colonies where sinful workers could be redeemed by religion, temperance, and strict discipline.[76] Removal of those trapped in an urban jungle of depravity into a utopia of forced labor and daily prayer was touted as the way to restore English workmen to full employment. Introduced in a small way in London in 1890, in Hadleigh, Essex, in 1893, and later in North America, the Army's training schemes for men got regular attention from politicians and philanthropists, primed to see in penal colonies for male vagrants an effective recipe for social reform. Although Conservative governments gave it respectful attention and flirted with the idea of public financing, the Salvation Army succeeded in gaining the powers over able-bodied workmen that it desired. Yet it set a powerful precedent linking job creation and spiritual reform. Work was to be redemptive, to change character as it filled purses. It was to discipline, punish, and test character and true need. Hopes for individual reformation, rather than the claims of economic growth or justice, dominated discussions of unemployment in the years between 1880 and 1905.

Welfare reformers in the later nineteenth century sought appropriate therapies for the problems of the destitute. They trusted an increasingly interventionist state to classify, cure, and put to work those left behind in the great race for income and independence. Where self-help did not succeed, state help would compensate. Many paupers accepted the rules of this changed welfare game and turned to state services to account for themselves and their families, although they probably did not enjoy the experience. Moreover, the crusade against outrelief made recourse to the state in times of need increasingly atypical. By the 1890s, few workers below the age of sixty-five used welfare or had any direct experience of the workhouse. What could be seen as success for the poor laws – a diminishing clientele – had diminished their legitimacy among ordinary citizens. As the strategies of the social workers moved the destitute out of their communities and cut down local experience of state aid, hostility to the poor laws among the actual and potential poor mounted.

[76] William Booth, *In Darkest England and the Way Out* (London: Salvation Army, 1890).

9

POPULAR REJECTION OF THE POOR LAWS

> A humble house, but neat and clean,
> When [workers] have strength and work.
> But when old age o'er them does creep
> And they can barely slave,
> Then they must leave; they do not reap
> So much as t' masters crave.
> Then to the workhouse they must go,
> What matters if they clem,
> So long as t' masters wealth do stow,
> They reap from t' working men.
>   Harry Robinson, 1892

In 1892, Harry Robinson, a sixteen-year-old boy from Halifax, Yorkshire, sent a poem called "Rich and Poor" into the *Workman's Times,* a newspaper that circulated in the north. Featured in the weekly poetry column, it told a simple story of the rich who danced in "gilded halls" and lived off "toiling souls" who slaved while young and then became paupers when they could no longer produce enough to satisfy their masters. Now divided into classes of capitalists and wage slaves, England had degenerated from its past of "valiant knights" and "noble dames" into a harsher, meaner place. Despite the glories of English freedom and individual acts of kindness and love, workers now met a dire fate in old age. Harry ignored poor law hospitals, schools, and pensions and cut to the heart of the matter: the workhouse. Any government welfare effort that meant confinement within its walls stood condemned in the world he sketched, which echoed workers' criticisms from the 1830s. The conceptualization of welfare as therapy and social work had made virtually no impact on Harry Robinson and other contributors to the *Workmen's Times.*

By the century's end, many workers had effectively distanced themselves from the poor laws, in both practical and psychological terms. Between early and late Victorian times, workers' direct experience of the poor laws diminished sharply. First, far fewer people received relief. During the 1840s, officials claimed to aid between 80 and 100 people per 1,000 of the total population; in 1900, the number had dropped to approximately 25 per 1,000.[1] As average real incomes rose, far fewer people asked for state aid. Many more insured themselves against risk, using friendly societies and trade union funds as shields against loss of income.[2] But if relatively few had experienced pauperism, most feared it. The familiar sources of dependency – unemployment, illness, old age, and disabilities – had scarcely disappeared. Some workers had absorbed the scorn of the better-off for the inferior beings who had fallen behind in the race for independence and respectability; others used a harsh rhetoric of class and hostility to capitalism to blast the workhouse and its denigration of the poor. As workers asserted their rights to political citizenship, they adopted a broader conception of social citizenship that made welfare in the form of "poor" laws unacceptable.

A Fate Worse Than Death

Readers of the *Workman's Times* found themselves in a world of trade unions, labor politics and stridently asserted rights. During the middle and later 1890s, campaigns for old-age pensions were being vigorously supported by the National Committee to Organized Labour, which held out a vision of alternative types of welfare. The paper exhorted: "In things Essential, Unity; in things Doubtful, Liberty; in all things, Charity." From the paper's point of view, the poor laws fell afoul of all those precepts, jailing paupers, removing them from their communities, and giving aid meanly. They pictured unforgiving, judgmental officials who punished, rather than relieved. Such actions violated workers' subjective sense of themselves and of their dignity, just as

---

[1] Karel Williams, *From Pauperism to Poverty* (London: Routledge, 1971), 158, 161; these figures average the numbers of people aided on the two days per year when data were collected and then relate them to population size. Although the ratio of the population aided on the sampled days to the total number who were aided during an entire year might well have shifted over time, it is unlikely that it increased between the 1840s and 1900. During the earlier period, authorities were more willing to give outrelief, the economy was in worse shape, and workers had fewer private resources. The figures from the 1840s probably underestimate use of the poor law more sharply than do the figures for 1900.

[2] Paul Johnson, "Private and Public Social Welfare in Britain, 1870–1939," in Michael Katz and Christophe Sachße, eds., *The Mixed Economy of Social Welfare* (Baden-Baden: NOMOS-Verlagsgesellschaft, 19929–147); Paul Johnson, *Saving and Spending* (Oxford: Oxford University Press, 1985).

they violated the paper's commitments to an egalitarian society. Interest in old-age pensions offered an alternative vision for treatment of the elderly, one that promised continued independence.

Readers of the *Workmen's Times* late in the century were regularly treated to maudlin attacks on welfare policies. Poems, such as "Frozen to Death" or "The Farm Labourer's Last Home," blamed "slaving masters" for the dismal fate of the poor.[3] In their pages, virtuous workers struggled for survival, whereas "prosperous pets of Providence" feasted on wine and walnuts, and denied the poor their due.[4] Elderly couples torn apart at the workhouse door, battles over pauper funerals, and unemployed workers forced out of their communities were staple items in a stark vision of public vice and private virtue. Writers reiterated stock images of the New Poor Law to attack welfare practices and to point toward alternatives. The major target for attack was the workhouse, coupled with strident refusal to accept its humiliations.

Widespread and long-standing fears of pauper funerals haunted the elderly. When Harry Woodford died after a few years in the workhouse, the *Workmen's Times* reported that four paupers had been appointed by the parish to carry his coffin from the cart to the churchyard. Unfortunately, the old and weak men dropped the coffin, smashing the lid and letting the body slide out onto the ground. At that point, mourners supposedly discovered a naked Mr. Woodford wearing only his socks and a small rag.[5] Tales of indignities at cemeteries and the meanness of the guardians effectively fanned popular fears of welfare authorities. Under present political and economic conditions, the reward for long lives of labor could only be a pauper's grave.

The *Workman's Times* reified the poor laws in the form of the workhouse, allowing the whole to be rejected along with its most objectionable part. Correspondents ignored public medical care and education and denounced an institution that they saw as robbing them of independence and status. Facts slid into fiction in the story of elderly Reuben Farnicombe and his wife, Martha, humble Christian laborers forced by guardians to go into the workhouse when they became ill and infirm. After sentimental goodbyes to their cottage and worldly goods, they tottered to the workhouse, only to be roughly separated by the relieving officer, Mr. Hardheart, who told them they could meet once a week for half an hour! Crying out in frustration, they embraced

---

[3] *Workman's Times*, 6 February 1892, 2; 16 January 1892, 2.

[4] J. Watson Grice, "Pensions for the People," *Workman's Times*, 6 February 1892, 4.

[5] "Terrible Scene at Pauper's Funeral," *Workman's Times*, 13 February 1892.

and both fell down dead.[6] A correspondent provoked much sympathy from readers in 1892, telling of Mr. Moseley, a man who had been a dues-paying member of the Ancient Order of Foresters for forty-eight years, but who nevertheless had had to go into the workhouse. The author was indignant: "Of what use is it to be banded together as 'brethren' if, when exceptional circumstances arise, the needy one is to be dealt with as if he were a stranger and unknown in the land."[7] For him, welfare aid was not a right, but a punishment that signaled workers' failure to look after their own.

The paper expressed rumor and readers' fears more than their direct experiences. In its pages, unionized and insured workers lashed out at a major symbol of the social inequality they so resented. If labor brought wealth and national prosperity and gave value to life, how could a just society exclude workers in their hour of need? The poor law's solution to the problem of destitution did not answer questions about equity and fairness posed by the many correspondents who shared a social democratic vision of a reformed England. The poor laws gave relief under "degrading and humiliating conditions." Therefore, they should be replaced by a better political and social order, one that correspondents identified with a more egalitarian distribution of wealth.

> There will be no empty cupboards,
> Nor ragged clothing to use,
> When Workers, and workers only,
> Will have the wealth they produce.
> Masters and servants for ever
> By and by will cease to be;
> All will be brothers and sisters –
> All equally noble and free.[8]

Alex Paterson of London contributed a poem, "Who Are the Paupers?" exalting the virtue of the dependent poor over that of the upper classes who did not work for a living; in a better world, there would be no need to use the poor laws. He proclaimed:

> Pauperize the working classes!
> Is it not a splendid joke?
> Laugh away, ye toiling masses,
> As ye sweat beneath your yoke.

---

[6] E. R. Callender, "The Labourer's Last Home," *Workman's Times*, 16 January 1892, 7.

[7] The Errand Boy, "Should Foresters Go into the Workhouse?" *Workman's Times*, 23 January 1892, 2.

[8] R. J. Derfel, "All the Land Will Be the People's," *Workman's Times*, 16 January 1892.

By and by will come revision
Of the country's pauper roll,
When Democracy's decision
Will be – sweep away the whole![9]

The author of "Should Foresters Go into the Workhouse?" demanded old age pensions, as did several other correspondents. They found support in the workhouse unacceptable; it clashed directly with their image of respectability and self-reliance.[10] Pat Thane argues that the theme of independence underlay the stances of a majority of trade unionists with reference to state welfare schemes.[11] If asked to choose between state aid and self-support, adequate wages and full employment would get the nod. For those who could no longer work, however, pensions provided a good alternative, winning the support of the vast majority of the early Labour candidates for elections and of the National Committee of Organized Labour. A variety of voices of people who saw themselves as representing workers, therefore, looked past the poor laws to another conception of welfare.

Consumer Dissatisfactions

Given the sharp cutback in outdoor relief carried out in the 1870s and the growing faith in institutional care, it is not surprising that workers' attitudes toward the New Poor Law continued to be hostile. Yet by the 1890s, workers expressed much more wide-ranging criticisms of welfare methods and standards than they had done in the 1830s. Not only did they reject the idea of the workhouse, but they also railed against the treatment of the poor by guardians and inspectors. Humility in the face of the overseer is less in evidence than pride and self-assertion. Indeed, respectability brought with it a revolution of rising expectations, as well as a growing concern for public reputation. Many workers rejected relief because it had come to be seen as stigmatizing; others who continued to need it resented demeaning procedures and any public loss of status. By 1900, criticisms of the poor laws had spread from their procedures to their tone, style, and cultural meaning, a much more fundamental attack and a devastating one in tightly knit workers' communities. As F. M. L. Thompson has argued, "Resort to poor relief . . . came to be equated with

---

[9] Alex Paterson, "Who Are the Paupers?" *Workman's Times,* 30 January 1892.

[10] Errand Boy, "Foresters," 2; see also Grice, "Pensions."

[11] Pat Thane, "The Labour Party and State Welfare." in K. D. Brown ed., *The First Labour Party, 1906–1914* (London: Routledge, 1985), 183–216.

the loss of respectability, a concept nourished and enforced by local communities and peer groups whose sanctions of disparagement, ridicule, or ostracism were far sharper and more potent than the disapproval of middle-class moralizers or administrators."[12]

At the same time that poor law aid became more avoidable, it seems to have become much more distasteful to many workers. Labor leaders could get roars of approval by attacking public welfare both in principle and in practice. Southampton dockers cheered Tom McCarthy when he told them in 1890 that "they were robbed of fourpence an hour and got a penny dinner in return." Ben Tillett rejected charity and welfare aid: "When they wanted soup, let them have the money to make it for themselves."[13] The themes of self-reliance and pride struck a responsive chord among organized workers in the late Victorian period.

In oral histories recorded during the last twenty-five years from people all over Great Britain, the vision of the poor law they conjured was not a pretty one. Many workers born before 1918 claimed strong memories of poverty and of childhood contacts with poor law officials; few had anything good to say about them. Informants, who had looked back at their childhoods through the eyes of those accustomed to the strongly equalitarian norms of the welfare state, did not like what they saw. Many claimed that their parents had refused, despite great poverty, to deal with the poor law, and those who did remember parish aid attacked it strongly. Several of the women interviewed in northwestern counties by Elizabeth Roberts recalled how family pride had kept parents from applying for relief.[14] Paul Thompson's informants from Scotland equated asking for relief with begging, and they insisted that parents had refused to take anything they had not earned.[15]

In northern industrial communities, at least, the path of virtue did not lead to the guardians of the poor. Robert Roberts reports a story that circulated during his childhood among older people in Salford about a poor man with a large family, which included his sick father. After much debate, the father insisted

---

[12] F. M. L. Thompson, *The Rise of Respectable Society* (Cambridge: Harvard University Press, 1988), 353.

[13] *Southampton Times*, 24 May 1890 and 7 June 1890; quoted in Ruth Hutchinson Crocker, "The Victorian Poor Law in Crisis and Change: Southampton, 1870–1895," *Albion* 19:1 (1987):40.

[14] Elizabeth Roberts, *A Woman's Place* (Oxford: Basil Blackwell, 1984), 142.

[15] Paul Thompson has collected interviews of people born in the years 1890 to about 1920, which are held at the University of Essex in the Famiy Life and Work Experience Archive (hereafter FLWEA); the people surveyed are designed to represent a cross-section of the British population in terms of region, social status, and religion. FLWEA no. 307, 83; no. 367, 45.

upon being taken to the workhouse. The son carried him part of the way there, but stopped to rest at a large rock. There the father announced, "It was here I rested too, carrying my father to the workhouse." Overcome, the son took his father back home, saying, "We'll manage somehow."[16] Several of the women interviewed by Elizabeth Roberts about their childhood in Lancashire talked of heroic efforts to avoid using poor law services. Kin took in orphaned children and elderly relations because of the generalized dread of the workhouse; these actions were incorporated into family legends of self-sacrifice and independence. One woman, whose father was a drunkard and whose mother died leaving five young children, described her grandmother's response: "Our Margaret Jane's children in the workhouse? Never. Not while I draw breath."[17]

This visceral hatred of the workhouse stemmed from far more than fear of it as a "bastille" or as a site for forced labor. Indeed, reluctance to enter it lasted well into the period of relaxed administration in the twentieth century. George Lansbury, who had helped to reform conditions in the Poplar workhouse, insisted in the mid-1920s that he would not "voluntarily be found dead" in that or any other workhouse. He recalled a conversation he had had around 1906 with Lord George Hamilton, who praised the cleanliness and comfort of a particularly well-run workhouse that they had just visited. Lansbury replied, "It is too damned clean, too well regulated. Get up with a bell, breakfast with a bell, dinner and supper likewise, then bed with a bell, and at the end, heaven or hell by a bell. You, Lord George, would not live here an hour. . . . What is not good enough for you and me is neither clean nor comfortable enough for others."[18] At the time that Lansbury began his work as a Labour representative on the Poplar board of guardians, he was still working in a local sawmill and veneer works. He had left school at age twelve and supported himself largely by manual labor until he was elected to Parliament in 1910. His denunciations of the workhouse began at a time he still belonged to a group threatened by it.

Within workers' neighborhoods in the industrial north, people who used the poor laws found themselves relegated to the margins of local society. Robert Roberts recalled that in Salford around the time of the First World War, "[p]aupers hardly registered as human beings at all," and he placed them in the social hierarchy just above beggars, thieves, prostitutes, homosexuals, bookies' runners, and brothel keepers. Workers interviewed by Paul Thompson

[16] Robert Roberts, *The Classic Slum* (London: Penguin, 1971), 74.

[17] Elizabeth Roberts, *Woman's Place*, 171.

[18] George Lansbury, *My Life* (London: Constable & Co., 1928), 132.

about their childhood in Edwardian England made similarly harsh judgments. People who attended schools where workhouse children were sent spoke of how different they were. An Essex ironworker's son thought the workhouse children were "not particularly intelligent . . . when I say low, don't misunderstand me. . . . They were extremely poor and conscious of it."[19] One woman from Lancashire remembered: "Now those children were pathetic, all their hair was cropped and they had . . . thick clogs and thick caps. Now they were something apart. . . . We knew they were workhouse children but we didn't bother with them because we didn't understand what those children were feeling, we didn't know, we had a good mother and father, you see."[20]

Public contact with the poor law stigmatized workers within their own communities by the early twentieth century in a way that it had not seventy-five years earlier. One Staffordshire woman from a large family supported by her mother's laundry work remembers being sent occasionally to relieving officers for the weekly grant of bread. She took an old bag to cover it so that no one on the streets would know what she carried.[21] One Lancashire man noted how "humiliating" it was when the poor law inspectors called overlookers in the mill to check the wage figures given them by applicants.[22] A counterexample to these northern workers' communities where poor law aid brought shame can be seen in the population of Campbell Bunk, known in police reports as early as the 1890s as "the worst street in North London." Desperately poor, families there used a variety of charitable and state services, along with casual labor, petty theft, and scrounging, in order to survive. Conning the poor law inspector with protestations of piety and good intentions showed resourcefulness, rather than a loss of status. But the Bunk housed a lumpenproletariat, people clearly on the wrong side of the respectable/rough divide.[23]

It is important to note that workers who used, as well as those who rejected, aid from the poor laws shared an active hostility toward support from that source. Many workers rejected social-work styles of relief, just as they did deterrent methods. Some simply voted with their feet and stayed away from the welfare bureaucracy. Others were more articulate in their dissatisfaction. Within the workhouses, inmates refused assigned work tasks or sneaked

---

[19] FLWEA, no. 12, 11–12.

[20] Ibid., no. 153, 17.

[21] Ibid., no. 213, 37–38.

[22] Ibid., no. 47, 51.

[23] Jerry White, *The Worst Street in North London* (London: Routledge, 1986), 23, 131.

away. They taunted employees, stayed up late, and went out and got drunk. Women refused the cleaning jobs assigned to them, and when food was withheld as punishment, they cursed and started fights. When told to pick oakum, some men worked slowly or not at all. How many? No one knows, but guardians in their meetings had to contend with regular complaints from workhouse authorities about their unruly charges. Not all paupers were cowed and accepting of workhouse discipline.[24] Children ran away from the district schools in large numbers. Paupers were willing and able to challenge relief officers and demand different styles of treatment. They usually lost, but at least they had the short-run satisfaction of thumbing their noses at authority. Kathleen Woodward wrote in 1928 of her childhood spent in a London slum. She lived with her invalid father, two siblings, and her mother, who barely supported them all by working as a laundress. When work was slack, the guardians helped the family with a weekly grant of rice, which the family loathed. After weeks of rice, she complained to the unsympathetic guardians, who refused to accept dislike as a valid reason for change. Woodward remembers the guardians as insolent, peremptory and badgering. Her mother had little success, Woodward decided, because she was too proud. "Superior persons . . . provoked her utmost contempt and impatience and ground a fine edge to her tongue." One of the female guardians announced to the mother, "Rice is very nutritious!" The mother stared at the guardian, who was suntanned rather than pale like Woodward's family, and mistaking her for a mulatto, replied, "It may be where you come from!" That ended the interview, and the family returned to its diet of rice.[25]

Even those who accepted relief often did so with resentment and disdain. In the oral histories recorded by Paul Thompson and his group from a wide sample of the British population, people from all over the country coupled reminiscences of childhood poverty with bitter attacks on the poor law. The core of their resentment was twofold: objections to the personal treatment they received, and disdain for the results of application. When workers remembered guardians, they described nosy, nasty men who would shout and humiliate applicants. In Lancashire, they were called "grubbers." A man whose father was a relatively well-paid railway goods checker recounted local lore about guardians. "If they could bombast you or shout the hardest because you went in with a bundle of nerves, they won the day. Those days

---

[24] See *Leicester Mercury,* 25 January 1890, 2 February 1890, 3 August 1890.

[25] Kathleen Woodward, *Jipping Street* (New York: Harper & Brothers, 1928), 17–19.

were torturing days and people said work if we can, rather than 'the grubber', rather than starvation, rather than the workhouse."[26] One woman, whose father was a guardian in Cornwall and who defended his good motives, described his associates as "rather hard," "rather on the stingy side." She judged "they did not show a lot of [the] milk of human kindness to people who were in poor positions."[27] Another woman remembers her sisters and mother being falsely accused of getting double payments for coal and having great difficulty in proving that the relieving officer was cheating them, rather than the other way round. She summarized: "They were beasts [in] them days – absolute beasts they were."[28] One man raised in Salford, whose mother once sent him to apply for relief, claimed that the guardians treated him "very roughly." "They talked down to you and . . . made you feel your position."[29] One man, born in 1911, recalled a meeting with Bradford poor law guardians in the 1920s: "I felt . . . er . . . degraded I did. I felt very degraded, having to go on my knees for something."[30]

One account by a Staffordshire miner's daughter shows some of the reasons for strong resentment. Under strong pressure from her mother, her father went once at Christmas to get some food for dinner. He had to stand in line and was asked many questions about his income and the family. As she recounts the story, her father became furious and told the relieving officer: "You can keep your tickets for your Christmas dinner and you know what to do with 'em." She says he walked away empty-handed because he refused to put up with the treatment. Her mother, she said, "could go and do it, but not him."[31] Others accused poor law inspectors of coming into their houses unannounced and checking the cupboards for food and smelling their breath for alcohol. The questions and the intrusiveness rankled. Looking backward, people took pride in describing their own family's independence in rejecting, or at least resenting, such interference. Even graffiti in the vagrant wards showed the effect of rising standards and expectations:

Its very unkind, nay, further, cruel,
To give here merely a drop of thin gruel;

[26] FLWEA, no. 47, 51.

[27] Ibid., no. 436, 75.

[28] Ibid., no. 126, 12, 14.

[29] Ibid., no. 89, 10.

[30] Bradford Oral History Collection, Bradford Public Library, no. AO 105.

[31] FLWEA, no. 329, 49.

But let them keep it, we can do without it –
And I mean to let half the town know about it![32]

Note, however, that this was a consumer's dissatisfaction. Alongside the majority who found it possible to avoid the poor laws, there remained those who occasionally had to ask for aid. But hostility, rather than gratitude, was a common response.

By the twentieth century, many workers had become accustomed to a higher standard of living than their counterparts had experienced before 1850, and they were less willing to make do with the pittance offered by their local poor law union. Part of the remembered hostility against relieving officers came from the little they offered and what they proposed to take away. Dealing with poor law authorities meant multiple sacrifices. A Lancashire miner's son claimed that guardians monitored behavior, forbidding applicants to do things that cost money or showed access to wealth. "You hadn't to ride on a car and you hadn't to do this and you hadn't to do t'other. . . . If you could have managed on dry bread you were best away."[33] The son of a Lancashire spinner complained that before they could get any aid when unemployed, they had to sell everything of value in their homes.[34] Others charged that guardians came into their houses and inventoried goods, requiring that chairs, mantles, or pianos be sold and the money used for self-support.[35] Norms of working-class respectability were breached by the poor laws, and this was deeply resented. The son of a Lancashire ironworker, who remembered his father once having had to break stones for six pence an hour relief, charged, "In his day, you wasn't to have a decent home. If you had a decent home you couldn't get relief – or they, they'd make you get rid of something. Sell it . . . and, oh, it was shocking, you know."[36] A cabinetmaker's son from London charged that anything appearing "comfortable" had to go before relief would be granted. He charged relieving officers with administering "a means test . . . in its filthiness and it was ugly."[37]

What poor law officials offered in exchange for their public and private

[32] Reports on Vagrancy by Poor Law Inspectors, PP 1866, XXXVI, 66; quoted by Rachael Vorspan, "Vagrancy and the New Poor Law in Late-Victorian and Edwardian England," *English Historical Review* 92:362 (1977):71.

[33] FLWEA, no. 139, 48.

[34] Ibid., no. 122, 38.

[35] Ibid., no. 208, no. 225, no. 240.

[36] Ibid., no. 52, 29.

[37] Ibid., no. 296, 54.

humiliations was judged to be too little by many workers. Many remembered aid being given only in kind – bread, oatmeal, tea, margarine. People remembered having to use specific stores and being told what grants could be used for: margarine not butter, treacle but not jam. The brown bread stuck in their imaginations as well as in their throats. The humiliation of having regulated amounts of poor-quality food added to the general nastiness of the application procedure. The bitterest charges seemed to come from adults whose own families had never applied for relief. A London stableman's son recalled that the poor were given a "terrible" kind of black bread.[38] The child of a Lancashire spinner told of a time in 1918 when the father's mill shut down. They refused to go to the poor law, he claimed, because "all as they'd have given you then was a . . . a voucher to go and get a little bit of food or offer you institutional accommodation."[39] A Welsh tinworker's son recalled weeks when his father was unemployed or ill, and they had pawned all their proper clothes so they had to remain inside their home. The family ran up debts in the shops and ate stews made from bones. Yet he added that they had gotten no help from the guardians. "If you asked for it [aid] you only got half a crown a week; wasn't worth having."[40]

By the early twentieth century, many skilled workers had acquired higher living standards and a strong sense of their own respectability. They were far less willing to trade deferential behavior and pitiful stories of need for scanty alms. At the same time, their sense of entitlement to poor law relief seems to have faded. Asking for money directly from the state put them in social categories to which they refused to belong. Those who could find no alternative sources of income writhed under the humiliating gaze of the guardians, whom they did not respect, and rejected in principle a system some felt forced to use in practice. By the twentieth century, the popular legitimacy of the Elizabethan poor law bargain had disappeared.

Demands by the Unemployed

Rejection of the poor laws was also rampant among workers much more directly threatened by destitution. Unemployment forced both skilled and unskilled men to confront poor law styles of relief. For the most part, they tried to ignore local guardians and to pressure public authorities for help in

[38] Ibid., no. 299, 24.

[39] Ibid., no. 122, 38.

[40] Ibid., no. 380, 66.

other forms. In 1904, men paraded down the streets in Bradford asking for work to be provided by the town. In Leicester in 1905, the Joint Committee of the Unemployed worked with the trades council, the town council, and the Citizens' Aid Society to try to find ways of helping the jobless and keeping them away from the poor laws.[41] In the nearby town of Loughborough, a "right to work" parade was organized. Unemployed men from Liverpool marched southward in the winter of 1906, getting food, shelter, and a lot of attention as they went from town to town. By the turn of the century, both in the capital and in provincial towns, the unemployed had organized in large numbers, one of their aims being to change poor law policies toward destitute males.[42]

Men out of work in Leicester in the summer of 1905 went regularly to the marketplace to hear Labour politicians and local trade unionists denounce the corrupt "system" that permitted unemployment and stigmatized the poor. Socialists called for rejection of the "status quo" and support for "social justice." Other speakers called on the government to pass its Unemployment Bill, which would mandate labor exchanges and public works and give those out of work alternatives to the workhouse or a dole. They found the poor laws ideologically unacceptable. Particularly those measures intended to test the reality of destitution or willingness to work came under criticism. One recently elected guardian of the poor suggested that men refuse the labor test and offer to go into the workhouse in such large numbers that they could not be accommodated. Speakers called for aid from the town council and rejected disenfranchisement and begging for relief in front of the guardians.[43] A worker sent a letter to the town paper demanding "justice and not charity," by which he meant the provision of jobs under "humane conditions." By 1905, the Leicester unemployed had turned away from the poor laws and branded their aid illegitimate.

During the summer of 1905, four hundred jobless men walked from Leicester to London, complete with bicycle escort, baggage wagons, ambulance, and the town band in attendance for part of the way. Their banner identified them as "Leicester's Unemployed March to London Representing 2,000 Men and Their Families." The men hoped to see the king and to demon-

---

[41] *Leicester Mercury*, 19 May 1905, 24 May 1905.

[42] *The Pioneer*, 18 November 1905, 2 December 1905, 3 February 1906; *Leicester Mercury*, 5 June 1905; Interview Transcripts, 1905: "Mr. Dunn of the Charity Organization Society," Webb Local Government Collection, The Poor Laws, vol. 341: Bradford, Yorkshire.

[43] *Leicester Mercury*, 17 May 1905, 19 May 1905.

strate in favor of legislation to authorize public employment. Once in the capital, they rallied in Trafalgar Square and heard speeches by J. Ramsay McDonald, other Labour politicians, and trade union leaders. Their rhetoric rang of patriotism, virtue, democracy, and justice. Speakers pointed to an exemplary marcher, a elderly man identified as a soldier in both the Crimean War and the India Mutiny, now "after fighting with all his strength for Queen and Country, . . . left to starve in the street!" Right was on his side, not that of the guardians. Reverend Donaldson of St. Mary's, Leicester, lauded the unemployed who "desired not charity, but work." Alderman Saunders of the London County Council directed their attention away from the king, "who was powerless," and toward Parliament, "which could help and would do so as soon as sufficient pressure was brought to bear upon its members. A bill should be passed to enable every honest workman to get work when he demanded it and could not get it from a present employer."[44] A right to work, not a right to relief, was at the center of their concerns.

By the early twentieth century, workers had become politically organized in a variety of groups that took positions on welfare issues. Certainly not a united "class," some swung behind Conservatives, whereas others voted Liberal; about 40 percent of all adult males still were barred from a national franchise. Support for the fledgling Labour party in early twentieth-century elections came from under 10 percent of all voters. Still, trade unions had begun to swing behind the new workers' party and to support pressure groups like the National Committee of Organized Labour. In the decade before 1914, a "socialist-flavoured Labourism" became the dominant ideology among trade unionists, according to Chris Wrigley.[45] Workers' groups of all sorts had begun to demand from the government a broadened attack on unemployment and poverty, and most of the early Labour candidates pledged to fight for new policies in these areas. After joint meetings among leaders of the Trades Union Congress, the General Federation of Trade Unions, and Labour members of Parliament in the winter of 1904–5, a delegation met with the prime minister to outline hoped-for changes in national and local policies toward workers. They wanted responsibility for the unemployed to belong not with the poor law, but with a Ministry of Labour, and they demanded that paupers no longer be disenfranchised. In the plan they outlined, the national government would act to abolish monopolies and organize industry so as to avoid

---

[44] *The Times,* 12 June 1905, 9.

[45] Chris Wrigley, "Labour and the Trades Unions," in Brown, *Labour Party,* 129.

cyclical changes in employment. Other policies were to be instituted on the local level: There, standard wages, the eight-hour day, public works, and public investment in reforestation and land reclamation should, they hoped, expand employment opportunities in towns and rural areas.[46] Labour leaders worried about declines in demand that followed decreases in real wages, and they showed a sophisticated awareness of alternative ways to expand the market for labor.

Both Labour leaders and the unemployed used a different discourse from that of the Charity Organization Society and professional social workers. They talked about economics and about status, rather than modes of treatment. The world they described was one that owed them work and a decent income. Leicester shoe factory workers protested insinuations that all men "worth their place" could find employment. Lacks in demand, they claimed, not defects of character had led to their discharge. The Shoe Finishers' Association blamed changes in technology and piecework procedures for their unemployment. Their banners proclaimed them "the unemployed," drawing on an up-to-date economic rhetoric rather than words invoking a humiliating poverty or dependence. Men marched to the home of a shoe manufacturer and demanded a retraction of his charge that any competent, energetic worker could find a job, and they denounced clergy who had insinuated that various criminals had joined the street marchers.[47] The marchers both insisted on their own virtue and attacked moral explanations of unemployment. Their rhetoric mixed new and old approaches to poverty. It was not, however, a rhetoric of class, but one of citizenship, in which they demanded the rights due them by virtue of their membership in a national community.

Patrick Joyce has recently described the "controlling narrative" used by English workers to make sense of the world as that of "radical populism." When they commented on the world as they wished to see it, notions of liberty, equality, and fraternity combined with a sense of mission: The ordinary people, the "decent folk" would combine to work against privilege and the illegitimate power of the rich. They set their awareness of poverty and insecurity into an explanatory framework that called for justice. When workers pointed to the opposition of rich and poor, virtue lay on the side of the latter. Reconciliation would come along with redistribution. As part of this story, the New Poor Law occupied a key role in a master narrative of past golden ages and utopian futures. Its adoption signaled a retreat by the rich from their

---

[46] José Harris, *Unemployment and Politics* (Oxford: Oxford University Press, 1972), 236–7.

[47] *Leicester Mercury,* 15 May 1905, 19 May 1905, 20 May 1905, 22 May 1905, 25 May 1905.

duties toward the poor; its demise would point to a revival of communal bonds and solidarities as well as the restoration of the rights of the "freeborn Englishman," who in a new and better world could eat roast beef and raise his family in peace and dignity.[48] In popular rhetoric, the word pauper was rarely used except to muster sympathy for those oppressed by unjust treatment. When thinking about the poor laws around 1909, workers were much less likely to muse about Majority or Minority Reports than they were to conjure up visions of Albert Chevalier on the music hall stage standing in front of workhouse doors marked "Men" and "Women," where he said goodbye to his wife of forty years, "My Old Dutch."[49]

[48] Patrick Joyce, *Visions of the People* (New York: Cambridge University Press, 1991), 247, 331.
[49] Martha Vicinus, *The Industrial Muse* (London: Routledge, 1974), 274–5.

10

NEW PRINCIPLES FOR SOCIAL ACTION, 1906–48

The problem of unemployment is the problem of the adjustment of the supply of labour and the demand for labour.
William Beveridge, 1909

I wish hon. Members would get it into their heads that a non-contributory scheme [for mothers' pensions] would not be a dispensing of charity, but a very definite payment for services that the widow had rendered to the State, and that it should enable the woman to bring up the children properly.
Ellen Wilkinson, 1925, in House of Commons

Deciding what to do about poverty in the twentieth century was no easy matter. Multiple voices, certainly not in harmony, chimed out "Family Allowances," "Jobs," "Pensions," "Labor Colonies," and even, "The Principles of 1834," invoking a poor law that had never worked as promised. Then disputes moved from theory into practice as philanthropists financed agricultural settlements for the unemployed, and newly elected pro-Labour guardians cheerfully ordered more money to be passed out to paupers. In London's East End, Oxford graduates residing in Toynbee Hall tried their hand at community organizing and social work, while Octavia Hill's rent collectors set out to civilize the inhabitants of renovated buildings. Experimentation in ideas and forms, rather than a firm insistence on one solution, dominated. This was not a carcereal society, or even a rigidly doctrinaire one, if the range of policies targeting the destitute is examined.

Two major new approaches stand out, however, from the disparate solutions and local activities pushed by philanthropists and elected officials. When people argued for changes in existing poor law and charitable practices, they usually adopted one of two strategies. The first to be articulated and the most powerful until the eve of the First World War was that offered primarily by charitable workers and poor law doctors, who sought to combine knowledge of individuals and families with personal interventions to help them solve their problems. Under this regime, the poor became "cases" to be investigated and labeled. Social workers would respond to distinctions of age, gender, health, and character; knowledge and classification could then point to an appropriate therapy. From this vantage point, poverty appeared as an individual disease, needing treatment by professionals who would use medical models to cure them. By splitting the poor into individual units, they could handle, treat, and save them. The state and private groups would use sociological and medical expertise to perfect the polity.

The alternative strategy looked more to statistics and economics than to sociology and medicine. The discourse was of risk, and the relevant influences, those of actuarial science. For advocates of this approach, poverty consisted primarily of a lack of income, which could be compensated for by insurance schemes designed to fit particular demographic groups. The aim was not to diagnose particular weaknesses but to raise income to a minimum standard, through either contributory insurance or a state-funded payment. Entitlement came via age, gender, and occupation, not moral worth. Introduced first by the Liberal government in 1909, then maintained and widened by Conservatives in the interwar period and later by the Labour government in 1948, this approach became identified as that of the welfare state. In it, citizens, backed by the state, stood together to maintain the weakest; the solidarities of strangers would strengthen the whole. It was the poor laws' failure to achieve their stated goals, along with the difficulties of reform and the hostility of workers and organized labor, that prompted politicians to look for other social welfare policies.

In the years 1905 to 1914, the most obvious alternative to the poor laws was social insurance, already in place and working effectively in Germany, Austria, and Denmark, and under active discussion in Sweden. Its adoption by the Liberal government avoided the political difficulties of poor law reform and secured the good will of organized labor, then joined to them in an electoral alliance. Parliament's approval of a second strategy for attacking poverty would in the end prove decisive: The poor laws were left to die by attrition and surgical removals of essential organs. In the meantime, treatment of the poor as defective members of society continued apace.

Statistics and Minimum Standards

People concerned with poverty around 1900 had hard choices to make: Which sort of panacea would they advocate? At issue were their images of an industrial society, their ideas of causation, their priorities for change. Many people had retreated from the strict ethic of individual responsibility and repayment according to just deserts that had triumphed in early Victorian times. Martin Wiener has written of the shift late in the nineteenth century from "moralism" to "causalism," which he defines as an outlook that sought to reduce harm and suffering irrespective of judgments about behavior and virtue.[1] That change was particularly in evidence among professionals willing to expand the power of the state. Their reconfiguration of solutions for the poverty problem went hand in hand with a reworking of social knowledge and investigation.

In an effort to extend the range of "scientific" observation and analysis, many social researchers turned to statistics for help, ignoring the fictive, socially constructed quality of numbers.[2] Frustrated by their inability to observe or to predict the outcomes of individual cases, they turned to the measurement of mass phenomena as an effective strategy for research. Numbers supposedly brought knowledge in a precise form. Consider the claim of a physicist, Lord Kelvin: "When you can measure what you are speaking about, and express it in numbers, you know something about it, but when you cannot measure it, . . . your knowledge is of a meager and unsatisfactory kind."[3] Many leading scientists in the late nineteenth century agreed with him. When mathematicians developed ways to measure uncertainty and deviation, they provided empirical science with a new technology for making causal statements about the world. Between 1890 and 1910, several of the major techniques of mathematical statistics were developed by Karl Pearson, G. Udny Yule, F. Y. Edgeworth, and Charles Spearman. Working with notions of probability, chance, and correlation, they developed ways to calculate causal relationships. Statistics became not only a privileged form of knowledge in the social and natural sciences, but one that charted causality and representativeness. With statistical tools in hand, social scientists expected to tackle Big Questions and provide answers in the form of normal curves, stan-

---

[1] Martin J. Wiener, *Reconstructing the Criminal* (New York: Cambridge University Press, 1990), 337–8.

[2] Mary Poovey, "Figures of Arithmetic, Figures of Speech: The Discourse of Statistics in the 1830's," *Critical Inquiry* (Winter 1993): 256–76.

[3] Quoted in Stephen M. Stigler, *The History of Statistics* (Cambridge: Harvard University Press, 1986), 1.

dard deviations, and regression analysis. They discovered "law and order in large numbers."[4]

Although Karl Pearson and Francis Galton did much of their pioneering work in the field of evolutionary theory and eugenics, others turned their attention to social problems. Statisticians graphed the distribution of social characteristics, calculated means, and worked to make precise depictions of the natural world that reduced a vast range of phenomena to the same terms of intelligibility. Indeed, Karl Pearson announced that "from paupers to cricket scores, from school-board classes to ox-eyed daisies, from crustaceans to birth rates, we find almost universally the same laws of frequency."[5] In 1895 and 1896, Udny Yule had applied Karl Pearson's skew curves to data on pauperism among the elderly, and he used a correlation table to challenge Booth's assertion that there was no relationship between the incidence of pauperism and the prevalence of outdoor relief.[6] Pauperism was therefore normal, predictable, and correlatable with other measurable characteristics. Between 1890 and 1914, new mathematical techniques transformed the collection of social statistics and the claims that could be made about them.

Elements of late Victorian analyses of urban poverty were superseded, battered down by new standards for evidence and representativeness. Even Seebohm Rowntree's pioneering study of York had relied heavily on impressionistic criteria. He based judgments about poverty upon income, the "appearance of poverty," and information on a family's drinking habits. Using those categories, he collected data on every wage-earning family in the city and then claimed that York was typical of the nation.[7] But when Rowntree offered his results to the Interdepartmental Committee on Physical Deterioration, which met in 1904 to examine the health and fitness of the British population, they rejected his effort to generalize his conclusions because of his research methods.

Other investigators had developed methods that could give representative results. Arthur Bowley, a lecturer in statistics at the London School of Economics and at the University of Reading, was able to apply advances in prob-

[4] Karl Pearson, "The Chances of Death," in *The Chances of Death and Other Studies in Evolution*, 2 vols. (London: Edward Arnold, 1897), 1:15. For an analysis of the early history of mathematical statistics, see Stigler, *Statistics,* and Theodore M. Porter, *The Rise of Statistical Thinking, 1820–1900* (Princeton: Princeton University Press, 1986).

[5] Porter, *Statistical Thinking,* 309.

[6] Stigler, *Statistics,* 346–7.

[7] B. Seebohm Rowntree, *Poverty: A Study of Town Life* (London: Macmillan, 1901), viii, 13; see also Karel Williams, *From Pauperism to Poverty* (London: Routledge, 1981), 358.

ability theory to issues of social investigation. He worked out a method of random sampling that permitted surveys to be based on small numbers of representative cases, and he calculated standard deviations to estimate the degree of error that would be present in his findings.[8] To illustrate his techniques, he analyzed a sample of one in twenty working-class households in Reading, Northampton, Warrington, and Stanley and generalized his findings about poverty in those places to all British towns of a similar size. Moreover, he conceptualized poverty as a simple, economic phenomenon created by the difference between incomes and living costs. Because it could be measured by collecting data on wages, rents, and family sizes, he constructed a precise profile of urban economic deprivation. Readers were told that 27 percent of the children and 16 percent of the total working-class population in the medium-sized towns were living in "primary" poverty with incomes below a standard necessary for a "healthy existence."[9] Moreover, he deflected criticism about the representativeness of his results by calculating a margin of error and showing it to be small. Bowley's work, unlike that of Booth and Rowntree, virtually ignored any connection between poverty and individual character. For him, poverty had economic causes and economic cures, and it could be quantified. The resulting picture showed poverty to be predictable, ubiquitous, and easily curable by economic means.

A similar language of numbers informed William Beveridge's work on unemployment, published in 1909. Using indexes, rates, and averages, he reduced the human tragedies of the jobless to numbers. Unemployment became "average," distributed in particular patterns among trades and age groups. Rather than aberrant, it became a normal attribute of the industrial economy. When he concluded that efforts to count the unemployed would never be sufficiently accurate because of the fluctuating, ambiguous nature of the phenomenon, he turned away from counting the individual cases to analysis of the larger process itself. He focused on unemployment, which he analyzed using neoclassical economic theory. Beveridge saw unemployment chiefly as a "problem of industrial organization," one that could be solved by better planning and interference with the labor market and with wage scales.[10] Character had disappeared as an important causal factor. Beveridge

---

[8] E. P. Hennock, "The Measurement of Poverty: From the Metropolis to the Nation, 1880–1920," *Economic History Review,* 2nd ser., 40:2 (May 1987): 219–22.

[9] A. L. Bowley and A. R. Burnett-Hurst, *Livelihood and Poverty* (London: G. Bell & Sons, 1915): 46–7.

[10] W. H. Beveridge, *Unemployment, a Problem of Industry,* new ed. (New York: AMS Press, 1969), 27, 236–7.

turned to collective solutions for the problem of unemployment. He recommended labor exchanges and fluctuating working hours to help match the supply of workers to the demand for them, and he suggested that insurance could help to stabilize income. Because he accepted some unemployment as an inevitable characteristic of the industrial economy, he worked to design compensatory measures. Social risks should be covered by social insurance.[11]

By the early twentieth century, thinking about poverty in Britain had shifted from an individualist to a collective, largely economic framework. Because all were menaced by the potential decline in national efficiency that stemmed from unemployment, physical deterioration, and environmental degradation, many felt that the collectivity ought to intervene in the interests of reform. This turn toward the group can be seen across a spectrum of social and political formations. Many workers had long since embraced collective solutions to social problems by joining trades unions and friendly societies. Some had strong religious identities that bound them to a wider community. Feminists asserted the ties of gender and family, claiming rights on their account. Conservatives exalted nation and empire as foci for identity, whereas socialists looked toward the state to provide the structures for action and support. From the 1870s, both Conservatives and Liberals built political organizations at the grass-roots level to foster allegiance to their parties. Despite continued belief in English rights and liberties, many ties bound the average citizen into collectivities where mutual responsibility went along with similarity of identity.

Acceptance of new forms of collective responsibility for poverty and the interruption of earnings grew in public debates over welfare legislation during the last quarter of the nineteenth century. In 1897, the Conservative government introduced and helped to pass a Workmen's Compensation Bill, which mandated payments for employees in railways, factories, building, mines, and engineering.[12] In the case of skilled male industrial workers, Parliament ordered employers to provide insurance against work-related accidents and illnesses. Herbert Asquith, speaking for the Liberal opposition, criticized the measure on the grounds of incompleteness, and he looked forward to a time when "the community at large" would pay compensation for such injuries.[13] In this particular case, both major parties clearly had jettisoned the notion of individual responsibility, although neither was willing to

---

[11] For an analysis of Beveridge's career and approach to social reform, see José Harris, *William Beveridge* (Oxford: Oxford University Press, 1977).

[12] E. P. Hennock, *British Social Reform and German Precedents* (Oxford: Oxford University Press, 1987), 63–79.

[13] *House of Commons Debates*, 15 July 1897, 208; quoted in Hennock, *British Social Reform*, 76.

extend such protection to females and to casual or service workers. They reserved public protection for the male industrial worker whose wages would support a family.

Public discussion of collective support had, however, come to embrace other groups, too, particularly those defined by age and gender. By the 1890s, the Women's Cooperative Guild had begun to lobby and demonstrate for various state social reforms to benefit women, children, and the elderly. Organized labor pushed for noncontributory pensions for the elderly, and by 1900 most sections of it, as well as some representatives of major friendly societies, had come to endorse a state-financed pension scheme.[14] The case for state responsibility toward wives and children was argued by socialists and feminists, who sketched out family-based welfare policies.[15] Slowly, public approval for opening a small umbrella of state care over dependent children increased. The National Society for the Prevention of Cruelty to Children garnered support from doctors and philanthropists for its efforts to remove the custody of neglected children from parents to the poor law. Town councils began to assign medical officers of health to schools. Even the *British Medical Journal,* which opposed direct state welfare activities, recommended publicly funded dental care for children, as well as medical inspection and physical training for the young. Although most efforts to improve children's health remained voluntarist in orientation until the early twentieth century, the line between public and private efforts to lower infant mortality became blurred in many towns, where locally run and funded infant welfare centers, mothers' schools, and public health visitors demonstrated the effectiveness of modest amounts of information and care, whatever its source of funding.[16] Ellen Ross argues that the British Left had made free meals for schoolchildren "a priority" from at least the 1880s and had pushed for public acceptance of this "right" by marches, demonstrations, and meetings with officials. The London County Council actively supported charities' ongoing efforts to feed hungry pupils in its elementary schools, while an army of volunteers in the metropolis provided funds and personnel for this new public-

---

[14] Pat Thane, "Non-Contributory Versus Insurance Pensions 1878–1908," in Pat Thane, ed., *The Origins of British Social Policy* (London: Routledge, 1978), 92–5; idem, "The Working Class and State 'Welfare' in Britain, 1880–1914," *Historical Journal* 27:4 (1984): 877–900.

[15] See Susan Pedersen, *Family, Dependence, and the Origins of the Welfare State* (New York: Cambridge University Press, 1993), 41–6.

[16] Pat Thane, "Infant Care in England and Wales, 1870s to 1930s," in Michael Katz and Christoph Sachße, eds., *The Mixed Economy of Social Welfare* (Baden-Baden: NOMOS-Verlagsgesellschaft, 1996), 253–9; Bentley B. Gilbert, *The Evolution of National Insurance in Great Britain* (London: Michael Joseph, 1966), 93.

private symbiosis. In 1903 and 1904, both the Royal Commission on Physical Training in Scotland and the Interdepartmental Committee on Physical Deterioration recommended joint public and private efforts to feed needy children. Passage of the 1906 Education (Provision of Meals) Act rested on a coalition of Labour, Liberal, and philanthropic support long in the making, augmented at the local level by activist mothers' pressure.[17]

By the early twentieth century, the notion of collective responsibility for children's health had become acceptable to a wide coalition of people with differing political allegiances. In fact, the Interdepartmental Committee on Physical Deterioration made improvement of children's health the centerpiece of its program of reform. Appalled by the disease and malnutrition that, in their opinion, had devastated the bodies and minds of the lower classes, they called upon the state to provide medical inspections and school meals, to encourage physical exercise, to teach mothers how to cook and how to care for their offspring, and to regulate health hazards in the environment.[18] Children's welfare proved an easy ground upon which to compromise yet again the principle of laissez-faire.

With the provision of school meals and state-funded medical inspections, the English government shifted into a much more active mode of providing welfare services. Rather than waiting for the poor to come and request help, it would authorize officials to look for the needy and to offer minimum standards of care. In this new world, poverty could be measured in terms of calories and body weight; it could be counted, charted, and compared, then counteracted with pea soup and porridge. Manchester bodies could be measured against those in Cornwall and Cumberland, and appropriate actions taken to upgrade them all. It placed poverty within an empirical framework of physical deprivation, for which there were clear physical remedies. Morality did not signify.

The Last Chance for Poor Law Reform

Spurred by a sense of mission and of their own expertise, aspiring social engineers offered differing remedies for poverty, ones that could be largely implemented within the framework of the poor law. To use Harold Perkin's terminology, a "professional social ideal" began to "infiltrate" the outlook of

[17] See Ellen Ross, "Hungry Children: Housewives and London Charity, 1870–1918," in Peter Mandler, ed., *The Uses of Charity* (Philadelphia: University of Pennsylvania Press, 1990), 176–80; see also Gilbert, *National Insurance*, 107–8.

[18] Gilbert, *National Insurance*, 89–91.

upper-, middle-, and working-class people between 1880 and 1914.[19] As they rose in power and influence, individuals who depended on human capital and expertise for status and income mounted an increasingly effective ideological challenge to older ways of thinking about society. In particular, they attacked laissez-faire, competition, and individualism in the name of justice and utilitarian outcomes. After pointing accusing fingers at the social disorder of the slums, they suggested that, if given a chance to act as expert managers, they would set the tumbledown British house in order. Professionals helped to demolish the walls of the minimalist state with the battering rams of knowledge and publicity, and then set about rebuilding a larger, more expensive edifice.

Beatrice Webb illustrates well the path from voluntarism to an ethic of professional interference. Her public career began in the 1880s when she worked as a rent collector for Octavia Hill and as a Charity Organization Society slum visitor, but by the 1890s, she had moved from the assumption that poverty could be cured by exhortation and will power to the position that expansion of state welfare services was necessary. After her marriage to Sidney Webb, she and he began to investigate English institutions, moving from historical analyses to recommendations for reform. Beatrice Webb spent the years between 1905 and 1909 looking into the history and operation of the poor laws, while designing schemes for their replacement. A dining club, the Coefficients, which met at the Webbs' London house, brought together a star-studded group of politicians and enthusiasts of social imperialism to debate, albeit ineffectually, ways of redesigning society in the interest of "national efficiency." Sidney Webb had, in fact, coined that phrase when in 1901 he called on Lord Rosebery to commit the Liberal party to implementing a "National Minimum" standard of life, which would permit "the rearing of an Imperial race."[20] Poor law reform, slum clearance, and improvements in housing were only a few of the changes he called for.

Efforts by professionals to redesign the nation intensified after the Boer War triggered an outpouring of anger against both the army and the national government for their ineptitude. Webb's slogan of "National Efficiency" became a label for wide-ranging criticism of public policy and alarm about public health. What would happen to the empire if workers had become so weak that they could be beaten by the Germans or even native populations?

---

[19] Harold Perkin, *The Rise of Professional Society* (London: Routledge, 1989), 116.

[20] Quoted in ibid., 158.

Eugenicists pointed to looming danger in the forms of physical deterioration and racial decay.[21] The government report investigating such matters concluded not surprisingly that workers' children did not get enough to eat, that they lacked adequate medical care, and that they lived in substandard housing.[22] By 1905, the topic of poverty had again become a lively public issue, but without any consensus on remedies.

Under pressure to think about issues of public health and welfare, the Conservative government decided in 1905 to appoint a Royal Commission to investigate the poor laws and to suggest reforms. Why Arthur Balfour and his colleagues made this decision at that moment is unclear. Perhaps Balfour hoped to gain favor with the unemployed and with working-class voters, or perhaps he wanted to show that he, as well as Joseph Chamberlain, was capable of creative action on the social front. In any case, Arthur Balfour and his brother, Gerald, who was President of the Local Government Board, launched the commission, selecting a diverse lot of social investigators, as well as the upper-class administrators needed for respectability. Lord George Hamilton, former Secretary of State for India, a Conservative who had organized Indian famine relief, headed the group. Several other career civil servants who worked with the English, Scottish, and Irish Local Government Boards joined him. Balfour also appointed six leading members of the Charity Organization Society (Helen Bosanquet, Octavia Hill, C. S. Loch, T. H. Nunn, T. G. Gardiner, and L. R. Phelps), a professor of political economy from Glasgow (William Smart), a Bradford businessman (F. H. Bentham), an Irish landlord who was soon replaced by a Roman Catholic bishop (C. O. O'Conor, and after 1906, Denis Kelly), and five prominent people of unorthodox, allegedly radical views (Charles Booth, Beatrice Webb, George Lansbury, Dr. H. R. Wakefield, and F. W. Chandler). Balfour had invited representatives of the major groups who worried about poor law policies; he excluded neither socialists nor trade union representatives, although the majority of the members sympathized with a C.O.S. point of view.[23]

During the months in which evidence was collected and witnesses were examined, the commission scrutinized major areas of poor law activity, which they found quite wanting. Helen Bosanquet looked into women's

---

[21] G. R. Searle, *The Quest for National Efficiency* (Berkeley: University of California Press, 1971).

[22] For an analysis of the Inter-Departmental Committee on Physical Deterioration, see Gilbert, *National Insurance*, 88–91.

[23] For the story of the designing of the commission, see A. M. McBriar, *An Edwardian Mixed Doubles: The Bosanquets Versus the Webbs* (Oxford: Oxford University Press, 1987), 176–94.

wages and outdoor relief; Beatrice Webb constructed a history of policies since 1834 and planned other inquiries into children on outdoor relief and into medical services. Members of the Documents Committee surveyed Scottish and Irish poor laws. The commission broke down the poor law's clientele into its constituent groups, implicitly recognizing differences among them. Enormous amounts of historical material were sifted to reconstruct what had actually been done since 1834, with the record, however, being read in multiple ways. At the same time, the group polled government departments, local authorities, Liberal economists, Socialist advocates, medical doctors, trade unionists, and welfare activists for suggestions. Opinions evolved on all sides as the mountain of disparate evidence accumulated.[24]

When the dust settled in 1909, the principles of 1834 had been left far behind, and none of the major players on the commission regretted their abandonment. Both sides had retreated from individualist solutions to the poverty problem and willingly delegated responsibility to the state for certain categories of the destitute. Helen Bosanquet and William Smart wrote most of the report for the majority. Webb's refusal to compromise with the C.O.S. group led her to produce a minority report, which she persuaded Lansbury, Wakefield, and Chandler to endorse. Both groups maneuvered for public support and energetically campaigned for adoption of their schemes for reform. From the standpoint of the 1990s, however, the most striking point about the two documents is not their differences, but the distance between both of them and the Royal Commission report of 1834.

In 1909, both the majority and minority reports worried more about poverty than about pauperism. The able-bodied pauper, the villain in 1834, was superseded by the unemployed worker. Moreover, the dependent poor had gained a demographic profile: They were recognized as the elderly, as children, and as adult males and females. Statisticians had charted their incidence in the population, as well as cyclical changes in their numbers. They became part of the total population, subject to its conjunctural rhythms. Moreover, the majority suggested linguistic means of reincorporating them in the larger communities. The destitute were to become the "necessitous"; the "poor law" would be renamed the "Public Assistance Authority." "Guardians of the Poor" would disappear to be replaced by Public Assistance Committees. The majority noted that the old names had about them "associations of harshness, and still more of hopelessness, which we fear might seriously

---

[24] For a discussion of the working of the commission, see ibid., 195–279, passim.

obstruct the reforms which we desire to see initiated." They wanted to sub-stitute "new traditions" for old.[25] Their linguistic turn signaled a retreat from the effort to marginalize the dependent poor by demonizing them.

Most of the commission acknowledged the impact of old age, casual labor, sickness, low wages, and unhealthy trades. Although familiar moral explana-tions – drinking, gambling, and thriftlessness – still figured high on their list of the causes of dependence, they had learned one of the lessons of late Vic-torian social investigations: Destitution had roots in the human life cycle and in the industrial economy. Punitive welfare provisions no longer seemed a sufficient solution to the poverty problem. Indeed, the majority condemned the use of the general workhouse as a test or deterrent and called on welfare institutions to provide "help, prevention, cure, and instruction." Provident dispensaries could aid the sick poor, whereas day nurseries and maternity homes would offer needed services to women and children. They endorsed outdoor relief to people "living respectable lives in decent houses," who could be identified by investigation, case papers, and cooperation with char-ities. The social work style of relief was given a central place in their blue-prints for redesigned welfare. For the unemployed, they approved of labor exchanges and counter-cyclical public works, as well as emigration, labor colonies, and detention colonies. Although their plans called for the survival of existing poor law institutions with different names and county administra-tion, the majority report recommended substantial changes in the functioning of workhouses, turning them away from the purposes of 1834.

The minority plan left the New Poor Law even farther behind. It urged dividing the dependent poor according to their stage in the life cycle and phys-ical condition, and then shifting their care to an appropriate department of government. Local health authorities would supervise birth and infancy through maternity hospitals, midwifery services, and day nurseries. An edu-cation authority, aided by an army of inspectors, would look after poor chil-dren, provide them with medical services and free meals, and investigate the foster families and boarding homes in which some would be placed. State pen-sions would enable most of the elderly to live independently, whereas the infirm would fall under public health officials. The minority plan completely removed the unemployed from poor law hands by mandating National Labour Exchanges, trade union insurance, a higher school-leaving age, and a Ministry of Labour. In essence, Beatrice Webb proposed to organize the national labor

[25] *Royal Commission on the Poor Law and Relief of Distress*, PP 1909, XXXVII, 596–7.

market by shifting, training, insuring, and exporting workers so that the supply would equal the demand.[26] The minority report proposed removing the destitute group by group from the care of the poor law and placing them under the care of newly designed public welfare institutions. The key figure in its state-run utopia was the civil servant, who would feed the hungry, bandage the wounded, and succor the homeless, providing a sheltering umbrella from cradle to grave. Beatrice Webb's vision went far beyond the political sensibilities of the time, although it did gain restrained approval of various socialist and labor groups that were eager to do away with the poor laws.

Both the majority and minority plans to replace the existing poor laws ended in failure. The plans had few defenders and many opponents who attacked the schemes aggressively. Unwilling to be consigned to the scrap heap of history, boards of guardians condemned the proposals effectively. They exploited divisions between majority and minority reports and pushed quite limited schemes of reform, which incidentally increased guardians' powers and left the basic structure of welfare administration intact. Equating Webb's proposals with socialism and calling compromise reforms too radical, they outmaneuvered experts supporting both the majority and the minority reports. Even the C.O.S. was disgusted: Its *Review,* then edited by Helen Bosanquet, complained of "the chorus . . . from Poor Law conferences all over the country that all is for the best in the best of all possible Poor Laws."[27] Moreover, the government knew that until local taxation procedures were reformed and decisions made about allocating financial responsibility for local services, any changes in welfare arrangements would be opposed in Parliament on the grounds of their cost.[28] Faced with vehement division among the welfare experts, opposition by elected officials, and only lukewarm endorsement of the minority report by the Trades Union Congress and the Labour party, the Liberal government had little to gain and much to lose by adopting any of the proposals presented. They wisely decided to ignore the lot.

Professionals' attempts to remake relief officially into social work went nowhere in the decade before the First World War.

---

[26] "Separate Report by H. Russell Wakefield, Francis Chandler, George Lansbury, and Mrs. Sidney Webb," *Royal Commission on the Poor Law,* PP 1909, XXXVII, 721–3, 799–800, 843–5, 889–90, 897, 926–7, 1215–17.

[27] *Charity Organization Review,* NS 26 (November 1909): 303; quoted in McBriar, *Edwardian Mixed Doubles,* 328–9.

[28] José Harris, *Unemployment and Politics* (Oxford: Oxford University Press, 1972), 267–8.

National Efficiency and Social Insurance

When Henry Campbell-Bannerman and the Liberal party consolidated their hold on power in 1906, they found themselves in a political world where multiple pressure groups jostled for influence over social policy, pushing the government in different directions. Friendly societies and insurance companies lobbied for self-help and their continued influence. On the opposite side, the Trades Union Congress and the Social Democratic Federation demanded state initiatives to improve workers' incomes and living conditions, whereas multiple workers' pressure groups weighed in on old-age pensions, housing, and the right to work. Although their influence was not great, M. A.Crowther wisely suggests that the labor movement defined what governments could not do.[29] On a more pragmatic level, women's groups and female reformers actively shaped state welfare institutions through their innovations in the private sector, and they were demanding additional policy changes in the areas of women's and children's health.[30] Much of the activity in social reform remained in the private sector, while public debate waxed and waned on particular issues.[31]

Social reform appeared on the national agenda again after 1905 with support both in- and outside of Parliament. When a new Labour M.P. introduced a bill for free school meals in 1905 and when a Liberal M.P. brought forward a proposal for medical inspection in 1906, the government decided to substitute their own versions of these measures to shape the result and to avoid more radical designs. The issue was not whether each of these bills would pass, but what would be enacted, once the issue of cost had been resolved. Bentley Gilbert argues, "Social legislation is the one form of legal enactment that an opposition responsible to a democratic electorate dare not fight."[32] Moreover, groups as diverse as social imperialists, feminists, trade unionists and eugenicists could agree on the utility of such measures.

The next beneficiaries of new state initiatives after children were the elderly. In the spring of 1906, a Labour M.P. introduced a resolution into Par-

[29] Thane, "Working Class and State 'Welfare,'" 877–9, 889–90; M. A. Crowther, *British Social Policy 1914–1939* (Basingstoke: Macmillan Education Ltd., 1988), 25.

[30] Seth Koven, "Borderlands: Women, Voluntary Action, and Child Welfare in Britain, 1840–1914," in S. Koven and S. Michel, eds., *Mothers of a New World* (New York: Routledge, 1993), 94–135; see also. S. Koven and S. Michel, "Mother Worlds," in ibid., 2.

[31] See Geoffrey Finlayson, *Citizen, State and Social Welfare in Britain, 1830–1890* (Oxford: Oxford University Press, 1994).

[32] Gilbert, *National Insurance*, 451.

liament calling for noncontributory old-age pensions, and the government came under increasing pressure from lobbyists and M.P.'s to take a stand on the issue.[33] By November of 1906, Campbell-Bannerman and Asquith, then Chancellor of the Exchequer, had committed the government to providing tax-funded pensions, although they fudged the issue of timing, amounts, and universality. Over the next year and a half, the Treasury collected data from friendly societies and surveyed existing pension schemes in Scandinavia, Germany, France, Belgium, Italy, New Zealand, and Australia, showing little interest in the German form of insurance paid for by workers and employers. After Asquith had introduced a graduated income tax, new funds became available, and a bill was written with the budgetary limits dictated by the Treasury in mind. (Hennock argues that, at the time, contributions by workmen and employers had been ruled out as politically impossible.) The resulting legislation, which came into effect in January of 1909, provided a five-shilling per week pension to people at age seventy who earned less than twenty-six pounds per year, who had not had poor relief since January of 1908, who had not been in jail during the previous ten years, and who had earlier demonstrated their willingness to work. To quote Pat Thane, "It was a pension for the very old, the very poor, and the very respectable."[34] Clearly, neither means tests nor morality had disappeared from calculations about welfare, although they had been used primarily as a method to keep down costs. The trade unions and the National Committee of Organized Labour accepted the measure as a first installment, declaring their intention to lower the age of qualification and to widen eligibility.

In 1908, no national consensus existed on possible alternatives to the poor laws. The issue of insurance and its funding divided the labor movement and charity activists. A few lonely voices, such as those of W. H. Dawson, William Beveridge, and Harold Cox, the Liberal M.P. for Preston, praised German insurance plans. The *Times* charged that the Pension Bill was "hastily flung together" and constructed without regard for "the great issues involved," and it worried that the bill "must render it extremely difficult if not impossible for the country to revert to any scheme based upon scientific or economic principle."[35]

---

[33] For the story of the writing and the passage of the bill, see Hennock, *British Social Reform,* 126–51; Gilbert, *National Insurance,* 159–233.

[34] Thane, "Non-Contributory Pensions," 103–4; the state also provided smaller pensions on a sliding scale for those who earned up to £31 per year, a wage far below that of the regularly employed unskilled laborer.

[35] *The Times,* 15 June 1908; quoted in Hennock, *British Social Reform,* 146.

Figure 10.1. "The Introduction of Old Age Pensions," *The Graphic,* 1 January 1909

During the political jockeying over the form and substance of the pension bill, statistics and economics had played major roles. Asquith had used data on the German insurance scheme to discredit it before Parliament; friendly societies had sent in actuarial calculations to defend their continued influence. Meanwhile, David Lloyd George, then Chancellor of the Exchequer, had estimated the cost of different ages and types of eligibility, retreating to age seventy in order to be able to pay for the scheme. Because the government had agreed to foot the entire bill, the demography of the population and its wage scales were very much at issue. In Hennock's opinion, Lloyd George learned early that the cost of universal welfare payments was high, and he saw that the Treasury could not pay for additional measures. During the debates, however, he learned enough about German insurance designs to prompt him to set off on a working vacation to that country in August of

1908. After visits to the Central Insurance Office in Berlin and talks with the Minister of the Interior, he came back convinced that German ways would suit English needs. Contributory insurance, he discovered, was cheap, popular, and effective. If the population at risk helped to pay in advance for a benefit, coverage could be universal, immediate, and low in cost.

Hennock argues that between June and December of 1908 the Liberal government was "converted to the German approach," accepting compulsory, contributory insurance as the model for their initiatives to provide protection against sickness, invalidity, and unemployment.[36] Instead of worrying about compulsion and state interference, the cabinet discovered the benefits of universality and equity. The National Insurance Act of 1911 was the result: In return for set weekly payments from employed workers, employers, and the state, those covered received a flat benefit in the case of sickness, invalidity, and unemployment. Actuaries worked out the implications of the funding decisions in order to keep the plan financially sound. Eligibility came from employment and contributions; it was a right, rather than a reward for merit or a boon offered to the destitute. The change in outlook came quickly and fairly easily.

That social insurance offered the government an easy way out of the political impasse created by pressure group politics and limited resources was quickly realized by younger Liberals, such as Lloyd George and Winston Churchill, who masterminded the new legislation.[37] Both had an intuitive grasp of the political issues and the opportunities involved, and neither balked at using the state to effect goals in which they believed. They were not social workers, but politicians on the make with a sensitivity for the social problems inherent in an advanced industrial society. Churchill had learned enough from the Webbs to accept the justice of minimum standards for all, and he was astute enough to figure out politically feasible ways of implementing that goal. Churchill claimed that the new insurance plans would give workers "a stake in the country," and turn their attention away from "revolutionary socialism." In any case, he argued that insurance was an unsentimental plan carrying "a strictly limited risk"; its chief result being to "remove the dangerous element of uncertainty from the existence of the industrial worker."[38] He combined an actuarial language with a vision of communal

---

[36] Hennock, *British Social Reform,* 201.

[37] For the story of the design and the passage of the legislation, see Gilbert, *National Insurance,* 289–399, and Hennock, *British Social Reform,* 152–79.

[38] "Insurance Against Unemployment. Mr. Churchill's Scheme," *Daily Mail,* 16 August 1909; quoted in Harris, *Unemployment,* 365–366.

responsibility, antithetical to the ethic of the New Poor Law. The solidarities he mandated were to be carefully restricted to specific populations. They could be calculated, enforced, and limited.

Who could enter the safeguarded community? Because much of the outside pressure on the government had come from organized labor and the friendly societies, as reflected in both lobbying groups and the ballot box, it is not surprising that the major beneficiaries were male industrial workers. Dependents, the self-employed, and the casually employed – certainly the poorest – were largely ignored. Although wives of insured workers received a maternity benefit, other insurance payments went to the wage earner to replace his interrupted earnings, not to underwrite family needs. Women, except for the very poor over seventy and the few who held manufacturing jobs over the long run, were excluded from the plans. Those who earned and contributed received; others did not. Susan Pedersen argues for the continuity with Victorian visions of the Liberals' new polity: Both were built around "the figure of the responsible, breadwinning, male citizen." Their social order rested upon the male-headed family; provide for him and all would thrive.[39] The insurance model poured old wine into new bottles, but it removed the label of pauper from all those who were allowed to drink.

In 1911, the Liberal party took a leap in the dark by substituting insurance for social work styles of welfare. Since it had worked in Europe, why not in the United Kingdom? The Liberal party embraced limited interference with labor markets and incomes in the interests of preserving the basic Victorian social, economic, and political order, as they saw it. To implement this vision, they turned away from the locally funded, means-tested, residualist system codified in the seventeenth century and reworked in the nineteenth century and substituted tax-funded, or contributory, insurance for those qualified by working in specified industries. The rest remained dependent on charities and the poor law.

Pauperism and Public Assistance, 1914–48

The poor law barely survived World War I, its demise delayed less by devotion to the principles of 1834 than by the grinding poverty of the 1930s and the government's inability to cope with mass unemployment, family dependence, and the ill health of the population. Between the two wars, the poor law was kept alive not by ideological fervor, but by a general failure of imag-

---

[39] Pedersen, *Family,* 50–1.

ination, by the tenacity of its local administrators, and by the depths of popular need. Unlamented, it eventually died quietly on a parliamentary dissecting table, as its various organs were slowly and painstakingly removed for assignment to younger ministries and units of local government. Final burial came with the National Assistance Act of 1948, which announced proudly that "the existing Poor Law shall cease to have effect."

For almost 250 years, welfare commitments within England and Wales had been tied to the concept of pauperism – a two-sided coin that matched aid with disapproval, resources with discrimination. That term officially disappeared in 1931, killed by evolving notions of entitlement and social justice. Interwar governments decided that social insurance and pensions should become the preferred modes of dealing with interrupted family incomes, but what of those who were not covered by state plans or those who had not worked long enough to qualify? How was the support of unemployed women and young children to be guaranteed? Even if administrative relabeling could eliminate "pauperism," the problem of destitution remained. Moreover, depression and economic decline raised the question of how to incorporate the very poor into a democratic state, where allegedly all were war veterans entitled to the spoils of victory. What share ought the dependent have in a reconstructed Britain? Continued inequalities and the practice of residualism bumped harshly against the heady rhetoric of social justice in the postwar world.

After 1914, the poor laws survived on sufferance, defended primarily by officials guarding their own turf. The war not only shifted national priorities, but also distracted politicians and reformers alike from the issue of welfare reform. As long as the guns thundered on, the poor laws seemed irrelevant. Besides, jobs were abundant, as employers sought to increase production and to replace workers who had joined the military. Nevertheless, the problems addressed by both the majority and minority reports on the poor laws did not disappear, and the war cabinet recognized that fact. Lloyd George, with his atypically expansive vision of possibilities, predicted that the end of the war would permit the "doing of big things," and he set up a Ministry of Reconstruction to begin planning for the future.[40] The McLean Committee, which he appointed and stacked with avid reformers such as Beatrice Webb, was given the job of redesigning parish relief and of placating the various interest groups involved; it promptly recommended the abolition of the boards of guardians and the parceling out of their welfare functions to various local

---

[40] *The Times,* 7 March 1917; quoted in Bentley B. Gilbert, *British Social Policy, 1914–1939* (Ithaca: Cornell University Press, 1970), 5.

authorities. The issue of poor law reform had again been put on a public agenda, although it was far from the top.[41]

Little of substance happened for another ten years. The head of the new Ministry of Health, Christopher Addison, took over administration of the poor laws from the Local Government Board, and began to plan an attack on the guardians, who mustered their own political supporters in self-defense. But reforming zeal quickly ebbed after the war as the Treasury began to set limits on funding for welfare plans. Then, too, the various approved societies, doctors, and insurance groups fussed about the consequences of expanded insurance, concerned to safeguard their own futures. Like snakes in the grass, the poor laws once again proved that those who tread upon them did so at their own peril. Addison's power and freedom of action ended along with the drive to give the British "Homes Fit for Heroes"; as the major architect of the government's housing program, he took the blame both for its cost and for its supposed ineffectiveness, leaving the government in 1921.[42] Economics and politics doomed poor law reform in 1920 and 1921, and by then, rising unemployment and decreasing revenues preempted attention. Politicians seemed able neither to deal with the poor laws nor to dispense with them.

Nevertheless, events of the 1920s made the inadequacies of the poor laws painfully clear to politicians of all parties. When the end of the wartime boom brought massive unemployment, hundreds of thousands retreated to the guardians for support. By December of 1921, guardians were relieving around 1.5 million people, almost 4 percent of the English and Welsh population. At the time of the general strike in the summer of 1926, nearly 2.5 million people were assisted under the poor laws. Not only did local authorities find themselves inundated by requests for aid, but they had been ordered in 1910 and 1911 to provide "adequate" relief. And what to do about men out of work? The familiar choice between the workhouse and the stoneyard had not gained in appeal after the experiences of military service or years of full employment.

In the postwar political environment, advocating a return to the principles of 1834 was impossible. The Ministry of Health had already in 1920 retreated from central supervision, telling guardians that they were in effect free to set their own relief policies. Moreover, it provided guidelines for a scale of payments to be used in London, which raised grants substantially above prewar

---

[41] For alternative views of the early negotiations undertaken by the McLean Committee, see McBriar, *Edwardian Mixed Doubles,* 354–5.

[42] For the story of reform efforts between 1917 and 1921, see Derek Fraser, *The Evolution of the British Welfare State* (London: Macmillan, 1973), 166–9; Gilbert, *British Social Policy,* 208–11.

levels. The net effect of its directives was to legitimate eased access to outrelief for the unemployed, a policy that had been pushed by Labourite guardians
since early in the century. Several unions – in particular Salford, Liverpool, a
few in East London, and those of the south Wales mining areas – began to subsidize the unemployed witout requiring labor service in return. The result, of
course, was skyrocketing expenditure, and who was to pay? When the borough
councillors of Poplar in East London refused to levy local rates high enough
to cover local relief costs, they were collectively brought into court and thrown
into jail. The government's ultimate solution to their defiance merely legitimated their policies: All of their costs for outrelief were shifted to a Metropolitan Common Poor Fund, supported primarily by the wealthier unions in
the West End. The Poplar guardians defended their position on ideological
grounds; they wanted the state to be more generous than the labor market. Why
punish people twice for their loss of work? Pat Ryan argues that "Poplarism"
demonstrated both a calculated rejection of the deterrent poor law and a measure of popular control over relief policies. In many of the Poplarite unions,
demonstrations by the unemployed and pressure by other Labour groups triggered action by relief officials.[43] Their actions proved difficult to curb and
deeply galling to the Conservative government, which was wedded to bal-
anced budgets and sound finance.

In the end, Neville Chamberlain, who became minister of health in Conservative cabinets, provided both the design and the political energy to
remodel welfare administration between 1926 and 1929. After the general
strike had weakened the Labour party and the unions, he could curb the powers of local Labour-dominated guardians with little opposition as he transferred more powers to central institutions.[44] Unfortunately, he cared more
about efficiency and finance than about human costs and benefits. His regime
of doles, benefit cuts, and niggardly means tests aroused popular ire and
resentment, although he dismantled the poor laws. Putting an end to the issue
of pauperism was no mean feat, but what was put in its place retained much of
the rank odor of the earlier regime and largely ignored demands for more equal
access by women and children to state payments.

Major changes arrived with the Widows', Orphans', and Old-Age Contributory Pensions Act of 1925 and with the Local Government Act of 1929.
Designed primarily for industrial workers, the first created a fund financed by

---

[43] P. A. Ryan, "'Poplarism' 1894–1930," in Pat Thane, *The Origins of British Social Policy*,
(Totowa: Rowman & Littlefield, 1978), 56–83.

[44] Crowther, *Social Policy*, 48–9.

employers, employees, and the state, giving those covered the unconditional right to a small pension between ages sixty-five and seventy and offering payments to widows who had children age fourteen and under. Pressed by strong demands for more generous pensions and by the mounting cost of the 1908 noncontributory scheme, the government turned to contributory insurance as the way out of their dilemma. In theory, the change ought to have permitted earlier retirement and insulated the insured from the poor laws; the reality was far different. Although the plan was actuarially sound and quickly transferred additional income into the hands of the elderly, it did little in the interwar period to reduce dependence on public relief. The number of people over age sixty-five getting poor law aid increased steadily during the later 1920s and 1930s, far faster than the size of the total population. In 1928, the elderly represented 15 percent of all paupers; in 1939, they accounted for 27 percent of the total.[45] The need for medical care, which they could not afford, and a lack of additional resources combined to force pensioners into the care of the state. Both the British Medical Association and the insurance companies blocked rationalization of the health care system and extension of medical benefits.

Finally, in 1929, the government remodeled poor law institutions as part of a more general revamping of local government and taxation. After much discussion and many objections, Parliament eliminated all boards of guardians and shifted their responsibilities to county councils and county borough councils. New Public Assistance Committees were to administer all the asylums, hospitals, and other facilities formerly run by the poor laws, but the counties could shift them to other local government departments. Although the status of pauper disappeared, actual reform of welfare practice was largely voluntary. Gilbert points out that county councils recruited former employees of the guardians into the new welfare staffs; moreover, guardians' committees continued to supervise the granting of outdoor relief to applicants. A new order had definitely not emerged from the ruins of the old.[46] Derek Fraser argues that from the standpoint of the unemployed, the changes were cosmetic. The Public Assistance Committees, which administered government grants to the unemployed when insurance payments had run out and when household incomes were sufficiently low, interfered and poked into family business, humiliating those whom they undertook to help.[47]

Removing the unemployed from the clutches of the poor laws took place

[45] Karel Williams, *From Pauperism to Poverty* (London: Routledge, 1981), 206–7.

[46] Gilbert, *British Social Policy*, 229–33.

[47] Fraser, *British Welfare State*, 180.

through the device of extending unemployment insurance. At the end of the war, only about one in four workers was covered by unemployment insurance, but it was clear that demobilization and the shift back to civilian modes of production would produce massive numbers of people out of work. To cover that dislocation, the coalition government announced temporary payments, first to soldiers and then to civilians, which would provide subsistence grants for the unemployed and their dependents. Extension of the National Insurance scheme, which had already been discussed, seemed a way out of the government's expensive dilemma. The 1920 Unemployment Act set up a compulsory insurance program for employed manual workers making less than £250 per year, although those in agriculture, domestic service, and the self-employed, fairly large groups, were excluded. In return for regular weekly contributions from employer and employee, insured workers got fifteen weeks of payments.[48]

The depression combined with political pressures and actuarial naiveté to doom any retreat to a self-funded insurance program. Instead of an insurance plan, the state committed itself to open-ended support for the unemployed. "Extended" and "transitional benefits" financed out of taxes were invented to keep industrial workers off the poor laws. By the later 1920s, such benefits could be held for an unlimited length of time. Pressured by bankers to cut benefits, the National Government in 1931 retreated to means tests and time limits on benefits, which drove tens of thousands more into the arms of the Public Assistance Committees over the next several years. Then, in 1934, the government shifted payments to those lacking insurance and those whose insurance benefits had been exhausted to an Unemployment Assistance Board, empowered to increase payments over levels mandated in the early 1930s and to grant support according to need. By 1937, care for the able-bodied had moved away from the Public Assistance Committees, finally breaking the link between the poor laws and those out of work.[49]

On the eve of World War II, the remodeled poor laws fulfilled residual, but not unimportant welfare functions. Despite the state's extension of insurance and pension schemes, in 1939, the successor agencies to the boards of guardians still supported 1,200,000 poor – almost 3 percent of the total population.[50] The poor law hospitals, infirmaries, and asylums had become part of a locally administered health service, and they were packed, although their

---

[48] Crowther, *Social Policy,* 40–3; Gilbert, *British Social Policy,* 73–97.

[49] Gilbert, *British Social Policy,* 162–81.

[50] Williams, *Pauperism,* 162.

inmates were no longer considered paupers. Those that remained in the renamed workhouses or on outrelief had slipped through the cracks of an emerging network of insurance, public services, and voluntary societies. Despite the vast array of private welfare agencies, there still remained a place for the remodeled poor law.

Workhouses and Welfare Between the Wars

Until 1929, much of the welfare machinery of the poor laws still moved in its long-accustomed, bureaucratically defined grooves. Many widows, their children, most of the elderly poor, but only some of the unemployed got out-relief – after careful investigation. The Leicester union kept meticulous books on settlements, removals, and family circumstances of applicants to verify their eligibility; Lancaster guardians recorded demographic details and descriptions of the aid given to the households in the union. In York, the guardians continued to apprentice a few orphaned or deserted boys to tailors, carpenters, and other local craftsmen.[51] As always, adult males presented the most difficult policy choices. Lancaster gave outrelief to those with large families and usually refused it to single workers.[52] One man's story of his reception in 1929 by the Bradford guardians shows how the unemployed were treated in his town. As an unemployed foundry worker, he initially qualified for insurance payments and transitional benefits, but when both were exhausted, he turned to the poor law. Three men interviewed him and then offered seven shillings a week in return for doing odd jobs at the workhouse. From nine to four daily, he dug, chopped, carried, washed, and bundled at a wage of a few pennies an hour.[53]

The amount of work exacted from him was probably atypical. Political opposition, as well as problems of scale, meant that efforts to put the unemployed to work usually failed. In general, the labor test seems to have been abandoned. In Wigan, the guardians refused to force paupers to do hard labor; in Norwich, the paupers themselves refused. Only in a few places were stoneyards opened and kept in operation. In fact, the Webbs argued that mass

---

[51] Board of Guardians, Leicester Poor Law Union, "Settlements, 1914–1915," vol. 8, 26/D68, no. 313, Leicestershire County Record Office; Board of Guardians, Lancaster Union, "Application and Report Book for the Half Year Ending March 31, 1921," PUL 23/1, Lancashire County Record Office; Board of Guardians, York Union, "Register of Apprentices, 1845–1929," Acc 2-954, York City Archive.

[52] Board of Guardians, Lancaster Union, "Application and Report Book for the Half Year Ending March 31, 1921."

[53] Bradford Heritage Recording Unit, Oral History Collection, AO 105, Bradford Public Library.

unemployment doomed efforts to force men on relief to do punishing work.[54] Guardians could not cope effectively with the thousands of applicants who besieged them wanting paid work or maintenance.

The era of quiet acceptance of poor law policies of discipline and deterrence had passed. The election of Labour guardians and the extensive lobbying both locally and nationally by the unemployed testified to widespread discontent with the poor laws. In both large and small ways, people attacked the perceived humiliations of pauperism. Stella Davies grew up in Lancashire, living on a street near a workhouse. She remembers popular responses in 1920 to the vicar's wife, who was also a guardian. When a local man asked for relief but was denied it because he owned a piano, Mrs. Iliffe had the nerve to lecture him on his behavior and potential resources. But the story spread. Workers threw stones and dirt at her after church, and for days after, she was greeted in the streets by taunts and boos. "Do you good to go without a meal; that'd learn you!" "Who do you think you are, God Almighty?"[55] Guardians' freedom of action was curbed by popular opposition.

During the later 1920s, the deterrent workhouse slowly became extinct for all groups except vagrants. Attempts to use it in the northeast during the General Strike to discipline miners had only short-term effects. Other unions with guardians more sympathetic to striking workers merely increased outrelief in line with "Poplarist" principles. Determined not to be bested in a political conflict over relief policies, the Ministry of Health sometimes stepped in and worked to curb outrelief, but it did not try to reinstate the heavy-handed use of the workhouse. By 1930, test workhouses for the able-bodied had in effect disappeared. One of the Ministry of Health inspectors complained in 1928 after a tour of London workhouses that "[t]he old corn mills are now regarded as museum pieces and stone-breaking is, I think, only done at one institution."[56]

Confinement in institutions, however, became an increasingly widespread mode of dealing with the poor. Orphans went into children's homes or boarding schools, "lunatics" found themselves locked up in asylums, and the sick entered hospitals or infirmaries. Pushed by medical opinion, Parliament authorized spending on new institutions for particular sorts of diseases and

---

[54] Sidney Webb and Beatrice Webb, *English Poor Law History, Part II: The Last Hundred Years*, vol. 2 (London: Longmans, 1929), 922–4.

[55] C. Stella Davies, *North Country Bred: A Working-Class Family Chronicle* (London: Routledge, 1963), 203.

[56] C. F. Roundell, 17 January 1928; quoted in M. A. Crowther, *The Workhouse System, 1834–1929* (London: Methuen, 1981), 108.

disabilities. The tubercular and the mentally defective were deemed in need of specialized, professional care. Meanwhile, the long-discredited mixed work-houses – now known as Poor Law Institutions – continued to shelter the destitute who either could not care for themselves or were deemed unable to do so. Most of their inhabitants were classified as sick, disabled, injured, infirm, or suffering from some sort of mental illness or weakness.[57] Dependent females were the one additional group brought in significant numbers into the workhouses. M. A. Crowther points out that at a time when able-bodied men had essentially vanished from such places, deserted or separated wives as well as unmarried mothers continued to be sent there, rather than given adequate outdoor relief. Confinement still seemed an appropriate solution for the economic troubles of single, adult women who had been sexually active.[58]

The effectiveness of such places in reforming their charges is open to doubt. During the war years, the Market Harborough and Lutterworth unions record in their punishment books lists of the refractory. Paupers fought or were insolent; one man punched the workhouse master. Women attacked one another in the laundries, stole food, and got into trouble for swearing. Paupers got drunk and came back late from leave; they were scarcely a docile crowd, awed by workhouse discipline.[59]

Poor law authorities still attempted to discipline vagrants who applied for relief by locking them up for at least a day. George Orwell, who entered a casual ward briefly in 1931, has described his confinement in "the spike" with a dingy crew of "urban riff-raff." After his personal possessions were confiscated and his compulsory bath was completed, he found himself in a "gloomy, chilly, lime-washed place, consisting only of a bathroom and dining-room and about a hundred narrow stone cells." Lists of rules and punishments decorated the walls, and the windows had been placed too high to permit looking outside. They fed on bread, margarine, and tea, spending the hours between meals and sleep huddled on wooden benches. The "stench of drains and soft soap" oppressed, but the worst problem was the boredom during the time of their forced confinement: "Ennui clogged our souls like cold mutton. Our bones ached because of it." Orwell himself got a favored assign-

---

[57] Ministry of Health, "Persons in Receipt of Poor-Law Relief, England and Wales, . . . 1st day of January, 1920," PP 1920, XXXVI, 36–7.

[58] Crowther, *Workhouse,* 100.

[59] Market Harborough Union, "Offences and Punishment Book, 1914–1917," G10/87/1, DE 723/2; Lutterworth Union, "Offences and Punishment Book, 1879–1932," G/8/87/1, DE427a, Leicestershire County Record Office.

ment – one afternoon in the workhouse kitchen, where he gorged himself and hid for a time in the potato storage shed. Task work had disappeared, even for the tramps and beggars.[60]

The physical structures of the disciplinary workhouse remained, although its muscle had turned flabby. After 1913, centrally set mealtimes, work hours, and classifications were no longer enforced. Guardians could finally change menus, plan Christmas dinners, and relax rules without approval from London. Trained medical staffs expanded with orders to improve treatment of both the sick and the children. In their final years, poor law institutions became more like refuges than prisons.[61]

The malleability of workhouses, as well as their remarkable longevity, deserves emphasis. Look at the history of the St. Marylebone workhouse in the twentieth century. Founded in 1752 but rebuilt in 1897, it occupied four acres of land in central London and could house 1,921 inmates. It had two five-story blocks plus a central building used for the sick and infirm, as well as separate units for able-bodied males, for casual paupers, and for cooking and dining. During World War I, the wards designed for vagrants housed Belgian refugees and, later, became military detention barracks. By 1922, they had become a center for granting outdoor relief, which they remained until 1948. After 1929, the London County Council turned the main buildings into a home for the elderly and the infirm. As a result, both the maternity ward and two sections for the mentally ill closed in the later 1930s. Children's wards were emptied by the evacuation of their charges from London in 1939. Meanwhile, the London County Council transferred all the adult males from the workhouse to farm colonies and other training centers. Then fearing air raids, they emptied the upper stories of the buildings and turned a few rooms into a recreation center for civil defense workers. Despite occasional hits by firebombs, several hundred elderly continued to live in the workhouse through the early 1940s, but by the end of the war, one of the buildings housed displaced persons; another became a hostel for homeless women. The final chapter in the long saga of the St. Marylebone workhouse came after the passage of the National Assistance Act in 1948. Rebaptized as Luxborough Lodge and modernized with television sets, elevators, and a canteen, the buildings became a home for about one thousand pensioners until 1965,

---

[60] Sonia Orwell and Ian Angus, *The Collected Essays, Journalism, and Letters of George Orwell, I: An Age Like This, 1920–1940* (New York: Harcourt Brace & World, 1968), 36–43.

[61] Crowther, *Workhouse*, 86–7.

when they were finally demolished.[62] Like clothes transferred from parent to child, poor law hand-me-downs furnished the welfare state.

Life on the Dole

George Orwell's travels to Wigan in 1936 took him into streets where "nobody has a job, where getting a job seems about as probable as owning an airplane and much less probable than winning fifty pounds in the Football Pool."[63] In the north, among the slag heaps and closed mines, he met families of idle men and overworked women, struggling to survive on government handouts. "The Dole," the centerpiece of official welfare strategies between the wars, kept them alive until the war brought full employment. Crafted by political expediency out of tax dollars, it masked relief with an insurance framework designed to deal only with short-term unemployment. To be sure, it provided subsistence-level grants to the unemployed and their families. Yet its difference from poor law payment consisted primarily in the name of the group dispensing the somewhat more generous grants. Carefully means tested during the 1930s, payments depended upon proof of need, thereby legitimating the state snooping so resented by workers. Indeed, Orwell claims it broke up families by driving elderly pensioners into lodging houses and turned neighbor against neighbor. Mean streets gave rise to mean-minded behavior.[64]

The dole and mass unemployment shifted life-cycle patterns and family relations. A female textile worker (b. 1921) from Hartlepool, Durham, described her family during the 1930s. Because her father was unemployed, her mother worked in the fields or took in laundry to help support the family and to earn enough to apprentice the sons. By dint of great effort, she placed four of them in the shipyards, but they were all fired at the end of their terms so that they would not have to be paid full wages. Thereafter they went on the dole, jacking up their grants by claiming to live in lodgings while remaining at home. A penny a night to a lodging house keeper "in on the fiddle" made money both for them and for him. She claims that none married until their thirties because they could not afford to.[65]

---

[62] Alan R. Neate, *The St. Marylebone Workhouse and Institution, 1730–1965* (London: St. Marylebone Society Publications, 1967), 31–7.

[63] George Orwell, *The Road to Wigan Pier* (New York: Berkeley Publishers, 1961), 80.

[64] Ibid., 75.

[65] Bradford Heritage Recording Unit, Oral History Collection A 0077, Bradford Public Library.

Others managed somewhat better. One man, born in Bradford in 1913, lost his job in a textile mill in 1935. Because he was insured, married with a child, and had a long work history in the same company, he fared rather well. His dole, plus family allowances, actually exceeded his normal wage, and he managed to supplement it by taking bets for a bookie and delivering newspapers. A steady job materialized only in 1939, when he joined the army.[66]

Female-headed households had much more difficulty managing to stay solvent. Because domestic servants and self-employed workers were not covered by insurance, their unemployment led directly to the poor laws, which many rejected on principle. Much more dependent upon charities than their male counterparts, women found themselves scrounging for clothes and fuel to supplement meager wages. Elsie Oman grew up in Manchester and Salford, raised by an aunt after her mother's death in 1911. The aunt, who had to support a paralyzed husband as well as three children, worked as both a charwoman and a laundress. She sent the children to the Wood Street Mission for treats and toys, and arranged that they got free breakfasts at school. Because Elsie's father was in the navy, she and her brother got a pint of milk a day, provided by the state. His dependents' allowance helped to support them during World War I. Their success in remaining "respectable and independent" was a source of pride to Elsie and her aunt. Yet the family lived in bug-infested rooms, and Elsie complained bitterly of the poverty and squalor around her.[67]

English social insurance was designed to maintain the wages of a largely male industrial labor force, and the dole followed the same pattern. Grants were given to men and to the limited numbers of wage-earning females in the covered trades because of their work histories and the size of their families. When they could no longer earn, the state stepped in and took over their responsibility for supporting themselves and their dependents. Susan Pedersen has written of the "male breadwinner logic of welfare" adopted by the British Parliament. Feminists' proposals to subsidize parenting directly were roundly rejected by politicians and civil servants, who refused to recognize married women's services to the state, unless they were independent wage earners. Indeed, even widows' pensions were justified in terms of debts owed to working men. In Pedersen's words, "Married women were insured not primarily against loss of wages but rather against loss of men."[68] This paternal-

---

[66] Ibid. Oral History Collection A 0045.

[67] Elsie Oman, *Salford Stepping Stones* (Swinton: N. Richardson, ND).

[68] Pedersen, *Family*, 354.

ist design for welfare directly disadvantaged married women and children, whose access to state funding depended not upon their own needs, but on the work history of husbands and fathers and male willingness to share grants with dependents.

"Welfare" in the interwar period, however, meant far more than just the dole. The host of charities, voluntary societies, and religious groups that had championed "good works" before the war forged on, supplying help as they saw fit. Cinderella Clubs provided clothing for poor children. The Charity Organization Society promoted self-help through grants of surgical stockings, ear trumpets, and other rehabilitative gifts. Thousands of branches of the Mothers' Union dotted the country, offering poor women advice, cheap sewing materials, Christmas treats, and free tea.[69] Using volunteer labor, School Care Committees followed up school medical exams, working to enforce orders for new glasses, ringworm treatments, and delousing.[70] Church groups continued to supply applicants with coal and clothing. Welfare practice in Britain remained a mixed system, combining efforts by charities, families, and the state.

For infants and children, new strategies developed for cooperation between public and private authorities. Extensive campaigns by the Women's Cooperative Guild and others helped to increase resources available to poor parents. Clinics for babies and their mothers multiplied during the war, and with the Maternity and Child Welfare Act of 1918, the government promised to pay local authorities for the cost of hiring health visitors and midwives, running crèches, and feeding poor children.[71] Their services, however, were quite limited: For the most part, health visitors and infant welfare clinics dispensed advice on "good mothering," rather than medical knowledge. Women could get attention during pregnancy and at parturition, but little thereafter. They could get free or subsidized food and milk, but they were not given birth control advice until after 1930.[72] For many harassed mothers, this little did not suffice. To quote one woman living on the dole interviewed in York

---

[69] Frank Prochaska, "A Mother's Country: Mothers' Meetings and Family Welfare in Britain, 1850–1950," *History* 74:242 (October 1989): 379–99; see also Finlayson, *Citizen.*

[70] See Ellen Ross, *Love and Toil: Motherhood in Outcast London, 1870–1918* (New York: Oxford University Press, 1993), 211–14.

[71] For information on the Infant Welfare movement, see Deborah Dwork, *War Is Good for Babies and Other Young Children: A History of the Infant and Child Welfare Movement in England 1898–1918* (London: Tavistock, 1987); and Ross, *Love and Toil,* 195–221.

[72] Thane, "Infant Care," 271–4.

around 1935: "They are asking for children to be born but they will not keep them. The population is big enough for the poor money they are giving us."[73]

The maternalist side of British welfare provision operated largely through voluntary societies and through limited services intended to reduce infant mortality provided by local government. Although high infant death rates were recognized as a social problem, the British government was far less willing than the French to subsidize childrearing. In Britain, the clinical side of child welfare was targeted through an emphasis on professional health care, whereas support for the broader needs of parenting was in short supply. Jane Lewis blames the preoccupations of "predominantly male, middle-class policy makers," who found the demands of feminist groups for family allowances politically unacceptable.[74] Susan Pedersen points out that family policies in Britain were shaped in large part by civil servants and trade unions interested in protecting wages from government interference, because their adversaries, the groups who articulated demands for family allowances and other maternalist welfare measures, had little political clout.[75] Although alternative designs for welfare services were discussed, Parliament consistently opted for a paternalist system that gave money to men in relation to their job histories and household size. Married women and families qualified through husbands' entitlements, not their own.

Feminists' dissatisfactions with interwar welfare arrangements have to be added to those of the unemployed, who through their organizations called for work and higher benefits. Life on the dole had few defenders. The psychological cost was considerable. Walter Greenwood's popular novel, *Love On the Dole,* which appeared in 1933, captured much of the anguish of men and women who spent their lives stretching a few shillings to cover subsistence costs and dreaming of something better.[76] The unemployed stayed alive through pawning and public assistance, their day filled with wandering around the streets and futile trips to the Labour Exchange. "The world is getting worse instead of better; so don't you think something can be done for the unemployed? Either more money or else work, but my husband prefers work. He is sick of doing nothing," a York woman told interviewers in 1936.[77]

---

[73] Rowntree Papers, "Family Budget Analyses," PP/1, Borthwick Institute, York.

[74] Jane Lewis, *The Politics of Motherhood: Child and Maternal Welfare in England, 1900–1939* (London: Croom Helm, 1980), 15, 51.

[75] Pedersen, *Family,* 19.

[76] Walter Greenwood, *Love on the Dole* (London: Penguin, 1969).

[77] Rowntree Papers, "Family Budget Analyses," PP/1, Borthwick Institute.

And their problems were more than psychological. The Pilgrim Trust did a study of men out of work in 1936 and 1937, attempting to calculate the long-term effects of unemployment. Using a standard based on the British Medical Association's estimate of minimum food requirements with small additions for clothes, light, and fuel, they compared the incomes of the unemployed with their needs in six industrial towns. Thirty percent of the long-term unemployed had incomes below subsistence and an additional 33 percent had incomes at or a little above the subsistence level.[78] Looked at simply as a problem of physical survival, unemployment required heroic efforts of self-denial that few could maintain consistently. The movies, football pools, and cheap sweets seemed far better choices than brown bread and carrots.

Assessing life on the dole presents the classic example of the glass partly filled with water: Should it be seen as half full or half empty? After World War I, the civilian population on average had lower mortality and was healthier than its prewar counterpart. Malnutrition decreased, and expansion of state-provided medical care helped to lower infant death rates, which continued to decline after the war, as did crude death rates for adults of both sexes.[79] On average, the British population lived longer in the 1920s and 1930s than did citizens in Edwardian times. Moreover, real wages rose for those with jobs, and the real levels of government subsidies were higher than in the prewar period. Public assistance grants allowed workers to buy more bread, meat, and milk than they had been able to in 1900. Insurance and the dole partly substituted for lost wages among those covered by government plans. Social scientists who studied workers' incomes in the 1920s and 1930s agreed that fewer people lived in poverty than had in 1900. Rowntree concluded, after surveying York households in 1936, that in comparison to the city in 1899 "the proportion of the working-class population living in abject poverty had been reduced by more than one half."[80]

At the same time, people were clearly less happy with what was given them. They saw the social glass as half full at best. Workers were far less inclined to accept deferentially grants from guardians or the Public Assistance Board. They wanted respectability, their hopes fed periodically by the political

---

[78] Pilgrim Trust, *Men Without Work* (New York: Cambridge University Press, 1938), 105, 109.

[79] See J. M. Winter, *The Great War and the British People* (Cambridge: Harvard University Press, 1986), 140–7; B. R. Mitchell, *Abstract of British Historical Statistics* (New York: Cambridge University Press, 1962), 39–41.

[80] B. Seebohm Rowntree, *Poverty and Progress* (London: Longmans, 1941), 451; for a similar survey done in 1924 in five towns, see A. L. Bowley and Margaret H. Hogg, *Has Poverty Diminished?* (London: P.S. King, 1925).

rhetoric of politicians seeking to get elected. Those reduced to pawning blankets for food money or sitting in a cold room could scarcely be expected to be content with what they had. Groveling for a voucher worth a few shillings at a local store infuriated them, even if they were prepared to do it. Rising expectations were part of the problem, certainly. One wife oppressed by life on the dole told investigators in 1936: "People think £1 6s. is a lot; it may be for old people, but not for young. . . . We've nothing, and I want lots!"[81] She had friends who could take vacations and buy clothes, whereas she and her husband could not even afford fish when they went to a chip shop for dinner. "Making do" involved endless battles with desires, fed by advertisements and films. The consumer society left the unemployed behind, and they felt cheated. The demise of the workhouse helped, of course, as did the dissolution of the boards of guardians. But even if pauperism had disappeared, destitution had not. The social contract of the interwar years barely provided the poor with maintenance, and placed "respectability" and "decency" definitely out of reach. Democratic rhetoric regularly promises more than it delivers, and it sounded particularly hollow in Britain during the 1930s.

[81] Rowntree Papers, "Family Budget Analyses."

EPILOGUE: RESIDUALISM
REDUX, 1948–95

Today destitution has been banished.
Labour party manifesto, 1950

I feel destitute, not poor.
Disabled pensioner, 1982

The poor laws were swept away with a great flourish in the social democratic climate of the later 1940s, their assumptions supposedly made obsolete by the egalitarian norms of wartime and of the postwar planners. The Labour party successfully wooed voters with a seductive picture of cradle-to-grave security, supported by full employment. Using the prescriptions of both William Beveridge and John Maynard Keynes, they promised to abolish want for all through a massive expansion of state-directed welfare expenditures. Building on the Beveridge Report of 1942 and wartime plans for reconstruction, Parliament quickly enacted National Insurance Acts, created the National Health Service, and nationalized the hospitals. Family allowances, unemployment benefits, and pensions, to be supplemented by state-provided housing and medical care, would shield citizens from the instabilities of life cycles and labor markets. Instead of tough measures to reform the "residuum," the state promised universal benefits that would end destitution and dampen the inequalities of class and region.[1]

The realities of enactment fell short of the promises, of course, but the hastily built structures of the post-1945 "welfare state" have proved remarkably stable and politically popular, even under the recent rule of Margaret

[1] For a recent treatment of the post-1945 welfare state, see John Brown, *The British Welfare State* (Oxford: Basil Blackwell, 1995).

343

Thatcher and free market Tories. The political center in Britain, which sees itself benefiting from existing arrangements, has proved wide enough to blunt major attacks by militants of both the Right and the Left. Tinkering, rather than major surgery, has been the response of Conservative as well as Labour governments during the past fifty years. The shift to earnings-related pensions, which Parliament enacted in 1975, stands out as one of the few major changes in entitlement that followed the initial bursts of legislation in the 1940s.

Continuities in practice lie behind the flashy promises of improvement touted by politicians at election time. Not until 1984 did a Conservative government reexamine insurance, health, and pension systems in a major way. Reviews resulted in retrenchment and shrinkage – the cutting of insurance benefits, the ending of graduated payments for sickness and unemployment, and the narrowing of eligibility – but Parliament and the public defeated more extensive plans to limit old-age pensions and child benefits, and the National Health Service has survived with little alteration. The Conservatives have managed, despite their harsh rhetorical attack, only incremental shifts in a structure that remains largely intact. But they have succeeded in undermining the postwar social consensus in favor of universalism. With an aging population and an economy in relative decline, the cost of adequate benefits to all regardless of need seems to many voters to be too high.

The resilience of state welfare through periods of Conservative assault rests upon its compatibility with earlier forms of welfare provision, with the strong tradition of English local government, and with the private sector's support for voluntarism. Individualism means charity as well as self-help in the British tradition. As Geoffrey Finlayson pointed out, Britain continues to have a "mixed economy of welfare," in which the central government shares support functions with families, cities, and voluntary organizations. Far from withering away under the welfare state, the voluntary sector remains alive and well, offering services and major amounts of aid outside the auspices of central governmental institutions. Churches, charities, and local social agencies in great abundance draw individuals into participatory modes of helping the destitute. For both moral and practical reasons, the British state continues to encourage private initiatives in the care of the poor. Even in the most universalist, egalitarian phases of Labour party dominance, voluntary groups have enjoyed a good press and lots of official support. Anglo-Saxon styles of welfare provision rely heavily on individual initiative, among both givers and recipients. Female care-givers continue to work aggressively in the voluntary sector to design services that fit their definitions of social needs, and insurance agencies offer those who can pay greater protection than is provided by the state. Private groups, therefore, make an integral contribution to British communal welfare.

State welfare, therefore, is only a partial system. Much of the cost of supporting the destitute has remained elsewhere. In consequence, the state's cradle-to-grave protection has offered far less than official rhetoric implies. For early planners, universal access to a uniform benefit was the aim, not the elimination of poverty. They set minimum standards for support, which even at the time were recognized as inadequate to eliminate destitution.[2] Moreover, budgetary constraints and the fear of discouraging incentives to work have kept benefit levels in Britain below the cost of subsistence. Then, too, Beveridge designed his system around the model of male workers and dependent wives. Working women and single mothers got lower benefits than their male counterparts, and child allowances were deliberately pegged at less than the cost of full maintenance. To quote Anne Digby, the Beveridge reforms "gave first place to marital security and only second place to social security."[3] The welfare state did not eliminate the inequalities of either class or gender.

The new legislation did, however, set a floor under incomes both through the provision of transfer payments and through the addition of a means-tested benefit provided under the National Assistance Act of 1948 and successor legislation of 1966 and 1988. Being both unwilling and unable to set grants high enough to raise the incomes of the poorest above subsistence, legislators provided for additional payments to the most disadvantaged. Those qualifying for these "supplementary benefits" have become the group officially considered poor because they fall below a socially set standard of an "acceptable" income. In 1949, 1.8 million people got such payments; in 1965, the total reached 2.8 million, and it stood at 3 million in 1983.[4] Moreover, these figures exclude the substantial number of people eligible for payments who did not claim them. Despite the official demise of the "pauper," many continued to receive means-tested payments from the state, and many others were poor enough to do so. Want has disappeared neither in theory nor in practice, although the net effect of subsidies from charities and other voluntary organizations is impossible to quantify with precision.

[2] Howard Glennerster, "Social Policy Since the Second World War," in John Hills, ed., *The State of Welfare: The Welfare State in Britain Since 1974* (Oxford: Oxford University Press, 1990), 13–15.

[3] Anne Digby, *British Welfare Policy: Workhouse to Workfare* (London: Faber & Faber, 1989), 62.

[4] John Scott, *Poverty and Wealth: Citizenship, Deprivation and Privilege* (London: Longmans, 1994), 77; G. C. Fiegehen, P. S. Lansley, and A. D. Smith, *Poverty and Progress in Britain. 1953–1973* (New York: Cambridge University Press, 1977), 111; A. W. Dilnot, J. A. Kay, and C. N. Norris, *The Reform of Social Security* (Oxford: Oxford University Press, 1984), 22.

Nevertheless, when measured in terms of absolute standards, the improvement in the condition of the poorest under the dual impact of universal benefits and economic growth looks spectacular. Using his 1936 definition of a subsistence income, Seebohm Rowntree concluded that the proportion of the York population living in poverty had fallen from 17.7 percent in the mid-1930s to 1.7 percent in 1950.[5] (Rowntree's original notion of a subsistence income rested on a computation of the minimum cost of the food, housing, and clothing necessary for physical health and efficiency, but for his survey of 1936, he expanded his definition to include several discretionary items, now labeled necessities – insurance payments, travel costs, newspapers, tobacco, beer, etc.) By looking back to the prewar era, Rowntree painted a rosy picture of progress. The combination of full employment and transfer payments from the state to those with inadequate earning power substantially raised the incomes of the poorest citizens above what they had been in prewar decades.

Moreover, this trend then continued. Surveys of several thousand British households done by the Ministry of Labour and, later, by the Department of Employment during the 1950s and 1960s permit comparisons of income shifts during those decades. Real household incomes (as measured in 1971 currency) of the bottom quintile of the United Kingdom's population had increased by about 75 percent and those of the bottom decile by 71 percent between 1953 and 1971. Clearly, standards of living among the poorest citizens on average improved substantially from the end of the war into the middle 1970s.[6] Economic growth has continued to benefit those on the bottom of British society as well as those on the top. Toilets, telephones, and televisions appeared in slum apartments. Nevertheless, little redistribution of income to the poorest has taken place: Both in 1953 and in 1971, the bottom fifth of individuals in the United Kingdom earned about half the national median income.[7] Their relative position remained static although their purchasing power rose. Moreover, such surveys said little about the actual living standards of the very poor. What kind of housing could they afford? What sort of education did their children obtain? The stench of deprivation had vanished under the antiseptic smell of statistical means.

The success of social democratic solutions to the poverty problem in Britain came under serious attack during the 1960s from the political Left.

[5] B. S. Rowntree and G. R. Lavers, *Poverty and the Welfare State* (London: Longmans, 1951), 39, 48.

[6] Fiegehen, et. al., 28–31.

[7] Ibid., 31, 111.

Trips into the back streets of major cities left little doubt that the new prosperity had bypassed many residents. Audrey Harvey, a social worker in London's East End, wrote about "Casualties of the Welfare State," and Dorothy Wedderburn and J. Utting described the dismal lives of low-income elderly. Ken Coates and Richard Silburn took their students into the slums of Nottingham to interview "forgotten Englishmen."[8] After Peter Townsend and Brian Abel-Smith showed that the number of people in poverty as measured by official standards had risen during the 1950s from 8 percent to 14 percent of the population, the debate resumed in earnest.[9] How much did the state owe its poorest citizens? Coates and Silburn called for "systematic, simultaneous, and integrated assault upon all . . . areas of deprivation."[10] But if subsistence was no longer enough, how much more should be provided and who should decide? Such questions continue to trouble social dialogues about welfare.

Peter Townsend, who has been one of the most effective critics of government policies, defends a relative standard of need. Defining poverty as "the lack of the resources necessary to permit participation in the activities, customs and diets commonly approved by society," he has called upon the state to provide low-income citizens with the resources for vacations, acceptable clothing, and entertainment.[11] He wants not minimum standards, as Beveridge had envisaged, but rising ones pegged to "normal" practices. Townsend has extended Marshall's concept of social citizenship into new areas. By his measurements, of course, poverty is a much greater problem in Britain than government statisticians wish to acknowledge, but many challenge his definition and his categories.

Defenders of the free market, largely drawn from the right wing of the Conservative party, have offered alternative analyses of state obligation, and not surprisingly they stress absolute rather than relative definitions of poverty. By their count, economic development has raised standards enough so that only the very poor require additional aid. In any case, as Britain's economic problems mounted during the 1970s, both parties tried to curb increases in welfare spending. Finally, during the 1980s, Margaret Thatcher's government eroded

---

[8] Audrey Harvey, "Casualties of the Welfare State," Fabian Tract no. 321 (London, 1960); Dorothy Wedderburn and J. Utting, "The Economic Circumstances of Old People," *Occasional Papers on Social Administration* 4 (London: Bell, 1962); Ken Coates and Richard Silburn, *Poverty: The Forgotten Englishmen* (London: Penguin, 1970).

[9] Brian Abel-Smith and Peter Townsend, "The Poor and the Poorest," *Occasional Papers on Social Administration* 17 (London: Bell, 1965).

[10] Coates and Silburn, *Poverty,* 217.

[11] Peter Townsend, *Poverty in the United Kingdom* (London: Penguin, 1979).

universalist and expanded residualist benefits, reinvigorating the device of means testing. The sphere of state insurance has been correspondingly reduced; in 1982, the state transferred the responsibility for sick pay to employers, and it handled maternity benefits similarly. The Social Security Act of 1980 reaffirmed the principle of means-tested payments to the poor, but relabeled them "income supports" and "family credits." Euphemisms shield much of the retreat from universalism, while defenses of market forces supply ideological justifications.[12]

Since 1980, the British welfare regime has turned strongly back toward residualism as a compromise between the pressures of those who want the community to protect the poor and those who wish to shift the balance of responsibility back to individuals and families. The high unemployment of the 1970s and 1980s pushed the costs of benefits higher and reduced tax revenues, while it virtually ended the appeal of Keynesian economics. Meanwhile, deindustrialization, in combination with low wages and high taxes, made universalism an easy target for those eager to reinvigorate British capitalism through reliance on the market. Many fear that benefit levels discourage the poor from working, and ill-conceived tax policies have clearly made it disadvantageous for the poor at certain income levels to move more strongly into the labor market. The rightward swing during the Thatcher and Major years has pushed British welfare practice closer to that of the poor laws: less for the able-bodied, while targeting destitute elderly, sick, and disabled for communal support of a minimal sort. By grafting poor law traditions back onto the benefit schemes of the 1940s, those who designed legislation have produced a hybrid universalist-residualist system.

The poor laws have set parameters for thinking about poverty in Britain for over four hundred years, legitimating not only residualism but also a wide variety of public services and payments to the poor. Since the late sixteenth century, the sphere of public action vis-à-vis the destitute has been large: Employment, medical care, job training, housing, and pensions came within its purview. Even if they operated residually, the poor laws when viewed over their entire history offered an expansive vision of communal responsibility for the destitute. Nevertheless, their legacy shifted along with their social and cultural context. Public representations of, and changing levels of toleration for, poverty profoundly shaped poor law practice. During the centuries when

---

[12] Paul Pierson, *Dismantling the Welfare State* (New York: Cambridge University Press, 1994), 107–10.

respectable opinion saw the poor as a natural part of a divinely ordained social hierarchy, elites not only accepted the need to mitigate an inevitable burden of adversity, but also tolerated a wide range of income supports and publicly offered services. But when public opinion blamed human character, rather than the human condition, punishment seemed preferable to a pension.

When in the public eye the dependent poor became paupers, they were pushed to the margins of their communities both literally and figuratively. Poor law unions sited new workhouses on the outskirts of towns and used walls and gates to separate their charges from the outside world; the resemblance of workhouses to prisons was scarcely an accident. The social distance implied by pauper status could be read at a glance from the uniforms, haircuts, and antiseptic smell. Even after the shift from punitive to more therapeutic styles of welfare, these markers remained. The poor laws worked through hierarchy, proclaiming and reinforcing inequalities of status. As long as bourgeois public opinion conflated virtue with self-support, the destitute found themselves outside the boundaries of respectability. But this exiling of the very poor meshed uneasily with the rhetoric of a democratizing society. With every expansion of the suffrage, the contradiction widened between full political participation and the exclusion inherent in pauper status. Both the voting power and the moral suasion of organized labor soon weighed in against the poor laws. The dilemma was solved only after 1945, when universalist benefits overrode residualism.

The changing story of the poor laws in Britain must be told against a backdrop of ideas about poverty, work, gender, and the state, as well as about individual responsibility; cultural and ideological shifts reshaped the theory and practice of welfare more directly than economic forces. Created by the Tudor and Stuart monarchies and Parliament in an era of strong controls on labor, the poor laws mandated public responsibility for the impotent poor while directing the unemployed to stay at home and work for a living at locally provided tasks. Age and health, rather than gender, determined the form of public subsidies. Poor men, women, and children alike had the duty of self-support. In the longer run, however, changing ideas about labor markets and gender reshaped treatment of the poor. Along with classical economic theory came a commitment to "free labor," which discouraged state provision of jobs and regulation of wages and gave added legitimacy to labor mobility. The ideas of Smith and Malthus stressed the responsibility of individuals, rather than the state, to determine their own economic destinies, and the state provision of manufacturing work soon ended. Women, however, were slowly shifted into a different set of categories than men as the acceptance of female domesticity spread beyond the middle class into working-class circles. When artisans, as well as liberals and later the Chartists, made a wife in the home the hallmark of respectability, the stage was set for gender-specific benefits and treatments. Under the New Poor Law, punitive treatment of males to force entry into the labor market was set against the provision of small pensions and child allowances for females, whereas the fact that many women had to work was conveniently ignored. By the 1850s, welfare provision came in gender-differentiated packages, and that has continued to be the case. The twin concepts of the male breadwinner wage and female work within the household became pillars of British welfare institutions, outlasting the poor laws and structuring the form of universalist benefits.

Work and welfare have been intertwined commitments in England and Wales since the later sixteenth century. Relief came as a quid pro quo for current work service, as a reward for past labor, or as support for those who would work in the future. Like the philosopher's stone that would transmute lead into gold, work would turn paupers into productive citizens. Yet at no point did poor law authorities succeed in designing a viable scheme for the extraction of profitable labor from the destitute, although they persisted in trying to do so. In the workhouse, paupers could provide goods and services for each other, cutting down the cost of maintenance, but little else. More expansive plans required interaction with local labor markets and employers, which raised a series of practical and philosophical problems. Make-work at sub-subsistence wages did little more than alienate both the destitute and their competitors, the working poor. Moreover, the involvement of the state in the labor market infuriated many taxpayers. Yet practical problems did not end the seductive appeal of work service. Work signaled discipline, independence, and acceptance of the duty of self-support – qualities deemed necessary for cultural survival. As a result, discourses about welfare continued to revolve around work, although the implicit requirements for efficiency and cost cutting that lie behind work rules mean that enthusiasts are soon disappointed. Viable nonpunitive work requirements, which can be justified for social and cultural reasons, are expensive, and they require much ingenuity to implement and much perseverance to maintain. Neoclassical faith that labor markets can solve the problem of social dependence refuses to recognize the realities of human debility and incompetence. In any case, where should the line of the work requirement be drawn? The Victorians pretended to exclude women with children; in today's world, the elderly are exempt. Effective work requirements need consensual answers to multiple questions. Who may provide jobs? For whom must they be provided and at what cost?

Because different moral imperatives shape answers, work requirements have been difficult to design and to enforce.

The long-term evolution of the poor laws took place against the economic backdrop of a capitalist, rapidly urbanizing society. Ordinary people had to support themselves within labor markets increasingly shaped by commercial agriculture and manufacturing for export. The growth of agricultural and industrial proletariats, with their rising dependence on the market for wages and food, increased the seasonal and cyclical vulnerability of workers, periodically intensifying the demand for poor law support. Although both the form and the extent of welfare provision rested upon cultural assumptions, individual needs fluctuated with the structure of the economy as well as that of the human life cycle. As industrialization and urbanization progressed, people moved more often and at greater distances, increasing their vulnerability and decreasing their access to family support. More and more of one's neighbors were strangers and short-term residents. Soon, parishes and townships no longer constituted effective communities or labor markets. Initial steps in bringing welfare practice in line with the exigencies of mobile labor and urban residence came in 1795 and then in 1834 with the New Poor Law; the insurance systems of the early twentieth century continued the process. Nationalizing welfare provision made the boundaries and scale of welfare entitlements symmetrical with those of the economy and the state, homogenizing practices that had differed substantially throughout the British Isles.

These long-run changes cannot be circumscribed within a story organized around the concept of class interest. Invented by Tudor administrators and local officials, the poor laws were passed and amended by a Parliament of landlords and merchants. Coalitions of aristocrats and bourgeois gentlemen, conservative as well as liberal, supported the shifts of 1834, whereas late nineteenth-century debates included organized labor, women's groups, and a wide range of voices arising from within a highly vocal civil society. The Liberal party, representing a coalition of workers and middle-class groups, introduced and passed the early shifts to social insurance, which the Labour party extended in the mid-1940s with the active support of the other parties. Coalitions rather than classes negotiated the specific forms of British welfare legislation.

Even if officially dead, the poor laws continue to offer a contentious legacy to the present. Recently, Gertrude Himmelfarb lauded the Victorians' ideas of welfare reform, praising "less eligibility," orphanages, and the stigmatizing of illegitimacy. In nineteenth-century Britain, she argues, clear standards of behavior helped individuals to behave according to their best interests, and we should emulate them. For Himmelfarb, the poor laws helped to maintain a moralized society. To counter that argument, Stefan Collini called the poor law of 1834 "one of the most thoroughly reviled and detested pieces of legislation passed in the nineteenth century."[13] He left no doubt that he shared that opinion, condemning its mean-spirited, destructive approach to destitution. Interestingly, both scholars identified English welfare history with its least generous, most deterrent phase, neglecting both earlier and later periods, when consensus outweighed contention.

Both are mistaken in this identification. The fundamental outlines of English and Welsh poor law practice were set in the seventeenth and eighteenth centuries. At that time, entitlement overrode moralization. The kind of social citizenship created by the Elizabethan poor law depended more upon communal membership than upon behavior. The poor laws more than any other legal mechanism defined the boundaries of community within England and Wales, linking rich and poor in a tight chain of dependency and responsibility. Moreover, they marked out for aid the entire range of human needs. Settlement, not condition, brought entitlement. The residualist form of benefits, however, necessitated other support systems. As a result, the poor laws fostered a mixed economy of welfare, which reconciled capitalist devotion to the free market with Christian admonitions to support the poor. Neither of these commitments disappeared under the pressures of social democratic rhetoric and the overlay of universalist benefits.

After 1834, however, the inequalities inherent in the welfare bargain intensified. As civil society came to identify work and wealth with virtue, destitution brought disgrace. This style of moralizing poverty was not tenable in the longer run in a society where a socialist party could capture political power and where social democratic ideas had their place in the rhetoric of all the major parties. Although the New Poor Law acquired a powerful hold on both British and American imaginations, its solution to the dilemma of the dependent poor was an unstable one, from which administrators retreated soon after its passage. By the late nineteenth century, treatment rather than punishment became the order of the day.

The essence of a successful welfare system lies in its ability, one, to encompass the needy and, two, to muster support from both givers and receivers. When both conditions are met, the polity has created an effective circle of social citizenship. The poor laws in their early years did this, enjoy-

---

[13] Gertrude Himmelfarb, "The Victorians Get a Bad Rap," *New York Times,* 9 January 1995; Stefan Collini, "We've Come Far Since the Victorians," *New York Times,* 15 January 1995.

ing a widespread legitimacy until the early nineteenth century. They defined both rights and obligations and set standards acceptable to taxpayers as well as the destitute. When measured against the welfare regimes of other European states in the early nineteenth century, this was no small achievement, and the polity benefited. The exclusion of the Irish, however, levied a high social cost, one that continues to be paid. When wars, population growth, and industrial development multiplied the poor, the earlier consensus disintegrated, to be replaced by divisive discourses of blame and failure. The solidarities of strangers became attenuated, only to be reestablished with the acceptance of social insurance in the twentieth century. But that consensus too now crumbles. Recent political shifts in both Western Europe and North America have eroded support for universalist social welfare regimes and reinvigorated interest in individualist, voluntarist solutions to social problems. The mounting cost of universalist benefits in countries with aging populations and deindustrializing regions has convinced many that the welfare state must be redesigned. Indeed, both pragmatic and philosophical objections mount. The return of individualist arguments has been strongest in the United States, where Congress has decreed that even means-tested payments to nondisabled poor must be temporary. The dividing line between communal and individual responsibility for the poor is being redrawn.

The welfare story, therefore, is not a Whiggish saga of progress toward the sunny land of egalitarian social citizenship. To the contrary, it is a tale shaped by the shifting winds of particular economic and social worlds. History and politics give it shape, and culture gives it meaning. Welfare regimes have been most successful when most widely accepted. According to Michael Ignatieff, "A decent and humane society requires a shared language of the good."[14] The English poor laws helped to provide that language for over two hundred years, after which they became a force for division leading in the twentieth century to a search for alternative solutions. Universalist benefits answered the needs of the polity in 1945, but today come under increasing attack. In the postsocialist era, as Britain adapts to a postindustrial world, the "shared language of the good" becomes ever more elusive. The question "what should the virtuous state do for individuals and communities?" excites passion and conflict, rather than consensus. Moreover, renegotiating the boundaries of social citizenship in the context of the European Union and international migration suggests expansion of state protection in ways that many Britons reject. The essentially localist legacy of the poor laws is incom-

[14] Michael Ignatieff, *The Needs of Strangers* (New York: Viking, 1985), 14.

patible with Britain's international commitments, but the identification of universalism with a now-defunct socialism tarnishes its appeal for many voters. In the past, social citizenship helped define the nature of the British polity, and it will continue to do so in the future, but adjudicating differences in a democratic, multicultural age remains extraordinarily difficult. The language of hierarchy and deference that bridged social differences in earlier centuries became inadequate by the time of the French Revolution, but universalism has lost support.

The universalist legacy has always been an ambiguous one. Despite the florid promises of 1945, it has proved compatible with poverty, with substantial amounts of social inequality, and with a continued need for means-tested payments from the government. Equality has not been one of its results. Yet in a world of multiple national needs and an aging population, the combination of limited universalist benefits with residual payments to the destitute may be the maximum that can be afforded and successfully maintained. By combining opposites, it offers something to everyone's taste, although at the cost of ideological purity. Even if there is no shared language of the good in Britain today, there is wide-ranging entitlement to widely defined welfare benefits, which, from the vantage point of the United States, look generous and inclusive. An expansive concept of social citizenship established by the Elizabethan Poor Law has been maintained, even through the punitive phases of the Victorian period. The most valuable legacy of the poor laws has been to draw strangers into a national community of shared obligation that has withstood multiple political and cultural challenges.

APPENDIX: COLLECTION AND ANALYSIS OF SETTLEMENT EXAMINATIONS

Urban settlement examinations, statements sworn before magistrates to establish the parish of an applicant's legal settlement for purposes of relief, include data on multiple social characteristics of poor individuals and families. For the mid and later nineteenth century, these materials can be supplemented by registers of applicants and decisions taken. The most thorough clerks and magistrates collected information on birthplace, age, marital status, occupation, type and place of settlement, apprenticeship, date of application, and family and household structures. In addition, examinations sometimes include material on wages, health, injuries, employment histories, earlier poor law applications, and decisions made about relief. Basic literacy of applicants can be inferred from their ability to sign their names to the documents. Because such examinations – first mandated by the 1662 Settlement Act – continued to be collected through the life of the poor laws, they form a unique source on the social life of the destitute population that is comparable over regions for a period of almost 300 years. Unfortunately, many places did not preserve a complete series of these documents, and it is impossible today to confirm the survival rate of documents for years before the Poor Law Commission began to collect statistics on the incidence of local relief. Even after 1850, the relationship between applicants, examinees, and the aided population is difficult to determine because complete lists of each of these separate groups were not kept.

This study began many years ago with a plan to use settlement documents to provide a profile of the family life of low income populations in British cities. To that end I visited about one-third of the county record offices in England, surveying the surviving sets of examinations and noting the differences in the recording practices of clerks. Finding the collections less extensive than I had anticipated, I scaled down my aspirations and collected materials on London (St. Giles in the Fields, St. Pancras, Hammersmith, St. Martin in the Fields, St. Martin, Vintry) and six medium sized county towns (York, Cheltenham, Bedford, Cambridge, Shrewsbury, Southampton) for two different periods, a year around 1820 and a second year around 1850 in order to capture shifts in clientele and policy introduced by the New Poor Law. My selection was guided by several considerations: 1) the detail in which information was kept; 2) the number and apparent completeness of the records; and 3) the region in which a town was located. For each place I chose a random sample of one in ten from the available cases with the aim of including at least 50 cases per sampled county town and at least 50 for each sampled London parish. These were then coded, counting as one case each family or individual who was examined. The examinee was treated as the head of the household, and s/he was the person whose social location, dependents, and co-residents were mapped. The codes for life cycle stages were adapted from Theodore Koditschek, *Class Formation and Urban Industrial Society, Bradford 1750–1850* (New York: Cambridge University Press, 1990), and those for household organization adapted from the work of James Lee and Jon Gjerde in "Comparative Household Morphology of Stem, Joint, and Nuclear Household Systems: Norway, China, and the United States," *Continuity and Change,* I (May, 1986), 93. In addition, I used files on 1163 households supported by the poor laws around 1890 in Stepney, which were collected and recorded by Charles Booth and his assistants for their study of pauperism in the East End (Booth Collection, Series B, Books A-E, and Series C, British Library of Political and Economic Science). In this case, I used a sample of one in ten cases to survey poor households in London at the end of the century. Information on the same variables as those surveyed for 1820 and 1850 was collected.

Because of the uneven recording of many variables and small sample sizes when the data were broken down finely, I retreated from plans to do an extensive study of the family structures of the destitute. Instead, I concentrated on differences among applicants by gender, ethnicity, and age, dividing the material into a London and a county town sample. When the data was sufficiently robust and interesting to be used in the manuscript, I have reported sample sizes and chi-square values to demonstrate that the results were unlikely to have been produced by chance.

The issue of the representativeness of the sample has been approached in two ways. The question of whether or not the six county towns chosen could represent the urban population outside of London was examined through a comparison of census data for those six towns with data from a random sample of seven towns drawn from the 1851 census. Summary statistics of total size, proportion male, mean age, age distributions, dependency rate, proportions married, and proportions born within the county were collected, and averages of each variable were calculated; comparisons were made using two-sample tests of a difference in means. The aim was to see whether the null hypothesis that there was no significant difference between the means could be rejected. No significant differences between the samples could be detected, except in the area of town sizes. In addition, census data from several different districts of London (St. Giles, Hammersmith, St. Pancras) were compared to figures for the metropolis as a whole to see which districts would best represent demographic averages for all of London. Since averages for each of the districts were quite close to London figures, I decided to use a combination of all three to represent the metropolis. Data on examined applicants to the poor laws from those districts was then assumed to represent the pauper population of the metropolis as a whole.

Overall, of course, pauper populations are not statistically representative of a total urban population. They differ in multiple ways – income, general health, age distribution, and family organization most particularly. To clarify this point, data on pauper family organization in St. Pancras was compared to data on family structure collected for the census of 1861 in the sub-district of St. Pancras. Pauper households in St. Pancras differed from all St. Pancras households in the proportion of households headed by a married couple and the proportion headed by a single adult. Differences were significant at the .05 level.

The sampled cases, however, give a detailed picture of the social characteristics of paupers in the larger towns and in the capital during the waning years of the Old Poor Law and the early years of the New.

BIBLIOGRAPHIC ESSAY

The footnotes provide the most complete guide to the range of sources used in the research for, and writing of, this book; full references appear in each chapter in the first citation. Some additional comments on primary sources will make clear the wide variety of materials available both in Britain and in the United States on the history of the poor laws and on attitudes toward poverty.

The Parliamentary Papers [hereinafter PP] are the place to begin an investigation of the poor laws. *The Report from Her Majesty's Commission on the Administration and Practical Operation of the Poor Laws,* PP 1834, vols. XXVII-XXXVIII and the *Royal Commission on the Poor Law and Relief of Distress,* PP 1909–10, vols. XXXVII-LV, give extensive information on both the theory and practice of the poor laws as they existed in the early nineteenth century and in the early twentieth century. George Cornewall Lewis's *Report on the State of the Irish Poor in Great Britain,* PP 1836, vol. XXXIV, provides rich material on attitudes among employers and government officials toward the Irish around 1830. Additional details on the Irish and their dealings with the poor law from the point of view of welfare administrators can be found in the *First Report from the Select Committee on Settlement and Removal,* PP 1847, vol. XI, and in the *Report from the Select Committee on Poor Removal,* PP 1854, vol. XVII, and the *Report from the Select Committee on the Removal of the Irish Poor,* 1854, vol. XVII. The issue of settlement and removal got extensive attention during the middle decades of the nineteenth century, the results being published both in select committee reports and in yearly returns of the numbers of orders of removal issued, which sometimes included information on the origins, destinations, sex, and occupations of the paupers removed.

In the *Annual Reports* of the Poor Law Commission, the Poor Law Board, and the Local Government Board, the slow building of a poor law bureaucracy after 1834 can be traced, and much material on local conditions and local concerns is included. The official statistics on the cost of relief and on the population relieved appear in these series as do the reports of the Assistant Commissioners who toured the country to survey the administration of the poor laws. Of particular interest is the essay by Henry Longley, "Report to the Local Government Board on Poor Law Administration in London," from the *Third Annual Report of the Local Government Board,* 1873–4, PP 1874, vol. XXV, 40–54.

Relatively little information on individual paupers and on the negotiations imbedded in poor law applications appears in national records, which concentrated on circulating regulations and on quantifying the problem of pauperism. Taking a closer look at the implementation of welfare policies and at the people who received aid requires a shift to local sources, which are available in county as well as city record offices and local libraries. Holdings of poor law examinations, certificates of settlement and removal, and application and report books are uneven throughout the country; not everything was saved for every year, and local recording practices varied to some extent. Although detailed sources are available for London, for example, little has been saved by the towns of Yorkshire and Lancashire. Local holdings for Bedford (Amthill Poor Law Union), Cambridge, Cheltenham, Leicester, Shrewsbury, Southampton, and York are comparatively rich, and I made extensive use of the Bedfordshire Record Office, the Cambridgeshire Record Office, the former Greater London Record Office, the Leicestershire County Record Office, the Shropshire County Record Office, the Southampton City Record Office, and the York City Archive and the library of the Borthwick Institute. In the case of London, additional materials on City parishes [of particular interest is St Martin, Vintry, "Examinations of the Poor, 1815–1826"] can be found in the Guildhall Library, and on St. Giles in the Fields and on Holborn in the Holborn Public Library. Scattered information on the operation of the New Poor Law in the textile districts can be found in the West Yorkshire Record Office, the Manchester City Library, the Lancaster Record Office, and the public libraries of Huddersfield and Bradford. The unique series of letters from emigrants applying for relief in Kirkby Lonsdale [Kirkby Lonsdale, "Township Letters, 1809–1846"], which are held in the Cumbria Record Office, I read on microfilm and am indebted to James Stephen Taylor for his generous loan. One particularly detailed set of records is available in the Shropshire County Record Office for the Atcham Union [Atcham Union, "Applications for Relief"; B10A–83/221–2]. These I consulted both in Shrewsbury and on microfilms owned by Vincent Walsh, whom I wish to thank for his kindness.

Another treasure trove of poor law materials relating to Stepney in the years around 1890 is part of Series B of the Booth Papers, held at the British Library of Political and Economic Science. Extensive case records both of inmates in Stepney institutions and of people receiving outrelief were kept, as well as a transcription of records from 1890 from the Stepney Committee of the Charity Organization Society. I am indebted to Michael Hughes for allowing me to borrow a microfilm of the Booth Papers, Series B. The *Webb Local Government Collection* can also be found at the British Library of Political and Economic Science. Part 2: *The Poor Law* contains materials on the working of the poor law organized by county.

Local boards of guardians also kept extensive records of their decisions and minutes of their meetings. Such materials, which are widely available under the heading "Signed Minutes," can be used to trace long-term changes in poor law policies. Reports by local inspectors, such as St. Luke's, Chelsea, Middlesex, "Inspectors' Reports on Paupers, 1833–1834," P 74/Luk 30 in the Greater London Council Archive, give commentary on particular cases and sometimes on criteria used for making decisions about welfare amounts and types. In addition to the holdings of such records in county and city archives, the Genealogical Society of the Church of Latter Day Saints has done extensive microfilming of nominal records relating to the poor in Britain. Their films are available from the central archive in Salt Lake City, Utah, and through local reading rooms run by the Church of Latter Day Saints.

To investigate workers' conceptions of poverty and their attitudes to the poor laws, I drew heavily from interviews transcribed in the twentieth century. The most extensive set of such materials comes from the Family Life and Work Experience Archive held by the Department of Sociology at the University of Essex. Collected by Paul Thompson and Thea Vigne, these oral histories include subjects from all parts of the British Isles and represent a range of social statuses. These recollections of the Edwardian period refer frequently to the topic of poverty and to the poor law. A more limited set of oral histories can be found in the Bradford Public Library. Done by the Bradford Heritage Recording Unit, the *Oral History Collection* used local workers as subjects for an investigation of social life in Bradford during the twentieth century. Workers' autobiographies, which exist in large numbers for the nineteenth and twentieth centuries, also include extensive comments on the problem of poverty and on personal experiences of deprivation. The best guide to using these sources is David Vincent, *Bread, Knowledge and Freedom* (London: Europa, 1981). Although these life stories should be seen as carefully constructed, selective narratives and not transparent outlines of past times, they provide a wealth of material on attitudes toward poverty. Among the more valuable of these life stories for the first decades of the nineteenth century are Joseph Barker, *The History of the Confessions of a Man, As Put Forth by Himself* (London, 1846), and Joseph Gutteridge, "Autobiography," printed in Valerie E. Chancellor, ed., *Master and Artisan in Victorian England* (London: Evelyn, Adams & Mackay, 1893). Also of interest is the journal of Elizabeth Browett, "Diary of a Seamstress," written in London in 1833–4 and held in the Haverford College Library; I am grateful to Trudi Abel for this reference. Local libraries and archives also hold locally printed life stories that had limited circulation; see, for example, Maggie Newbery, *Reminiscences of a Bradford Mill Girl* (Bradford: City of Bradford Municipal Council Libraries Division-Local Studies Department, 1980).

Additional material on popular attitudes toward poverty can be found in the ballads sold on street corners and purchased by workers. Although the issue of whose voice they represent is a thorny one, I accept Patrick Joyce's willingness to see within the ballads a popular world view; see Patrick Joyce, *Visions of the People: Industrial England and the Question of Class, 1848–1914* (New York: Cambridge University Press, 1991). Among the major ballad collections I have consulted are the Baring-Gould Ballad Collection and the Crampton Ballad Collection at the British Library. Other substantial collections of broadside ballads can be found at the Cambridge University Library and at the Lewis Walpole Library in Farmington, Connecticut.

Regional newspapers in their coverage of poor law issues and controversies provide valuable insights into local definitions of welfare problems. Unrest or insubordination in the workhouse got attention as did particular scandals concerning relief decisions. Among the newspapers I used were the *Leicester Mercury,* the *Wolverhampton Chronicle,* and the *Leeds Mercury.* They also did extensive reporting on the range of charitable activities mounted to collect money for the poor. Moreover, they provide good coverage of early efforts to mount citywide public relief programs. The *Workman's Times,* a union paper published in Yorkshire and London offers scathing commentary on the poor laws, as well as observations on workers' pensions. The British Library at Colindale holds the most extensive collection of such papers.

Photographs, engravings, and cartoons of the poor are available in many places. The best source in the United States for eighteenth-century printed material is the Lewis Walpole Library in Farmington, Connecticut. In addition, the Yale Library of British Art has a superb collection of paintings, printed books, and watercolors, and it is easy to use. Julian Treuherz's catalogue, *Hard Times* (Mt. Kisco, NY: Moyer Bell, 1987), of an exhibition at the Yale Library of British Art surveys a wide range of material on the English poor and gives details on their locations. The Van Pelt Library of the University of Pennsylvania has excellent sources for both the nineteenth and twentieth centuries in its regular holdings and in its special collections. Of particular interest is *The Graphic,* printed in London from 1869 to 1896, whose artists presented a relatively realistic, sympathetic view of the poor. In Britain, both the British Library and the Victoria and Albert Museum have major holdings of pictorial materials. Good collections of photographs of local people and their neighborhoods can be found in the Manchester City Library and in the Greater London Council Archive. Most of the materials cited represent the urban poor, who received much more attention than did their rural counterparts. For an introduction to early treatments of the rural poor by English painters, see John Barrell, *The Dark Side of the Landscape* (New York: Cambridge University Press, 1980).

Contemporary discussions of the poor in Britain abound. Among the more important sources are periodicals such as *Blackwood's Magazine,* the *Edinburgh Review, Fraser's Magazine, Macmillan's Magazine,* the *National Review,* and the *Quarterly Review,* which published essays on poverty and welfare issues by intellectuals and reformers of various sorts. The *Journal of the [Royal] Statistical Society,* published in London from 1837, contains regular reports on the London poor and their neighborhoods, which infuse numerical profiles with diagnoses of poverty. An excellent source for early poor law administration and issues of settlement is the handbook by Richard Burn, *The Justice of the Peace and the Parish Officer,* which was reprinted and revised repeatedly between 1755 and the mid-nineteenth century. More detailed material on poor law practices in eighteenth century can be found in Sir Frederick Eden, *The State of the Poor: Or an History of the Labouring Classes in England* (London, 1797).

The many representations of the poor by doctors and by reporters are well known and easily accessible. Particularly interesting commentary linking physical and moral environments can be found in George Godwin, *A Glance at the 'Homes' of the Thousands* (London, 1854), and Hugh Shimmin, *Liverpool Life: The Courts and Alleys of Liverpool Described from Personal Inspection* (Liverpool, 1864). For the early twentieth century, George Sims, *Living London,* 3 vols. (London, 1902), combines photographs with a survey of workhouses, schools, refuges, and other reformist institutions.

The issue of the incomes of the poor produced a series of detailed reports in the later nineteenth and in the twentieth centuries. The reader who wishes to go beyond the surveys of London by Charles Booth, *Life and Labour of the People of London,* 1st ser, *Poverty,* 5 vols. (London, 1902), and of York by Benjamin Seebohm Rowntree, *Poverty: A Study of Town Life* (London, 1901), and idem, *Poverty and Progress* (London, 1941), should look at E. Collet and M. Robertson, *Family Budgets: Being the Income and Expenses of 28 British*

Households, 1891–1894 (London, 1896), and A. L. Bowley and Margaret H. Hogg, *Has Poverty Diminished?* (London, 1925).

Prescriptions about poverty and the poor take many forms. The contributions of activists in the Charity Organization Society deserve special attention. See Helen Bosanquet, *Social Work in London, 1869–1912: A History of the Charity Organization Society* (London, 1914), Charles B. P. Bosanquet, *A Handy Book for Visitors of the Poor in London* (London, 1879), and Sir William Chance, *The Better Administration of the Poor Law* (London, 1895). Among the many other analyses of poverty and dependence that deserve mention are Patrick Colquhoun, *The State of Indigence and the Situation of the Casual Poor in the Metropolis Explained* (London, 1799), J. H. Stallard, *London Pauperism Amongst Christians and Jews* (London, 1867), Louisa Twining, *Workhouses and Pauperism and Women's Work in the Administration of the Poor Law* (London, 1898), and Eleanor Rathbone, *The Disinherited Family* (London: Edward Arnold, 1924). Novels and stories represent the poor in alternative ways, even if many of the moral points remain the same. Harriet Martineau's *Cousin Marshall* (London, 1832) and her *Poor Laws and Paupers Illustrated* (Exeter, 1855) typify the ideology of the New Poor Law, while Arthur Morrison's *A Child of the Jago* (London, 1896) and his *Tales of Mean Streets* (London, 1892) present a sympathetic view of the problems of the poor and the constraints upon them.

INDEX

Printed in the United Kingdom
by Lightning Source UK Ltd.
9834900001B/55-57